RED GLOBALIZATION

Was the Soviet Union a superpower? *Red Globalization* is a significant rereading of the Cold War as an economic struggle shaped by the global economy. Oscar Sanchez-Sibony challenges the idea that the Soviet Union represented a parallel socio-economic construct to the liberal world economy. Instead, he shows that the Soviet Union, a middle-income country more often than not at the mercy of global economic forces, tracked the same path as other countries in the world, moving from 1930s autarky to the globalizing processes of the postwar period. Far from an economic force in the world, the Soviets managed only to become dependent providers of energy to the rich world, and second-best partners to the global South. In examining the constraints and opportunities afforded the Soviets in their engagement of the capitalist world, Oscar Sanchez-Sibony questions the very foundations of the Cold War narrative as a contest between superpowers in a bipolar world.

OSCAR SANCHEZ-SIBONY is Assistant Professor of World History at the University of Macau, China, where he teaches courses on Soviet history, the Cold War, and global capitalism.

NEW STUDIES IN EUROPEAN HISTORY

The aim of this series in early modern and modern European history is to publish outstanding works of research, addressed to important themes across a wide geographical range, from southern and central Europe, to Scandinavia and Russia, from the time of the Renaissance to the present. As it develops the series will comprise focused works of wide contextual range and intellectual ambition.

A full list of titles published in the series can be found at:
www.cambridge.org/newstudiesineuropeanhistory

RED GLOBALIZATION

The Political Economy of the Soviet Cold War from Stalin to Khrushchev

OSCAR SANCHEZ-SIBONY

CAMBRIDGE
UNIVERSITY PRESS

CAMBRIDGE
UNIVERSITY PRESS

University Printing House, Cambridge CB2 8BS, United Kingdom

Cambridge University Press is part of the University of Cambridge.

It furthers the University's mission by disseminating knowledge in the pursuit of education, learning and research at the highest international levels of excellence.

www.cambridge.org
Information on this title: www.cambridge.org/9781107040250

First published 2014

A catalogue record for this publication is available from the British Library

Library of Congress Cataloguing in Publication data
Sanchez-Sibony, Oscar, 1977-author.
Red globalization : the political economy of the Soviet Cold War from Stalin to Khrushchev / Oscar Sanchez-Sibony.
pages ; cm. – (New studies in European history)
ISBN 978-1-107-04025-0 (Hardback)
1. Soviet Union–Foreign economic relations. 2. Foreign trade regulation–Soviet Union. 3. Cold War–Economic aspects–Soviet Union. 4. Soviet Union–Economic conditions–1945–1955. 5. Soviet Union–Economic conditions–1955–1965. I. Title. II. Series: New studies in European history.
HF3628.S26 2014
337.47009′045–dc23
2013035760

ISBN 978-1-107-04025-0 Hardback

This first book I've written is dedicated to my parents.
No sequence of sentences, no short narrative can explicate their presence in this book.
Because I am him they made, this book is also theirs.

Contents

Figures

Acknowledgements

Thank you, Sheila. You were unimpressed with my first idea of what a book might look like, and limited yourself simply to reminding me of those interests that brought me to the University of Chicago in the first place and which I had put behind me during my immersion into the field. The fog lifted; you supported my next idea for a book. And when that one crumbled against the gates of the foreign ministry archives, you supported a new, impromptu book scheme. You showed confidence in my strengths and interests, and the dissertation, the first incarnation of this book, owed much to that blend of constancy and flexibility that has made you one of the field's great advisors. Later, while on a trip back to Moscow to temper the dissertation into a book, you pointed me to some excellent sources that have served this book well. The content of the book itself was perhaps somewhat outside of your usual Soviet stomping grounds, and for its wild assertions, combative tone (against your better judgment), and mistakes I alone must answer. But what use it might be to colleagues and general readers owes most to your guidance. Thank you.

To my fellow Chicago cohort, I owe you much as well. For years we discussed each other's work, at workshops and bars, while walking and eating. We did not always have the most enlightening things to tell of each other's work, but the continuous intellectual agitation the exchange itself created was the point, I think. Those conversations, on endless Soviet subjects, echoed in the recesses of my brain, finding outlet in arguments, expressions, and writing methods throughout this book. Surely my instincts are wrong when they try to take credit for the voice of the book. Perhaps more importantly, the example of your individual strengths was a thing to aspire to, and a constant motivation: the work ethic, the commitment to history and its Soviet experience, the archival expertise. Stacey Manley, Andrey Shlyakhter, Ken Roh, Michael Westren, Andy Janco, Ke-chin Hsia, Mie Nakachi, Ben Zajicek, Ed Cohn, Jennifer Amos, Alan Barenberg, Julia Fein, Rachel Applebaum, Julie Bashkin, Leah

Goldman, Flora Roberts, and Natalie Belsky, thank you for your companionship in Chicago. I am particularly thankful to have coincided in Chicago with one of its many talented students, one by the name of Sloin. Andrew, not too long ago I rediscovered the very first email that you wrote me. It was a response to a draft of some chapter, perhaps the first one I wrote for the dissertation. I can't remember what I must have thought of your email then, probably that it was irrelevant and somewhat eccentric. I reread it more recently with increasing embarrassment in seeing so many of the underlying arguments I had struggled so painstakingly to construct in this book reflected – anticipated – so effortlessly in your email. I think this book has, in some subliminal manner, been chasing that vision, probably because it was given greater substance over the many beers and emails we later shared and exchanged.

In Chicago there were three somewhat more distant figures that nevertheless continue to shape my academic identity, and therefore this book. The late Richard Hellie was often inclined toward ideas I did not share, but he was a dedicated teacher. He was sometimes provocative, always gruff, and his praise was as reluctant as it was encouraging. He was unimpeachably collegial – a walking lesson on the matter – and one I will endeavor always to emulate. Ronald Suny rounded out the remarkable team in Chicago in Russian–Soviet history. Ron, your talent to size up an argument and leave it better than when you encountered it is a bit more difficult to emulate, but it has always been enlightening to behold at the Chicago workshop and in private consultations. It was an equal privilege to have had the advice of Bruce Cumings. Your touch was light, Bruce, and all the more convincing for it. What intellectual value this book carries derives in large part from an interaction with your ideas. These were not always easy to grasp, but rereading your prose was always a pleasure anyway. This book does not yet show that commitment to good writing that you preach and practice, but I am converted, and what scant literary pleasures might be found here owe to your example.

Bruce Cumings came, once upon a time, from the field of International Political Economy (IPE), a general approach to understanding power and international relations that is generally uncontroversial among political scientists but which the conservative field of Cold War history processed, impossibly, as Marxist "revisionism" and "economic determinism." If Bruce planted the seeds, Omar, brother, you guided me through the IPE thicket that obtained. You read, reread, advised, and goaded. You critiqued, encouraged, and then advised some more. As did our sister Olivia's, your guidance started long ago, before the edge of memory, and it continues. There would have been no impromptu plan for Sheila Fitzpatrick to support, nor a follow-through for her to believe in; this book might not have been but for you, or it might have been something else entirely, and certainly less interesting.

It's not only my own family, or Chicago, that has provided moral support and intellectual sustenance. Elizabeth McGuire provided both. At key moments of particular intellectual solitude, you appeared as if by magic to provide a readership of one that was as good as ten thousand, and a critical appraisal that was the essence of encouragement. Your latest act of magic came in the form of a dissertation review (for which I also thank the editors of the eponymous website) right as I was making the last push to finish the book. Thank you for that. Ben Loring, Brigid O'Keeffe, Ben Sawyer, Kelly Kolar, and others have continued the conversation on matters Soviet and otherwise well after the dissertation stage – sporadically to be sure, now that I am far – and theirs has been a reassuring continuity. Steve Maddox, Christian Teichmann, Josh Sanborn, Jesse Ferris, Arch Getty, Sean Guillory, Maya Haber, Greg Kveberg, Alex Oberlaender, Christoph Gumb, and the many others that gathered faithfully every Friday evening long ago in Moscow during the time I spent there doing the bulk of the research for this book, thank you for your companionship and conversation.

Institutions that have provided the critical money and infrastructure necessary for the book's production have been many. A Fulbright-Hayes fellowship and an unexpected IREX fellowship fronted the money for its initial dissertation form. I ended up with a product rather different than the one I sold these fine institutions, for which I always felt somewhat guilty, especially since the new topic, the one that is the subject of this book, never again found the enthusiastic backing of the one I aborted on Soviet–Cuban relations. Back in Chicago, a University of Chicago Trustees fellowship afforded me the time to write the bulk of the dissertation. The archivists at the State Archive of the Russian Federation (GARF), the Russian State Archive of the Economy (RGAE), and the Russian State Archive of Contemporary History (RGANI), as well as the librarians at the Lamont Library in Harvard, and June Farris at the University of Chicago library were invariably competent and helpful. And although no institution thought this subject matter worthy of further support, it did finally find its reward in the Association for Slavic, East European, and Eurasian Studies (ASEEES) with the Tucker/Cohen Dissertation Prize; I will always be grateful to its 2010 committee, and especially its chair, Lewis Siegelbaum, for the morale boost that vote of confidence signified.

Later still, an early draft of the book was given a thorough mauling while in beautiful Poland. I thank Andrzej Kaminski and Jim Collins for the invitation to the conference on Recovering Forgotten History: The Image of East–Central Europe in Anglo-Saxon Textbooks, the people at Lazarski University for the impeccable organization and the lesson in hospitality, and Daria Nałęcz and Andrzej Nowak for taking time out of their busy schedules to read through the draft and critique it. A return trip to Moscow in 2011 introduced me to the helpful staff of the Russian State Archive of Socio-Political History (RGASPI), to whom I am also much obliged. Money for that trip was provided by the always-generous University of Macau, where I must particularly thank Tim Simpson for his decisive help in unlocking the funds in time.

Kai, you never did like this book much, did you? By the time you even think of reading it, its ideas will be old. Whether useful or not, the book will be remembered, if at all, for the things it missed or got wrong altogether. Kai, the book kept me from you, as future ones will also do. They will keep me from your brother Luka too (not born as I write this, he will yet be older than this book). Kai, don't be mad. I must start on this journey, and this book is where the conversation starts. I don't know where this conversation will lead, Kai, but it forms now part of the effort to illuminate things that were dark, so you may walk in the world with more confidence. Your mother also wants you poised and wise. She has sacrificed more than anyone else in making this humble addition, and this is as much her project as it is mine, as many more will be. Kai, don't be mad. I hope one day you too will join the conversation. Its forms are many and varied, and you may choose your own. Until such a day, your mother and I will talk with you, and with your brother Luka, and also with the many thousands that we now journey with. Thank you, Yin, for that.

Introduction

Lorenzo traveled light. An exile from Spain living in Paris, and roughing it under bridges when money could not rent a bed, he was on a train heading east with a few shirts, an unwisely light jacket, rubber shoes his mother had sent from Spain and – his most precious possession – an article clipping from *Le Monde* in his pocket. It was early in 1963 and getting cold throughout Europe. Lorenzo was not yet twenty, and despite traveling as the representative of a Spanish Communist student organization (FUDE in its Spanish acronym), he was not quite a student either. It is true that he had received a very thorough education in the works of Karl Marx, but his educational institution had been one of Francisco Franco's correctional facilities for political hooligans. Lorenzo's lessons in Marxism had been carried out amidst discreet sessions of torture. He had entered jail an anti-Francoist, and had come out of it and gone into exile a committed Communist. Now he was heading past the Iron Curtain for a meeting in Warsaw of the International Union of Students, where he and hundreds of students from across Europe were to be welcomed by the Polish Minister of Foreign Affairs at the Palace of Culture and Science, a magnificent eyesore recalling the old Warsaw Citadel that symbolized Russian rule over Poland a century earlier. Lorenzo's plan was to take out his *Le Monde* clipping at the meeting.

The Communist Bloc was a thorough disappointment for Lorenzo. Upon crossing the border into East Berlin, only recently ornamented with a long wall, he noticed a distinct surplus of machine guns hanging about the station. His Polish cabin companion, an aging teacher of French returning home, had become conspicuously taciturn after the crossing. Upon arriving in Warsaw, she addressed Lorenzo one last time to advise him not to change his French francs with the official money-changer on the train. "He is a thief," she spat, and Lorenzo could get four times the amount of zlotys in the street. Lorenzo thought her reactionary and bourgeois, but nevertheless changed only a small part of his meager wealth on the train, only to find that in addition to being bourgeois and reactionary, his companion was also quite right.

At the dormitory in Warsaw, Lorenzo found a woman on duty surveilling every floor and she was not shy to irrupt into a room if any local female students happened to be socializing with the foreigners. Lorenzo found Communist Poland to have almost as many churches as Francoist Spain, and they were distinctly more popular here. If a New Man were to be born in these conditions, he would have the definite whiff of the traditional priggish man of God he knew so well back home, the same who taught in Catholic schools, thought education a bloody process, and took so many of Lorenzo's young classmates into rooms where no woman on duty would interrupt.

A warmer experience, perhaps one closer to the Communist Bloc of his imagination, might have mollified Lorenzo and kept him in line during the anticipated meeting with the Polish Foreign Minister. Instead he felt surer than ever. He must take out his article from *Le Monde*, his incontrovertible proof, and demand answers. What was written in the article? It was a simple story of trade. Poland had been selling coal to Spain throughout the year. Hard currency, as Lorenzo had already found out for himself, was much prized in the Communist Bloc after all. This seemed an innocuous item of information, and it was in fact a routine bit of profitable commercial exchange by this time, as far as Communist officials were concerned. But the actions of the Polish Communist Party also constituted an act of immense treachery against Lorenzo and his fellow exiled comrades.

The locus of anti-Francoist agitation in Spain was in the coal mines of the northern region of Asturias. In the spring of 1962, miners in that rugged land went on a massive strike, and the exiled Spanish Communists supported them in every possible way. This often meant clandestine trips back into Spain for the likes of young Lorenzo, a risky activity that could end up in capture or worse. In the event, the strikes of the unruly, courageous Asturians spread across the country and bowed the regime itself, inaugurating a new Spain in which workers had earned the right to organize and strike. It would not be too much of an exaggeration to say that the coal strikes of 1962 sounded the death knell of the Spain Franco forged in the interwar era and became the year of inception of a social movement in Spain that culminated in the formation of a new European social democracy after Franco's death in 1975; and no thanks to the Polish Communist Party.

At the Palace of Culture and Science, Lorenzo waited until the end of the minister's speech to speak. With a knot in his throat but drawing strength from his piece of newspaper, he was now waving it and demanding to know why the Polish Communists were undermining the single most important fight for socialism in Spain since it was extinguished there in 1939. The minister, taken aback by this unexpected turn, mumbled something about the friendship of the peoples and quickly changed the subject. The minister was right of course, and his comments were very much in line with the policy of the Kremlin and the whole of the Communist Bloc.

After this anticlimax, Lorenzo thawed in Paris and soon after quit the Communist Party and returned to Spain, just barely avoiding the fate of many of his comrades who went on to fight against the right-wing dictatorships of Latin America only to be burned to a crisp by American napalm. Yet there was a curious convergence between the successive American administrations that murdered Lorenzo's friends in their jungle hideouts and Lorenzo himself, and it had to do with how both imagined the Soviet Union and the Communist Bloc. For the US government, Lorenzo, and indeed most academic scholars, the Soviet Bloc was a world apart, an experiment being carried out behind high walls that intersected with the rest of the world mostly in the realm of ideas. As such, when acting beyond its borders, it was supposed to be relentlessly ideological, putting its messianic mission ahead of crass financial concerns; only political prerogatives concerning security and grand geopolitical games could trump ideological interests now and again. What the friends and enemies of Communism shared, then, was an imagined Communist Bloc that bore little relation to the actual policies, and indeed rhetoric, of Communist officials. Trade as a vehicle for world peace and a palliative for Cold War tensions appeared to Lorenzo – and was in fact – a terrible betrayal. This credo also sounded to Lorenzo, the US government, and generations of Western scholars as a cynical excuse, necessarily masking something more subversive.

This book argues that this was nothing of the sort. The Polish minister's excuse was, in fact, commercial policy of long standing in the Soviet Union and its post-World War II empire.[1] One of the most consistent areas of agreement among Westerners of all political stripes is a conception of the postwar international regime as strictly bipolar. This belief is an essential constituent of a Western European and North American narrative for

[1] Poland, alas, is not within the book's purview, although it can be assumed that their commercial policy was in keeping with that of the Soviets, and if anything, more aggressively integrationist with the liberal world order.

understanding themselves and the world around them; only such a distribution of global power could explain the very real division of Europe. Integral to this bipolarity framework is the idea that the Soviet Union was autarkic to its core. Autarky, often an unremarked condition but always foundational to any analysis of the Soviet Union, has allowed two sets of different but related scholarly artifice. On the one hand, autarky has enabled Sovietologists to construct a narrative of the country as an antagonistically illiberal and willful socio-political construction that could only be erected as a purely ideological undertaking: the "Soviet experiment." The totalitarian paradigm that became so influential for understanding the Soviet Union in Western academia and societies at large was precisely built on those notions of autarky; only complete seclusion from the world could have deviated a country so far from the more organic liberal course that so often serves as the normative benchmark for historical development.[2] But on the Left, autarky was also enthusiastically embraced; the idea of the Soviet Union as an experiment embodied the hope that processes were in motion there unsullied by the commercialized, exploitative capitalism of societies in the West. In the related field of Cold War studies, autarky served scholars in constructing a narrative that required a clear delineation of the two camps. The powers that be, above all the US Department of State, acted on this assumption and justified much of American foreign policy by it – often activating immense reserves of ignorance, racism, and cynicism to do so (see Guatemala circa 1954). There have not been many permutations of these assumptions in the Cold War scholarship; bipolarity is still the name of the game, and autarky its mostly unacknowledged foundation.

The problem is that Soviet autarky is wrong. It is wrong as a matter of statistical fact. It is wrong as a matter of clear and consistent political intent on the part of the Soviet leadership. It is wrong. Using domestic prices for foreign trade items – rather than the foreign prices converted to rubles at the exchange rate that the official foreign trade statistics use – the economist Vladimir Treml calculated that the share of foreign trade to

[2] A useful guide to totalitarianism as a conceptual framework is Abbot Gleason, *Totalitarianism. The Inner History of the Cold War* (Oxford: Oxford University Press, 1995). The most recent iteration of this narrative is the modernity paradigm, which at least places the USSR within a larger pan-European narrative but sees it as a particularly nasty embodiment of Enlightenment logic precisely because it was so thoroughly illiberal, so thoroughly, willfully apart from the prevailing liberal order. The first and best statement in this line of inquiry is Stephen Kotkin, "Modern Times: The Soviet Union and the Interwar Conjunction," *Kritika: Explorations in Russian and Eurasian History* 2:1 (2001): 111–64.

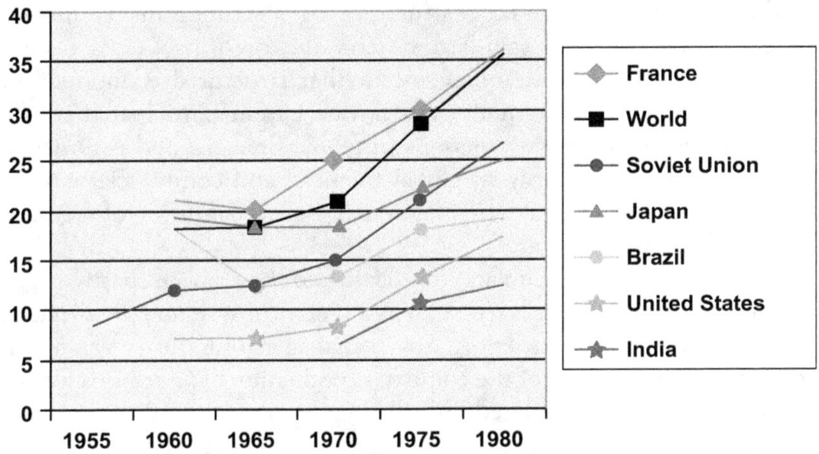

Figure 1 Trade as percentage of national economy

national income increased from 12 percent in 1960 to 21 percent in 1975 and about 27 percent in 1980 (see Figure 1). In other words, the Soviet Union had a level of "autarky" comparable to that of Japan, which followed a similar progression from the near autarky of the early 1950s to a more globalized economy two decades later.[3]

The Soviet Union throughout the postwar era was more sensitive to changes in the world economy than other large countries such as the United States, Brazil, India, and by the late 1970s, even Japan. But Treml's suggestive figures failed to percolate through the field; there was no place to integrate them within existing master narratives of the "Soviet experiment." Likewise, the field largely ignored the four-decade-old work of Michael Dohan, which itself seemed to take its cue from the fast growth of Soviet economic relations through the 1960s and 1970s.[4] Dohan argued that autarky in the 1930s was not a political choice, but an outcome of the Great Depression. This book confirms and builds on his impeccable scholarship. The fact is that the Soviet economy was in large measure

[3] Japan began the postwar Bretton Woods era in abject dependence to the United States, which accounts for the higher trade-to-GDP ratio early on. It ended the era less globalized than the USSR, whose trade-to-GDP ratio Treml guessed would be above 30 percent in the 1980s, in Vladimir G. Treml, "Soviet Dependence on Foreign Trade," in NATO Economics Directorate, *External Economic Relations of CMEA Countries. Their Significance and Impact in Global Perspective*, Colloquium 1983 (Brussels: NATO, 1983), 35.

[4] Michael R. Dohan, "Soviet Foreign Trade in the NEP Economy and Soviet Industrialization Strategy" (PhD diss., MIT, 1969).

embedded in global economic structures at all times in its history. Whether it was the gold standard system, the Bretton Woods system, or the post-Bretton Woods quasi-system that structured economic and political relations internationally, the Soviet Union participated mostly directly in the trends and tribulations of global financial and commercial exchange – if not necessarily in global financial and commercial governance, which was dominated by the much richer countries of Western Europe and the United States.

Only one group of scholars can claim to have been partly right: economic Sovietologists. It is true that as a matter of systemic predilection, the Soviet system abhorred export. Soviet managers of industry wanted no involvement in the export of the country's production. The reasons for this have not yet been fully explored, but the beginning of an answer probably has to do with the problem that a manager would find in having his (always his) enterprise selected for export duties. This dislike of exportation led to the Kremlin commandeering production and taking that production out of the industrial black market (another immensely important area of Soviet economic life we know little about). Inasmuch as the industrial black market helped these same managers deal with the pressures of plan fulfillment, export was to be avoided at all costs. But of course this is only one-half of the story of Soviet trade. The other half is importation, which the Soviet Union craved probably more keenly than more liberal countries. It was part of the well-known phenomenon of the Soviet economic system whereby enterprises hoarded inputs and then demanded more in order, again, to mitigate the strain of Gosplan's production demands.[5] But where the system was conflicted in its relationship with the world outside Soviet borders, the Kremlin was not. The outcome of the Soviet leadership's single-minded policy to engage the world is incontrovertible: The Soviet economy became first autarkic and then globalized in roughly the same measure and on roughly the same timetable as the world first became autarkic in the interwar period and then globalized in the postwar.

If Soviet trade was not conducted within a framework of a free global market, it is not because the Soviets generally emphasized political concerns over commercial ones, as conventional wisdom has it. Politics certainly intruded on Soviet commerce, but more often than not in the form of constraints enforced by American power through institutions like

[5] This systemic contradiction (the irony!) is the subject of Oscar Sanchez-Sibony, "Soviet Industry in the World Spotlight: The Domestic Dilemmas of Soviet Foreign Economic Relations, 1955–1965," *Europe-Asia Studies* 62:9 (2010): 1555–78.

the Coordinating Committee for Multilateral Export Controls (CoCom) in the industrialized world, or through implicit and overt threats to the commercial well-being of non-industrialized countries. It was the drive to lift these American-made constraints that guided Soviet commercial efforts during the first two decades of its trade expansion. This is an important point to grasp and internalize when analyzing Soviet foreign policy. Cold War literature has focused too much on short-term political decisions made during headline-grabbing Cold War flashpoints, rather than on the Soviet elite's understanding – often perfectly sensible – of the political and economic realities that circumscribed their actions and shaped longer-term policy.

This book recovers that general financial and commercial architecture that delimited Soviet foreign policy. But it does not set out simply to illuminate what Cold War historians refer to as the "economic dimension" of the Cold War or to prove that economics somehow trumps politics. Rather, it is predicated on the idea that economic developments constrain and enable certain politics in at least the same measure that politics constrain and enable economic policymaking. These dynamics shaped the worldview and preconceived notions of policymakers, what in the field is often but inadequately denoted as ideology, an unfortunate notion that often implies doctrinal texts and rigidity of thought – usually depicted as a Soviet characteristic, but rarely attributed to American innocents abroad. This is not to deny that some ideas in the Soviet Union were perfectly autonomous and fairly unchanging. For example, Soviet policymakers clearly favored importing capital goods (machine tools, ships, cables, etc.) to the consumer goods that industrialized countries often tried to peddle in the Soviet Union. Why this should be so had little to do with preferences shaped by economic incentives and conjunctures and probably owed much to notions of exploitation, privilege, and economic waste derived from ways of thinking established well before the Bolsheviks were even in power. One could view this as a Marxist notion and chalk it up to rigid Kremlin ideology, but then too many non-Marxists around the world shared the notion for it to be so easily labeled. We will find throughout the book that this is true of other ideas – for example, planning – that have usually been ascribed to the Kremlin's commitment to a disembodied and absolute "Marxist ideology."

This book examines exactly what the underlying logic and actual practice of Soviet economic policy was and how it changed over time in tandem with the global economy. The idea for the book started with the clear and ubiquitous evidence – in internal communications in the archives, in public speeches, and in all Soviet publications on the matter – that autarky was nowhere near the expressed desire of anyone in the Soviet Union. What Soviet officials did express was an abiding sense of the limitations of the country and the preponderance of Western economic might. The Cold War literature, so good at transcribing the tone and substance of US State Department officials' attitudes, consistently misrepresents these two fundamental characteristics of Soviet officials' discourse. Instead, many historians have imagined an equivalence of interests between West and East. The Cold War of this bipolar equivalence was a zero-sum game of enlarging one's camp. But the fact is that Soviet economic interests exhibited little of the competitive thrust assumed by most historians (and to be fair, prevalent in Soviet ideational discourse). Rather, the reality of the country's economic relations was characterized largely by accommodation and cooperation with the West and the search for an elementary admission to the markets of the global South.

To understand this commercial policy one needs first to understand the degree to which Soviet successes in physics (i.e., Sputnik and nuclear technology) and economic growth in the 1950s hid an abiding comparative underdevelopment in the realm of economy. This barely registers in most histories of the Cold War, and it is instructive that those few historians who acknowledge Soviet economic reality then find it necessary to dismiss the idea that material resources bear much of a relationship to global power. In the *Cambridge History of the Cold War*, for example, historian Odd Arne Westad wrote: "But even though Soviet capabilities overall were more on the scale of Britain and France than on those of the United States, the militarization of the Soviet economy and its society made it a formidable opponent in international affairs. First and foremost it constituted the other superpower as a result of its oppositional ideology: it was the only great power that throughout the Cold War steadfastly opposed US objectives and refused to be integrated into the global capitalist economy. By doing so it carved out a primary role for itself in international affairs, at great expense to its development over time."[6] A curious thing

[6] Odd Arne Westad, "The Cold War and the International History of the Twentieth Century," in Melvyn P. Leffler and Odd Arne Westad, eds., *The Cambridge History of the Cold War*, vol. 1 (Cambridge: Cambridge University Press, 2010), 11. This criticism of Westad's emphasis on ideology and his dismissal of the variegated importance of the Soviet Union's comparative underdevelopment is not meant to lump his scholarship with that of a more obfuscating pedigree that barely admits the constraints imposed by Soviet economic weakness. In fact, the Cambridge volumes he edited are laudable for their incorporation of views that conflict with that of his most recent scholarship on this matter. For example, in his essay in the same volume Charles Maier contends that "distinctions between socialism and capitalism seemed fundamental to ideological identity and to bloc cohesion in

that: dismissing economy when it comes to assessing Soviet global power. Of course Osama Bin Laden proves Westad right in the power that is garnered in the simple act of opposing. But to close that logical loop, Westad further requires Soviet autarky (its refusal "to be integrated into the global capitalist economy"). And Soviet autarky is wrong.[7] Rather than dismissing it, histories of the Cold War would do better to come to terms with the reality of Soviet economic underdevelopment before any arguments about "superpower" rivalry can be engaged.[8]

This book has much to say about the Soviet Union's economic engagement of the global South, but argues that Western Europe (and to some extent Japan) was the real focus of Soviet commercial and economic ambitions. There is a pivot in progress in the literature of the Cold War toward the global South.[9] The argument is that with the building of the Berlin Wall (that great signifier of Soviet autarky) the Cold War stagnated in Europe, whereupon Soviet and American energies were redirected south.[10]

the 1950s," (in ibid., 44) a formulation that seems to see the ideological conflict as more a matter of discourse than practice, whereas he perceives economic international policymaking on both sides as much more convergent than Westad and much Cold War scholarship allows. Maier's formulation points to another theme that this book addresses only in passing but that has been developed most forcefully by Mary Kaldor: The Cold War's ideological discourse so redolent of martial conflict on both sides was a tool more important to the cohesion and discipline of domestic audiences in America, Europe, and the Soviet Union than for the battle for minds and hearts abroad – which is a formulation not intended to deny that the battle for hearts and minds abroad was inexistent or even irrelevant, it was simply less consequential and useful a tool for international audiences, as at least Soviet leaders often acknowledged when abroad. See Mary Kaldor, *The Imaginary War. Understanding the East–West Conflict* (Oxford: Blackwell, 1990).

7 His insistence on the power of ideas is also perplexing. In his often excellent and important *The Global Cold War. Third World Interventions and the Making of Our Times* (Cambridge: Cambridge University Press, 2005) Westad achieved the dubious narrative feat of combining a discursive origin to the Cold War that ignores the power of economy to constrain and structure with a structural denouement to the Cold War that is dependent almost wholly on it, all in the space of one volume.

8 Appleman Williams pointed out the limitations of Soviet power long ago. "Startling as it may seem," he wrote, "in view of the constant emphasis on Soviet military power, the central fact confronting any past or present Russian leader is the imbalance of the economic and political development of the nation. Czarist and Soviet history is the record of a continuous, all-pervading struggle to reach a minimum level of material well-being, let alone relative prosperity or actual wealth." William Appleman Williams, *The Tragedy of American Diplomacy* (Cleveland: World Publishing Company, 1959), 280. Alexander Gerschenkron calculated that on the eve of World War I the industrial output of large-scale industry of Russia was 6.9 percent that of the output of the United States. See Gerschenkron, "The Rate of Growth in Russia: The Rate of Industrial Growth in Russia, Since 1885," *The Journal of Economic History* Vol. 7, Supplement: Economic Growth: A Symposium (1974): 155.

9 Inaugurated most forcefully by Westad, *The Global Cold War.*

10 Jeremi Suri's idiosyncratic *Power and Protest. Global Revolution and the Rise of Détente* (Cambridge: Harvard University Press, 2003) uses this trope to a different purpose, one that compels the two superpowers to look inward in defense of their legitimacy rather than outward toward the South. This is certainly a step in the right direction, causing his book to lie uncomfortably in the canon of Cold War literature.

In fact, the Cold War remained very dynamic in Europe, particularly commercially and financially. But inasmuch as Cold War historians have moved away from the importance of commerce and finance to chase the chimera of ideology, they have found it necessary to move away from post-Berlin Wall Europe. It has also proven difficult to sustain a Cold War narrative of bipolar struggle in a context (Europe) in which the Soviets are seeking accommodation and a modicum of integration. But Europe remained a much more important arena than any in the global South, and erasing it from the Cold War master narrative after the early 1960s obscures the unremitting, hypocritical American hostility to Soviet economic interests in Western Europe that informed Soviet policy everywhere else.[11]

This book also reconsiders East–South relations in light of the material resources that informed each country. Much ink today is spilled over the idea that the Third World was presented with two models of development to choose from, whereby the choice placed a country in one camp or the other. But the reality was complex enough to make this academic formulation unintelligible. In the global South, the choice was not a matter of premeditation and implementation. Choices were made within an evolving structure of constraints and possibilities continuously generated by a global liberal economic order and an international politics largely dominated by the United States and the existing and then former empires of Europe. Indeed the middle-income economy of the Soviet Union was subject to these same dynamics, as this book illustrates.

In the course of telling the story of Soviet trade, the narrative tries to do away with a persistent idea that has very little evidence behind it. In relating the transition between Joseph Stalin and Nikita Khrushchev, historians have often talked about Soviet agents "fanning out" and "wooing" the Third World.[12] This is introduced as an absolutely new policy that radically distinguished Khrushchev from his more careful predecessor. This kind of language is particularly problematic. In using it, historians perpetuate the racialized and gendered worldview with which the State Department looked at the world. The Third World is made to lack ambition and initiative, both manly characteristics found more readily

[11] The crucial importance of Western Europe to the Soviet Union has been recovered in Jonathan Haslam, *Russia's Cold War. From the October Revolution to the Fall of the Wall* (New Haven: Yale University Press, 2011).

[12] In keeping with the practice of using particularly good histories to make critical commentary on the field, see Aleksandr Fursenko and Timothy Naftali, *Khrushchev's Cold War. The Inside Story of an American Adversary* (New York: W. W. Norton & Company, 2006), 58, for an example of this language.

in the two Cold War poles. The Soviet archival evidence, however, shows almost exactly the opposite of this. The Soviets more often than not waited for others to initiate relations; it is difficult to read the relevant documents in any way other than as responding to initiatives from outside (whether coming from rich businessmen or Third World leaders), and there is a marked dearth of documents suggesting the contrary.[13] Moreover, this idea of a new leadership sending its emissaries all over the world upon Stalin's death obscures a clear continuity in Soviet commercial policy, which was after all carried out during and after Stalin's rule by the same top official, Anastas Mikoyan. It is of course undeniable that Soviet foreign affairs, economic and otherwise, became much more active from the middle of the 1950s, at around the time of Khrushchev's ascension to power. But it is more accurate to view this increased activity as provoked by the radical global reorderings of decolonization than by any willful, autonomous change at the Kremlin. Though this book focuses squarely on the Soviet Union, it makes clear that the new leaders of the global South were not languid, effeminate, child-like creatures seeking ideological guidance from dynamic white men. They were – every single one of them – men of ambition who used the Soviet Union to their advantage to better negotiate a hierarchical world order that punished insubordination to Western dictates. If there were shared attributes to their distinct worldviews, the reason does not lie in Soviet guidance or subversion, but in large measure in the shared economic and political circumstances in which they exercised their agency.

Three important areas of Soviet commercial history are not covered in this book: trade within the Communist Bloc, the brief but important economic exchange with China in the wake of Mao's triumph there, and military trade. The first two of these important topics have received good treatments already, although much work remains to be done, while the trade in Soviet armaments simply cannot be carried out given the current state of archival access in Moscow.[14] It is unclear, however, that

[13] A few other historians have noted this tendency as well, for example Vojtech Mastny with respect to India. See Vojtech Mastny, "The Soviet Union's Partnership with India," *Journal of Cold War Studies* 12:3 (2010): 51.

[14] The best book on Soviet economic relations with countries in East–Central Europe is the underappreciated Randall W. Stone, *Satellites and Commissars. Strategy and Conflict in the Politics of Soviet-Bloc Trade* (Princeton: Princeton University Press, 1996). The history of the massive Soviet economic transfer to China of the 1950s has not yet received the focus it deserves. The best, indeed only, book on the subject, Shen Zhihua's *Sulian zhuanjia zai Zhongguo, 1948–1960* [Soviet Experts in China, 1948–1960] (Beijing: Zhonguo guoji chubanshe, 2003) is still awaiting English translation, though an earlier volume, Odd Arne Westad, ed., *Brothers in Arms. The Rise and Fall of the Sino-Soviet Alliance, 1945–1963* (Washington, DC: Woodrow Wilson Center Press, 1998) covers some preliminary work on the subject.

consideration of any of these three areas changes the basic outline of Soviet international political economy sketched in this book. The massive economic and technological transfer that was the Soviet aid program to China seems to have left little in the way of a legacy with respect to Soviet aid programs later on – even if its legacy in China was far-reaching. Meanwhile, economic exchange within the Communist Bloc was derided by those involved as "an exchange of inefficiencies."[15] Despite the fact that trade within the Bloc constituted the lion's share of Soviet commercial volume, it not only decreased continuously from the mid 1950s as a share of total trade, but was almost surely overvalued in Soviet statistics with respect to trade in hard currency. Should any of the conclusions drawn in this book require revision after future scholars research these areas of economic exchange, or indeed after more complete histories of Soviet bilateral economic exchanges with particular countries are written than was possible in this volume, the book will have served its purpose in reconnecting economy with the debates on Soviet history, Soviet foreign policy, the Cold War, and the international history of the twentieth century more generally.

The debate over the size of the Soviet economy

Before going on with the story of Soviet globalization, I would like to briefly discuss the debate over the size of the Soviet economy, since an understanding of the issues concerning this debate goes a long way in informing much of what the reader will encounter throughout the book. The debate over the relative size of the Soviet economy is far from closed. Given the arbitrariness of domestic prices and the immeasurability of the idiosyncrasies of the Soviet system – pervasiveness of shortages, systemic misrepresentation of production, etc. – the subject is likely unknowable and thus will sustain a wide array of opinions for a long time to come. As economic historian Mark Harrison put it, "there is no single, objective truth waiting to be discovered beneath the surface of the lie. The Soviet GNP is not a hidden number awaiting discovery, but an aggregation of assumptions and hypotheses about a multi-dimensional reality which resists reduction to a unique figure."[16]

[15] Philip Hanson's *The Rise and Fall of the Soviet Economy. An Economic History of the USSR from 1945* (New York: Longman, 2003), 120.

[16] Mark Harrison, *Accounting for War. Soviet Production, Employment and the Defence Burden, 1940–1945* (Cambridge: Cambridge University Press, 1996), 4.

The first attempt at a survey of Soviet national income was carried out by British economist Colin Clark, one of the pioneers of the concept of gross national product (GNP) as a way to analyze national economies. Clark's first work on the Soviet economy appeared in 1939, and it was of necessity characterized by very poor data.[17] The main issue was prices; how can one make a comparative assessment of an economy with an inconvertible currency and a command system that does not set prices according to supply and demand, and thus cannot measure relative scarcities? Would it be better to compute quantities in rubles, or should an economist try to find a dollar amount for a comparable good in the West and produce a system of accounts comparable to those in market economies? Clark decided on the latter. Although more complete statistical sets would not be made available by the Soviets until 1956, Clark was nevertheless able to work out different data sets of a limited array of products. Contrary to later analyses, Clark concluded that from 1928 to World War II, Soviet national income grew by less than 50 percent, at an annual rate of 3.1 percent.[18]

Clark's deep-seated skepticism of Soviet statistics was shared by Naum Jasny, a former Menshevik émigré whose work on the Soviet economy first brought to the fore the economic disaster of Soviet agriculture. Jasny was also sensitive to the inadequacies of publicly available statistical data in depicting the lived experience inside the Soviet Union; his conclusion on the growth of the Soviet economy, although more than double the rate of growth suggested by Clark, was still far below the official Soviet figure. While the Central Statistical Administration (*Tsentral'noe statisticheskoe upravlenie* [TsSU]) calculated a five-fold increase from the First Five-Year Plan to World War II, Jasny posited a near-doubling of Soviet real national product from 1928 to 1940.[19]

The greatest sustained effort at an analysis of Soviet national accounts, however, was Abram Bergson's project. Bergson gathered a number of scholars under his direction and came to work under the auspices of the RAND Corporation of the United States Air Force.[20] Together they developed the Soviet national income and product (SNIP) project.

[17] Colin Clark, *A Critique of Soviet Statistics* (London: Macmillan & Co., 1939).

[18] Colin Clark, *The Conditions of Economic Progress* (New York: St. Martin's Press, 1957), 247.

[19] Naum Jasny, *Soviet Industrialization, 1928–1952* (Chicago: University of Chicago Press, 1961), 444. While arguing that "exactness is impossible," and that only orders of magnitude could be attempted, Jasny calculated that gross national product at real 1926–27 prices amounted to 29.8 billion rubles in 1928 and 56.4 billion in 1940. This figure nearly doubled again by 1955, amounting to 111.5 billion.

[20] His colleagues included Raymond Powell, Janet Chapman, Roman Bernaut, Abram S. Becker, Richard Moorsteen, Lynn Turgeon and Jerzy F. Karcz.

Bergson was more trustful than his predecessors of Soviet statistical publications, arguing that were the Soviets freely inventing figures, they would not have gone to the lengths they did in hiding certain data such as that relating to defense spending. Moreover, captured archives during World War II confirmed the correspondence between published and secret figures. There was thus a fair amount of conflict between the Bergson school and earlier assessments. Bergson and his colleagues were particularly critical of Jasny, condemning his work for being unscientific and for displaying political biases against the Soviet Union. Jasny, for his part, soon saw that he was having difficulties publishing in American journals, with only the University of Glasgow's *Soviet Studies* available to him. The idea that Soviet statistics were basically honest was so entrenched in American academia that he was rarely invited to conferences and symposiums there, and could not find funding for his work.[21] Bergson's numbers were proved to be more generous than any that had come before, but the spread in the conclusions he presented also presaged methodological problems. When computed in 1928 ruble prices, Bergson's calculations arrived at a near tripling of the Soviet Union's GNP in the nine years to 1937, whereas the same exercise in 1937 prices showed only 60 percent increase for the same time period.[22] Much of this disparity was later attributed to what economists call the Gerschenkron effect, the change in an index's growth rate that comes about when different base years are chosen.[23] At any rate, it would be the work of Bergson and his associates that would set the methodological standard for later elaborations of Soviet national income.

It was most importantly the Central Intelligence Agency (CIA) that continued Bergson's trustful tradition of Soviet statistics and reworked them into statistical sets of Soviet national accounts more comprehensive

[21] For a good synopsis of Jasny's troubles see John Howard Wilhelm, "The Failure of the American Sovietological Economics Profession," *Europe-Asia Studies* 55:1 (2003): 59–74.

[22] Abram Bergson, *The Real National Income of Soviet Russia since 1928* (Cambridge: Harvard University Press, 1961), 128, 153.

[23] This happens because as an economy develops, the structure of prices in that economy changes, so that, for example, capital-intensive goods may become less expensive when compared to labor-intensive goods, as happened in the Soviet Union through the 1930s. Growth in machinery, comparatively expensive in 1928, will seem high in 1928 prices, but less so in 1937 prices, when machinery became less expensive in relation to labor-intensive products such as foodstuffs. In other words, the use of price weights of an earlier year will give higher growth rates than the use of prices of later years, at least in rapidly growing economies. Soviet statistics were notorious for this kind of bias, which they used systematically in their publications. For a good, concise explanation of how the Gerschenkron effect influenced economic computations of Soviet national income see Harrison, *Accounting for War*, 51–53.

than any that had come before. Following Bergson, the CIA aggregated official physical output series into branch, sector, and GNP indexes, and then weighted them to an adjusted factor cost standard, that is, clean of indirect taxation. This generally reduced official growth rates, but not by much; mostly the CIA replicated much of TsSU's work. Published annually, the CIA's statistical handbooks became the most influential reference on the Soviet economy in Western scholarship. Naturally, given their source-base and methodology, the agency's conclusions were alarming to American policymakers. The Soviet Union, according to CIA statistics, was the second biggest economy in the world, by 1965 already more than three times the size of the British economy.[24] Its GNP as a percentage of American GNP went from not quite 49 percent in 1965 to 57 percent in 1974, where it hovered until about the mid 1980s.[25]

British economists never shared their American counterparts' positivist attitude toward Soviet statistics, or even the meaningfulness of a straightforward comparison between the United States and the Soviet Union in GNP terms, which was after all a Western concept developed for market economies.[26] The figures calculated by the CIA were never universally adopted in the field, but the trickle of criticism did not become a flood until British economists brought the skepticism of economists within the Soviet Union to the attention of Western scholarship. The debates that ensued focused mostly on two issues: the perennial misgivings about the reliability of Soviet statistics, and the debates over Soviet investment and hidden inflation that played out mostly in the pages of the journal *Soviet Studies.*

Alec Nove was the first to make this connection. Introducing the research of Viktor Krasovskii and Vladimir Fal'tsman, Nove argued that far from the respectable increases in Soviet investment tabulated by both TsSU and the CIA, the volume of investment may indeed have been falling in the late 1970s and early 1980s.[27] The statistics were wrong because they hid a significant degree of inflation that arose from the growing disparity between the rising price of a given product and that product's real use characteristics, which often remained unaltered. In other words, higher prices that benefited an enterprise's success indicators were

24 The numbers, in 1973 dollars, were 463.7 billion for the Soviet Union compared to 142.4 billion for the British economy. CIA, *Handbook of Economic Statistics* (Washington, DC, 1975), 29.

25 CIA, *Handbook of Economic Statistics* (Washington, DC, 1991), 34.

26 For a representative example of this skepticism see the discussion in Alec Nove, *The Soviet Economic System* (London: Allen & Unwin, 1977), 353–65.

27 Alec Nove, "A Note on Growth, Investment and Price-Indices," *Soviet Studies* 33:1 (1981).

all too often justified by fictitious improvements in quality. This, coupled with the systemic exaggeration of output that characterized the Soviet system, rendered both official statistics and their CIA parallel suspect. Capital-intensive and fast-changing technological products were generally more vulnerable to these processes of exaggeration and falsification than more homogeneous commodity-type products.

Peter Wiles and Philip Hanson further developed the issue of hidden inflation and exaggerated Soviet investment indexes, with Wiles arguing that economics should measure utility output rather than goods output and Hanson bringing to the discussion the work of Grigorii Khanin and Konstantin Val'tukh.[28] Yet another Soviet émigré and Soviet-trained economist, Igor Birman, sounded the alarm on the possibility that Soviet growth in the late 1970s and early 1980s may already have been negative, rather than the two percent the CIA computed.[29] Birman never made an attempt at an encompassing study of Soviet GNP, but he remained critical of CIA estimates and argued – against the general consensus in the United States – that the Soviet economy was on the brink of collapse through the 1980s, a prescient analysis for which he later got little credit.[30] The argument, then, became one between conclusions drawn from sophisticated but methodologically problematic statistical representations of the Soviet economy, and the lived reality of the Soviet economy. The ghost of Jasny continued its challenge to Bergson and his legacy.

[28] Peter Wiles, "Soviet Consumption and Investment Prices, and the Meaningfulness of Real Investment," *Soviet Studies* 34:2 (1982): 289–95 and Philip Hanson, "The CIA, the TsSU and the Real Growth of Soviet Investment," *Soviet Studies* 36:4 (1984): 571–81. Hanson summarized the eventual debate best when he concluded that "as in many of the arguments between Soviet emigrés and the US intelligence community, the question is whether you back the insider who uses the back of an envelope or the outsider with a computer. Either or both may be wrong, but both are handicapped by the sheer paucity of the data." Ibid., 578. More recently, and with the benefit of previously unpublished archival data, Byung-Yeon Kim argued that state retail price subsidies, which came to amount in the late 1980s to about 20 percent of the state budget, had the effect of squeezing credit for enterprises and constricting investment in general, which in turn caused greater subsidies. These distorting subsidies, which may have started as early as the 1950s, picked up steam after the 1965 reforms and became particularly detrimental in the late 1970s and through the 1980s. They created retail shortages and hidden inflation of a magnitude that contributed to the collapse of the Soviet economy, especially after oil revenues dried up with the oil price collapse in 1985, so diminishing state resources further. See Byung-Yeon Kim, "Causes of Repressed Inflation in the Soviet Consumer Market, 1965–1989: Retail Price Subsidies, the Siphoning Effect, and the Budget Deficit," *Economic History Review* 55:1 (2002): 105–27.

[29] In Igor Birman, "The Financial Crisis in the USSR," *Soviet Studies* 32:1 (1980): 84–105, Birman was already arguing for very significant budget deficits obscured by hidden inflation. The famed economist Abel Aganbegian, who came to be one of the main economic advisors of Mikhail Gorbachev, later confirmed that, official statistics notwithstanding, the government was indeed working under the more pessimistic assessments of the Russian economists.

[30] Igor Birman, "The Imbalance of the Soviet Economy," *Soviet Studies* 40:2 (1988): 210–21.

The one economist who went furthest in the downward revision of TsSU and CIA statistics was Grigorii Khanin. His harsh criticism of official Soviet statistics made him an outcast in the field within the Soviet Union, where he found it hard to publish his work, or even to find a job. In 1987, however, with the coming of glasnost and the help of journalist Vasilii Selyunin, he published his famous – among economists – "*Lukavaia tsifra*" (the cunning figure) in *Novyi Mir*, a journal not specialized in economics.[31] Khanin made the most sustained argument for statistical analyses that bear ground realities in mind. As he argued in his review of Western economic Sovietology, and particularly in his criticism of the Bergson School, "nowhere was I able to find proof that scholars of this [the Bergson] school read the daily Soviet press, the satirical publications of Soviet reality, the journal *Krokodil*, the books of émigré writers, etc., exactly that literature where one will find, more or less, a truthful description of Soviet reality."[32] Given the poor quality and assortment of products, and the severe shortages that resulted from artificial price stability, it was eminently evident that the Soviets did not live even near the consumption levels of Western countries, whatever the statistics appeared to evince. Khanin tried his hand, perhaps quixotically, at quantifying his everyday reality.

Deeming official aggregate statistics hopelessly deceptive, Khanin calculated a set of alternative statistics based on figures he felt could not be as systematically corrupted as the aggregate figures used by the CIA and the TsSU.[33] He argued that more homogeneous products tended to produce more reliable data because managers and bureaucrats dealing with their production had a more difficult time claiming nonexistent improvements in quality and assortment. Thus he consulted Soviet input–output tables to measure the growth of raw material consumption and electrical power consumption, among other items. He calculated that the Soviet economy increased by about seven times from 1928 until the end of the Soviet Union, rather than the ninety times stipulated by official statistics.

[31] For an English-language discussion of Khanin's work before a more substantial clarification of his work came out in books in the 1990s see Richard E. Ericson, "The Soviet Statistical Debate: Khanin versus the TsSU," in Henry S. Rowen and Charles Wolf, Jr., eds., *The Impoverished Superpower. Perestroika and the Soviet Military Burden* (San Francisco: Institute for Contemporary Studies Press, 1990). Khanin eventually gathered his arguments in G. Khanin, *Dinamika ekonomicheskogo rasvitiia SSSR* (Novosibirsk: Nauka, 1991).

[32] G. I. Khanin, *Sovetskii ekonomischeskii rost. Analiz zapadnykh otsenok* (Novosibirsk: Ekor, 1993), 92–93.

[33] For an excellent critical assessment of the problems with Soviet statistics and the many biases they accumulate see Anders Åslund, "How Small is Soviet National Income," in Henry S. Rowen and Charles Wolf, Jr., eds., *The Impoverished Superpower. Perestroika and the Soviet Military Burden* (San Francisco: Institute for Contemporary Studies Press, 1990).

Depending on the base size of the Soviet economy in 1928, this would put the Soviet economy at the end of the 1980s at anywhere between 8 and 20 percent of the US economy. In other words, rather than the behemoth more than three times the size of Great Britain the CIA fantasized about, Khanin's Soviet Union had an economy roughly on par with that of Great Britain by the 1980s – unless it was much smaller. Incidentally, Khanin's picture of the Soviet economy mirrored Federal Reserve estimates, notwithstanding the alarming numbers emanating from Langley just across the Potomac River. When Alan Greenspan alighted on Russia in 1990 ready to help avert a possible financial crisis, he reckoned the Soviet economy to be "about the same size as the United Kingdom's, or about one-sixth the size of all Europe's."[34]

Khanin's calculations and conclusions were politely received in the Western academic establishment, but not necessarily adopted.[35] Other calculations of Soviet national income had already come to the fore that revised downward the impossible CIA figures, and so scholars could have their pick according to their particular inclinations.[36] One last observation is worth making for its relevance to estimates of Soviet national income.

[34] Alan Greenspan, *The Age of Turbulence. Adventures in a New World* (New York: The Penguin Press, 2007), 135.

[35] Neither was Khanin criticized much, at least not by Western economists, who generally think Khanin's numbers as plausible as anybody else's. The most extensive critical overview of Khanin's work is Mark Harrison, "Soviet Economic Growth since 1928: The Alternative Statistics of G. I. Khanin," *Europe-Asia Studies* 45:1 (1993): 141–67. Harrison's most adamant criticism is Khanin's disregard for the Gerschenkron effect, as Khanin tends to attribute to methodological errors the effect's (legitimate) inflation of results in Western calculations, and which Khanin, in his own calculations, tends to (unfairly) add to hidden inflation. Harrison praises Khanin's models for being "consistent and well-founded." Interestingly, Harrison points out that the main point of deviation between Khanin's calculations and those of the CIA pertain to the prewar era. Khanin, like Clark before him, estimated only a 50 percent increase in the Soviet economy from 1928 to 1940. For the postwar period until the 1980s, Khanin's figures resemble those of the CIA; he estimates more rapid growth than the CIA in the 1950s and a sharper slowdown in the 1960s and 1970s. Khanin estimated no growth – and so negative growth on a per capita basis – in the 1980s, rather than the CIA's two percent growth. The large discrepancy between the two in the final outcome, then, obtains largely from the smaller economic base in the postwar period that, for Khanin, was the result of an unimpressive economic expansion in the 1930s.

[36] These mostly coincided at a Soviet per capita income of about a third that of the United States, while acknowledging that methodological difficulties tend to overestimate Soviet growth. Among the most important were World Bank studies carried out in Paul Marer, *Dollar GNPs of the USSR and Eastern Europe* (Baltimore: The Johns Hopkins University Press, 1985), Imogene Edwards and Gertrude Schroeder, *Consumption in the USSR: An International Comparison*, a study prepared for the use of the Joint Economic Committee (Washington, DC: Government Printing Office, 1981), and the immensely useful Angus Maddison, *The World Economy. A Millennial Perspective* (Paris: Development Centre of the Organization for Economic Cooperation and Development, 2001), which is CIA-based with a downward revision that makes the Soviet economy the fourth biggest economy in 1990 after the United States, Japan and, strangely, China.

Anders Åslund reported that, upon the collapse of the Soviet economy, at least one-fifth of the Soviet production decline should have been attributed to its utter uselessness. In other words, when production finally came to cater to actual demand, much of it turned out not to be in demand at all; the drop in production of this useless output, computed statistically as a sudden and real contraction of the Soviet economy, should have been seen, he argued, as a desirable development, an end to wasteful production. "Russia's level of economic development," Åslund concluded, "remains where it was during the Soviet era, roughly on par with Brazil."[37]

There are reasons for this book to take the British and Russian criticisms of American economic Sovietology seriously, regardless of the impossibility of arriving at a magic GNP number. We will see that it was generally issues of quality and assortment that prevented the Soviet leadership from furthering their international economic engagement. Rich countries found little use for Soviet manufactured products, and poor countries that imported Soviet industrial equipment and technological products also found them sorely wanting. Despite the hard currency woes that afflicted much of the global South and motivated them to establish barter trade with the Soviet Union, the import of Soviet products remained, throughout the Cold War, a second-best solution to the challenges of economic development. In the industrialized world, the Soviets found a disappointingly small market for their manufactured products, particularly their capital-intensive products, the selling of which would have announced to the world the great technological strides made by the Soviet economic system. What's more, the change in the structure of their foreign trade with the rich, industrialized countries was more representative of a middle-income country slipping toward the single commodity production reminiscent of poor, primary-producing countries. Whereas in 1955, manufactured goods made up 28 percent of Soviet exports to Western Europe, in 1983 the figure was 6 percent.[38] In the mid 1980s, some three-fourths of their exports to the developed countries consisted of oil, natural gas, and gold.

[37] Anders Åslund, "Russia," *Foreign Policy* 125:4 (2001): 20. The corollary to this view, of course, is that the "collapse" was not as destructive and extensive as the 44 percent decline indicated by official statistics.

[38] A more international perspective substantiates the decline. While in 1965 the Soviets provided 0.82 percent of the Organisation for Economic Co-operation and Development (OECD) imports of manufactured goods, by 1981 the figure was 0.51. In that same period the share of imports from newly industrialized countries increased from 2.74 percent to 6.95 percent. Anders Åslund, "How Small is Soviet National Income," 43.

Imports of Western manufactures into the Soviet Union were the other side of the coin. We have already seen how in the 1970s Vladimir Treml noted a large increase in the importance of trade to the Soviet economy, over one-fifth by the 1970s when measured in domestic prices.[39] The larger share of that growth came from imports, which increased from 7 percent of national income in 1960 to almost 15 percent in 1976.[40] This faster rate of nominal import growth was the result of shifts in trade patterns. The Soviets had become more reliant on fuel exports, which were domestically undervalued, especially after world prices skyrocketed in 1973; at the same time they increased Western machinery imports, which rose from 17 percent of total machinery imports in 1970 to almost 40 percent seven years later.[41] The Soviet Union was by no means a banana republic, but the pattern of greater dependence on primary commodity exports to finance the importation of more Western manufactures was as unmistakable as it was a sign of mounting economic limitations. These patterns were markedly different from those experienced by industrial heavyweights such as Japan and Germany.

For the purposes of this study, the vague and perhaps unscientific observations of Greenspan and Khanin are a much better guide than the methodical and alarming – to Americans – statistical compendiums of the CIA. As the narrative unfolds it will become apparent why. The ruble amounts used in this book usually denote foreign trade rubles – although it is not always immediately clear in the archival material. These were basically an accounting unit that transformed convertible currency into ruble figures according to a meaningless exchange rate set by the Soviet government.[42] The value of exports, then, was difficult to judge, except when exports were bought for hard currency. Commercial relations

[39] Vladimir G. Treml, "Foreign Trade and the Soviet Economy: Changing Parameters and Interrelations," in Egon Neuberger and Laura D'Andrea Tyson, eds., *The Impact of International Economic Disturbances on the Soviet Union and Eastern Europe. Transmission and Response* (New York: Pergamon Press, 1980).

[40] Imports and exports remained in balance in convertible currency, that is, the Soviets were not financing imports through debt. The disparity was a function of domestic prices only.

[41] Treml, "Foreign Trade and the Soviet Economy," 190.

[42] Throughout the book, unless otherwise noted, ruble figures are current for that year. The exchange rate to the US dollar was about four rubles to the dollar from 1950 to 1961, whereupon it was decided that the conversion rate would be 1.1 dollar per ruble. This may well have been viewed as an incredible revaluation of the ruble; Soviet strength in other words. However, domestically, rubles were exchanged at the rate of ten old ones for one new one, and prices were slashed by ten. Not that this meant the ruble had been devalued vis-à-vis the dollar. In fact, none of it meant much at all, except for accounting for actually convertible currency in rubles. For a breakdown of ruble values and conversion coefficients of foreign trade rubles to 1961 see Dohan, "Soviet Foreign Trade in the NEP Economy," 703–08.

with Third World countries, however, were rarely on a hard currency basis; they were characterized by barter agreements. It is here, particularly, that the quality problems swept under the carpet by TsSU statistical methodologies become politically prominent.

The fate of eight Soviet Ilyushin IL-18 airplanes sold to Ghana in the early 1960s will serve by way of illustration. A Soviet delegation to Ghana ascertained Ghanaian claims that of the eight airplanes sold to that country, only four worked regularly, but clocking a mere fifteen hours of flying time each month on average. By comparison, the single Bristol Britannia airplane in the country's fleet was flying 113 hours monthly, and costing the government less in repairs.[43] It would seem, then, that the value of the one British plane – all other characteristics being equal – was almost twice that of the eight Soviet planes. Value readjustments here do not necessarily have to be calculated by the historian, however; the Soviet Union's trade partners themselves readjusted the value of continuing economic relations with the Soviets by often turning away from Soviet markets and back to world markets. In other words, Soviet comparative underdevelopment constrained the Soviets politically and economically in ways the Cold War literature has yet to fully assimilate.

Inasmuch as the foreign trade sector became – and remained – one of the fastest growing sectors of the Soviet postwar economy, it could be argued that the leadership was broadly successful in stimulating the country's foreign trade. This success, however, was highly qualified. The archival evidence shows a Soviet leadership that was under persistent economic constraints in relations with the West and South. It is not the CIA calculations, but rather Khanin's speculations and Greenspan's cursory observations that most closely conform to this picture. The volume of the Soviet Union's foreign economic relations was consonant with the country's size and level of economic development. The constraints and frustrations at the top that this book documents should help situate the Soviet Union in the world economy of the twentieth century, and reconfigure the country's capability for power projection to more modest dimensions than has up to now been the case in the literature of international history. The postwar Soviet emergence in the world arena occurred against the background of – and was enabled by – an embryonic economic globalization. This is the story of the Soviet experience of first the ebb and then the flow of the great globalizing process of the twentieth century.

[43] GARF, f. 5446, op. 97, d. 1382, ll. 63–64.

PART I

Isolation

CHAPTER I

Depression Stalinism

Karl Polanyi's *Great Transformation*, written in 1944, concentrated on the international underpinning of capitalism, and explained how one of its pillars, the gold standard, fell apart, bringing to the fore the forces of economic nationalism that led to a disintegration of Europe's political order. Polanyi deemed bolshevism one of these radical forces, but categorized Russia as a special case in the short passage in which he discussed that country. As many historians would later do, Polanyi counted two Russian revolutions, the first, in 1917, "embodied traditional Western European ideals, while the second formed part of the utterly new development of the thirties."[1] The first, he argued, was merely a Russian event, while the second "formed part of a simultaneous universal transformation."[2] The pressures of a dysfunctional gold standard were felt throughout the globe, homogenizing many of the outcomes:

> By 1924 "War Communism" was a forgotten incident and Russia had reestablished a free domestic grain market, while maintaining state control of foreign trade and key industries. She was now bent on increasing her foreign trade, which depended mainly on exports of grain, timber, furs, and some other organic raw materials, the prices of which were slumping heavily in the course of the agrarian depression which preceded the general break in trade. Russia's inability to develop an export trade on favorable terms restricted her imports of machinery and hence the establishment of a national industry; this, again, affected the terms of barter between town and countryside – the so-called "scissors" – unfavorably, thus increasing the antagonism of the peasantry to the rule of the urban workers. In this way the disintegration of world economy increased the strain on the makeshift solutions of the agrarian question in Russia and hastened the coming of the *kolkhoz*. The failure of the traditional political system of Europe to provide

[1] Karl Polanyi, *The Great Transformation. The Political and Economic Origins of Our Time* (Boston: Beacon Press, 1944), 255.
[2] Ibid., 256.

> safety and security worked in the same direction since it induced the need for armaments, thus enhancing the burdens of high-pressure industrialization. The absence of the nineteenth-century balance-of-power system, as well as the inability of the world market to absorb Russia's agricultural produce, forced her reluctantly into the paths of self-sufficiency. Socialism in one country was brought about by the incapacity of market economy to provide a link between all countries; what appeared as Russian autarchy was merely the passing of capitalist internationalism.[3]

Later explanations for Soviet autarky would imagine a purposeful effort at an import substitution strategy that quickly succeeded.[4] On the face of it, this seemed a logical conclusion. Soviet trade volume increased rapidly during the period of the First Five-Year Plan, only to drop dramatically thereafter. Initial imports of Western technology seemed to have paid off in productivity gains and general economic growth, and import substitution was a leitmotif in Soviet propaganda during the second half of the 1930s. This argument does not, however, take into account the fast-changing international developments that Polanyi and scholars of international political economy have described as seminal to later decades.

In fact, Polanyi's analysis has roughly held up to the scrutiny of later economists of the Soviet Union. In the 1920s, the world began to experience the mechanization and modernization of agriculture.[5] Although mechanization did not increase yields, it raised worker productivity, reducing the need for farm labor, swelling urban populations, and encouraging the occupation of productive, arable plains in Argentina, Australia, and other regions of recent settlement. Improvements in transport also brought these new, higher-yielding grain-producing regions into the world market. The overall effect was to depress the world price of grain and, in Europe, to cripple the agricultural sector and incur protection and subsidies from

[3] Ibid.

[4] See Alexander Gerschenkron's arguments in his *Economic Relations with the USSR* (New York, 1945), later developed by Franklyn Holzman in his otherwise excellent *Foreign Trade under Central Planning* (Cambridge: Harvard University Press, 1974), especially in chapter 6, which timidly took up some of Polanyi's points, but stressed a domestic drive to autarky, rather than international pressure for it. See also E. H. Carr and R. W. Davies, *Foundations of a Planned Economy, 1926–1929*, vol. 1 (New York: The Macmillan Company, 1969), 402–13, which overemphasizes Preobrazhenskii's arguments on foreign dependence and discounts the arguments on the right by Sokol'nikov and the more centrist Bazarov. The latter two argued for a development of agricultural exports as a first priority, in order that the Soviet Union may be able to import industrial equipment. It is not clear why Carr and Davies thought that the leadership did not take these opinions seriously when Sokol'nikov was, by any measure, part of the leadership and when his faction had, in the first instance, won the argument.

[5] See Jeffry A. Frieden, *Global Capitalism. Its Fall and Rise in the Twentieth Century* (New York: W. W. Norton & Company, 2006), 167–68.

European governments. As Charles Kindleberger noted, it was the grain-exporting countries, among them the Soviet Union, which first felt the cold grip of what would become the Great Depression.

In the Soviet Union, by and large, Soviet grain prices fluctuated in relation to two developments. While greater domestic demand increased prices within the Soviet Union, Soviet officials were under pressure to set prices low in an attempt to export grain on profitable terms, an effort made difficult by falling world prices.[6] Official purchase prices thus oscillated according to the need for export profits and the conflicting need to encourage grain marketings. The peasants responded by using grain to increase livestock and the more profitable marketing of meat and other livestock products, the prices of which were mostly set by the domestic market and were rising sharply on increased demand.

The price of industrial goods also increased dramatically within the Soviet Union as a result of the success of the New Economic Policy (NEP), which increased overall demand. The deliberate decision on the part of the Soviet government to suppress these rising prices brought about shortages, the so-called goods famine, or inflation by another name.[7] Peasants responded to the dismal situation in their terms of trade by withdrawing from the market and waiting for a more propitious time, turning the grain into feed and stores rather than exchanging it for industrial products and consumer items produced in urban areas. Robert Allen calculated the substantial elasticity enjoyed by peasants' grain marketings before the end of NEP, amounting to a 7 percent increase in grain marketing to every 10 percent rise in its price;[8] an improvement in the countryside's terms of trade might indeed have substantially increased the marketing of grain to the cities.[9] Many in the leadership had a fair

[6] Michael R. Dohan, "Soviet Foreign Trade in the NEP Economy and Soviet Industrialization Strategy" (PhD dissertation, MIT, 1969), 343–45. True as it was of grain, this concern was particularly acute in the case of other agricultural products, especially eggs, butter and flax.

[7] See R. W. Davies' discussion in *The Socialist Offensive. The Collectivisation of Soviet Agriculture, 1929–1930* (Cambridge: Harvard University Press, 1980), 38–41.

[8] For an opposite view see Paul R. Gregory, *Before Command. An Economic History of Russia from Emancipation to the First Five-Year Plan* (Princeton: Princeton University Press, 1994), 107.

[9] Robert C. Allen, "Agricultural Marketing and the Possibilities for Industrialisation in the Soviet Union in the 1930s," *Explorations in Economic History* 34:4 (1997): 387–410. Another reason for the failure of grain marketings was the substantial decrease in average farm size that occurred upon the onset of the revolution. Estates and large farms had provided most of the surplus grain exported by tsarist Russia; however these had been eliminated during the Bolshevik revolution, resulting in smaller farms and greater consumption of grain in the farms, a development compounded by population growth in the countryside. With subsistence farming on the rise, marketings to the cities decreased. Allen calculated that "the decline in surplus extraction was responsible for about one-quarter of the decline in marketing, while the deterioration in the terms of trade accounted for the

notion that this was the case, but then, domestic grain markets were not the only moving targets. There were also the world markets to contend with, after all, and these were not being very cooperative with Soviet industrialization plans in the late 1920s.

In pre-revolutionary times, while the gold standard underpinned worldwide economic integration and growth, the Russian economy had been able to secure foreign credit to fuel growth in the industrial sector, even as erratic but generally growing agricultural exports supported most of the necessary foreign investment and technology transfer that was transforming Russian industry. This was not at all the situation during the industrialization debates of the second half of the 1920s. Indeed, at just the time when foreign trade surpluses were needed to complement the great push in industrial investment that the Soviet government envisioned in the aftermath of a largely restored economy, the state barely managed to export a fifth of tsarist-era grain exports in 1926–27, and less than a tenth in 1928.[10] In a reversal of policy, and one that would become a staple of Stalinist foreign trade, 1927–28 marked the first time in which exports of most products were forced according to export quotas rather than commercial profitability.[11] As the world economy began its descent into the void of the 1930s, the market mechanism in the Soviet Union was being discarded in favor of central command.

Lenin's legacy: The gold standard

No other sector of the Russian economy was as hard hit by the Bolshevik revolution and the Civil War as the foreign trade sector. As Michael Dohan wrote, "the entire infrastructure of tsarist foreign trade including skilled personnel, trade treaties, tariff and trade policies, exchange rates, financial institutions, and a functioning market system, was swept away. The restoration of foreign trade, therefore, depended not only on the physical production of exports and the distribution of imports, but also on rebuilding this foreign trade structure."[12] The task was complicated by a

three other quarters," in Robert C. Allen, *Farm to Factory. A Reinterpretation of the Soviet Industrial Revolution* (Princeton: Princeton University Press, 2003), 84.

10 Stephen Wheatcroft, "Agriculture," in R. W. Davies, ed., *From Tsarism to the New Economic Policy. Continuity and Change in the Economy of the USSR* (Ithaca: Cornell University Press, 1991), 99.

11 Dohan, "Soviet Foreign Trade in the NEP," 482–83.

12 Michael R. Dohan, "Foreign Trade," in R. W. Davies, ed., *From Tsarism to the New Economic Policy. Continuity and Change in the Economy of the USSR* (Ithaca: Cornell University Press, 1991), 217.

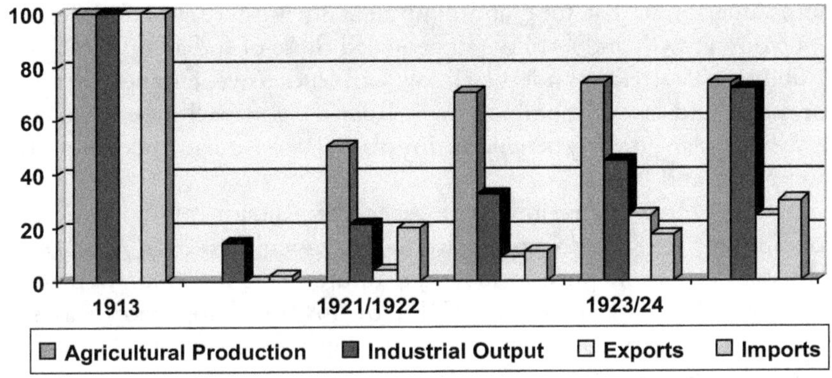

Figure 1.1 NEP economic recovery (1913 = 100)*
*Dohan, "Soviet Foreign Trade in the NEP," 177. By 1928, exports were still only a little more than a third of 1913 levels whereas the weight of imports were about two-thirds. The relatively good performance of imports stemmed from the Soviet government's willingness to finance the resulting balance of payments deficit with gold and other precious metals. Industrial and agricultural production had, by 1928, handily surpassed 1913 levels. See ibid., 471–72.

comparative lack of expertise in foreign trade, which after all had mostly been handled by foreigners during tsarist times. In other words, the Bolsheviks could not do as they did in domestic industry and simply recall bourgeois experts (see Figure 1.1).[13]

Upon seizing power, the Bolsheviks inherited a largely agrarian economy; one with as much, if not more, in common with non-Western developing economies than with the economies of Europe that have so often served as markers for Russian progress. Russia's income, economic structure, and demography all pointed to this.[14] Its income was above that of India and China, but well below the poorest of the European Mediterranean and Scandinavian periphery.[15] Despite industrial growth at a rate similar to that of European countries during the last two decades of tsarist rule, Russia's economy remained mostly agrarian, with three-quarters of its population engaged in agriculture, a proportion higher than in much of

[13] John Quigley, "Foreign Trade Agencies Abroad: A Note," *Law and Contemporary Problems* 37:3 (1972), 467.

[14] Robert C. Allen, *Farm to Factory. A Reinterpretation of the Soviet Industrial Revolution* (Princeton: Princeton University Press, 2003), 11–13.

[15] Ibid., 5, based on Angus Maddison's survey of the world economy, Allen calculated Russia's per capita income in 1913 at $1,488, compared with $2,263 in the Mediterranean periphery, $2,652 in the Scandinavian periphery, $1,694 in Eastern Europe, $3,439 in Latin American's Southern Cone, $1,095 for the rest of Latin America, and close to $1,000 for Southeast Asia.

South America at that time and equivalent to most Asian countries. Its population growth and fertility rates equaled those of India, suggesting the possibility that, had it not been for war, successive famines, Stalinist repression, and fast economic growth, Russia might well have fallen into the Malthusian trap experienced in places like India, Indonesia, the Philippines, and Brazil.[16]

But the single most important aspect of Russia's pre-revolutionary economy was the way it revolved around its agricultural base. At the start of Russia's economic push in 1885, agriculture made up about 59 percent of its gross domestic product (GDP); by 1913 the proportion was still 51 percent. Industry had risen in weight from 6.6 percent in 1885 to 14.9 percent in 1913, whereas transportation had risen from 2.3 percent to 5.8 percent in the same time period. "Russia was developing a modern economy," Allen concluded, "but the pace was glacial."[17] In other words, the impressive 3.3 percent annual GDP growth experienced during that same span of time had, in large part – almost half in fact – been produced by growth in the agricultural sector.

This last point is important because growth in Russian agriculture had largely been a consequence of global economic integration.[18] Railways reached deeper into Russia's countryside, allowing its rural inhabitants to market their grain in world markets, to which the ruble's gold-backed convertibility was allowing access in greater quantity. Rising prices for most agricultural produce, and particularly wheat – the so-called wheat boom of the first era of globalization – improved the countryside's terms of trade and encouraged the settlement of uncultivated land in places as disparate as Canada, Australia, and Argentina. This, in turn, fomented improvements in agricultural productivity in Russia as in much of the world.[19]

[16] Ibid., chapter 6. [17] Ibid., 25.

[18] Paul Gregory, for example, looked at investment cycles in England, France, Germany, Sweden, the United Kingdom, and the United States between 1885 and 1913. Despite having misgivings about the data, he makes three interesting observations: "First, Russian investment cycles are generally related to investment cycles in other countries: Russia participated in the general upswing in investment spending during the 1890s, in the general decline near the turn of the century, and in the upswing in investment spending between 1908 and 1913. Second, the Russian investment cycle seems most closely related to the German and Swedish cycles. Third, the turning points occur first in the larger economies (the United Kingdom, France, and Germany) and then are transmitted to the smaller economies (Sweden and Russia)." Only 1905 and its economic consequences distinguish the Russian investment cycle in any major way. In terms of GDP growth cycles, the picture becomes a bit more complicated, with growth more affected by civil unrest in 1905 and 1906 than by the world economic slowdown at the turn of the century. Gregory, *Before Command*, 77–80.

[19] See Frieden's discussion in *Global Capitalism*, 68–72.

It is no surprise, then, that more than three-quarters of Russia's exports before the war came from the agricultural sector, with grain alone making up 50 percent of total exports, whereas other primary products such as timber and oil accounted for most of the remaining quarter. Russia's foreign trade was a classic example of exchange based on comparative advantage, as its imports consisted of industrial materials such as wool fiber, paper, rubber, and lead, which accounted for 42 percent of total imports; manufactured goods, which made up 22 percent; foodstuffs, particularly tea and herring, amounting to 20 percent; and industrial equipment, 15 percent.[20] It was necessary, however, to run a trade surplus in order for Russia to balance its payments, as it found itself needing to service an increasingly onerous debt with which important segments of its industry and communications, such as the railroads, were being financed.[21] But despite the fact that imports were on average about 75 percent of exports, there was still a considerable deficit in Russia's balance of payments. Russia's major trade partner was Germany and accounted for 30 percent of its exports and almost 50 percent of its imports, with Great Britain accounting for almost 18 percent of its exports and providing less than 13 percent of its imports, and the Netherlands buying 12 percent of its exports and supplying barely 1.5 percent of its imports.[22] Broadly speaking then, Russia sold its grain and timber to Great Britain and the Netherlands to buy industrial material and industrial and manufactured consumer goods from Germany. And the gold standard underpinned it all.

War predictably collapsed Russia's balance of payments.[23] The country started importing large quantities of war materiel while exports nearly

[20] See table 58 for a breakdown on the value of imports during the last four years of the Russian Empire and the NEP in R. W. Davies, ed., *From Tsarism to the New Economic Policy. Continuity and Change in the Economy of the USSR* (Ithaca: Cornell University Press, 1991), 326.

[21] Robert Lewis, "Foreign Economic Relations," in R. W. Davies, Mark Harrison and S. G. Wheatcroft, eds., *The Economic Transformation of the Soviet Union, 1913–1945* (Cambridge: Cambridge University Press, 1994), 200. In fact, the cost of servicing Russian debt, along with remittances of profits by foreign investors and the substantial expenses of Russian tourists abroad, exceeded imports of new capital in the last few years of the empire, a situation generally experienced by dependent Third World countries.

[22] Calculated from Ministry of Foreign Trade, *Vneshniaia torgovlia SSSR za 1918–1940 gg. Statisticheskii obzor* (Moscow: Vneshtorgizdat, 1960), 21, 23.

[23] Peter Gatrell, *Russia's First World War. A Social and Economic History* (Harlow: Pearson/Longman, 2005), chapter 6. Gatrell has estimated that total war-related state spending amounted to 38,650 million rubles, compared to 2,295 million rubles spent on the Russo-Japanese War. In a bit of continuity in economic policy, the tsarist government financed much of the war effort by printing money; this inflationary policy would be continued by the Bolshevik government after 1917, and would not end until 1923 and the introduction into circulation of the chervonets ruble.

vanished, with output being redirected toward the war effort and transportation links suffering from devastating interruptions.[24] The decisive blow was dealt by the Bolshevik Revolution, as the policies of its young government brought with it a general blockade from the rest of Russia's major trading partners that were not already at war with Russia. The new revolutionary government had moved quickly to continue the creeping monopolization of foreign trade that both the tsarist and provisional governments had begun during the war, extending a system of import and export licenses that had already been introduced by the tsarist government. Under the tsarist government, the policy had been carried out by the Ministry of Trade and Industry as part of the general efforts at economic mobilization to strengthen the war effort and assert greater state control over it. This development picked up steam in May 1915 with the establishment of the special councils and the effective nationalization of the Putilov Company in November of that year.[25] As demand for imports of pyrites and other materials for the war industry increased, the state went from control through licenses to direct participation in foreign trade to secure these materials and to make sure exported goods were not needed for domestic consumption. By May 1916, in a move that prefigured the People's Commissariat of Foreign Trade, exporters were made to deposit their foreign currency receipts with the Ministry of Finance.[26]

With the road thus paved, the process continued after the revolution, culminating in the repudiation of all foreign debts in January 1918 by a government no longer beholden to the same financial networks as the previous one, and the final nationalization of foreign trade in April of that year. The repudiation of tsarist debt, besides its ideological presumptions, was also quite practical, since acquisition of new foreign credits would have been highly unlikely given the hostile environment, and interest payments would have quickly evaporated the fledgling revolutionary state's reserves.[27] The nationalization of foreign trade was partly a practical

[24] The tsarist state's abject dependence on foreign armaments and war materiel during World War I was a lesson the Soviets would not forget, and certainly a factor both on the Soviet government's industrialization drive and on its emphasis on heavy industry, machine building, and the development of industrial materials and transportation. See Dohan's discussion in "Soviet Foreign Trade in the NEP," 154–57.

[25] On the special councils see Peter Gatrell, *Russia's First World War*, 108–27. It is interesting to note that almost immediately after the establishment of the councils, a great amount of tension grew between those responsible for trade and industry and the Special Council on Transport. The tension would continue through the NEP, Stalin, and Khrushchev eras.

[26] Alexander Baykov, *Soviet Foreign Trade* (Princeton: Princeton University Press, 1946), 5–6.

[27] Lewis, "Foreign Economic Relations," 201–02.

response to the stipulations of the Treaty of Brest-Litovsk of a month earlier, which required the Soviet government to raise neither tariffs against German goods nor export duties on timber and mining products required by the Germans. In any event, it was peace with Germany that finally incurred the blockade, and the embargo was again tightened the following year with the seizure of Russian assets abroad.[28]

The blockade signified the end of the technological transfer upon which much of Russia's nascent industrialization drive had been based. The market mechanism at the root of tsarist Russia's foreign trade had also been swept away by the war, taking with it the credits and networks that had been built around it. Despite the reestablishment of foreign economic relations with the end of the blockade in 1920 and the signing of a trade treaty with Great Britain the next year, the Bolshevik government was never able restore the flow of foreign technology that had served as one of the main pillars of the pre-revolutionary industrialization process. This was not for lack of trying. In a makeshift manner, the foreign political economy of Lenin's NEP was built around the tsarist model; commercial profitability was to be the main referent for exports, even as the Bolsheviks embarked on a policy of foreign concessions to promote technology transfer. Concessions, however, only ever amounted to about 0.5 percent of total output at their apogee in the second half of the NEP period.[29] The keystone to this market-based edifice, and the seed of its destruction, was to be the reconnection with the liberal world economy through the gold standard and the creation of a new currency whose value would be insured by gold reserves and hard currency: the chervonets.[30]

Although the NEP was quite successful in restoring Russia's former economic output, foreign trade languished through the 1920s causing Russia's technological level to fall further behind the West's. In fact, the foreign trade sector, having come under the state's control as one of

[28] Dohan, "Foreign Trade," 218.

[29] R. W. Davies, *The Soviet Economy in Turmoil, 1929–1930* (Cambridge: Harvard University Press, 1989), 33, footnote 129. Particularly successful were future American Ambassador Averell Harriman's manganese concession in Georgia, the Lena Goldfields concession, which reestablished an old British investment, and the pencil company of the American Armand Hammer, who also exported pharmaceuticals to the Soviet Union and would eventually control Occidental Petroleum.

[30] Its role in the debates of 1925–1926 is recounted in David M. Woodruff, "The Politburo on Gold, Industrialization, and the International Economy, 1925–1926" in Paul R. Gregory and Norman Naimark, eds., *The Lost Politburo Transcripts. From Collective Rule to Stalin's Dictatorship* (New Haven: Yale University Press, 2008), based on newly available stenograms of the discussions in the Politburo. As Woodruff notes, these stenograms show "the absolute centrality of the international economy as a concern for Bolshevik policymakers in the period." Woodruff, "The Politburo on Gold," 200.

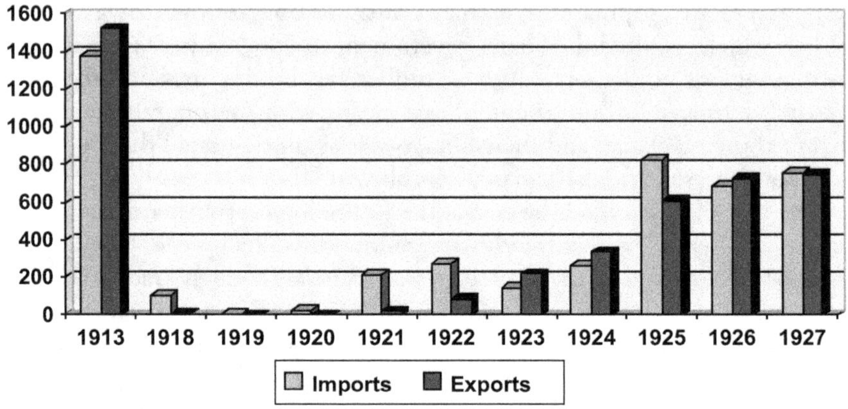

Figure 1.2 Russian and Soviet foreign trade in current prices, 1913, 1918–28 (million rubles)*
**Vneshniaia torgovlia SSSR za 1918–1940 gg.*, 14.

Lenin's commanding heights, was one of the worst-performing sectors of the young Soviet Union's economy (see Figure 1.2). Operations had been taken over by the People's Commissariat of Foreign Trade in June 1920, with the acting Commissar of Trade and Industry Leonid Krasin at its helm. Krasin himself had emphasized Western credits, concessions, trade, and loans to reinstate the economy's tsarist model, and he wanted to establish a commissariat that focused on those goals.[31]

At the root of the foreign trade failure in the NEP era was, predictably, the failure of grain marketing. Imports in the early 1920s were largely financed through the depletion of hard currency and gold reserves.[32] These having been exhausted by 1922, a more controlled foreign trade plan was drawn up that more or less succeeded in nearly balancing the trade deficit for the 1922–23 accounting year. From 1923, the People's Commissariat of Finance would orchestrate the campaign for fiscal discipline needed to restore the country to the gold standard; its decrees should be regarded as

[31] A good account of this early period is Timothy Edward O'Connor, *The Engineer of Revolution. L. B. Krasin and the Bolsheviks, 1870–1926* (Boulder: Westview Press, 1992).

[32] The main cause of the exhaustion of gold reserves, by and large, was an attempt to modernize the railway system through large-scale imports of foreign locomotives and other equipment. Up to 30 percent of Russia's gold reserves were mobilized for this first, simple-minded attempt at a quick reconstruction strategy through the rapid modernization of the communications system. The story is detailed in Anthony Heywood, *Modernising Lenin's Russia. Economic Reconstruction, Foreign Trade and the Railways* (Cambridge: Cambridge University Press, 1999).

battle commands, the commissariat's head, Grigorii Sokol'nikov, told the regional party organs in 1924.[33] That year, with the stabilization of the European economies under the Dawes Plan, a sudden surge in grain exports, with the famine of two years earlier overcome, brought about an astonishing trade surplus of ninety-four million rubles; alas the first and last balance of payments surplus of the NEP era. The surge generated much optimism and allowed the country the reconstruction of its gold and hard currency reserves and its reconnection to the international system of currency convertibility, the gold standard.[34] Ambitious foreign trade plans were drawn up for subsequent years, although currency stability did little to stabilize the weather, and a poor harvest in 1924–25 brought the country sharply back into deficit. That year, the Soviet Union was a net importer of grain, reducing the state's hard-earned reserves of gold and hard currency to levels that endangered the chervonets' gold peg.[35]

The loss of reserves along with the end of the non-inflationary remonetization of the economy – whereby the supply of money was doubled without a significant increase in inflation – began to constrain state action by the end of 1925. As we shall see, this prompted much debate in the leadership leading up to the Fourteenth Party Congress at the end of that year.[36] Credit issues for grain appropriations had to be curtailed as domestic grain prices started to rise and diverge sharply with respect to those in world markets, a profitless development for a government bent on using grain exports to fuel industry (see Figures 1.3 and 1.4). Balancing domestic and international markets was proving to be beyond the capacity of Soviet power.

[33] L. N. Dobrokhotov, V. H. Kolodezhnyi, V. S. Pushkarev, eds., *Denezhnaia reforma 1921–1924 gg.: sozdanie tverdoi valiuty. Dokumenty i materialy* (Moscow: Rosspen, 2008), 577–78.

[34] The reconnection was a matter of acquiring the means – i.e. gold and hard currency reserves – to intervene in markets both domestic and foreign to keep the gold value of the chervonets constant. The government never undertook the commitment of exchanging the chervonets for gold at a fixed rate, as other governments did for their currencies during the interwar period. The definitive account of the short but important history of the chervonets is Yurii Goland, "Currency Regulation in the NEP Period," *Europe-Asia Studies* 46:8 (1994).

[35] According to Sokol'nikov, the Soviets spent 115 million rubles in gold to balance payments. See K. M. Anderson, A. Iu. Vatlin, P. Gregory, A. K. Sorokin, R. Suza and O. V. Khlevniuk, eds., *Stenogrammy zasedanii Politbiuro TsK RKP(b)-VKP(b) 1923–1926*, vol. 1 (Moscow: Rosspen, 2007), 334.

[36] David M. Woodruff, "The Politburo on Gold, Industrialization, and the International Economy, 1925–1926" in Paul R. Gregory and Norman Naimark, eds., *The Lost Politburo Transcripts. From Collective Rule to Stalin's Dictatorship* (New Haven: Yale University Press, 2008), 202–04. Yurii Goland looked at this same debate, only mostly within the lower-rung, more specialist confines of the Council of Labor and Defense (STO), in "Currency Regulation in the NEP Period."

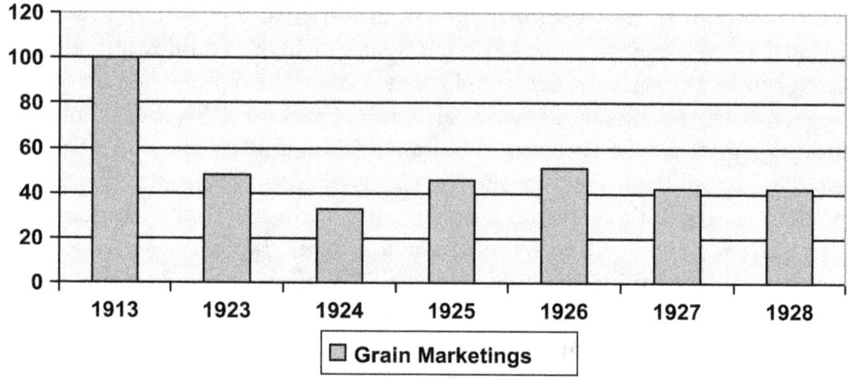

Figure 1.3 Value of grain marketings (1913 = 100)*
*Davies, *From Tsarism to the New Economic Policy*, 279.

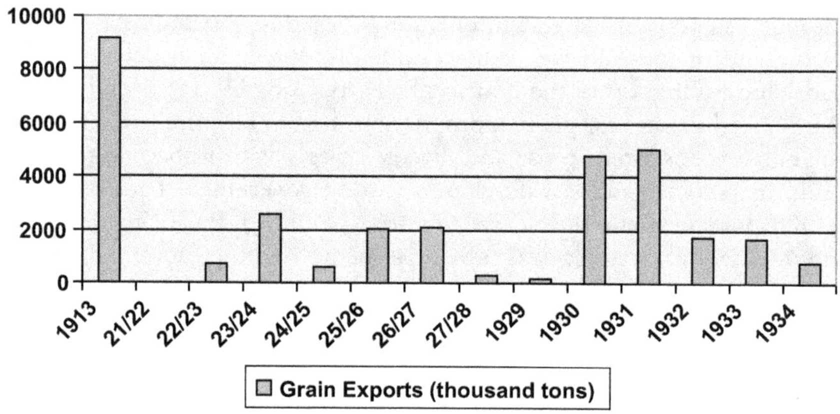

Figure 1.4 Volume of grain exports, 1913, 1922/23–1934*
*In Davies, Harrison and Wheatcroft, *The Economic Transformation of the Soviet Union*, 316. Calculated from *Vneshniaia torgovlia SSSR za 1918–1940 gg.*, 84, 110, 144, 179.

Foreign trade and the Soviet industrialization debate

It is a mostly fruitless endeavor to look for similarities between the Bolshevik leadership and the Hoover Administration – or indeed for similarities with the leaderships of most industrialized countries. But there is one revealing parallel. When confronted with economic crisis in the 1920s, they both chose to follow the liberal prescription of gold standard orthodoxy, namely austerity. The history between the death of Lenin and the enactment of the First Five-Year Plan has generally been told as a political struggle based on theoretical positions; permanent revolution versus socialism in one country, or the so-called industrialization debate of Right versus Left, followed by Stalin's turn against the advocates of balanced industrialization on the right.[37] This narrative entails an apparent freedom of policy options at a time when options were becoming rather constrained. It is also odd and misleading. It portrays a leadership willfully fighting ideological battles – what better sport for communists! – when, in fact, it was in the midst of resolving a thorny economic crisis. It is in that crisis that the debate should be contextualized.

The more open and well-known industrialization debate in the Soviet Union was shadowed by a more hands-on discussion in the Politburo on policymaking in the face of an uncooperative world economy. At issue was how best to use the financial and commodity assets of the country to industrialize and modernize its economy within a market framework. That this had become an issue at all was the result, not of ideological qualms, but of unexpected pressures on the chervonets and on the government's gold reserves. This, in turn, threatened the credibility of the state's commitment to monetary stability both domestically and abroad. One option was to defend the gold parity of the chervonets by selling gold in the open market and hope for exports and industrial development to pick up in time to salve the chronic balance-of-payment deficits and replenish gold and foreign currency reserves. This is the option the leadership unanimously agreed upon. Not defending the chervonets would entail a run on the currency, market-busting inflation, and the possible exclusion from international capital markets; this latter option was not countenanced until it became inevitable. Growth within market parameters for a largely agrarian economy, the Bolsheviks would discover at length, was incompatible with the deflationary global markets of the second half of the 1920s.

But no one could have predicted that in the heady months of the mid-decade. And so, over the course of many months starting in the autumn of 1925, the Politburo exhaustively discussed foreign trade and finance in a rather hopeful tone. As its members rather self-consciously admitted, they were engaged in the reconstruction of the tsarist-era Witte system, in which peasants were exploited and grain was exchanged abroad for

[37] For a narrative typical in the field, indeed unfortunately borrowed from the field, see Ivan T. Berend, *Decades of Crisis. Central and Eastern Europe before World War II* (Berkeley: University of California Press, 1998), 210–19.

industrial inputs and technology.[38] The linchpin of this political economy was, of course, a functioning world market system. Unfortunately, most accounts of the industrialization debate minimize its most important feature – perhaps rightly, since the theoretical benefits of greater engagement of the world economy went largely unchallenged, making for uninteresting reading from a narrative standpoint.[39] One historiographical exception to this rule is instructive. Richard Day's study of the debate correctly emphasized the discussion over integration with the world economy. He erred, however, in projecting the post–Great Depression, autarky-mongering Stalin back half a decade and making Leon Trotsky the sole champion of the integrationist cause.[40]

In fact, the Politburo discussions show Stalin to be a loyal defender of austerity and the gold parity of the chervonets – in other words, a staunch integrationist and a market optimist who held out hope for the promise of foreign capital.[41] For the members of the Politburo, the crisis at this stage was turbulence, serious but eventually surmountable under current institutions. As historian Yurii Goland has explained, what administrative measures they undertook at this time of crisis were designed to prevent "a fall in confidence and the creditworthiness of the country as a whole."[42] Indeed, the commissariats of domestic and foreign trade had recently been merged in 1925 into one commissariat precisely because the leadership expected the market, through the gold standard, to continue as the keystone of their economic project.[43]

In the Politburo, it was Feliks Dzerzhinskii who was least pleased with the austerity-dictated cuts to the budget of VSNKh, the organization responsible for the country's industrial development, which he chaired at

38 "The goals are different," an unidentified Politburo member was quick to interject when Kalinin reminded his colleagues that that was, in practice, what they were doing. In Anderson et al., eds., *Stenogrammy zasedanii Politbiuro*, 616.

39 Apparent in the classic Alexander Erlich, *The Soviet Industrialization Debate, 1924–1928* (Cambridge: Harvard University Press, 1960).

40 Richard B. Day, *Leon Trotsky & the Politics of Economic Isolation* (Cambridge: Cambridge University Press, 1973). In fact, Trotsky was arguably the least committed to integration, although committed nonetheless.

41 "We must fix this error. Otherwise we risk a financial crisis. In this area our regulatory organs should aim for absolute strictness, otherwise the currency can leap down, and we will find ourselves in great danger," Anderson et al., eds., *Stenogrammy zasedanii Politbiuro*, vol. 1, 342.

42 Goland, "Currency Regulation in the NEP Period," 1279.

43 The better to manage the now "inextricable link" between the domestic and world economies, as A. D. Tsiurupa explained it to the public in an article published the day after the merger of the two commissariats. In RGAE f. 5240, op. 1, d. 1, ll. 2–3. They were separated in 1931, another telling clue as to when the leadership accepted its mistake and changed, or rather postponed, its integrationist policy.

the time. "The program outlined by the commission's decree, does not, of course, satisfy VSNKh," a sour Dzerzhinskii told his colleagues in the Politburo in February 1926 in reference to the need to cut industrial imports and replenish the state's gold reserves. "But it is clear that you cannot pour from an empty bucket" (*iz pustogo ne nal'esh'*).[44] Both Dzerzhinskii and Trotsky stood for forcing exports to balance payments, for which Dzerzhinskii hinted at an unspecified agenda to forcefully increase grain exports.[45] They did not shy from suggesting more administrative methods to overcome the crisis, but neither put forward a vision of an economic system without the chervonets.

Stalin's intervention, meanwhile, was not exactly Erlich's "exercise in evasion."[46] Here David Woodruff, in his masterly account of the Politburo debates, notes an interesting dichotomy in Stalin's political rhetoric in 1925–26. Stalin's position in the Fourteenth Party Congress was substantially similar to Sokol'nikov's, calling for "a positive trade balance, restraint in the pace of industrialization and the importance of avoiding inflation." As a political weapon, however, he adopted the rhetoric of the industrial lobby, which accused the finance minister of wanting to keep the Soviet Union in economic dependence to the West.[47] Political infighting notwithstanding, Sokol'nikov's austerity program went into effect all the same in 1926: budgets were slashed, taxes raised, imports restricted, and credit curtailed.[48] Bolshevik financial rectitude was soon rewarded when in April the Germans broke a Western financial taboo by lending 300 million marks to Soviet trade agencies. These were good times for the confident, pro-agrarian right.[49]

Austerity has ever been an inherently optimistic policy, but we know in hindsight the Bolsheviks were being buffeted by the first gusts of the storm to come. And they waited reasonably and expectantly for fairer winds that

[44] Anderson et al., eds., *Stenogrammy zasedanii Politbiuro*, vol. 1, 613.

[45] See their interventions in the Politburo meeting of January 11, 1926. Ibid., 543–90.

[46] Erlich, *The Soviet Industrialization Debate*, 90–98. This is Erlich's term, connoting a centrist, noncommittal Stalin in the industrialization debates. This description does not quite work when examining the leadership's resolve to remain within the market framework of the gold standard, which found in Stalin one of its most steadfast proponents.

[47] Woodruff, "The Politburo on Gold," 214–15. It should be noted that Sokol'nikov similarly attacked Stalin at the Fourteenth Party Congress on factional grounds. A good account of this underappreciated Bolshevik's 1920s political life is Samuel A. Oppenheim, "Between the Right and the Left: G. Ia. Sokolnikov and the Development of the Soviet State, 1921–1929," *Slavic Review* 48:4 (1989): 592–613.

[48] As laid out by Narkomfin's head of currency adminsitration L. Iurovskii in Anderson et al., eds., *Stenogrammy zasedanii Politbiuro*, vol. 1, 602.

[49] This optimism extended to agricultural exports, which were expected to grow by 38 percent from the previous year. RGASPI, f. 84, op. 2, d. 1, ll. 184–96.

never came. Already the end of the Politburo discussions had been punctuated by a small reversal of policy that proved to be far-reaching. In the spring of 1926, diminishing gold reserves forced the state to stop defending the chervonets in the currency markets in Moscow, temporarily they hoped. This led to a fatal loss of confidence in the chervonets, which made it increasingly difficult for the state to attract private domestic savings for industrial investment.[50] Conversely, it made administrative solutions to mobilizing investment resources more attractive, although the situation would have to worsen still before that psychological barrier was overcome.

The austerity measures adopted earlier in the year maintained a measure of monetary stability during the second half of 1926; not enough to rebuild gold reserves, but enough to maintain some semblance of hope. But the trade and financial crisis only deepened the next year when credit again flooded the economy to induce greater marketings of grain and to accelerate industrial development. Inflation gathered speed and the peasantry once again held on to their grain; only large outlays of precious metals and the forced exports of non-grain commodities such as eggs, timber, oil, and cotton cloth, averted disaster.[51] The resulting shortages of both domestic and imported material slowed growth in light and heavy industry, stalling the party's industrialization plans.[52]

This was certainly not the first economic crisis of the NEP period. Similar "scissors" crises occurred in 1923 and 1925, and both had been overcome. This time, however, the international economic and political climate was turning unexpectedly hostile, putting pressure on the Soviet leadership just as state authority was converging on Stalin. In April, the Soviet embassy in Beijing was raided by Jiang Jieshi's (Chiang Kai-shek) forces; in May, Britain first raided the Soviet Union's trade mission in London and then broke diplomatic and trade relations with the Soviet Union; in June, the Soviet ambassador to Poland was assassinated; and in September, trade negotiations with France broke down. This followed a two-year flow of alarmist intelligence gathered by Dzerzhinskii and warning of imminent military action against the Soviets by a French–British

[50] Because people increasingly refused to keep their wealth in a persistently depreciating chervonets. Goland, "Currency Regulation in the NEP Period," 1293.

[51] Dohan, "Foreign Trade," 223. For example, oil and timber exports equaled 13.7 and 12.2 percent of total exports respectively in 1927–28, as opposed to 3.3 and 11 percent in 1913. Dohan, "Soviet Foreign Trade in the NEP," 409.

[52] Dohan, "Foreign Trade," 223–24.

anti-Communist coalition.[53] These events elevated the sense of threat among the Soviet leadership, reversing even Nikolai Bukharin's opinion, who now called for greater investment in heavy industry and particularly the defense industry to improve the Soviet Union's military preparedness.[54] Industrialization and fast economic growth came to be seen as the only means to persuade the British and the French that a decision for war with the Soviet Union would be a costly one.[55]

Stalin, nevertheless, still hoped to entice business circles in Europe and the United States into financial deals and profitable economic exchange. As he told the Politburo in a letter in December 1927, "it is absolutely no sign of weakness if we admit openly among ourselves that our financial and economic situation is extremely serious and that we are suffering from a chronic lack of money and a lack of intelligent economic forces so that we are unable to carry out our program with our own resources alone, to create the economic dictatorship of the proletariat as well as its political dictatorship. Therefore, to be able to realize our program, we have to make use of foreign help."[56]

The international environment remained uncooperative, however. With England's markets frosty to Soviet trade in 1928, the Soviets once again had to rely on precious metals and their hard currency reserves to balance their payments. Gold exports for 1927–28 amounted to 145 million rubles, with the export of other precious metals adding another 10 million rubles; in 1928 alone, Soviet hard currency reserves fell 30 percent.[57] More worryingly for the leadership, pressure was mounting as foreign banks started to doubt the Soviet Union's ability to pay its debts. Notices were circulating around German firms urging caution on extending credits to the Soviets.

[53] James Harris, "Encircled By Enemies: Stalin's Perceptions of the Capitalist World, 1918–1941," *The Journal of Strategic Studies* 30:3 (2007), 515–21.

[54] John P. Sontag, "The Soviet War Scare of 1926–27," *Russian Review* 34:1 (1974), 74–75.

[55] Harris, "Encircled By Enemies," 522–23. It should be noted that interpretations of the war scare have varied radically. It has been interpreted, rather vaguely and indirectly, as Stalin's cynical ploy to attack Trotsky, in David R. Stone, *Hammer & Rifle. The Militarization of the Soviet Union, 1926–1933* (Lawrence: University Press of Kansas, 2000), and more convincingly as a real panic that served to reenergize the Left Opposition into a last challenge to the Stalin–Bukharin leadership, in Jon Jacobson, *When the Soviet Union Entered World Politics* (Berkeley: University of California Press, 1994), 216–32. What is clear is the very real anxiety it generated in the society at large, as analyzed in A. V. Golubev, *"Esli mir obrushitsia na nashu Respubliku." Sovetskoe obshchestvo i vneshniaia ugroza v 1920–1940-e gg.* (Moscow: Kuchkovo Pole, 2008). Corroborating the earnest rather than the cynical view is David Brandenberger's conclusion that the panic caused a thorough reassessment in the ideological propaganda of the state it directed to its people. David Brandenberger, *Propaganda State in Crisis. Soviet Ideology, Indoctrination, and Terror under Stalin, 1927–1941* (New Haven: Yale University Press, 2012).

[56] The letter is printed in full in Michal Reiman, *The Birth of Stalinsim. The USSR on the Eve of the "Second Revolution"* (Bloomington: Indiana University Press, 1987), 128–33.

[57] Lewis, "Foreign Economic Relations," 204–05.

Not coincidentally, German doubts arose at the same time that the flow of capital to Germany from the United States abruptly decreased, forcing the Reichsbank to tighten credit and spelling the end of the hard-earned stability brought on by the Dawes Plan four years earlier.[58] The consequences were quickly felt. "This dictates the necessity to cut down the import plan; we'll have to cut where it hurts (*rezat' po zhivomu mestu*)," the young Commissar for Foreign and Domestic Trade Anastas Mikoyan wrote to Stalin. "This year there will be large reductions in our pace of development where imports are concerned."[59]

In July, Mikoyan informed the Central Committee about the difficult state of affairs in the foreign trade sector, which was then in an "extraordinarily strained situation, more strained than in the last two years."[60] He related it in particular to the grain marketing failure of the last campaign, and the expected failure of the current one. The problem was with exports, where the modest success of non-agricultural exports such as oil could not quite make up for the disaster in agricultural exports. Without these, Mikoyan declared, it would prove impossible to restore exports to prewar levels, which is why "attention to other export items does not remove the problem of grain exports." Exports of grain had made up more than half of total exports before the war, he reminded his audience, and now "it amounts to such an insignificant figure that it should not even be taken into account."[61]

The global economy had the Soviet economy in check, leaving the leadership with a stark choice that Mikoyan summarized for the Central Committee in spring 1928. He proposed to mobilize all organs of the state and party, and all export resources in order to rebuild the reserves by all means available. Even that promised "only" some 10 percent growth in light industry under current global conditions. Sokol'nikov, M. I. Frumkin, and A. L. Sheinman, on the other hand, proposed further cuts to imports and more austerity, which Mikoyan asserted would not only guarantee no growth for the year 1928–29, but would also wreck industrial and financial plans for the rest of the current year.[62] Pushing exports and

[58] Barry Eichengreen, *Golden Fetters. The Gold Standard and the Great Depression, 1919–1939* (Oxford: Oxford University Press, 1992), 241–46.

[59] V. P. Danilov, O. V. Khlevniuk, A. Iu. Vatlin, eds., *Kak lomali NEP. Stenogrammy plenumov TsK VKP(b), 1928–1929 gg.*, vol. 3 (Moscow: Izdatel'stvo Materik, 2000), 592.

[60] Mikoyan gave his report during a Central Committee Plenum that lasted from July 4 to 12, 1928. V. P. Danilov, O. V. Khlevniuk, A. Iu. Vatlin, eds., *Kak lomali NEP. Stenogrammy plenumov TsK VKP(b), 1928–1929 gg.*, vol. 2 (Moscow: Izdatel'stvo Materik, 2000), 184–87.

[61] Ibid., 186. [62] RGASPI, f. 84, op. 2, d. 5, ll. 143–51.

keeping to the import plan would at least maintain levels of industrial production. But this was a temporary salve; future import growth, and hence the future of Soviet industry, ultimately depended on getting a grasp on agricultural production and grain marketings.[63]

Even as the commitment to export agricultural production remained operative, it became clear that the foreign trade mechanism was becoming unreliable. The arguments of the Left had made little sense in 1925, when winds were fair and the Soviet leadership expected a substantial increase in foreign trade turnover based on an expected expansion of grain marketings. People on both the Right and the Left agreed that the large-scale development of heavy industry would allow for ample growth in light industry and for the mechanization of the countryside. But in 1925, mostly rightists thought that the necessary inputs could reasonably be expected to be obtained more rapidly and harmoniously through imports. The economic trends of the period amply justified their approach, and discredited the Left. By 1928, the Left had been thoroughly defeated and Stalin famously took over their economic platform. By now, however, an export expansion could no longer be expected without a radical change in the state's relationship with its rural population. If, in 1925, the world economy had obliged the arguments of the Right and encouraged a reasonable optimism, by 1928, these arguments seemed to be built on increasingly implausible prospects. Stalin's shift from right to left was not the move of a sinister political master tactician; it was the precursor of a global political and ideological shift structured by the shackles of the gold standard in an unbalanced world economy.

The great vanishing act of the world economy

The Great Depression was not set in motion by the dramatic bang of the October 1929 stock market crash in New York. It began with an economic slowdown in important parts of the world. First, it happened in Australia and the Dutch East Indies at the end of 1927; in 1928, it spread to Brazil and Germany; and during the first half of 1929, Canada and Poland were showing evidence of recession. Before October 1929, large parts of Central

[63] In an exchange with Stalin later in the session, Mikoyan argued that the idea was not necessarily to fully restore prewar levels of grain exports. Exports at 30 to 50 percent of prewar levels would suffice to begin building hard currency reserves and resolve the problem of imports, which Mikoyan called "the main bottleneck in our industry." Danilov et al., eds., *Kak lomali NEP*, vol. 2, 448.

Europe, Latin America, and Asia had edged into recession.[64] This, in turn, ebbed the flow of American capital abroad, especially to the old continent.

In the wake of World War I, New York had emphatically taken over London as the financial capital of the world. The postwar economic reconstruction in Europe had been financed by American capital. Germany, in particular, was fully dependent on such capital to stave off defaulting on its reparations to England and France, who themselves needed the money from Germany to pay debts to the United States incurred during the war. This triangular shuffling of capital, formalized in the 1924 Dawes Plan, had maintained a delicate economic stability in Europe for four years. Now, finding smaller profit margins in a more or less reconstructed Europe, much of the American capital that underwrote the reconstruction had started to find its way back to the United States, where both the economy and the stock market were booming.[65] And so, if in the first half of 1928 lending to foreigners averaged $140 million a month, the next twelve months saw the rate slow down to $70 million, and by the second half of 1929 lending slowed down to $35 million.[66] As capital left European markets, investors changed foreign European currencies into American dollars. Since currencies were pegged to gold, that essentially meant a dangerous outflow of gold from Europe to the United States. In an attempt to retain gold and their membership to the gold standard, European governments responded by raising interest rates and cutting back spending. Eventually, interest rates were also raised in the United States to cool down an overheating stock market, which had doubled in less than two years by the fall of 1929. Outside of the United States, these policies combined had the effect of deepening the recession. Deflation intensified worldwide; already indebted companies, governments, and consumers reduced their consumption levels even as credit dried up. With consumption down, businesses failed, unemployment rose, debtors defaulted, and banks went bankrupt. Then the situation grew worse.

Many of the problems confronted by the Soviet state during the First Five-Year Plan can be contextualized into this larger story of the world depression. It was not, for example, the only country suffering from a hemorrhage of gold. Countries whose main exports were primary products

[64] Eichengreen, *Golden Fetters*, 222.

[65] The most readable history of the establishment of this financial house of cards and its denouement is Liaquat Ahamed, *Lords of Finance. The Bankers Who Broke the World* (New York: Penguin Books, 2009).

[66] Taking into consideration debt repayment, a net outflow of $900 million in 1927–28 slowed down to an outflow of merely $86 annually from 1929 to 1931. Frieden, *Global Capitalism*, 174.

tended to rely on gold outlays when hard currency reserves were low, a sign generally of weakened commodity prices. The Soviet Union was simply one more victim of this general process, which took its toll particularly in South America and the Far East. Wheat-exporting countries such as Australia and Canada lost gold before those with other export commodities. Argentina started losing its hard currency during the second half of 1928 – the same year that saw a 30 percent reduction in Soviet hard currency reserves – and Hungary, the largest European wheat exporter, did so in 1929.[67] Concomitant to this development was the scramble for foreign exchange; the Soviets joined other primary producers, especially in Latin America, in pushing exports for this purpose. Mikoyan's exhortations to the Central Committee were but an echo of similar appeals elsewhere in government cabinets around the globe. The main outcome of this scramble, however, was to accelerate the decline in commodity prices and exacerbate primary producers' problems with their respective balance of payments.[68]

Neither were the Soviets alone in seeing imbalances between town and country during the 1920s. The much-vaunted NEP crises were part of a global phenomenon. With the attachment to the gold standard at its nucleus, NEP had been designed precisely to take advantage of the coming global economic expansion; what the Bolsheviks got instead was the full measure of the world economy's 1920s fluctuations. Farm products, and particularly grain, suffered from deflationary pressures throughout the decade, where in the Soviet Union it brought about crises in 1923, 1925, and the extended crisis from 1927 to collectivization. The deflationary pressure was an outcome of the quick restoration of agricultural production in postwar Europe after production had expanded in other parts of the world to make up for lost production during the European war.[69] Agricultural overproduction was the result, and farmers worldwide came to suffer from very unfavorable terms of trade with industry. Depressed prices and increased stockpiles of grain were as familiar a sight in Uruguay and Canada as they were in the Soviet Union.

Finally, there was little particularly unique about the actions undertaken by the Soviet leadership to cope with the crisis, at least in their

[67] Charles P. Kindleberger, *The World in Depression, 1929–1939* (Berkeley: University of California Press, 1973), 87–89.

[68] Eichengreen, *Golden Fetters*, 222–23.

[69] Kindleberger, *The World in Depression*, 72–74. Aggregate prices of world agricultural products declined about 30 percent from 1925 until 1929, while stockpiles increased some 75 percent. From there, prices plunged to less than a quarter in 1932 of what they had been in 1925.

international activities; the country's problems were structural, and the reaction of its leaders was as pragmatic as that of leaders everywhere in the indebted, commodity-exporting economies. The policy was etched in the very ideological fabric of the gold standard. Deflation was the only prescribed answer to a discrepancy between domestic and world price structures. That is, the drain of gold reserves, such as the one commodity exporters were experiencing in the late 1920s, could only be staunched by raising interest rates, imposing austerity measures, and waiting for industrial wages and farm incomes to contract until external balance was restored. Such economic contraction, however, was a solution neither the Soviets nor any government could tolerate for long without suffering social unrest.[70]

The way out was to suspend the gold standard. Letting the currency depreciate allowed governments to pursue expansionary policies, or at the very least defend domestic wage levels, which minimized domestic unrest and made exports more competitive. Greater exports would allow governments to maintain debt payments and thus ensure continued access to international capital markets.[71] Australia's reaction to the deepening crisis in 1929, for example, echoed the Soviet Union's in 1926 when the latter went off gold.[72] From 1928 until the end of 1929, Australia's export prices fell by about 25 percent. Australia coped by drawing down the hard currency reserves it possessed in London banks; eventually, it had to start settling accounts with gold, losing a fifth of its gold reserves in 1929. The main objective was to maintain creditworthiness, making the discontinuation of debt payments unthinkable. Currency depreciation became the default solution. To staunch the loss of hard currency, the Australian government rationed reserves to importers, immediately spawning a black market in hard currency quoting higher prices than the official exchange. The government went on to impose import duties and to requisition gold remaining in private hands. It adopted measures to improve the efficiency with which foreign currency was spent by pooling the reserves of the major banks in the country. With no formal controls and a flourishing black market where foreign currency could purchase a higher price, banks defected and rationing collapsed. Australia's currency went into freefall, and was repegged at 30 percent below its former value. All these

[70] For the Soviet case and its political and social implications see Reiman, *The Birth of Stalinism*, 51–66.

[71] Eichengreen, *Golden Fetters*, 231–32.

[72] The following account is taken from Eichengreen, *Golden Fetters*, 232–36.

maneuvers, however, had saved nominal wages in the country from falling to levels that reflected the fall in price levels.[73]

The political effects of Australia's economic instabilities were quickly felt throughout the world. The Labor Party in both Australia and the UK took over the reins of government in 1929. Parties less ideologically beholden to the gold standard triumphed throughout this period. It is intriguing that in the Soviet Union a similar process began in 1926, when along with an end to the ruble's convertibility came the political ascendance of S. G. Strumilin's Gosplan and the Worker-Peasant Inspection (Rabkrin), and the slow descent into oblivion of Grigorii Sokol'nikov's People's Commissariat of Finance, whose leadership had guided the Soviet Union into the gold standard in 1924.[74] Furthermore, although import duties in the Soviet context were obviated by the monopoly of foreign trade, the Soviets anticipated the Australians in pursuing a campaign to increase efficiency in imports and tried – though often failed – to ration import licenses to its industry. And always they pushed exports.

Domestically, and against Sokol'nikov's advice, the government slowly moved toward the stimulation of industry through the inflationary printing of rubles, although this policy was not really unleashed until the second half of 1927 when industrial growth and capital construction began to be built on the basis of inflationary credit. It was then that the free rate of the ruble, which had lost 10 to 15 percent of its value against the dollar but had remained in that range since early 1926, plummeted. Through 1927 it lost 30 to 40 percent of its value.[75] Domestically, this meant that it became harder for the government to tap into domestic savings without the use of coercion and propaganda. Internationally, remaining creditworthy would become a bit of an obsession, particularly for Stalin, who would prove quite willing to implement whatever policies were needed to achieve this purpose, both in the 1930s and after World War II, even if it compounded times of starvation.

Coping with disaster, or 1930s foreign trade policy

Given the consensus on the intensification of foreign trade, it should be no surprise that the First Five-Year Plan intended to do just that. As Dohan

[73] Although this did not save the country from worker unrest, particularly in the mining and timber industries.

[74] I thank Andrew Sloin for bringing this crucial development to my attention.

[75] Yurii Goland, "Currency Regulation in the NEP Period," *Europe-Asia Studies* 46:8 (1994): 1293.

long ago argued, the deliberations leading to the First Five-Year Plan discussed economic independence "not in terms of reducing foreign trade, but rather in terms of securing military needs and freeing the economy from limits imposed directly by foreign trade problems and indirectly by the peasants' failure to market grain and other produce."[76] Predictably, far from implementing autarkic policies, the plan sought to overcome the problems laid out by Mikoyan in July 1928 by projecting a surge in exports of 21 percent a year, making it one of the most rapidly growing sectors.[77]

This, at least, was the optimal plan; the minimum variant projected a still impressive 18.5 percent increase. Dohan pointed out that "these planned growth rates exceeded the growth rate of exports during NEP, exceeded by a large margin the historical growth rate of Tsarist Russia trade and exceeded the historical growth of exports in most large industrialized countries."[78] To achieve this growth, the Soviets planned a major increase in investment in industries that produced for export, such as timber and oil industries, the food industry, textiles, and various minerals (see Figure 1.5). They were ostensibly undaunted by the possibility of dependence on the world economy, an issue that had been brought up intermittently throughout the 1920s, noticeably without conviction.[79]

Trade expanded during the first three years of the plan, in large part because of the forcing of timber, oil, and flax exports despite domestic shortages.[80] The period saw the final institutionalization of the policy of the forcing of exports (*forsirovanie eksporta*), that is, the total disregard for commercial profitability in favor of hard currency, which in turn triggered the perennial Western concern with Soviet dumping.[81] Stalin wrote furiously to his colleagues in government to implement this policy ruthlessly, as in two August 1930 letters to his colleague Vyacheslav Molotov:

76 Michael R. Dohan, "The Economic Origins of Soviet Autarky, 1927/8–1934," *Slavic Review* 35:4 (1976): 609.

77 Ibid. 78 Dohan, "Soviet Foreign Trade in the NEP," 523.

79 Ibid., 557. As Dohan points out, the discourse of import substitution, on which pervasiveness many Western scholars argued that the Soviets had always pursued an autarkic foreign trade policy, did not begin to appear until 1931, with the coming of a debilitating hard currency crisis.

80 Dohan, "Soviet Foreign Trade in the NEP," 561.

81 Dohan, "The Economic Origins of Soviet Autarky," 621. The Soviets, in turn, spent great efforts defending themselves from such accusations, trying to assuage Western fears and using the economic weapon to reward positive outcomes. The greatest success was arguably US political recognition of the Soviet Union, which was a function of Soviet willingness to import American technology and know-how. See Jonathan Haslam, *Soviet Foreign Policy, 1930–1933. The Impact of Depression* (New York: St. Martin's Press, 1983).

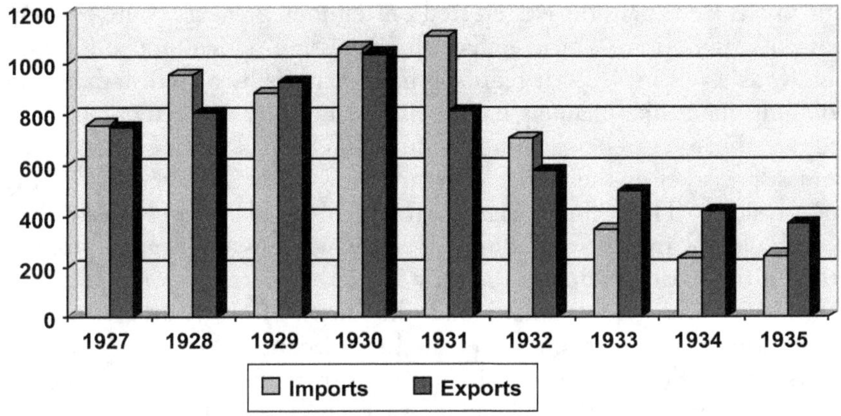

Figure 1.5 Soviet foreign trade in current prices, 1927–35 (million rubles)*
**Vneshniaia torgovlia SSSR za 1918–1940 gg.*, 14.

> We have one and a half months left to export grain: starting in late October (perhaps even earlier), American grain will come on to the market in massive quantities, and we won't be able to withstand that. If we don't export 130–150 million poods of grain in these six weeks, our hard currency situation could become really desperate. Once again: We must force through grain exports with all our might.[82]

And a day later:

> Mikoian reports that grain procurements are growing, and each day we are shipping 1 to 1.5 million poods of grain. I think that's not enough. The quota for daily shipments (now) should be raised to 3–4 million poods at a minimum. Otherwise we risk being left without our new iron and steel and machine-building factories (Avtozavod, Cheliabzavod, etc.). Some clever people will come along and propose holding off on the shipments until the price of grain on the world markets rises "to its ceiling." There are quite a few of these clever people in Trade. They ought to be horsewhipped, because they're dragging us into a trap. In order to hold off, we must have hard currency reserves. But we don't have them. In order to hold off, we would have to have a secure position on the international grain exchange. And we haven't had any position at all for a long time there – we'll only obtain it now if we can exploit conditions that have arisen at the present moment and are particularly favorable to us.
>
> In short, we must push grain exports furiously.[83]

[82] In Lars T. Lih, Oleg V. Naumov, Oleg V. Khlevniuk, eds., *Stalin's Letters to Molotov* (New Haven: Yale University Press, 1995), 203.

[83] Ibid., 205.

But this trade expansion was erected on tenuous premises. One of them was collectivization, which ended up depressing agricultural output to disastrous levels in 1931–32, reducing grain exports by a third rather than doubling them like planners had envisaged in 1928. Collectivization also redirected hard currency-earning products, such as oil, from exports to the domestic market as the Soviet government was forced to mechanize the countryside.[84] The second pillar upon which the planned expansion had been built was the liberal trading system, which saw the general proliferation of trade barriers during the early 1930s that were the consequence of the end of the gold standard and the onset of the world economic depression. The depression exacerbated the decline in commodity export prices worldwide, although the situation was particularly dire for the Soviet Union. Compared with 1928 ratios, for example, machinery imports in 1931 required two and one-half to three times as much grain to be exported per unit imported.[85]

But perhaps more catastrophically, credit availability also became scarcer and more insecure. Even as imports in 1931 were financed by net increases in borrowing, credit was becoming increasingly costly and less available.[86] If the first shock of the Great Depression had been the halt to the flow of capital from the United States to Europe in 1928, and the second the bursting of the stock market bubble in New York the next year, then 1931 brought about a more insidious problem: credit liquidity dried up after a series of banking panics in the United States. By the summer of that year, confidence in the solvency of European banks and the stability of the continent's currencies collapsed. Germany, along with much of Eastern Europe, was forced to sharply increase interest rates and implement capital controls to stem the flow of gold out of their reserves.[87]

The Soviet leadership only slowly came to understand the catastrophe unfolding around them. In August of that year, Lazar Kaganovich reported the worsening situation with German credits for imports to Stalin, considering that "the main issue regarding orders at present is the interest rate, it keeps leaping upward, and now it has already reached 17 percent. . . . It turned out that the soaring interest rate covers not only the orders that we

[84] Dohan, "Economic Origins of Soviet Autarky," 619–20.

[85] By 1932 most Soviet export prices had fallen by 50–60 percent, while import prices declined much more slowly, ibid., 622–23.

[86] Dohan calculates the share of imports purchased on credit at 20–25 percent. The Soviet Union's main creditor was Germany, which after 1932 cared only for repayment, in ibid., 625.

[87] This characterization of the Great Depression as the succession of a series of crises ricocheting off each other, rather than as a single crisis, is taken from Ahamed, *Lords of Finance*, 497–500.

are placing now, but also a large number of previous orders. Some said that they cover a range of orders totaling up to 500 million marks, nobody can say exactly, so we gave instructions that a precise accounting be submitted to us."[88]

As in the world economy, the year 1930 had not gone altogether badly for the Soviet Union compared with 1931. Short-term credits and above-planned exports buttressed the Soviet Union's balance of payments. A reduction of planned imports during the second half of the year helped bring foreign trade to near balance. Had the terms of trade remained at 1928 levels, the Soviets should have expected quite a large surplus.[89] By the second half of 1931, however, it had become all too clear that foreign trade would not generate the industrial inputs specified in the plan. After a sharp increase in imports during the first half of the year, the Soviet Union simply stopped placing machinery orders in the West and was resigned to pay off most of its debts with gold and trade surpluses.[90] A characteristic lack of organization, along with Vesenkha's[91] great hunger for imports may have been the main culprits of this debacle. As Kaganovich reported to Stalin:

> A few days ago, in the Vesenkha commission on the foreign-currency plan for August, we had to decide, on the one hand, to increase payments in America above what Rozengolts had proposed, and, on the other hand, to curtail Vesenkha's demands. We are not placing new orders now, but we have to pay for the old ones, which are already 40 percent paid. Vesenkha demanded 8–9 million rubles. After calculating what must really be paid, we arrived at 6 million, but the foreign-currency situation is extremely strained. I must tell you, Comrade Stalin, that the whole manner in which the import situation is organized has made a very bad impression on me, they can't answer the question of what equipment we are importing specifically in August, and as a result maybe we are rushing to import things in August that will then become idle capital for six months, which is the case at a number of plants. We do not know what our payments are on

88 R. W. Davies, Oleg V. Khlevniuk, E. A. Rees, Liudmila P. Khosheleva and Larisa A. Rogovaya, eds., *The Stalin–Kaganovich Correspondence, 1931–36* (New Haven: Yale University Press, 2003), 50. It also seems that, with no system of quality control in place, the Germans were sending subpar equipment to the Soviets.

89 Dohan, "Economic Origins of Soviet Autarky," 623.

90 Soviet indebtedness was liquidated by 1935. The international circulation of Soviet gold during the 1930s puts the Soviet Union in the ironic position of being one of the main pillars in the doomed prolongation of the liberal order during these years, as the Soviets provided much-needed liquidity for the operation of the gold standard.

91 Vesenkha was the Supreme Council for the National Economy, responsible especially for the country's industrial development.

> a quarterly basis, whom we are paying and for what. One gets the sense that there is no unity between order, the movement of equipment, and the movement of payments.[92]

It was only after this unforeseen debacle that the Soviet press lionized the draconian and shortage-ridden import substitution strategies of the rest of the 1930s.[93] Dohan concluded that "crash import-substitution programs and accompanying publicity were pragmatic responses to contemporary import crises."[94] Although the discourse on the desirability of economic independence, well established in Marxist literature, existed before 1931, the absence of an actual campaign to this end before that year supports Dohan's contention of the discourse of import substitution as a fig leaf. To balance payments, the Soviets would have to start achieving trade surpluses.

Stalin continued to harangue his colleagues to this end:

> I strongly object to the Politburo decision to replace butter and egg exports with other food exports. This is senseless from the standpoint of current market conditions. You push grain exports as hard as you can when grain fetches pennies, and you want to hold back and do away with butter and egg exports, which are more profitable export commodities. What sense does that make? Wouldn't it be better to hold back grain exports and increase butter exports, or even to increase both, if you really want to make some hard currency and not just play some export game?[95]

The road to foreign trade surplus was a long one. The years 1931 and 1932 still saw foreign trade deficits, with imports financed by expensive short-term credit. It was at this time that the disaster of collectivization made itself felt. At a time when the Soviet leadership had planned for grain, along with its attendant agricultural derivatives such as meat, to become once again the mainstay of exports that it had once been, the Soviet Union suffered the worst harvest since 1925. In 1932, total export volume fell by 19 percent, while export value fell by 29 percent. The next year the value of exports fell by 37 percent, even as volume fell only by a few percentage points.[96] Planned increases in exports for those years were 31 percent for 1932 and 23 percent for 1933.[97] Only a cutback in imports to about

[92] Davies et al., eds., *The Stalin–Kaganovich Correspondence*, 58–59.
[93] Dohan, "Economic Origins of Soviet Autarky," 633–34. [94] Ibid., 633.
[95] Davies et al., eds., *The Stalin–Kaganovich Correspondence*, 71.
[96] In 1931, grain exports made up about 20 percent of exports, despite the fact that the Soviets had not planned to export that much grain that year. Dohan, "Soviet Foreign Trade in the NEP," 593.
[97] Ibid., 594.

one-third of their 1931 value kept the Soviet Union solvent in 1933. The lag between orders and deliveries of industrial equipment made it difficult for the Soviets to cut imports in 1932; debt levels had to be maintained that year to sustain imports. By 1933, however, the Soviets managed to implement the austerity measures that allowed them to pay off the country's debt by 1935.[98] Politically, the Nazi party's ascension to Germany's government in January 1933 and yet another embargo from the British in March of that same year meant an end to the loans the Soviets had relied on to keep up import levels. American diplomatic recognition of the Soviet Union in November, a decision largely carried out for economic reasons, did little to halt the trend.[99]

The years 1932 and 1933 were a nadir for world trade. It was no surprise that they were also the most difficult years for Soviet foreign economic relations. The surprise was that the Soviet Union, unlike many economically emerging countries during those years, did not default on its debt,[100] preferring to starve the Soviet population instead and gamble the full faith and credit of their government with those they ruled rather than with the bankers and large enterprises that might finance their experiment. Although one might be tempted to characterize the nature of foreign trade during the next few years as import substitution, the reality is that the Soviets stayed solvent through the imposition of a harsh import deprivation policy. Import reductions were not offset by increased domestic production, but rather were ad hoc and caused harm to such priority goals as expanding machine-building capacity and the allocation of tractors to rural areas.[101] Exports, in turn, continued to be forced in many products that were in severe shortage, notably grain in times of famine, but also cotton, timber, and other foodstuffs. The gravity of the situation was probably best represented in the development of Torgsin stores, which were used to siphon off from the Soviet populace valuables easily convertible to hard currency, which the Soviet state exchanged for a little food. It is no coincidence that citizens were allowed to enter these stores starting in

98 Ibid., 596–600.

99 Davies et al., eds., *The Stalin–Kaganovich Correspondence*, 104–14 details the immense care with which the Soviets handled the possibility of achieving US diplomatic recognition. Stalin even became involved in the canceling of a Langston Hughes-backed movie critical of American race relations simply because a visiting colonel learned of its filming while visiting the Soviet Union and expressed his displeasure with it.

100 See Carmen M. Reinhart and Kenneth S. Rogoff, *This Time is Different. Eight Centuries of Financial Folly* (Princeton: Princeton University Press, 2009), 96, table 6.4, for a full list of countries that defaulted.

101 Dohan, "Economic Origins of Soviet Autarky," 632.

1931, nor was it mere happenstance that stipulations on what these stores could accept kept expanding. From gold jewelry, medals, and coins, Torgsin stores steadily broadened their business by allowing silver, platinum, diamonds, and antiques to be traded for food, and eventually hard currency that may have been acquired abroad or sent as remittance from families abroad.[102] The operation was not trivial; if sales reached a respectable 49.3 million rubles in 1932, the next year sales more than doubled to 105.4 million rubles, with the stores doing their briskest business when famine was at its worst during the first five months of that year.[103]

With the crisis years over and most debt retired by 1935, it made little sense to continue forcing exports in the face of such unfavorable terms of trade; the proliferation of trade blocks further complicated the situation.[104] Moreover, an industrial base had been built, and domestic industrial demand now hungered more than ever for raw materials that had traditionally been export staples such as oil.[105] But then, by world standards, the Soviet Union can hardly be characterized as particularly autarkic. Although the value of exports fell by half from 1931 to 1934, export volume was only 28 percent less, and still 18 percent above 1929's volume. As Dohan pointed out, world trade was 20 percent below its 1929 level; Soviet foreign trade was, even in retreat, expansionary when compared to that of most other countries.[106]

Trade did not revive much thereafter. Volumes decreased, although slow improvements in the terms of trade kept its value steady during the second half of the 1930s. Perhaps preparations for war had made dependence on imports a foolhardy proposition; or perhaps the Soviet leaders had

102 The exchange rates were very unfavorable, usually amounting to 25 percent of the hard currency's real value. Torgsin services were astounding by Soviet standards, even allowing for family members living abroad to send hard currency directly to a Torgsin in direct exchange for food for their Soviet relatives. See Elena Osokina, *Our Daily Bread. Socialist Distribution and the Art of Survival in Stalin's Russia, 1927–1941* (Armonk: M. E. Sharpe, 2001), 121–29.

103 Ibid., 122–23. Osokina puts Torgsin's success in useful perspective. During its existence, Torgsin made 287.2 million rubles. Imports of equipment for some of the most important industrial projects of the time amounted to 42.3 million rubles for the Gorky Auto Factory, 35 million for the Stalingrad Tractor Factory, 27.9 million for the Stalin Auto Factory, 31 million for Dneprostroi, 22.5 million for Gospodshipnik, 23 million for the Cheliabinsk Tractor Factory, 15.3 million for the Kharkov Tractor Factory, 44 million for Magnitka, 25.9 million for Kuznetsk, and 15 million for Uralmash. In ibid., 127.

104 It is of interest to note that the subject of foreign trade, which had been one of the most prominent in Stalin's correspondence with his colleagues during his summer retreats to Sochi, almost disappears entirely from such correspondence after 1933.

105 The export of oil crude and oil products was reduced from its 1932 peak of 6,117,700 tons to 1,930,000 tons in 1937. *Vneshniaia torgovlia SSSR za 1918–1940 gg.*, 129, 163.

106 Dohan, "Economic Origins of Soviet Autarky," 632–33.

come to believe their own ideological propaganda on the virtues of economic independence. Imports of equipment were no longer as critical as they were in the beginning of the industrialization drive, and imports of industrial raw materials for domestic industrial needs increased. Imported technology tended to be of a military nature as the Soviets started to gear their economy toward defense. In August 1936, for example, Stalin insisted that what remained of a British credit be used in the purchase of naval equipment. "I am against the plan of orders for the remaining portion of the British credit as approved by Sergo [Ordzhonikidze]. I insist that three-fourths of the remaining credit be used for the needs of naval shipbuilding, for turbines or turbine parts for destroyers, cruisers, battleships, for models of large naval artillery or even entire batteries, and for equipment for the Arkhangelsk plant."[107]

In fact that relative commercial expansion may have been its most unique feature; otherwise, the Soviet foreign trade story was fairly common. Ivan T. Berend found within the larger geography of Eastern European economic backwardness the same constraints and outcomes conditioning Eastern European socio-political developments as conditioned those of the Soviet Union.[108] More globally, with American investors growing weary of foreign bonds and international lending, trade barriers proliferated and private capital markets died. In this context, countries turned inward. Where the United Kingdom had carried out 51 percent of exports and 42 percent of imports within the Commonwealth in 1929, the respective figures for 1938 had increased to 62 and 55 percent. The weight of Japan's trade within its empire in Korea, Taiwan, and Manchuria more than doubled during the same time period.[109] The political outcome of such economic disintegration was embodied in the rearmament policies carried out throughout the world, although with considerable zeal in Germany and Italy. The industrializing effects of these policies were felt from Brazil, to South Africa, Germany, and India, although perhaps few were as effective at the task as the Soviet Union. The Soviets continued to be dictated terms by the world economy against their plans and best interests. In an assessment validated in the postwar period, Alexander Baykov concluded long ago that "had it been possible to increase exports, or to obtain regular long-term foreign credits, it can be assumed that Soviet import, particularly the import of consumer goods, would have been on a far larger scale than in 1933–1938."[110]

107 Davies et al., eds., *The Stalin–Kaganovich Correspondence*, 344.

108 Berend, *Decades of Crisis*, chapter 10.

109 Kindleberger, *The World in Depression*, 279–80.

110 Baykov, *Soviet Foreign Trade*, 63.

Conclusion

In one of the best treatises on the origins of Stalinism, Michal Reiman echoed Polanyi in concluding that Stalinism "was not a product of positive social development or the positive development of a social doctrine or conception, but the result of a deep and all-embracing crisis; it evolved as a special kind of instrument or means of finding a way out of this crisis."[III] Sadly, this crucial international context is mostly absent from the academic conversation – and most textbooks. Certainly factors other than the world economy were important in the Great Break and collectivization policies. Ideological inclinations, the Civil War experience, and perhaps most decisively, Stalin's personal ambitions and boundless ruthlessness during this period all irrevocably steered the course of Soviet history. But it is difficult to analyze even the decisive role of Stalin the man, without understanding the ways in which the structural breakdowns of the late 1920s and early 1930s opened the socio-political space for the grim agency he exercised. We may ask, for example, what would have happened had the Soviet state developed in a globalizing, inflationary world economy more akin to the triumph of the 1950s rather than the disaster of the interwar period? A more cooperative world economy would certainly have pulled the rug from under the feet of those who argued for a more confrontational approach to grain procurement, as indeed it did during the comparatively smoother years of 1924 and 1925. And perhaps a Pax Britannica or Americana, as existed before and after the interwar period, might have diluted the concerns that led to the vast investments in the industrial sector and the defense industry in particular.

None of this happened, of course. Instead international economic crises constrained the Soviet Union along the same broadly unavoidable patterns that structured political and social changes around the world. These crises compelled a response from both the leadership and society at large, and continued to condition that response as the crises evolved. As in the world, it was so in the Soviet Union. The Bolsheviks had tied their project with chains of gold to a fragile international economic construct. That construct's inadequacies and eventual dissolution drastically structured the history of the NEP era and the Stalinist socio-political formation that obtained in the 1930s. In the postwar era, a new economic architecture would be constructed far from Soviet borders that would come to have equally decisive consequences for Soviet society.

[III] Reiman, *The Birth of Stalinism*, 115.

CHAPTER 2

Postwar: *The Bretton Woods Cold War*

Discussions on the origins of the Cold War in the mid 1940s have invariably fastened themselves around the question of ideology like a coil. Scholars have generally shown US policymakers the benefit of the doubt on this count, describing US policy as a sensible response to either Soviet initiatives or the situation on the ground. On the other hand, Stalin's foreign policy has engendered essentially two categories of analysis: security versus revolutionary agitation, or *realpolitik* versus ideology.[1] Strangely, these are presented as generally mutually exclusive, ensuring a debate now decades-long with little theoretical progress to commend it. Current academic fashion has scholars overwhelmingly gravitating toward an analysis of ideological determinism that arches ever closer to that of the State Department at the time of the American chargé d'affaires George Kennan's famous telegram.[2] The Soviet decision-making process, we are told, is subject to an ideology that relentlessly distorts reality. This ideology is invariably understood as "Marxist–Leninist," which is an invocation meant to bear all the opprobrium of its current failure. The argument confirms itself in our present-day certainties.

Yet the similarities in the economic assessments of both Soviets and Americans tell a different tale, one not so easily encased in an ideology

[1] An emphasis on security is central in Vojtech Mastny, *The Cold War and Soviet Insecurity. The Stalin Years* (New York: Oxford University Press, 1996) and Caroline Kennedy-Pipe, *Stalin's Cold War. Soviet Strategies in Europe, 1943 to 1956* (Manchester: Manchester University Press, 1995).

[2] The two books by Melvyn P. Leffler show this academic progression from the geopolitical and economic concerns described so extensively in *A Preponderance of Power. National Security, the Truman Administration, and the Cold War* (Stanford: Stanford University Press, 1992), to the ideas-driven policymaking in the more recent *For the Soul of Mankind. The United States, the Soviet Union, and the Cold War* (New York: Hill & Wang, 2007). See also Vladislav Zubok, *A Failed Empire. The Soviet Union in the Cold War from Stalin to Gorbachev* (Chapel Hill: The University of North Carolina Press, 2007) and Westad, *The Global Cold War.* Despite much academic disagreement, these authors are ultimately following a trend set by John Lewis Gaddis in his many works, albeit without Gaddis' unabashed American triumphalism. The pinnacle of Gaddis' influence was *We Now Know. Rethinking Cold War History* (New York: Oxford University Press, 1997).

versus security framework. After the war, when Stalin began to restore a system that had been explicitly designed to withstand the meltdown of the liberal order in the 1930s – and the subsequent wars – he had in mind the certainty of another global market failure.[3] But the Marshall Plan was animated by the very same fears, as were the creation of the Bretton Woods institutions and the many experiments in social democracy across Western Europe; they were all enacted to forestall a relapse of the cataclysmic 1930s. A dogmatic fear born of recent experience drove the policies of both sides. Whether mass poverty led to Communism in Western Europe – the American position – or to imperialist contradictions and a third world war – the Soviet one – the fear made for an alluring yet simplistic prediction. Today these predictions are of little value to the historian when assessing the relative "irrationality" of one ideology or another. They do suggest, however, that there was an extensive, ideologically-blind consensus in the immediate postwar era concerning the existential threat of the unregulated market and the fragility of the postwar economic recovery.[4] Basing policy on those grounds after three decades of global socio-political disintegration should hardly be viewed as an aberration in sensible policymaking or an abrogation of common sense. Yet this is all too often what is implied in describing Stalin's foreign policy as "ideological."[5] A clearer account of the material realities surrounding these decisions and of the economic aspirations of the Soviets should clarify our discussion.

Despite the many narratives of the origins of the Cold War that essentially assume an equivalence of ambition and resources between East and West, the Soviet Union was in fact an exhausted country. All European countries in the West and the East – and including the Soviet Union – looked to the United States for the resources necessary for the postwar reconstruction. In early 1946, Kennan warned that the Soviet Union was "a political force committed fanatically to the belief that with US there can be no permanent modus vivendi, that it is desirable and necessary that the internal harmony of our society be disrupted, our traditional way of life be destroyed, the international authority of our state

[3] The best description of Stalin's foreign policy thinking at this time is Vladimir O. Pechatnov, "The Soviet Union and the World, 1944–1953," in Melvyn P. Leffler and Odd Arne Westad, eds., *The Cambridge History of the Cold War*, vol. 1 (Cambridge: Cambridge University Press, 2010).

[4] For two examples covering the political spectrum see Friedrich Pollock, "State Capitalism: Its Possibilities and Limitations", *Studies in Philosophy and Social Science* 9:2 (1941): 200–55 and Joseph A. Schumpeter, *Capitalism, Socialism and Democracy* (New York: Harper & Row, 1950).

[5] As Zubok and Gaddis so often do in the aforementioned books.

be broken, if Soviet power is to be secure."[6] Not that the US State Department was paying attention, but Kennan could hardly have been more wrong. Even as Stalin expected those imperialist contradictions to erupt in another war,[7] the Soviets sought to buy into the very system of financial and commercial exchange that could guarantee the quick recovery of fortress Soviet Union. Even as the United States ostracized the Soviet Union and surrounded it with military bases, the permanent US occupation of West Germany meant that the Soviets would enjoy more security than they had ever known since coming to power in 1917.[8] Even as the official Soviet discourse hardened around an existential conflict with capitalism – in tandem with domestic repression – the financial and commercial practices of the Soviet state were marked not by enmity and subversion, as virtually all Cold War texts assume, but by a search for accommodation, cooperation, and ultimately acquiescence. The Cold War signified a stability the Soviet leadership had not known in the interwar period, but it was not the result of equilibrium in a bipolar world, as some Cold War texts suggest.[9] Soviet commercial and financial practices suggest a stability born of American – and then Western – economic hegemony with which the ostracized Soviets sought a modus operandi, and ultimately gainful participation.

War's foretaste

The early months of the war in the West offered novel commercial opportunities for the Soviets, who had spent the past decade in a severely harmful autarky. In February 1940, during the time of the Nazi–Soviet alliance, Mikoyan reported to Stalin and Molotov about the possibility of importing American oil to Vladivostok paid for by Germany, presumably sent by

[6] Kenneth M. Jensen, ed., *Origins of the Cold War. The Novikov, Kennan, and Roberts 'Long Telegrams' of 1946* (Washington, DC: United States Institute of Peace Press, 1993), 28.

[7] Felix Chuev, *Molotov Remembers. Inside Kremlin Politics* (Chicago: Ivan R. Dee, 1993), 63. See also Vladislav Zubok and Constantine Pleshakov, *Inside the Kremlin's Cold War. From Stalin to Khrushchev* (Cambridge: Harvard University Press, 1996), 47.

[8] As Tony Judt counterintuitively argued in *Postwar. A History of Europe since 1945* (New York: The Penguin Press, 2005), 243. This is not to say that the Soviets did not feel militarily encircled, as they often proclaimed. But this was a far cry from the terrifying and imminent danger posed by the Nazis, or even, in the weary Bolshevik imagination of the post-foreign intervention 1920s, the British. In fact, upon hearing at Yalta that Roosevelt would only be committing American troops in Europe for two years, Stalin, far from smacking his lips at the possibilities for subversion in a defenseless Europe, immediately compromised on a larger French role in the German occupation than he had previously allowed. See Serhii M. Plokhy, *Yalta. The Price of Peace* (New York: Penguin Books, 2010), 107.

[9] Most influentially in John Lewis Gaddis, *The Long Peace. Inquiries into the History of the Cold War* (Oxford: Oxford University Press, 1987), which in turn takes its theoretical inspiration from the work of realist political scientists.

friends of the Führer in the United States. The Soviet Union would then compensate Germany with the equivalent amount of oil from Baku. This strange business offer would save the Soviets some hard currency as well as free up train, wagon, and freight traffic along the Trans-Siberian railway, since the Eastern regions would be supplied with oil from West of the Urals.[10] Those same American oilmen were also willing to send oil to Murmansk, where the Germans had offered to build tanks to store the oil before transporting it to Germany. This was a way to send American oil to Nazi Germany surreptitiously. Although the Soviets would not have a right to that oil, they would get to keep the storage tanks at the end of the war and to make use of them during the war.[11] The alliance with Germany also briefly revived the traditional Soviet–German exchange of primary commodities for industrial equipment, a recurrent and ultimately triumphant arrangement that thrived whenever economic and geopolitical circumstances allowed.

The German attack in the summer of 1941, however, put an end to that trade and brought about economic exchange, in the form of the Lend-Lease program, that was of a different dimension altogether. It has long been the standing notion, one established by Gosplan Chairman Nikolai Voznesenskii in his Stalin-approved *Voennaia ekonomika SSSR v period Otechestvennoi voiny* [War economy of the Soviet Union in the period of the Patriotic War], that British and American Lend-Lease aid amounted to a mere 4 percent of total Soviet war production. In his authoritative study of the Soviet wartime economy,[12] however, economic historian Mark Harrison calculated that Lend-Lease and other US and British assistance added about 8 percent on average to the domestically produced GNP during the war.[13] The volume of aid in dollar terms was

[10] RGASPI, f. 84, op. 1, d. 15, l. 45.

[11] Ibid., l. 46. The documents do not state who these American oilmen are. In fact, several US oil companies had already been cooperating with the Fascists during the Spanish Civil War, but the pro-Nazi CEO of Texaco Thorkild Rieber is the best bet, as he had already been flouting American neutrality laws for several years by then and had cooperated with the Nazis to set up similarly intricate arrangements to provide oil to both Franco and the Nazis in their respective wars.

[12] The book is based on a perusal of the planning agencies and the Ministry of Finance. See the discussion of Voznesenskii's numbers in Mark Harrison, *Accounting for War. Soviet Production, Employment and the Defence Burden, 1940–1945* (Cambridge: Cambridge University Press, 1996), 17–19, 131–39. For an example of Soviet disparagement of Lend-Lease's help to Soviet wartime production see Kumykin, ed., *50 let sovetskoi vneshnei torgovli*, 58–62.

[13] See Harrison, *Accounting for War*, 142–45. See also Ibid., 134 for the American reaction, particularly Gerschenkron's argument that "the tremendous contribution to the Russian war economy made by the scarce commodities delivered under Lend-Lease cannot be significantly measured in terms of a global percentage."

$11.93 billion;[14] however, it was unevenly distributed, with most of it coming in during the last two years of the war, while only a small fraction of it came to Soviet ports during the Soviet Union's darkest months before and during the battle of Stalingrad.[15]

Such a figure may have constituted a wartime annual tripling of Soviet imports at their peak in 1931.[16] And its contribution to Soviet resources should not be minimized. Lend-Lease's biggest contributions were in transport, in the form of aircraft, tanks, and especially motor vehicles; in communications, in the form of radios; in industrial materials, especially iron, nonferrous metals, fuels, and rubber; and in foodstuffs. This meant that the Soviets were able to fight the last two years of the war with more speed and coordination, and with fuller stomachs. With the Soviet economy at the edge of collapse, the fungibility of Lend-Lease aid allowed the Soviets to invest severely scarce resources to mitigate starvation and the depreciation of capital stock. It also had a compounding effect on the ability of the Soviets to recuperate productive capabilities and territories more speedily after the war, as well as to stave off greater losses of labor capital – as economists might say.[17] Furthermore, because much of the aid was in the form of advanced technologies new to the Soviet economy, its reverse engineering and incorporation into domestic production raised productivity levels higher than they would have been otherwise.[18] Indeed it would not be until the late 1950s, with Khrushchev's penchant for turnkey projects and his general attempts to intensify economic engagement with the West, that the Soviet Union would begin to see Western technology inputs once again.

[14] The United States alone sent $10.6 billion, which, as the Soviets liked to point out, was only one-fourth of total Lend-Lease aid, the rest of which mostly went to Great Britain. Ibid., 132.

[15] If one follows Khanin's numbers on the size of the Soviet economy during the first half of the 1940s, rather than the Abram Bergson's numbers that Harrison uses, the more than $10 billion may well have been more than the 10 percent of Soviet production Harrison surmises. Khanin computed much less growth during the 1930s than Bergson did.

[16] Baykov made this case. The figure might well be rather nonsensical, given that he simply calculated the annual amount in rubles according to the official 1938 Soviet exchange rate of 5.3 rubles per dollar. Baykov, *Soviet Foreign Trade*, 78–79. A more interesting figure was arrived at by the Soviets themselves, who in order to tabulate Lend-Lease aid into their own accounts, added different tariffs to the aid, levying up to 160 percent in the first few payments. Later amounts were tabulated using a 20 percent mark-up. Such account keeping was arbitrary, but it seems to suggest the extent to which the Soviet state thought its currency overvalued, and thus the extent to which Western products were undervalued. Harrison, *Accounting for War*, 135–37.

[17] Not everything was positive. British munitions and tanks, for example, had a particularly bad reputation in the Soviet army, while the wartime Soviet economy's lack of absorptive capacity meant that some Western equipment was left to rust. See ibid., 147–48.

[18] Philip Hanson, *The Rise and Fall of the Soviet Economy. An Economic History of the USSR from 1945* (New York: Longman, 2003), 24.

Like the rest of Europe, the Soviet Union saw the war ravage its balance of payments. By 1945, the Soviet Union was importing ten times the amount of goods that it was exporting.[19] As they had after World War I, the Soviets found themselves rapidly depleting their gold reserves, and they would continue to use gold to settle accounts for several years.[20] It is thus no surprise that the Soviet leadership not only welcomed, but pursued American credit; Stalin and Molotov, in fact, expected to get it ever since victory in Stalingrad allayed Stalin's fears of a possible détente between the Anglo-Saxon powers and Hitler.[21] The pursuit of Western credits was very much in keeping with prewar foreign economic policy. Indeed, after having taken the brunt of the German war machine and shouldered most of the burden of war against the Nazis, and particularly given the excessive – from the Soviet perspective – delay of the Second Front, the expectation of a large credit took on a moral dimension.

As Mikoyan later remembered, his pursuit of postwar reconstruction credits took up a fair amount of his responsibilities during the latter stages of the war. The Roosevelt Administration authorized US Ambassador Averell Harriman to talk about postwar credits as early as February 1944.[22] Mikoyan recalled that it was Harriman who first offered $1 billion worth of credits to the Soviet Union sometime before the Yalta Conference.[23] Perhaps a quick Soviet acceptance of this offer might have actually produced an American loan, but Stalin insisted in asking for $6 billion instead. Stalin's position surprised Mikoyan, who had suggested asking for $2 billion, and counseled Stalin that asking for $6 billion would be a

[19] Alec Nove, *An Economic History of the USSR, 1917–1991* (London: Penguin Books, 1992), 296. The numbers were 1,433 million rubles of exports and 14,805 million rubles worth of imports.

[20] See for example Mikoyan's request dated April 26, 1945 for ten tons of gold to pay off debts to the United Kingdom and imports of gas pipes from the United States, in RGASPI, f. 84, op. 1, d. 28, l. 3. A year-and-a-half later, Mikoyan is found asking for thirty-five tons of gold to pay off loans to the British and assorted imports, in RGASPI, f. 84, op. 1, d. 29, ll. 103–04.

[21] A lull in Lend-Lease deliveries in late 1941, along with the seemingly endless postponement of the Second Front, persuaded Stalin that Churchill and Roosevelt were planning to come to terms with Hitler. Geoffrey Roberts, *Stalin's Wars. From World War to Cold War, 1939–1953* (New Haven: Yale University Press, 2006), 140–42. According to Roberts, his confidence in the alliance, and his full willingness to maintain the Grand Alliance after the war, returned with the victory at Stalingrad.

[22] Hull to Harriman, 2 February 1944, in US Department of State, *Foreign Relations of the United States Diplomatic Papers, 1944*, Vol. 4 (Washington, DC: US Government Printing Office, 1966), 1042–43.

[23] Anastas Ivanovich Mikoyan, *Tak bylo. Razmyshleniia o minuvshem* (Moscow: Varius, 1999), 493–94. The credit was at a 3 percent interest rate for thirty years, which were fairly good terms. Mikoyan recalls how Gosplan Chairman Voznesenskii surprised both him and Stalin by coming out against the offer, arguing that it was disadvantageous, as the Soviet government would end up paying twice what would be lent to it. I frankly share Stalin and Mikoyan's purported surprise, and suspect that Voznesenskii's intervention may have been slightly more sophisticated than Mikoyan recalls.

nonstarter. In fact, unbeknownst to Mikoyan, the State Department was willing to countenance "several billion" at that time.[24] Secretary of the Treasury Henry Morgenthau made a request to President Roosevelt for $10 billion.[25] But doubts over whether such quantities could pass through Congress fatally delayed the credit offer. Its importance was nevertheless clear to everyone, and Mikoyan would continue his stubborn pursuit for credits for as long as the two sides continued to talk to each other. "Being occupied in economic questions, and knowing well the domestic requirements of the country," he wrote later, "I understood that postwar export resources would prove rather insufficient considering the economic destruction and the enormous domestic needs of the country. Therefore without large credits it would be impossible to develop foreign trade and have the large amounts of imports we needed."[26]

Throughout the Tehran and Yalta negotiations of 1943 and 1944, Stalin dangled the possibility of great rewards for US firms in Soviet markets, a positive prospect for the US leadership.[27] After all, it had been the contraction of world economic exchange, rather than any willful policy of the Soviet leadership, that had constricted Soviet import demand during the 1930s. Although export potential could be expected to remain restricted in the immediate future, German reparations would speed up Soviet economic reconstruction, while American credits could expedite the restoration of its foreign trade sector.[28] Evidently both sides were of the same mind. In the many discussions in the State Department on this issue during the final year of the war, the only other constraining factor in the amount of the loan besides congressional approval was Soviet export capacity and consequently their ability to pay back the loan. The Roosevelt Administration expected in return to put the great wealth of Soviet

[24] Memorandum by the Chief of the Division of Financial and Monetary Affairs, 4 January 1945, in US Department of State, *Foreign Relations of the United States Diplomatic Papers, 1945*, Vol. 5 (Washington, DC: US Government Printing Office, 1967), 938–39.

[25] Memorandum by Morgenthau, 10 January 1945, in ibid., 948–49.

[26] Mikoyan, *Tak bylo*, 494.

[27] See for example Stalin and Roosevelt's exchange on the first day of the Tehran Conference, with Roosevelt singling out Soviet reserves of raw materials as particularly promising. In Roberts, *Stalin's Wars*, 181.

[28] Large Soviet reparations, in the order of $20 billion, half of which would go to the Soviets, were fully supported by US Secretary of State Edward Stettinius, who went as far as to suggest that, moreover, millions of German workers should be involved in Soviet economic reconstruction during the next five to six years. Mikoyan, *Tak bylo*, 494. Fortunately no doubt for millions of Germans, Stalin hesitated at the last minute to ask for German labor at the Yalta Conference. Thinking that the allies would bristle at the request, Stalin misunderstood Roosevelt's eagerness to concede this to his ally as a sign of good will when the American brought up the issue on the second day of the conference. Plokhy, *Yalta*, 110.

primary resources at the service of the world economy and possibly to receive some political concessions in the bargain.

It was a deeply embedded belief of the Soviet leadership that long-term credit arrangements would normalize trade and thus political relations. With tensions escalating rapidly through 1946, Stalin compromised down to $1 billion on the credit request and prioritized it over most other items of discussion with the Americans. Whether it concerned talks on civilian aviation, free and open navigation on rivers of international significance, complaints from American citizens against the Soviet government, international copyright laws, or any cooperation between the two powers concerning economic aid to Europeans, no item suggested by the State Department was to go forward without a resolution on the American loan.[29] Meanwhile, the Soviets were busy obtaining loans from other European countries. They were most successful with Sweden, which in mid-1946 offered a 200 kronor (about $55 million) long-term credit line for the purchase of Swedish goods.[30]

The main impediment, in the eyes of the Soviets, was America's progressively more transformative plans for the postwar period. Credit negotiations would come with many strings attached, the Soviets soon found out.[31] They might have saved themselves the disappointment if only they had taken notice of the British example; as early as 1941 the British were having to compromise on imperial preference and tariff arrangements in order to receive Lend-Lease aid from the Americans. As American plans for the reconstruction of both Europe and the world economy became gradually more ambitious, the Soviets would increasingly come to be seen as a threat, rather than a partner, to these ambitions.

The Soviets opt out

It is an oft-repeated statistic that, at the end of the war, US production made up about half of world economic output. And indeed, the alacrity with which the United States had become an economic behemoth is unparalleled in human history. Its economy, dominant already in 1939 at about half the size of the combined economies of Europe, Japan, and the

[29] As per directives on negotiations with the US State Department from May 23, 1946, in RGASPI, f. 84, op. 1, d. 28, ll. 68–70.

[30] RGASPI, f. 84, op. 1, d. 29, ll. 1–16.

[31] Ibid., ll. 61–63. As Mikoyan noted in this report from July 9, 1946, this was a change from the time of the $1 billion offer a year before, which had no strings attached.

Soviet Union, was larger than all of them put together seven years later. US steel output by 1946, for example, was more than twice that of Germany, Great Britain, and the Soviet Union combined, whereas it had been at 85 percent in 1939.[32] The Great Depression, its consequent war and, most of all, the sheer economic preponderance of the United States in trade and finance convinced American leaders that it was the United States that had the most to lose from a return to worldwide autarky and beggar-thy-neighbor policies. The more evident the economic weakness of other powers became, the more vigorously the United States took on the burden of leadership of the world economy.

A conference in Bretton Woods, New Hampshire in 1944 set up financial and commercial institutions that would oversee the gradual reduction of barriers to trade and capital necessary for the smooth functioning of an international liberal economy. The path to the implementation of the Bretton Woods system was strewn with obstacles, not least of which was European recalcitrance in giving up the discredited system of imperial preferences. In desperate need of American credit, however, the European powers relented to American pressure in that and other issues, such as European economic integration. Postwar reconstruction was not smooth; a dollar shortage in Europe hampered necessary imports from the United States, and the traditional markets and resources of Eastern Europe slowly closed up to Western capital. The Marshall Plan, a widespread devaluation of European currencies in 1949 vis-à-vis the dollar, the Korean War, and the use of the raw materials from Europe's troubled colonies to earn dollars for their respective colonial masters slowly changed the situation. The Bretton Woods system would not hit its stride until the end of the 1950s, when the major world currencies finally became convertible.[33]

In their postwar planning, Soviet leaders had failed to appreciate the extent to which the United States would take over the reins of leadership and transform the world's economic landscape. The Soviet system had been built in response to the expiration of the previous gold standard-based liberal order. Victory in war had not only ensured the Soviet system's survival, it had legitimated its structure. Indeed the idea that the state

[32] Frieden, *Global Capitalism*, 262.

[33] A. G. Kenwood and A. L. Lougheed, *The Growth of the International Economy, 1820–1990. An Introductory Text* (London: Routledge, 1992), chapters 16 and 17. On the use of European colonies and their dollar-earning commodities for Europe's economic recovery see Robert E. Wood, "From the Marshall Plan to the Third World," in Melvyn P. Leffler and David S. Painter, eds., *Origins of the Cold War. An International History* (London: Routledge, 1994).

should be at the heart of a country's economic life was not in ascendance just in the Soviet Union; state control over social and economic affairs became the defining feature of the postwar political economy in both Europe and North America.[34] For the United States, this was not sufficient; American policymakers envisioned a world economy governed through institution-based, cooperative governance that would avoid the mistakes of the interwar period. For the Soviet Union, however, integration into this global architecture would have entailed the complete reorganization of its system, including the end of the state's monopoly over foreign trade and a return to the failed financial policies of the 1920s, when the government achieved the convertibility of the ruble only to be pushed out a few years later. Full integration, then, was a nonstarter, and indeed the Soviets showed little interest in the negotiations taking place in Bretton Woods, New Hampshire. They nevertheless hoped to take advantage of a revived world economy and a reopening of world financial markets.

In fact, Stalin fully expected to maintain good relations with his wartime allies. Apocalyptic imperial rivalries were not without their silver lining. Stalin's beliefs had been reinforced by some of the early analytical reports of Molotov's foreign policy team, which examined ways of how to weather the coming storms and how to best secure the Soviet Union and the revolution's gains from the West's future economic struggles. These reports, written during the waning months of the war, took Western goodwill for granted. Indeed, the Soviets expected to be wooed for support by the competing powers.[35] Moreover, they calculated that any economic revival in Europe, and America's continued economic

[34] See Tony Judt's excellent discussion of planning as an institutional legacy of the war in Judt, *Postwar*, 66–68. Judt stresses the many shades the idea of planning had in Europe, none of which tended to be of a Soviet sort. He expands on it in Tony Judt with Timothy Snyder, *Thinking the Twentieth Century* (New York: Penguin Press, 2012), 333–54. This history is also concisely recovered in Ivan T. Berend, *An Economic History of Twentieth-Century Europe. Economic Regimes from Laissez-Faire to Globalization* (Cambridge: Cambridge University Press, 2006), 223–26. Nevertheless, so much has been made of 1945 as a liberal moment, the best argument for which can be found in Robert Latham's excellent *The Liberal Moment. Modernity, Security and the Making of Postwar International Order* (New York: Columbia University Press, 1997), that it is easy to forget the extent to which the liberal world order was discredited in 1945. It would take almost four decades to see its idea triumph worldwide once again.

[35] See Vladimir O. Pechatnov, "The Big Three After World War II: New Documents on Soviet Thinking about Post War Relations with the United States and Great Britain," Cold War International History Project, Working paper No. 13, Woodrow Wilson Center, July 1995. Of special interest is the uniform stress on cooperation with the West in all the reports, which their authors believed to be the only effective means to protect Soviet interests. This was, as it happens, also the official line of the press and speeches by Soviet officials.

prosperity, would require Soviet raw materials as well as its market, ever hungry for Western products and technology.[36]

For two years, as political disagreements over Eastern Europe and Germany turned into impasses, Stalin continued to depend on that premise. It is thus no surprise that even as lines on both sides hardened during those two years, Stalin and Molotov's first reaction to the Marshall Plan announced in June 1947 was to roll up their sleeves and get to the bottom of the American offer. That same month, upon meeting his British and French counterparts at the Quai d'Orsay in Paris to discuss the plan, Molotov's first words were to ask if they had received more information from the Americans other than that contained in Marshall's speech.[37] The Soviet Minister of Foreign Affairs had come to Paris with a hundred-strong delegation to negotiate the terms of inclusion, if not in the liberal world order, at least in a system of European economic exchange funded by American capital.

He was soon disappointed. As early as May 23 of that year, Kennan, the then director of policy planning staff, had written to Undersecretary of State Dean Acheson that any plan for the economic recovery of Europe should be written in a way by which "the Russian satellite countries would either exclude themselves by unwillingness to accept the proposed conditions or agree to abandon the exclusive orientation of their economies."[38] As for Britain and France, as early as June 18 the American Ambassador to France Jefferson Caffery was informing Secretary of State Marshall that "the British feel that Russian participation would tend greatly to complicate things and that it might be best if Russians refused invitation. They tell me the French also [appear] to share this feeling."[39] It was followed later on that day by a much stronger commitment. "[British

[36] As argued extensively in Roberts, *Stalin's Wars*. The argument, now fully documented with archival material, relies to some extent on the evidence of developments in Eastern Europe. Where some scholars see an early blueprint for the Sovietization of Eastern Europe, Roberts sees a plurality of outcomes in Eastern Europe that connotes a basic Soviet willingness to compromise, thus reinventing the wheel since Joyce and Gabriel Kolko's *The Limits of Power. The World and the United States Foreign Policy, 1945–1954* (New York: Harper & Row, 1972). After much politicking and rhetorical hostility, it tellingly took the implicit economic exclusion of the Marshall Plan for Stalin to finally give up on compromise. For recent reiterations of the stubborn argument of a Soviet master plan see Georges-Henri Soutou, *La guerre de Cinquante Ans. Le conflit Est–Ouest, 1943–1990* (Paris: Fayard, 2001) and Anne Applebaum, *Iron Curtain. The Crushing of Eastern Europe* (New York: Doubleday, 2012).

[37] Quoted in Charles L. Mee, *The Marshall Plan. The Launching of Pax Americana* (New York: Simon and Schuster, 1984), 130.

[38] Kennan to Acheson, 23 May 1947, in US Department of State, *Foreign Relations of the United States* (FRUS), Vol. 3 (Washington, DC: US Government Printing Office, 1972), 228.

[39] Caffery to Secretary of State, 18 June 1947, FRUS, Vol. 3, 258.

Foreign Secretary Ernest] Bevin and [French Foreign Minister Georges] Bidault also both told me separately that they hope the Soviets will refuse to cooperate and that in any event they will be prepared 'to go ahead full steam even if the Soviets refuse to do so.'"[40]

After a few days of negotiation, during which Molotov had asked for secrecy and had been more accommodating than usual, according to Caffery, it soon became clear that the West fully meant to exclude the Soviet Union, unless the latter were willing to completely give up control over Eastern Europe.[41] "Both Britain and France are now in dire straits and they do not have at their disposal any serious levers to overcome their economic difficulties," Molotov wrote to Stalin while still in Paris. "Their only hope is the United States, which demands that Britain and France set up some kind of European body to facilitate US interference in the economic and political affairs of European countries."[42] Differing ideological lenses notwithstanding, both sides understood the situation in the same exact light. "We did not feel the Soviet Union would accept American verification of the use of the goods and funds," Marshall's close assistant Charles Bohlen later wrote. "Furthermore, we did not think the Soviet Union would be able to maintain its control over Eastern Europe if those countries were able to participate in the cooperative venture."[43] The United States indeed made great strides during the following years in breaking up imperial preferences and prompting European integration. It was precisely that price that the Soviet Union, no matter how eager for American credit, was unwilling to pay.[44]

Instead, the Soviets resolved to get the necessary resources through the wholesale pillaging of the defeated countries, along with some of their allies.[45]

40 Caffery to Secretary of State, 18 June 1947, FRUS, Vol. 3, 260.

41 Caffery believed "that the Soviets wish at all cost to avoid giving the French or the British a valid text to break with them." See Caffery to Secretary of State, 29 June 1947, FRUS, Vol. 3, 300.

42 The cipher telegram dates July 1, 1947. Quoted in Mikhail M. Narinsky, "New Evidence on the Soviet Rejection of the Marshall Plan, 1947: Two Reports," Cold War International History Project, Working paper No. 9, Woodrow Wilson Center, March 1994, 43.

43 Charles E. Bohlen, *Witness to History, 1929–1969* (New York: W. W. Norton & Company, 1973), 264–65.

44 For a similar appraisal that sees the Marshall Plan as the watershed that turned a reluctant Stalin decisively away from cooperation, see Michael Cox and Caroline Kennedy-Pipe, "The Tragedy of American Diplomacy? Rethinking the Marshall Plan," *Journal of Cold War Studies* 7:1 (2005): 97–134.

45 In Manchuria the Chinese found that many factories had been taken away, see Nove, *An Economic History of the USSR*, 296. Even in friendly Czechoslovakia the Soviets dismantled factories to be taken to the Soviet Union, arguing that they had belonged to German companies during the war. In the end, the Germans paid the greatest amount of reparations, followed by Romania and Hungary. See Randall W. Stone, *Satellites and Commissars. Strategy and Conflict in the Politics of Soviet-Bloc Trade* (Princeton: Princeton University Press, 1996), 27.

They did this in three ways: the bluntest was to simply uproot whole factories and replant them on Soviet soil; they also forced countries to sell resources to the Soviet Union at very low prices; and they took a 50 percent stake in many large firms throughout Eastern Europe. It is difficult to measure the extent to which the Soviet Union benefited from these arrangements. Poland famously provided the Soviet Union with coal at prices well below world market prices, but the Soviet Union, in turn, also supplied goods at prices lower than those in the world market. This practice would become endemic in Communist-Bloc trade; arbitrary pricing was one of its hallmarks. However, at least two ministers of foreign trade, in Bulgaria and Czechoslovakia, were executed for bargaining too hard with the Soviet Union, and it is fair to say that the benefits accrued to the Soviet Union of the postwar reparations were significant.

Yet the pillaging soon abated. Even before the success of the Marshall Plan, the Soviet Union started normalizing trade relations with Eastern Europe – inasmuch as relations could be normal under Soviet military occupation. Already in early 1947, Soviet leaders were studying ways to ease the "excessive tax burden" on joint-stock companies throughout Eastern Europe.[46] From 1947 through 1948 the Soviets negotiated credit agreements with Bulgaria and Czechoslovakia and cut in half the Romanian and Hungarian reparations. In 1950 they did the same for East Germany.[47] The Soviets also created the Council for Mutual Economic Assistance (CMEA) in 1949. This institution was supposed to coordinate production and help integrate the economies of the Eastern Bloc; however, it was never really able to overcome the bilateral system of intra-bloc trade. Although the CMEA was based in Moscow and followed agendas set there, the Soviet Union, unlike the United States, was never able to persuade its allies to accept its commercial leadership. The reason was simple; as political scientist Randall Stone argued, "The politics of trade in the Soviet bloc swirled and eddied around opportunities created by the distorted prices mandated by the Council for Mutual Economic Assistance."[48] Although loosely based on prices quoted in world markets, CMEA prices largely benefited Eastern European countries and created perverse incentives to evade international obligations that may well have benefited everyone as a whole; that, coupled with the institutional disorganization

46 RGASPI, f. 84, op. 1, d. 30, ll. 14–19. Mikoyan's letter dates from January 23, 1947. The suggestion was both to reduce taxes and to take more taxes in the form of production from those enterprises at reduced prices.

47 Nove, *An Economic History of the USSR*, 322–23.

48 Stone, *Satellites and Commissars*, 5.

in the Soviet Union meant that the smaller satellites were able to consistently resist Soviet pressure for fairer trade. The satellites were effectively subsidized by a country that was, in fact, less developed than many of them.

The Soviet leadership did succeed in one thing: It raised levels of trade with Eastern European countries. Presaging developments in the second half of the 1950s, when world political and economic developments finally allowed the Soviet leadership to engage the world in commercial exchange, Soviet trade with Eastern European countries expanded at an astonishing rate – albeit, as in the later expansion of trade with the rest of the world, from very low levels. From 1946 to 1950, foreign trade turnover more than doubled, from 1.3 billion to 2.9 billion rubles.[49] It again almost doubled in the next five years. The growth, particularly to 1950, came almost exclusively from the expansion of trade with Eastern Europe and China.

The issue of when postwar exploitation of Eastern Europe became subsidization is one not easily resolved. Czechoslovak planners interviewed by Stone stated that terms of trade were already pretty comfortable for Czechoslovakia when the CMEA was established in 1949, reporting that they could sell almost any industrial product they wished to the Soviets. East Germany, the other economically advanced region in the bloc probably also experienced positive terms of trade after its reparations were cancelled in 1954.[50] Whatever the case may be, postwar Eastern Europe presented the Soviets with their first opportunity ever to trade with other countries without overwhelming economic or political complications. It was telling that they seized the opportunity; it heralded the explosion to come (see Figure 2.1).

Bretton Woods interrupted: The economics of political ostracism

But even as the Soviet Union was orchestrating the rapid growth of trade within its new domains, economic exchange in the West was slow off the mark. The interwar years had shown the dangers of an international financial system that allowed capital complete freedom of mobility, especially in a financial landscape beset by large, war-generated imbalances in capital reserves. This postwar was not much different than the last one;

[49] Ministry of Foreign Trade, *Vneshniaia torgovlia SSSR za 1970 god. Statisticheskii obzor* (Moscow: Izdatel'stvo "Mezhdunarodnye otnosheniia," 1971), 8.

[50] Stone, *Satellites and Commissars*, 31. Stone mentions the 1953 uprisings in East Germany as the catalyst for the change.

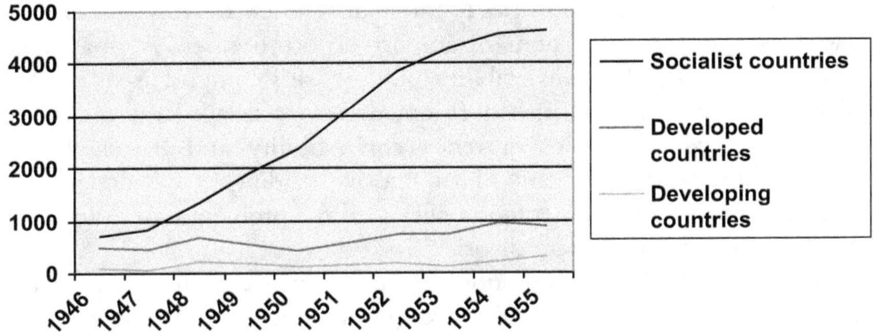

Figure 2.1 Foreign trade turnover by region (in millions of 1961 rubles)*
*Ministry of Foreign Trade, *Vneshniaia torgovlia SSSR. Statisticheskii obzor, 1918–1966* (Moscow: Izdatel'stvo "Mezhdunarodnye otnosheniia," 1967), 62.

in both, the United States accumulated inordinate amounts of capital. In 1948 the United States held two-thirds of global monetary reserves.[51] American capital flows to Europe had restored the European economies in the interwar period; trouble had begun when these abruptly diminished. A perverse adjustment policy – austerity – coupled with an absence of international financial cooperation had doomed the interwar financial system. The Bretton Woods system of the post-1945 era was designed with these mistakes in mind, particularly once it faced its first challenge: a severe dollar shortage in Europe.

A main objective of the Bretton Woods talks was the eventual convertibility of the European and Japanese currencies. These were to be pegged to the dollar, therefore maintaining one of the most clearly positive features of the gold standard: exchange rate predictability. Capital controls were to be widely used to achieve this goal while allowing governments the freedom to pursue domestic Keynesian policies. This was a freedom they had not had under the much more stringent peg of the gold standard. International institutions such as the International Monetary Fund (IMF) and the World Bank would keep vigil over the good functioning of the system. The problem was that in the immediate postwar, Europe found it very difficult to earn dollars from the United States – to export to the United States, in other words. And yet these dollars were sorely needed to import the raw and manufactured American products necessary for reconstruction. The corresponding deficits created a dollar shortage that

[51] Barry Eichengreen, *Globalizing Capital. A History of the International Monetary System* (Princeton: Princeton University Press, 2008), 112.

compelled the European countries to implement strict controls over capital as well as a draconian system of import–export licenses. A disastrous decision to restore the convertibility of the British pound in 1947, an American rather than a British decision, decisively delayed the objective of a general restoration of currency convertibility and hastened the coming of the Marshall Plan.[52] That massive lending of US dollars for the sake of European reconstruction alleviated the problem, but it was not really overcome until the late 1950s.

The Soviet Union could not aspire to convertibility and keep its economic system; its centralized economy was such that it made a nonsense of active participation in the Bretton Woods system. But despite the equivalence so prevalent in most Cold War narratives, this did not mean that the Soviets set up some kind of parallel system of economic and financial exchange. The Warsaw Pact might have been some kind of equivalent of the North Atlantic Treaty Organization (NATO), but the CMEA was far from anything remotely as effective or far-reaching as the Bretton Woods system. The Soviet Union, along with its CMEA partners, remained appendages to the much larger and dominant liberal construct. Commercial and financial interaction between East and West would resume only when the system's dollar shortage resolved itself and the stringent European currency controls gradually receded. Until that time, the Soviets could do little else but complain about commercial discrimination and embargo – mostly rightly – and gripe about the import–export licensing system, which they bumped into as soon as economic relations with Western Europe started to pick up with Marshall's financial tonic. The few written works on the economic Cold War tend to focus on that first feature of the early Cold War era, the US-orchestrated economic blockade that discriminated against the Soviets.[53] But the system of import licenses necessary for the functioning of Bretton Woods would prove a far more frustrating regime for the Soviets, who were apt to see politics whenever their deal-making with private enterprises hit a licensing wall at the government level. Which of the two should the historian focus on? Despite strenuous US efforts to get Europe and Japan to comply with the embargo of strategic goods, these embargo lists would not survive

[52] The story is succinctly told in Eichengreen, *Globalizing Capital*, 100–04.

[53] For example Ian Jackson, *The Economic Cold War. America, Britain and East–West Trade, 1948–63* (New York: Palgrave, 2001) and Shuguang Zhang, *Economic Cold War: America's Embargo against China and the Sino-Soviet Alliance, 1949–1963* (Washington, DC: Woodrow Wilson Center Press, 2001).

the end of the dollar shortage and therefore of US leverage over their allies – at least in anything close to their initial incarnation.

On the other hand, systemic constraints tended to delineate the space of Soviet economic action more forcefully than political ones. This was especially true of the system's most fundamental compulsion: As the Soviets sought to accumulate gold under the gold standard, they now strove to accumulate dollar reserves. A small episode of financial anxiety best captures the nature of power relations in the new liberal order the Soviets encountered against their best predictions. In the middle of 1948, with Cold War tensions at an all-time high and rising, the Soviets grew afraid that their meager reserves were in danger. Of their $74.5 million in reserves, more than two-thirds lay in American banks, and almost one-half of that was already committed to imports of rubber. They were afraid the United States might block their hard-earned savings – famously achieved in no small part from sales of grain while Soviet citizens starved in 1947.[54] They decided to transfer it to European banks, where the long arm of Uncle Sam might still prevail, but they hoped at least friendly financial relations might be more expediently developed there than in the by-now hopeless atmosphere of the North American colossus.[55] This was a portent of the Eurodollar market that came into being in the mid 1950s – a pool of dollars held outside of the United States and thus outside of its regulatory prescript.[56] Over time, the growing pools of these unregulated dollars grew to immense proportions and drowned the Bretton Woods system whole.[57] Ironically, the single most harmful anti-systemic initiative the Soviets ever undertook came from an attempt to protect their participation in the liberal world system.

[54] Although, it should be said, nothing like on the scale of what they exported during the much more dire 1930s famine. See Michael Ellman, "The 1947 Soviet famine and the entitlement approach to famines," *Cambridge Journal of Economics*, 24:5 (2000): 603–30.

[55] RGASPI, f. 84, op. 1, d. 32, l. 207.

[56] Catherine R. Schenk, "The Origins of the Eurodollar Market in London: 1955–1963," *Explorations in Economic History* 35:2 (1998): 221–38. Schenk convincingly foregrounds the particular financial conjuncture in 1955 as the catalyst for the formation of the Eurodollar market. But the Soviet Union's fears for its dollar reserves still played a role in providing liquidity to the market, and these fears preceded by almost a decade the usual explanation scholars give concerning Soviet fears of American reprisals following the 1956 Hungarian uprising.

[57] The number was $2.5 trillion by the mid-1980s, according to Ron Chernow, *The House of Morgan. An American Banking Dynasty and the Rise of Modern Finance* (New York: Grove Press, 1990), 545. These vast pools of capital seeking profit became the main means for speculation against the dollar toward the end of the 1960s, forcing the Nixon Administration to give up on the dollar's peg to gold that was the basis of the Bretton Woods system. This initiated the floating exchange rate regime and nigh-uninhibited movement of capital that has been the source of so many financial crises over the last three decades.

Credit negotiations with the British also reveal a compromising leadership trying to get through a year that wreaked havoc on their balance of payments and thus on their ability to pay their war debts. As they had done during the Great Depression, they resisted defaulting in the hope of defending their credit within the liberal financial architecture of the postwar period.[58] It was in turn the British who first negotiated commercial agreements in earnest with the Soviets. This was not a reflection of the celebrated commercial instinct of the British, but a reflection of the British Empire's endurance. When it came to multilateral trade and currency flexibility, the Bretton Woods system constrained Great Britain less than other European states. The pound sterling had a wider economic zone from which to draw, and England had, historically, a balance of payments deficit with the Soviets, allowing the latter to use the surplus sterling in other regions in the zone. The upshot was that Great Britain could afford a negative balance of payments with the Soviets as long as the British could maintain a trade surplus with their colonies. The Soviets were in turn happy to accumulate pound sterling and spend it in those colonies.

Both Western trade officials and academic scholars have often assumed that because one of the defining aspects of Soviet economic life was an essential dearth of consumer goods, the Soviet state would be primarily interested in alleviating these shortages. It is with this assumption in mind that the British approached their commercial negotiations with the Soviets. The British offered consumer trinkets in exchange for needful commodities, but quickly discovered this would not work. Instead, they found themselves scrambling to satisfy the Soviet Union's insatiable demand for industrial equipment and other technological inputs.[59] This pattern would invariably repeat itself during the course of negotiations with other rich countries over the next decade. Indeed the British themselves would periodically try to sell consumer goods, only to be told, as they were told by Stalin in June 1952, that the Soviet Union was interested only in the traditional Soviet–British exchange of raw materials for industrial equipment and technology.[60]

With this misconception rectified, the exceptionally constrained situation of the early Bretton Woods period assured a continued rocky relationship between the Soviet Union and Great Britain. A trade plan between the two former allies was drawn up in December 1947 and a year

[58] RGASPI, f. 84, op. 1, d. 30, ll. 222, 284–86.

[59] RGASPI, f. 84, op. 1, d. 32, ll. 208–11.

[60] RGASPI, f. 84, op. 1, d. 77, l. 153. Although Stalin was open to an exchange of consumer goods from both countries as well, an idea that invariably failed to stir much interest among Europeans.

later the Soviets had fulfilled their end of the bargain. The British, however, had been forbidden by the Americans to sell the ships and industrial equipment necessary to finance Soviet commodity imports. Even after accounting for Soviet purchases in the sterling area, the Soviet government still had some ten million pounds in British banks, which in the exasperated words of a report on the matter, "amounts to a forced extension of credit to Great Britain."[61] The Soviets seemed unaware of the fact that they were merely echoing the discontented rumblings of those forced to accumulate another country's legal tender as reserve currency. For the Soviets, buying into this particular iteration of a liberal financial system started with ten million unspent pounds.

Not all was sour. At least the 1949 devaluation of the British pound was probably profitable for the Soviets. The devaluation had not come as a surprise. It had been in the making ever since the US recession the year before wiped out what little demand there was in the United States for European goods, and European countries' dollar reserves along with it. The Soviets were assessing the damage a general devaluation might have on Soviet reserves almost a month before it happened. The assessment was positive. Their reserves in most European countries were protected by provisos that postulated payment in gold should the Soviets wish it. Only in England were their agreements unprotected. But there they stood to gain, since the Soviets still had a large wartime debt to pay in sterling and a devaluation would only make that debt cheaper.[62] Gains made in the debt repayment would offset the losses in the diminished purchase the Soviets would get from sterling reserves that Gosbank held in foreign accounts. The report advised a spending spree to reduce the balance on those sterling accounts; commodities in perennial demand like rubber and cotton would do nicely.[63]

The 1949 devaluations put an end to the crisis situation in Europe, and the advent of the Korean War, like the Marshall Plan before it, pumped billions of dollars into the world economy, curbing the dollar shortage even further. But the road to the dollar glut of the 1960s would

[61] Ibid., ll. 212–14. The recommendation was a cessation of grain exports to Britain.

[62] RGASPI, f. 84, op. 1, d. 51, l. 77. As of September 1949, the outstanding debt was 35.3 million pounds.

[63] Ibid. It looks like they managed to spend some two million pounds before the devaluation, as I calculated from a later report on the devaluation found in RGASPI, f. 84, op. 1, d. 51, ll. 147–151. The Soviets still had seven million pounds left in those accounts at the time of devaluation. The report calculated that general gains would be around 250 million rubles or almost eighteen million pounds once trade commitments were factored in, although this was little more than a guess.

be a long one, and along the way the Soviet Union came to play a very useful role, that of barter partner. Barter obviated the need for dollars, which constrained trade in many European countries and made it difficult for countries without empires to exploit to get a hold of basic commodities. Enter the Soviets, who under Stalin were bent on exploiting any advantage to improve their terms of trade. When, in early 1950, excess grain supply from the Americas decreased the world price of grain well below Soviet expectations, the Soviets looked around for countries under balance of payments pressure. Mikhail Men'shikov, then minister of foreign trade, suggested that Mexican, Austrian, and Egyptian firms might exchange their cotton production for grain, while Dutch and Ceylonese firms might be approached for their rubber, and even Belgian ones might be interested in an exchange of grain for rolled iron.[64]

Men'shikov's suggestion followed a request from an Egyptian firm that received a license from its government for an exchange of Soviet grain for Egyptian cotton and rice. An initial request by the Egyptian ambassador in the summer of 1948 for economic exchange and a trade agreement had also been met with a positive response from the Soviets, but the Egyptian government had failed to follow up on it, perhaps fearing Western retaliation.[65] By early 1950, Egypt was a country with chronic balance of payments problems, tight hard currency reserves, and a sudden enthusiasm for a barter deal with the Soviets. All three, as it turned out, at the behest of the Egyptians, whose rising desperation over their dwindling dollar reserves was matched by the rising price of wheat the Soviets sold them.[66] The next year the relationship continued to grow, even when it meant cutting already negotiated deliveries to Belgian firms, which paid a lower price for grain than the Egyptians.[67] The occasional payment in British pounds in times of emergency made the Egyptian relationship especially attractive.[68]

64 RGASPI, f. 84, op. 1, d. 61, ll. 139–144. The report dates January 18, 1950.

65 Vitalii Naumkin et al., eds., *Blizhnevostochnyi konflikt. Iz dokumentov arkhiva vneshnei politiki Rossiiskoi Federatsii*, Vol. 1 (Moscow: Mezhdunarodnyi fond "Demokratiia," 2003), 43–45 for the request and ibid., 49–50 for the response, including the observation that the Egyptian ambassador received the news without great enthusiasm, as if he was not expecting a positive answer.

66 In fact toward the end of that year, the Egyptians were paying in British pounds, which the Soviets always welcomed as a means to acquire rubber in other parts of the sterling area. Men'shikov's reports to Stalin on these negotiations can be found in RGASPI, f. 84, op. 1, d. 61, l. 200; RGASPI, f. 84, op. 1, d. 63, ll. 211–12; RGASPI, f. 84, op. 1, d. 64, l. 1; RGASPI, f. 84, op. 1, d. 67, l. 283.

67 RGASPI, f. 84, op. 1, d. 68, ll. 208–09.

68 As happened, for example, in December 1950. See RGASPI, f. 84, op. 1, d. 67, l. 48.

In Italy, a thorny situation resolved itself after a standoff over the high price of Soviet grain. Both parties had agreed to exchange Italian rail for Soviet grain. The Italians, however, refused to pay the ninety dollars per ton the Soviets demanded since American grain could be bought much more cheaply. But a lack of dollar reserves meant the Italians had to relent and agree to the Soviet price when the Communists threatened to pull out of the deal altogether.[69] In the end, the deal allowed the Soviets to keep their purchases and add tractors, excavators, cranes, and an array of other Italian heavy construction equipment.

These kinds of barter exchanges were a harbinger of future relations with the new countries that appeared in the wake of Europe's imperial collapse. But widespread decolonization was still a decade in the future, and Stalin would not live to see it. In Stalin's time, expanding engagement with the world economy meant doing business with Europe, which in turn meant dealing with the United States. In fact in the last years of Stalin's rule, Soviet barter practices were merely mitigating a diminishing trade with Europe. But a snapshot of trade in June 1950 reveals an interesting picture. Within a general context of diminishing trade over the previous twelve months, the Soviets essentially operated evenly in two currency areas: the sterling and the dollar (see Figure 2.2).[70] In the sterling area, they turned exports of grain and timber to England and grain to Egypt into imports of deficit resources from the empire, coupled with some imports of British industrial equipment and payments on the wartime debt to Britain. In Europe, the Soviets imported deficit resources – mainly from Europe's empires – and industrial equipment and technology with dollars earned from resource exports to both Europe and the United States. To a large extent, an increase in imports from dollar-strapped Europe would require an increase in trade with the United States itself, an ill prospect in the McCarthy Era. And even though the sterling area gave the British greater room to maneuver, much of the decrease in trade during those twelve months had come from a British refusal to go through with an exchange of Soviet manganese and asbestos for tin and uncut diamonds after the Americans put pressure on them. The French had also been dissuaded to sell tankers to the Soviets in 1949.[71] And as the new decade dawned, prospects were about to get much worse.

[69] RGASPI, f. 84, op. 1, d. 64, ll. 135–36. Mikhail Men'shikov, who had replaced Mikoyan at the head of the Foreign Trade Ministry in 1949, suggested in this August 30, 1950 report to Stalin that he take the deal, lest a refusal complicate the Italian market for the Soviets.

[70] The snapshot can be found in RGASPI, f. 84, op. 1, d. 66, ll. 79–87.

[71] Ibid., l. 84.

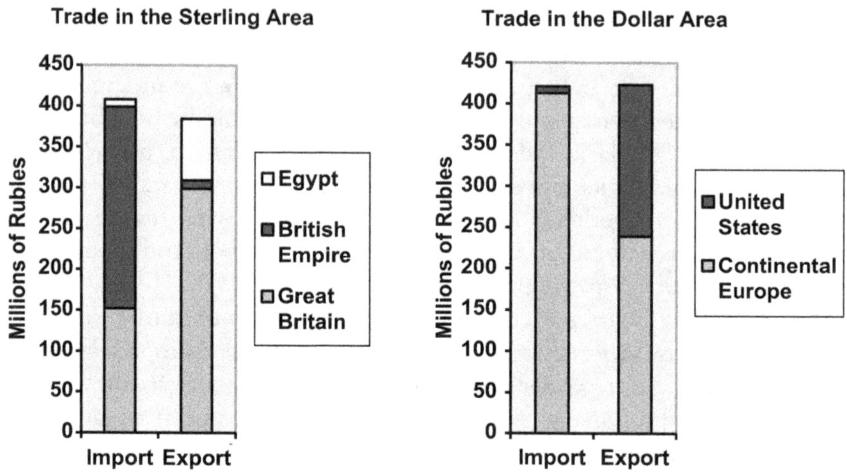

Figure 2.2 Soviet trade with the capitalist world, June 1949 to June 1950*
*Calculated from RGASPI, f. 84, op. 1, d. 66, ll. 79–87.

The acute shortage of dollars, the principal currency used in intra-European trade, was making European economic integration nigh impossible, despite the creation of the Organization of European Economic Cooperation (OEEC) to manage the Marshall Plan funds coming from America. The solution was found in the summer of 1950 with the creation of the European Payments Union (EPU), which allowed member states to settle accounts multilaterally and committed them to the coordinated liberalization of commercial and financial barriers. What this meant for the Soviet Union was a more subtle and effective form of exclusion. Whereas earlier the Soviet Union had been one more participant in a hapless network of ineffective barter practices, the EPU lowered the cost of trade immensely within Western Europe, which now drew upon itself to accelerate trade and initiate the famous long economic boom. The upshot for the Soviets was a relative irrelevance. The suddenly slow-moving Soviets could only watch from the sidelines and rage about the subversive American influence as the "Marshallized countries" (*marshallizirovannye strany*) lowered tariffs and generally did away with obstacles to the intensification of economic exchange among themselves.[72]

The success of the coordinated efforts under the auspices of the Bretton Woods practices of cooperation and negotiation would soon

[72] Ibid., ll. 138–39.

eclipse the importance of the Victorian-era trade in raw materials, and with it the imperative for empire. As the European Empire gave way to decolonization and its political offspring, the Soviet Union was able to finally establish direct links to the sources of those deficit resources that had played a significant role in Soviet–European commerce. This would be registered as "growth" in the Soviet Union's trade relations with the newfound "developing" countries, a mirage that would also register alarm among Western cold warriors. Ultimately this trade would lose importance for the Soviets as well; as they experienced their own 1950s economic boom, the future lay in the intensified import and exploitation of technological manufactures and services rather than in a nineteenth-century style mandate for raw materials. For the Soviets, the future lay with the industrialized world, whatever the US State Department's anxiety over the soon-to-be burgeoning East–South relations.

For now, however, the problem was adaptation. If Soviet trade in the waning years of Stalin's rule displayed all the adaptive dexterity of a woolly mammoth, that lack of agility had one name: Stalin. The official policy was still very much welcoming of trade relations, even if frustrated by what the Soviets perceived as a lack of interest or political will among Europeans to export the types of products in actual demand in the Soviet Union.[73] But the vehemence of anti-Communism among the industrialized countries had made Stalin overly cautious in commercial matters. On the one hand he wanted trade expansion, and fired Men'shikov as head of the Ministry of Foreign Trade for failing to exercise initiative and decisiveness toward that goal.[74] On the other hand, micromanagement, unclear directives, and a penchant for accusation froze the very initiative that would restore that nimble quality Stalin sought. Instead, Politburo members, as well as members of the Ministry of Foreign Trade, acted in groups and in constant communication with the Politburo.[75] Fear of individual missteps congested the system.

[73] As the Soviets told Executive Secretary of the UN Economic Commission for Europe Gunnar Myrdal when he called for greater economic integration between East and West in March 21, 1951. In RGASPI, f. 84, op. 1, d. 70, l. 59.

[74] RGASPI, f. 84, op. 1, d. 74, l. 9. On November 1, 1951 he was replaced by Pavel Nikolaevich Kumykin.

[75] This is a reflection of a much larger systemic congestion going on at all levels of government in the last years of Stalinism. Particularly striking is the number of signatures in seemingly innocuous documents; no one dared act alone. A more thorough description of this late Stalinism phenomenon can be found in Yoram Gorlizki and Oleg Khlevniuk, *Cold Peace. Stalin and the Soviet Ruling Circle, 1945–1953* (Oxford: Oxford University Press, 2004).

A tentative rapprochement between Soviets and Japanese businessmen serves as an example. On October 29, 1951, Soviet Foreign Minister Andrey Vyshinskii and Men'shikov, trade minister still for one more day, asked the Politburo to approve the Soviet trade representatives in Japan to meet with a group of Japanese businessmen and members of parliament. They were to propose the reestablishment of the kind of trade both countries had carried out before the war with each other, namely an exchange of ships and other Japanese manufactures for timber and coal.[76] The Japanese, who had made the approach in the first place, invited the Soviet trade representatives to Osaka or Kobe to carry out the talks. Mikoyan, dressing himself in an extreme sense of caution that he would later shed as soon as Stalin died, advised against the trip, arguing that the foreign press would pick up on this and allege that the Soviet Union had a special interest in trade with Japan, an innocuous enough development that in the foreign press would often acquire a connotation of subversive goings on.[77] He was pessimistic that the Americans or Prime Minister Yoshida Shigeru's government would allow commerce to develop, but nevertheless the Soviet trade representatives were to acquaint the Japanese with Soviet exports, catalogs, and Soviet import interests, as well as to study the Japanese market. Inasmuch as the Japanese also suffered from a taut situation with their balance of payments, they were to be acquainted with the barter system the Soviets had to offer, which excluded dollars and other hard currency.[78] Despite all the caution and deliberation, in the end the representatives got it all wrong. They had to agree on a later date to continue talks because the Japanese asked such a barrage of questions that the hapless Soviet representatives, unsure of how to answer and with very narrow guidance on what they were allowed to say, decided to check with the Politburo again. Less forgivable in the eyes of Stalin, they had not asked questions of the Japanese and had failed to learn their intentions. With nothing to show for it, the press would now write about a Soviet initiative that, as Mikoyan asserted, was neither true nor politically advantageous.[79] The representatives were to be reprimanded, although the reason is unfathomable: perhaps they were too cautious; perhaps they were not cautious enough.

[76] RGASPI, f. 84, op. 1, d. 73, l. 46. [77] RGASPI, f. 84, op. 1, d. 74, ll. 85–87.

[78] Ibid. By this point, in mid-November, Reuters had already written about a preliminary meeting, describing it as a Soviet initiative. Mikoyan proposed that the Soviet press set the record straight.

[79] RGASPI, f. 84, op. 1, d. 75, l. 28.

Bait and switch: The world after Stalin

The 1950s saw a seemingly profound transformation in both Soviet foreign policy and Soviet economic policy. The decade also saw a change of leadership in the Kremlin. It is easy to add these two events and arrive at a simple conclusion: Personality matters, and in autocratic Soviet Union, personality is all. Scholars have found it a bit more complicated to hold ideology to account, since the ideological premise of the Soviet Union did not change in its essence, nor, when it comes down to it, did the personalities carrying out Soviet affairs, by and large. But certainly the discourse remained recognizably Marxist and messianic, so ideology remained an important category of the analysis of this period for Cold War historians.[80] If the Soviet Union is autarkic, and its leaders bent on keeping it so, change in the Soviet Union can only come from its leaders or some internal systemic source. But we have seen that Soviet leaders wished to participate fully in what they called the "international division of labor," and were not in the least interested in autarky. Unlike almost all countries at their level of development, they never defaulted on a debt – except for the one incurred by the tsarist government – and in the Great Depression Soviet foreign trade was comparatively expansionary, as we have seen. Soviet leaders assiduously followed international political and socio-economic trends, and had an acute sense of the Soviet Union's place in that world, and certainly a much more accurate idea than the US Department of State. In other words, personalities and ideology were not bounded and constant, but rather responded to a fluid international order, as they had in the interwar area. The main development in Soviet policy went well beyond a changing of the guard within the walls of the Kremlin. The unexpected triumph of America's international liberal system over the next decade undermined almost all aspects of world politics and economy as they had emerged in 1945. The prospects of renewed depression and systemic breakdown had passed for good, and with it went the foundation upon which Stalin had been rebuilding his fortress. And if its 1930s blueprint was no longer operative, that meant Stalin's successors would have to improvise once again, but this time with a much larger institutional burden than anything Stalin inherited

80 Not altogether convincingly, since it is often made to explain everything, no matter how disparate, and therefore nothing. Notorious in this regard is Zubok's revolutionary-imperial paradigm, which he sees as a constant framework informing Soviet foreign policy from Stalin to Brezhnev.

in the late 1920s.[81] Men make their own history, but they do not make as they please, not even in a Marxist Zion.

After Stalin died, it soon became clear that his leadership had been a real impediment to the introduction of new policies that other Soviet officials and leaders had been mulling over for years.[82] One of these officials was Nikita Sergeevich Khrushchev, who quickly proved to be bursting with new ideas on where to take the quickly industrializing enterprise that was the Soviet Union. Upon the September 1953 plenary session of the Central Committee that elected him first secretary, Khrushchev laid down some of the new policies that would develop agriculture and the Soviet economy in general. As a whole, these entailed a switch from heavy industry to a focus on growth of consumer products.[83] The government would henceforth initiate an effort, long delayed by Stalin, to attenuate the severe suppression of consumption in the Soviet economy. In Stalin's time "we did not have the means for high-speed, simultaneous development of heavy industry, agriculture and light industry," Khrushchev explained. "Now these prerequisites exist."[84] In meeting after meeting and in party plenary sessions throughout his rule, Khrushchev would stress this point in his search for more efficient management of the economy and greater production of consumer goods.

The most immediate beneficiaries of these policies were the much-exploited peasants, who finally saw the terms of trade between city and country turn to their favor. But Khrushchev did not stop at reforming agriculture. Besides encouraging the building of a chemical industry almost from scratch to help develop agriculture and the textile industry, he also initiated reforms in internal trade and organized a construction boom that aimed to finally and forever do away with the much-maligned communal apartment that had prevailed under Stalin.[85] As economist Margaret Miller wrote, Khrushchev presided over the rise of the Soviet consumer. As time passed and he was replaced, no new leader would ever dare tighten the consumer's belt again, as Stalin had so often

[81] This takes somewhat from Kotkin's highly schematic "cunning of history," in which he points out that "above all else after World War II, the geopolitical framework changed." Kotkin, "Modern times," 161–64.

[82] Gorlizki and Khlevniuk, *Cold Peace*, 166–67.

[83] Whitney, Thomas P., ed., *Khrushchev Speaks. Selected Speeches, Articles, and Press Conferences, 1941–1961* (Ann Arbor: The University of Michigan Press, 1963), 79–149.

[84] Ibid., 83.

[85] See Steven Harris, "In Search of Ordinary Russia. Everyday Life in the NEP, the Thaw, and the Communal Apartment," *Kritika* 6:3 (2005): 583–614. Although this "strange turn of events," the officially approved reintroduction of material incentives, is less novel in the 1950s than Harris supposes. See also RGANI, f. 5, op. 30, d. 31, ll. 25–67 on the overhaul of the infrastructure for domestic trade that Mikoyan presented to Khrushchev in August 1953.

done.[86] Indeed toward the end of the Soviet Union as a political entity, placating the consumer, in the form of state subsidies for consumer goods, would play at least as important a role in the country's economic difficulties as the much-hyped military burden, if only because the growth of subsidies for consumer goods played a much more sudden and economically destabilizing role.[87]

Khrushchev's new emphasis on "creating an abundance of consumers' goods in our country"[88] was constitutive of the adoption of "peaceful coexistence" as the principal policy in Soviet international affairs. Khrushchev believed in the superiority of the Soviet system over the market and he envisioned a type of world economic and political competition that would prove him right. His ally in this ideological shift was Marshal Georgii Zhukov, quite possibly still the most admired man in the Soviet Union a decade after the Great Fatherland War. During his power struggle with Malenkov and Molotov, Khrushchev placed Zhukov at the helm of the Ministry of Defense, and soon made use of him to blunt Molotov's Stalinist foreign policy positions. Zhukov's May Day speech of 1955 signaled the beginning of Molotov's fall as the main reference in Soviet foreign policy. "The foreign policy of the Soviet Union," Zhukov orated, "proceeds from the wise counsel of the Great Lenin of the possibility of peaceful coexistence and economic competition of states, irrespective of their social or state structure."[89] Zhukov's appropriation of Lenin, although standard in Soviet oration practices, was not preposterous. Lenin's legacy, after all, had not been

[86] This was true not only of those who replaced Khrushchev, namely Brezhnev and Kosygin, but interestingly, it was also true of Malenkov, whose brief spell as head of state was also marked by similar policies benefiting consumers. For these developments see Margaret Miller, *Rise of the Russian Consumer* (London: Merrit & Hatcher Ltd., 1965). Yet another interesting point is that much of Miller's work, based as it was on a close reading of *Pravda*, is still very much valid at this time of archival access. When it comes to economic management, archives have provided only more detailed numbers, while the debates around what Philip Hanson termed the "treadmill of reform," seem to have been public and open.

[87] In a late addition to the long debate on hidden inflation, Byung-Yeon Kim estimates that, in trying to stabilize retail prices in consumer goods, the Soviet government went from spending 4 percent of its 1965 budget on this subsidy to 20 percent, or 12 percent of the Soviet Union's GDP, by the late 1980s. Byung-Yeon Kim, "Causes of Repressed Inflation in the Soviet Consumer Market, 1965–1989: Retail Price Subsidies, the Siphoning Effect, and the Budget Deficit," *Economic History Review* 55:1 (2002): 105–27.

[88] Whitney, *Khrushchev Speaks*, 79.

[89] Quoted in Aleksandr Fursenko and Timothy Naftali, *Khrushchev's Cold War. The Inside Story of an American Adversary* (New York: W. W. Norton & Company, 2006), 28. The authors further detail Molotov's disagreements with Zhukov's position, which came to a head on May 19, 1955 at a presidium meeting, when he called the minister of defense "anti-Leninist" upon which Bulganin and Mikoyan quickly defended both Zhukov and, by implication, the policy of peaceful coexistence. See ibid., 29.

Stalinism but NEP, not autarky but the gold standard. Soon Khrushchev and his foreign policy team had overturned many of Stalin and Molotov's long-standing foreign policies, achieving a rapprochement with Yugoslavia's Josip Broz Tito and finally signing a peace treaty with Austria, among other initiatives. His goal was to attenuate Western pressure on the Soviet political and economic situation. But ultimately, it was the Soviet Union's effective economic and political engagement of the world outside the Communist Bloc, some three decades after the failure of the 1920s, that gave meaning, immediacy, and legitimacy to the discourse of peaceful coexistence.

It was a momentous change, given the earlier ideological premise of "capitalist encirclement" and the inevitability of armed conflict. It was Stalin's conviction that as capitalist contradictions plunged the world again into war, the Soviet Union would be dragged into war with it. In the 1930s, predictions of war had been painfully validated; in the immediate postwar period Stalin thought only of reconstructing his fortress. And yet, much like in the 1930s, this did not mean autarky; Stalin had wanted to have economic relations, particularly with the rich countries, but he had balked at the price the United States had demanded, namely the surrender of political control over Eastern Europe and an unknown quantity of what were likely to be unacceptable stipulations attached to the much-needed reconstruction loans.

A decade later the web of worldwide relations had changed drastically. After their initial American-dependent economic reconstruction, Europe and Japan were proving ever more recalcitrant in allowing the United States to set the terms of their relations with the Communist Bloc. Furthermore, the slow disentangling of imperial ties meant both that the European powers had to diversify their suppliers of raw materials and that the colonies were free to seek other industrialized partners for their development goals. With these two sets of bilateral economic organization – Europe/Japan–US and colony–metropole – rapidly unraveling, the Soviet Union became suddenly attractive everywhere other than in the United States. Strategies of economic triangulation all around the world set in motion the injection of the Soviet Union into the world economy.

It helped that Khrushchev was so very responsive to foreign advances, but it would not be fully accurate to ascribe the turn to "peaceful coexistence" solely to his ascension to power and his personality.[90] His rise was

[90] This is one of the main themes in Fursenko and Naftali's *Khrushchev's Cold War*, which begins grandly by stating that "[t]here are times when the personality of a single human being can rival ideologies, institutions, or social movements as a cause of great international events." Not surprisingly, the backbone of their study is documentary material from presidium meetings; furthermore the authors choose to focus the study on the numerous Cold War crises of the time,

famously surprising, a notion that is de rigueur to note in all histories on the subject, and it is probably a counterfactual futility to speculate whether a neo-Stalinist such as Molotov had any reasonable chance of seizing the reins of power at that particular juncture in Soviet history. It is not merely wistful, however, to note that most of the major players in the Soviet leadership were willing to demilitarize to some extent both the domestic and foreign political economy of the Soviet Union; after the late-Stalinist freeze came the post-Stalin consensus.[91]

The relatively polite – by Soviet standards – succession struggle between Malenkov and Khrushchev during the years of collective leadership was not fought over fundamental discrepancies over what direction to take the Soviet economy, but rather over the issue of the role of the Communist Party in the management of the Soviet economy.[92] Like Stalin before him, Khrushchev used confrontational and alarmist language to maneuver politically while advocating for centrist positions of broad agreement.[93] Where the general thrust of the economic reforms and international affairs was concerned, though details varied, there was a broad consensus for agricultural reform, demilitarization, and a general shift from a focus on heavy industry to the encouragement of growth in the light industries.[94] Importantly, this was a consensus that carried smoothly down the bureaucratic ladder. The many officials of the different concerned ministries worked assiduously to look for new venues of international economic engagement, pushing Soviet products abroad and working hard on the infrastructure necessary to keep up the breakneck speed of Soviet commercial growth.[95]

ignoring the humdrum, everyday decisions and effort that go into the business of foreign relations, and through which one may discern the context and assumptions within which the work was done.

91 As George W. Breslauer called it in *Khrushchev and Brezhnev as Leaders. Building Authority in Soviet Politics* (London: George Allen & Unwin, 1982), 31.

92 Yoram Gorlizki, "Party Revivalism and the Death of Stalin," *Slavic Review* 54:1 (1995): 1–22.

93 Stalin's politics of the mid-1920s were covered in the first chapter. For Khrushchev, see Breslauer's discussion in Breslauer, *Khrushchev and Brezhnev as Leaders*, 34–38.

94 See Gorlizki and Khlevniuk, *Cold Peace*, conclusion. On the similarity of Malenkov, Khrushchev, and even Beria's positions on nuclear issues see David Holloway, *Stalin and the Bomb. The Soviet Union and Atomic Energy, 1939–1956* (New Haven: Yale University Press, 1994). On the possibility that the switch from heavy industry to light industry may have been intended even in Stalin's time see Timothy Dunmore, *Soviet Politics, 1945–53* (New York: St. Martin's Press, 1984).

95 For example see the Ministry of Foreign Trade's attempts to sell their low quality pyrites in West Germany, Belgium, and other rich countries where the technology was advanced enough to make use of the mineral. RGAE, f. 413, op. 13, d. 7931, ll. 100–01. Or complaints from the Ministry of the Oil Industry on the unsatisfactory performance of the Ministry of Ways of Communication in setting up the infrastructure necessary to accommodate the big growth in exports of oil to the West, which was causing the foreigners to complain. See RGAE, f. 413, op. 13, d. 7931, ll. 9–11. Besides the Ministry of Ways of Communication, another one that struggled to keep up with the pace of expansion was the Ministry of the Sea Fleet, which often did not have enough ships to carry out

We will see later in the book that by the 1960s, both Khrushchev and officials down the bureaucratic hierarchy were even willing to learn from and emulate capitalist practices in order to gain market share abroad.

The new guiding principle of peaceful coexistence in Soviet international political and economic affairs was given a scholarly body in the establishment (or reestablishment) of the Institute of the World Economy and International Relations (*Institut mirovoi ekonomiki i mezhdunarodnoi otnoshenii* [IMEMO]) in 1956. Of significance was the appointment of Anushavan Arzumanian, a close associate of Anastas Mikoyan, as the institute's chairman.[96] The institute was, in effect, a restoration of Evgenii Varga's Institute of World Economy and World Politics (IMKhMP), which had played a leading advisory role during Stalin's time in power.[97] The mandates of IMEMO and IMKhMP were essentially the same: "to require the Institute of World Economy and International Relations to inform the decision-making organs on the new processes in the economics and politics of the capitalist countries," according to the April 1956 decree for the establishment of IMEMO.[98] It is interesting to note that the dissolution of IMKhMP happened in 1947, the last year of Soviet hope for some form of accommodation between the two systems, and that its revival took place in the mid 1950s, when that hope became realizable once again.[99]

The Institute's journal, *The World Economy and Foreign Relations*, first published in the summer of 1957, quickly provided the theoretical

deliveries, and was sometimes made to sacrifice imports of new ships in order to import more cranes for Soviet ports. They often found they could not fill ships up fast enough. See RGAE, f. 4372, op. 57, d. 384, l. 236.

96 Almost a decade earlier Arzumanian had married the younger sister of Mikoyan's wife, after which the two Armenians developed a close friendship. Indeed, Mikoyan's son would become one of the institute's founding members and a frequent contributor to the institute's journal.

97 For a history of the Institute of World Economy and World Politics that disentangles historiographical misconceptions on the role of the institute and the Soviet leadership's relationship with it see Kyung Deok Roh, "Stalin's Think Tank. The Varga Institute and the Making of the Stalinist Idea of World Economy and Politics, 1927–1953" (PhD dissertation, University of Chicago, 2010). Arzumanian had met Varga and his cohorts when he was appointed in 1952 to the Academy of Science's Economic Institute, where he became deputy director a year later.

98 In Petr Cherkasov, *IMEMO. Portret na fone epokhi* (Moscow: Ves' Mir, 2004), 105–06.

99 This is not to make an argument of intention on the part of the Soviet leadership. The reasons for the dissolution of the IMKhMP were primarily of a political and cultural nature, with Andrei Zhdanov as the main instigator behind the dissolution of the institute and Stalin as its main protector. See Roh, "Stalin's Think Tank." Although the institute was wound up, all its workers were, almost without exception, taken under the umbrella of the Institute of the Economy of the Academy of Science, where they worked on the same issues and in fact increased their production of reports for state consumption. It is nevertheless suggestive that the institutional framework for such work was destroyed and reconstructed at key periods that paralleled the downs and ups of the Soviet Union's relationship with the world economy.

framework for the government's intentions in international commerce and politics. The journal's propaganda-laden editorials and articles echoed Zhukov's assertions on the Leninist nature of the paradigm of peaceful coexistence and gave them deeper theoretical gravity.[100] For good measure, Mikoyan made sure to raise the stature of the institute and its journal by using it to publish his own thoughts on what peaceful coexistence meant to the Soviet Union's foreign economic relations. He used his space to convey the same message he communicated to business legations whenever he met them. "In the West," he wrote, "one can often hear that socialist countries, joined to the Council of Mutual Economic Assistance, supposedly created their own 'trade block,' shut themselves off from the rest of the world, want to build a self-sufficient economy, and even would not want to develop trade with other countries. This, of course, is far from the truth."[101] It all might have sounded like empty propaganda, but the statistical record spoke for itself, a fact Mikoyan often made sure to highlight.

But the single most important factor in the Soviet Union's new commercial fortunes was the global economic context of the 1950s, and the myriad of possibilities it brought about in the aftermath of its restructuring. This is how a standard text on the international economy describes the situation of the early 1950s:

> By the early 1950s the first stage in the post-war recovery of the international economy had been largely completed. A significant proportion of the displaced people of the world had been repatriated or resettled in other countries willing to accept them. The European economies had been reconstructed, and normal peacetime production had been resumed in most of them. Inflation had given way to price stability and currency overvaluation had been corrected by the widespread devaluations in 1949. With the revival of the economic fortunes of Europe came a rising world demand for primary products, much inflated by the requirements of the Korean War, which contributed to an upsurge of growth in the underdeveloped regions of the world. These signs of widespread economic improvement set the stage for a

[100] For some of these propagandistic editorials and articles see "Leninskaia politika mirnogo sosushchestvovaniia," *Mirovaia ekonomika i mezhdunarodnye otnosheniia* 1:2 (1957): 3–12; or L. Fituni, "Ekonomicheskie I politicheskie osnovy mirnogo sosushchestvovaniia," *Mirovaia ekonomika i mezhdunarodnye otnosheniia* 1:3 (1957): 12–26. Yet another important theme, following Khrushchev's statements at the 20th Party Congress, was the need for a more creative and less dogmatic approach to the analysis of the capitalist world economy, in other words, to follow the legacy of Varga rather than that of Zhdanov. See "Za tvorcheskuiu razrabotku problem mirovoi ekonomiki," *Mirovaia ekonomika i mezhdunarodnye otnosheniia* 1:3 (1957): 3–11.

[101] A. Mikoyan, "O nekotorykh voprosakh mezhdunarodnoi torgovli," *Mirovaia ekonomika i mezhdunarodnye otnosheniia* 4:6 (1960): 9.

> burst of economic prosperity which confronted the highly developed countries at least with a new kind of economic problem – that of affluence.[102]

Significantly, and in sharp contrast to the international political situation of the 1930s, there was no breakdown of worldwide security arrangements. If 1930s insecurity had been one of the primary factors in the form and content of Stalin's industrialization strategies, then the Pax Americana of the 1950s was likewise an essential factor in the generalized assessment reached by a broad Soviet majority that there was much to gain from engagement. Khrushchev's personal penchant for slashing the military budget in favor of developing the civilian economy has been as widely noted as it was an unthinkable option for Stalin during the industrialization drive.[103]

There was, then, a self-reinforcing confluence of new understandings that allowed for the analytical and ideological development of the strategy of peaceful coexistence. There were the capitalists knocking at the Soviet door, more willing than they had ever been to profit from the Soviet Union. There was a bureaucracy pervaded by a new technocratic elite that was no longer paralyzed by fear and so more agile when it came to fulfilling the Soviet promise of greater consumer abundance. There was a civilian leadership, with Khrushchev following Mikoyan's lead, who saw the chance to seek legitimacy in economic superiority rather than military security. And there was a booming world economy that was the quintessential picture of "hegemonic stability," that is, the committed provision by one preponderant power of international public goods, in the form of international security and global macroeconomic stability, as well as committed leadership in forming and maintaining international regimes, as in the management of trade and money.[104] You would not know it from the average text on Cold War history, but in the more than three decades of Soviet history, the international political and economic outlook had never been this positive, and Soviet leaders, armed now with the premise of peaceful coexistence, were quick to seize it.

[102] A. G. Kenwood and A. L. Lougheed, *The Growth of the International Economy, 1820–1990. An Introductory Text* (London: Routledge, 1992), 245.

[103] See especially William Taubman, *Khrushchev. The Man and His Era* (New York: Norton, 2003), which often notes this particular proclivity. The most poignant story concerning this theme was toward the end of his rule, when he asked Defense Minister Rodion Malinovskii what was the use of spending more money on conventional weapons at a time when they already had a nuclear deterrent. Excessive spending was a drain on the civilian economy and it should be cut, he suggested, "otherwise we'll all lose our pants because of you." Taubman, *Khrushchev*, 618.

[104] As the concept has been developed by political economists. The term "theory of hegemonic stability" was coined by Robert Keohane in "The Theory of Hegemonic Stability and Changes in International Economic Regimes, 1967–1977," in Ole R. Holsti, Randolph M. Siverson, and Alexander L. George, eds., *Change in the International System* (Boulder: Westview Press, 1980).

PART II
Aspiration

CHAPTER 3

Restoration:
Resuming the relationship with Capitalism

Khrushchev came to full power toward the end of what turned out to be the biggest economic expansion in the Soviet Union's seventy-year-old history. In the 1950s, the Soviet Union experienced growth rates equaled only by Japan, approximated only by West Germany during its "miracle" that same decade and far above the growth rates clocked by Great Britain and the United States.[1] The new Soviet leader would soon play a role in hindering further economic progress, especially with his decentralization campaigns that regionalized economic decision-making into special economic councils (*sovnarkhozy*), but the disastrous effects of those policies would only become apparent in the following decade. In the 1950s, however, Khrushchev could be forgiven his enthusiasm; the economic winds had been fair a long while.[2] Moreover, the empires of the Western powers were dissolving in revolutionary upheavals. The Soviets seemed, and were, ascendant; the West, so manifestly preponderant, could only decline. With the world now free to choose their political and economic destiny, and the Soviet economy doing so pointedly well, it was difficult to resist the messianic impulse. The energetic, manic-depressive Khrushchev embraced it. The Soviet leadership would shed the caution enforced by Stalin's dangerous gaze and would enter into the now opened world economic arena with swagger and confidence. The foreign trade numbers told the tale.

[1] Khanin, "The 1950s – The Triumph of the Soviet Economy," *Europe-Asia Studies* 55:8 (2003): 1191–94.

[2] Indeed a parallel can be seen toward the end of the American expansion of the 1990s, when not a few enthusiastic economists were busy writing the obituary of the business cycle, or with that of the first decade of this century, when it was seemingly plausible to talk about "Dow 36,000." Charles P. Kindleberger analyzed the cyclical nature of these views in the "free market" world starting in seventeenth-century Netherlands in his masterful *Manias, Panics, and Crashes. A History of Financial Crises*, Fifth Edition (Hoboken: John Wiley & Sons, 2005). It is no surprise to see economists in the recent era learn little from history; over time, Kindleberger finds, financial vagaries and the concomitant euphorias have become ever more pronounced.

As the Soviet economy grew at already dizzying rates of 8–10 percent during the 1950s, foreign trade grew even faster at an average rate of more than 13 percent for that decade.[3] Foreign trade grew 87 percent during the first half of the 1950s, while world trade grew only by 38 percent, a 1955 report to the Central Committee noted proudly.[4] During the 1960s, foreign trade growth slowed down to about 8–9 percent, but was still well above Soviet gross domestic product (GDP) growth and in keeping with global commercial trends. Furthermore, trade expanded on all fronts. The world was globalizing, and the Soviets along with it (see Table 3.1).

This was a new development in the Soviet Union's four-decade-long history. Much of the postwar Stalin-era growth can be attributed to trade with (and pillaging of) the newly "friendly" regimes of Eastern Europe. Trade expansion on all fronts had to wait two developments. The first one was decolonization, which quickly presented the Soviets with new partners and allowed direct access to resources previously acquired only through Western imperial intermediaries. The second one was the end of the dollar shortage that allowed Europe and Japan greater commercial maneuverability and limited American leverage in imposing on their relations with the Soviet Union the embargo lists worked out by the Coordinating Committee for Multilateral Export Controls (CoCom).[5]

But one of these developments was more important than the other, as revealed by the steady change in the Soviet Union's trade structure. In 1955 almost 80 percent of Soviet trade was with communist countries, 16 percent with industrialized countries, and a mere 4 percent with developing countries.[6] Decolonization quickly raised the weight of developing

[3] Calculated from Franklyn Holzman, *Foreign Trade under Central Planning* (Cambridge: Harvard University Press, 1974), tables 2.1 and 2.2, 40–41. A rate of growth higher in trade than in a nation's economy as a whole usually means that trade is becoming increasingly important to that particular economy.

[4] RGANI, f. 5, op. 30, d. 113, l. 71. The world trade figure matches the figure computed by the WTO, which can be found in World Trade Organization, *International Trade Statistics 2008* (Geneva: WTO Publications, 2008), 173. More detailed statistics than the rounded numbers of the printed compendium can be found in http://www.wto.org/english/res_e/statis_e/its2008_e/its08_appendix_e.htm, last accessed June 25, 2012.

[5] The CoCom was established in 1949, but differing views between European and American leaders over the goals and content of the embargo created tensions from the beginning. See Ian Jackson, *The Economic Cold War. America, Britain and East–West Trade, 1948–63* (New York: Palgrave, 2001) for European, and especially British recalcitrance over maintaining a strict trade embargo against the Soviet Union, especially during the second half of the 1950s.

[6] Calculated from Ministry of Foreign Trade, *Vneshniaia torgovlia SSSR za 1956 god. Statisticheskii obzor* (Moscow: Vneshtorgizdat, 1958), 7–10. The numbers are, again, problematic. They are valued in rubles. When it comes to trade with the West, prices and value are simply translated into rubles at the official exchange rate, and so prices are at market value. However, for the barter trade with Eastern Europe or barter deals with developing countries, prices are not established by the market,

Table 3.1 *Soviet foreign trade in billions of rubles, 1938–70**

Year	Import	Export	Total Turnover
1938	0.3	0.2	0.5
1946	0.7	0.6	1.3
1950	1.3	1.6	2.9
1955	2.7	3.1	5.8
1956	3.2	3.3	6.5
1957	3.6	3.9	7.5
1958	3.9	3.9	7.8
1959	4.6	4.9	9.5
1960	5.1	5.0	10.1
1961	5.2	5.4	10.6
1962	5.8	6.3	12.1
1963	6.4	6.5	12.9
1964	7.0	6.9	13.9
1965	7.2	7.4	14.6
1966	7.1	8.0	15.1
1967	7.7	8.7	16.4
1968	8.4	9.6	18.0
1969	9.3	10.5	19.8
1970	10.6	11.5	22.1

* Ministry of Foreign Trade, *Vneshniaia torgovlia SSSR za 1970 god. Statisticheskii obzor* (Moscow: Izdatel'stvo "Mezhdunarodnye otnosheniia," 1971), 8. The figures are, of course, problematic. Prices, for example, are not constant. But nevertheless it's a good approximation of the growth of foreign trade at the time. The Soviet statisticians that made this table chose 1938 as the starting point because that year was the nadir of Soviet trade, thus exaggerating growth in future years. In fact, trade turnover did not approach the level reached in 1930 until the first half of the 1950s. It is nevertheless useful in highlighting the continuity of trade growth throughout the changes in the Soviet leadership.

countries in Soviet trade, so that by 1963 it had reached 10 percent. Of course much of that growth was really a transfer of trade previously carried out through Western European markets, such as the Southeast Asian rubber the Soviets used to buy in Dutch and English markets.

and although the Soviets tended to generally follow the world market in setting their own prices, they are essentially not a signifier of value. The generally low quality of the products exchanged among the countries of Eastern Europe meant that their products were most likely overpriced. In the 1980s, for example, the CIA adjusted for this by cutting the value of this trade in half, effectively implying that trade was half that found in official statistics, see Ed A. Hewett with Clifford G. Gaddy, *Open for Business. Russia's Return to the Global Economy* (Washington: The Brookings Institution, 1992), 11. For the 1960s no one has done such calculations that I know, but at any rate they are often little more than educated guesses, and given that hidden inflation was not such a big problem then as it would become in the 1980s, following the techniques of the CIA would probably make for too drastic a cut.

After that transfer was complete – and supplemented with a dose of real growth – the numbers reached a plateau, hovering around 10–13 percent for the rest of the Soviet Union's history.[7] Did that reflect some sort of natural ceiling, or did it entail a certain disappointment with the benefits of trade with the poor countries of the world?

The weight of trade with the West proved more resilient, growing unrelentingly despite the converse statistical loss for the West of the colonies' exports to the Soviet Union. Economist Philip Hanson has argued that trade with the West was probably the only sort of trade that actually came close to fulfilling classical economic predictions of increased productivity, as they were net inflows of quality technology. Demand for Western technology within the Soviet Union would seem to confirm this, as imports for the second half of the 1960s grew by 11.2 percent, faster than foreign trade in general.[8] These technology imports were exchanged generally for raw materials such as oil and timber, in other words, the classic Ricardian exchange based on comparative advantage that prevails to this day in Russia's trade. By 1970, and on an even more exacerbated version of these terms, almost a fourth of the Soviet Union's trade was with the developed West.[9]

The comparative "losers" of these two developments were the Soviet Union's communist allies, and that despite the creation of the Council for Mutual Economic Assistance (CMEA), also known as the Comecon, in 1949 – although of course that trade also grew over time, just not as fast as trade outside the CMEA. The reasons have been laid down by Randall Stone in his excellent monograph *Satellites and Commissars*. Through use of Soviet archival evidence and dozens of interviews with the government officials who carried out trade negotiations in both Russia

[7] Calculated from Ministry of Foreign Trade, *Vneshniaia torgovlia SSSR za 1964 god. Statisticheskii obzor* (Moscow: Vneshtorgizdat, 1965), 8. The growth was mostly in the Soviet export of industrial equipment and other manufactures to these countries in exchange for those deficit resources, which the Soviets had earlier paid to European countries with primary commodities of their own.

[8] Philip Hanson's *The Rise and Fall of the Soviet Economy. An Economic History of the USSR from 1945* (New York: Longman, 2003), 120.

[9] Calculated from Ministry of Foreign Trade, *Vneshniaia torgovlia SSSR za 1970 god*, 10. It bears repeating that if prices of all Soviet foreign trade had been allowed to be set by the market, the percentage of trade with the West would have looked quite a bit higher, since its real value vis-à-vis the value of trade with Eastern Europe would have been brought to bear on pricing. Vladimir Treml found that the ratio of domestic prices to foreign prices for imported goods from the West was more than double, which amounted to an admission that the ruble was much overvalued at official exchange rates. Vladimir G. Treml, "Foreign Trade and the Soviet Economy: Changing Parameters and Interrelations," in Egon Neuberger and Laura D'Andrea Tyson, eds., *The Impact of International Economic Disturbances on the Soviet Union and Eastern Europe. Transmission and Response* (New York: Pergamon Press, 1980), 186–91.

and Eastern Europe, Stone has convincingly laid bare both the criteria the negotiators used in the course of their work and the institutional weaknesses that obstructed the Soviet Union in conducting negotiations or even projecting its power to produce reciprocally beneficial collaboration. In the struggle for the commodity structure of trade, a struggle that arose from the logic of the artificial prices used in communist trade, the East Europeans were consistently able to outmaneuver the Soviets, thus exchanging their relatively overpriced machinery products for relatively underpriced Soviet raw materials. As a consequence, the satellites "planned their trade in order to maximize the Soviet trade subsidy, rather than to specialize efficiently or to exploit comparative advantage."[10] Moreover, the Soviets tried time and again to raise the quality of Eastern European exported goods, attempts that, much like efforts to improve accountability and promote general objectives, were effectively defused by the satellites.[11] We will see that systemic problems of this kind, further exacerbated by the Soviet Union's inherently weak position in international politics, were also exploited by other alleged allies in the developing world.

But before we get too far ahead, let us start with a look to the West. The commercial relationship with the West was the longest lasting, largely because it was the most mutually profitable and complementary. Its legacy saw the rise of the Russian oligarchs in the 1990s and formed the basis of Putin's power in the twenty-first century. The origin of this enduring geopolitical and economic reality lay in the 1950s and 1960s, and it is a story that has largely been obscured by, indeed subsumed under, another story of much less durable quality: the Cold War. It is time to recover it.

[10] Stone, *Satellites and Commissars*, 239. In the context of made up prices, it would have been hard to figure out comparative advantage anyway.

[11] This was not because the Eastern Europeans wanted to minimize dependence on the Soviet economy, as Zbigniew Brzezinski and others have argued. To the contrary, the satellites were always keen on increasing trade, but what they had in mind was exacerbating the trade subsidy through more imports of raw materials and more exports of industrial goods. When the Soviet Union was not forthcoming in this respect, they resisted. See Stone's three case studies, in ibid., 89–112. It is also important to note that Stone does not argue, as others have, for a grand political agreement whereby Eastern European countries would acquiesce to Soviet hegemony in exchange for this implicit subsidy of their economies. There is absolutely no evidence for that argument, and likely never will be. In fact, the Soviets were fully aware of this implicit subsidy, and Stone details throughout his book their many attempts to end it, or at the very least to diminish it. Unfortunately much of the latest literature still reflects this early, erroneous assessment. See for example Barry Eichengreen, *The European Economy Since 1945. Coordinated Capitalism and Beyond* (Princeton: Princeton University Press, 2007), 160.

Slouching towards convertibility

This book has been arguing that the ability of the Soviets to participate in foreign trade depended largely on systemic junctures rather than ideological prescript. In the first half of the 1950s, however, these constraints were matched by the Stalinist legacy of institutional immobility and terror, which was yet operational while the Kremlin leadership was sorting itself out. In the summer of 1954, for example, the Ministry of Foreign Trade's innocuous suggestion to publish ads for export goods in the newspaper *Novosti* would still be unsettled after a month-and-a-half's discussion.[12] Even as the advertisement conundrum was methodically contemplated, Tekhnopromimport, responsible as the name suggests for trade in technical equipment, was defending its Stalinist obduracy to its superiors. The agency had refused to renegotiate the sale of Soviet tractors with a Greek firm even after it became clear that the tractors would not work well in Greek conditions.[13] The Greek firm complained to Khrushchev directly that Tekhnopromimport did not seem interested in trade. This called for an energetic defense of bureaucratic rectitude; in its summary of the affair, Tekhnopromimport felt obliged to plaintively offer proof to the Politburo that the trade agency followed procedure, showing how it answered the telegrams on time and abided by the agreement that the Greeks now wanted changed. For the immediate survivors of Stalinism, procedure and alibi were more important than results.

Meanwhile, during the middle of the decade, relations with the Soviet Union's more important trading partners were still hampered by politics and dollar shortages. Bretton Woods was still a project, rather than an institution, and would continue as a project for as long as European currencies were not fully convertible. Western governments still had to carefully manage their dollar reserves through a strict system of import–export licenses, foreign exchange controls, and other administrative arrangements. These restrictions were making what few relations the Soviets had with the governments of the European West contentious. The Soviets preferred to trade through long-term agreements. These were usually three- or five-year agreements that stipulated the general amount of trade and its growth over those years. They also stipulated the basic quantities to be exchanged of a variety of staple trade goods, which brought the Soviets a measure of commercial stability and predictability

[12] RGAE, f. 413, op. 13, d. 7363, ll. 1–4. The letters date April 28 and June 4, 1954.
[13] RGAE, f. 413, op. 13, d. 7363, ll. 8–10.

with which to elaborate their own domestic economic plans. Every year, delegations from the two governments would meet to hammer out more specific lists of goods to be exchanged. The exchange had to be balanced on a clearing basis. In other words, once an agreed framework was instituted, the exchange was no longer the same as the opportunistic barter agreements of the 1940s. Generally, the Soviets would open an account in one of their partner's banks and use that country's currency to clear imports and exports. Balance could also be reached through the expense of dollars, preferably, or pound sterling when necessary. Importantly, these lists, though more specific, were merely indicative of what was to be pursued as both governments set themselves to the task of contacting providers within each other's countries and negotiating prices with them.[14] They were not to be, indeed could not be, strictly followed, but they did provide a set of expectations. Of course, the Soviets could more easily mobilize what their partners asked for and so keep their end of the bargain. European governments, working as they did within more unruly market parameters, were not so efficient. Nor was the government bureaucracy in the West as focused and disciplined; often what the European trade delegates negotiated, another branch of that same government obstructed.

The arrangement led to many misunderstandings, some of them willful. In the constant battle for hard currency, for example, the French demanded that goods not on the annual list be paid for in dollars rather than allow them to be added to the lists on a clearing basis.[15] The problem for the Soviets, however, was that after negotiations with private enterprises were completed to buy items on the list, the licensing bureau would fail to issue the necessary license. Sometimes this was political, as in the sale of certain kinds of technical equipment prohibited by the United States. But often it was simply mysterious, as in the sale of ferrous metals in the spring of 1956 for which a French firm had petitioned and failed to get an export license. In meetings with their French counterparts, Soviet trade officials had often to ask for such licenses on behalf of their private French providers.[16]

[14] Indeed, at one meeting between French and Soviet trade delegations, when the French complained that the Soviets sold canned crab in France at higher prices than the crab they sold elsewhere, the Soviets argued that price was a matter for buyers and sellers, and not trade delegations. In RGAE, f. 413, op. 13, d. 7769, l. 19.

[15] RGAE, f. 413, op. 13, d. 7769, ll. 8–9, as requested in a meeting on March 15, 1956. The Soviet representative quickly reminded the French that the agreement stipulated that items could be added to and removed from the list as the year progressed.

[16] RGAE, f. 413, op. 13, d. 7769, l. 18.

Scholars of Soviet trade, and indeed scholars in general, have long labored under the assumption that Soviet trade was always subordinate to its politics. Yet reading through their negotiations with Western European governments, it is hard not to sympathize with Soviet officials in their claim that they were far more attuned to commercial considerations than their liberal European counterparts. The claim soon became a refrain and a rebuke: "In composing the list for French deliveries, the Soviet side was not ruled by political considerations," a Soviet negotiator, in a common version of the practice, told his French counterpart at another meeting in 1956. The Soviets had been denied the purchase of radio relay equipment and machine tools, which fell within the lists of forbidden exports to the Soviet Union. "We proceeded instead from commercial considerations and so stipulated the type of equipment we are interested in," he pointedly informed when told he was not being sensitive of French political commitments.[17] A suggestion later in the meeting bears out the pragmatism with which the Soviets approached relations with the economically developed world. In trying to persuade the French delegation to consider entering a long-term trade agreement, the Soviets had few illusions that the exchange would be one between industrial equals. The trade would entail "deliveries from France of various machinery and equipment, ferrous metals, cork, alcohol and citrus and from the USSR to France deliveries of oil, oil products, hard coal, timber, cotton, chromium and manganese ore, coal tar pitch, canned crab."[18] This was to be a hard-headed attempt to get at French industrial technology as well as scarce goods controlled by the French Empire, not an exchange redolent of propaganda potential and political gain.

But then again, there was one overriding and enduring political aim that underlay the whole of Soviet commercial policy. This was the politics of the ostracized, the evicted seeking entry, the powerless and marginalized in search of recognition. The case was succinctly stated by Deputy Minister of Foreign Trade Pavel N. Kumykin in his initial remarks during the 1957 talks that led to the long-term trade agreement between the Soviet Union and West Germany. "We proceed from the fact that trade between countries allows for the use of advantages and profits that emanate from the international division of labor, and is also a good foundation for the improvement in mutual understanding and the strengthening of

[17] RGAE, f. 413, op. 13, d. 7769, l. 21

[18] Ibid., l. 23. The cork and the citrus were of course colonial products that the Soviets would soon be able to obtain directly from their source, most likely Morocco and Tunisia.

relationships among nations," he told his audience of Soviet and German negotiators.[19] This was not a simple case of dull diplomatic rhetoric devoid of substance. Kumykin, representing a state without significant economic leverage, had little time for guile. The Soviets were ready to buy West German equipment and boats worth 1.9 billion marks (1.8 billion rubles at the prevailing exchange rate) over the next four years, as well as 1.6 billion marks worth of ferrous metals, steel pipes, assorted cables, copper, and medicines and medical equipment. He offered in exchange an increase in those goods the Germans were already buying: timber, paper, cotton and flax fiber, oil and its derivatives, coal, manganese, chromium, zinc, and other such primary commodities.[20]

The two sides implemented this general plan over the next six months. As would become routine in Soviet foreign relations, the institutionalization of this trade in 1957 had little to do with the Soviet Union and much to do with the other side. For two years the Soviets had been using all channels in diplomatic and business circles to put pressure on the Chancellor of Germany Konrad Adenauer's government to sign a trade treaty. In this endeavor they could count on German industrialists and businessmen as partners. Everywhere Soviet specialists went in West Germany, they met German businessmen hoping for commercial relations to be revived between the two countries, and everywhere the Soviets fed wood to the fire.[21] But Soviet officials and German businessmen had to wait for Adenauer to modify his "policy of strength" into a more accommodating attitude toward the Soviet Union. It seems the chancellor's turning point came in the summer of 1957, that is, not before achieving his overriding goal of integrating West Germany firmly within the European fold, which he accomplished in March when he signed the Treaty of Rome. As historian Robert Spaulding has argued, the Adenauer government was guided primarily by political goals in their consent to a long-term trade agreement with the Soviets.[22] The two countries had established diplomatic relations only two years earlier, after Adenauer parlayed a trip to Moscow into the repatriation of thousands of German POWs. In agreeing to conduct trade talks with the Soviets in 1957, the Adenauer government officials often invoked the political gains that might be had from the Soviets, particularly in the form of further repatriations.

[19] RGAE, f. 413, op. 13, d. 7988, l. 19. Negotiations started on July 24, 1957. [20] Ibid., l. 20.

[21] For an example see a delegation's report from a May 1957 trip to West Germany in GARF, f. 5446, op. 120, d. 1358, ll. 83–93.

[22] Robert Mark Spaulding, *Osthandel and Ostpolitik. German Foreign Trade Policies in Eastern Europe from Bismarck to Adenauer* (Providence: Berghahn Books, 1997).

But the outcome of the talks belied somewhat the Germans' assertions about the primacy of politics. Throughout the negotiations, the Soviets stubbornly refused to be drawn into political negotiations, focusing solely on commercial exchange and making concessions only – but not very extensively – on the commodities to be exchanged and their quantities. If the negotiations dragged on for seven months, it was the Germans who did the dragging, stalling when they found that their political demands were not being addressed.[23] Another point of contention was the German insistence that at least 10 percent of Soviet purchases in Germany be agricultural products such as cheese, fruit juice, and flour. It was left to the Soviets to be the voice of economic reason, noting that the product lists offered by the Germans often had no relation to the needs of the Soviet economy.[24] This attempt to dump consumer goods on the Soviet economy echoed that of the British ten years earlier, and would be echoed in turn by the Japanese a few years later. In the end, the Germans gave way on both these issues. In fact, it was the Soviets that ended up with the strictly commercial treaty they wanted, despite all private assertions by Chairman of the German Delegation Rolf Lahr and his colleagues that they were under less pressure to compromise than their Soviet counterparts.[25] It was not that Lahr was wrong in noting that West Germany's less interested approach to the talks should have afforded the German side more leverage; it was that time was working against the capacity and ambition of the German government to have absolute control over international trade and finance.

In his welcoming speech Kumykin had already pointed out the context of the negotiation: Trade between the two countries had only started in 1954, and it was already at 450 million rubles.[26] As Spaulding noted, this fast growth in the absence of a treaty made a nonsense of the Soviet position that the long-term treaty was absolutely necessary for commercial growth. But it also meant that the Adenauer government's window to use

[23] This was the reason for the break lasting from August through November, 1957, as the Chairman of the German Delegation Rolf Lahr wrote in his report, in which he blamed the Russians for the failure because they had shown no interest in discussing the repatriation issue. RGAE, f. 413, op. 13, d. 7988, ll. 58–60. The Soviets found it interesting that Lahr published his report in the German press on September 19. This came after two long absences in the summer during which Lahr claimed he had to go back to consult with his government, as Kumykin reported on August 26. In RGAE, f. 413, op. 13, d. 7988, l. 41–46.

[24] For example in RGAE, f. 413, op. 13, d. 7988, l. 108–14, 130–37, 228–38 and 239–41 in late November meetings, and then again with renewed vigor in early February, 1958, in RGAE, f. 413, op. 13, d. 8269, l. 5–7.

[25] As quoted in Spaulding, *Osthandel and Ostpolitik*, 451–52.

[26] RGAE, f. 413, op. 13, d. 7988, l. 19.

the trade treaty to wrest political concessions from the Soviets was quickly closing. The dollar shortage that had incurred such a decisive government presence in all international economic transactions was quickly turning into a dollar glut. The full convertibility of the German mark, which would bring about the further liberalization of international commerce and finance, was little more than a year away. In the final outcome, the Germans went back to Bonn with no resolution to the political questions they had brought to Moscow, and having compromised on most of the tough economic positions they had planned to take. But after seven months of haggling and wrangling they had come around to the opinion expressed by Kumykin at the very start of the process: Ever-increasing commercial exchange between the two countries would bring about greater mutual understanding and a strengthening political relationship. In the years ahead, the intensification of commercial exchange between the two countries would shrug off successive crises over Berlin.[27] By the 1970s it would once again become the most important economic relationship of the Soviet Union, resuming the position the Weimar Republic had occupied in the 1920s.

News of the Soviet–West German long-term commercial agreement, which came into effect in 1958, spurred others to approach the Soviets about a similar arrangement. The British were first off the mark, although they wondered out loud to Soviet officials whether such an agreement was possible given the British government's less coordinated approach to capitalist production than that of the Germans.[28] Their qualms were baseless; the treaty would operate in Great Britain as it did in Germany. A five-year Anglo-Soviet trade agreement was signed in May 1959. Many soon followed.

Reencounter with Japan

As interest in the untapped Soviet Union mounted in the West, an old adversary from the East made a solicitous appearance. Japan's economy had not weathered well the postwar 1940s under American occupation. Despite the famous reverse course in 1947, Japan's industry continued to suffer from a lack of capital, and its economy from a crippling inflation that rendered exports uncompetitive and thus starved the country of hard currency. In 1949, a harsh austerity program coordinated by General

[27] A similar argument with respect to Great Britain and the Suez and Hungarian crises of 1956 is made in Mark B. Smith, "Peaceful Coexistence at All Costs: Cold War Exchanges between Britain and the Soviet Union in 1956," *Cold War History* 12:3 (2012): 537–558.

[28] RGAE, f. 413, op. 13, d. 8259, ll. 59–61.

Douglas MacArthur's government, the Supreme Commander of the Allied Powers (SCAP) – which referred to his administration as much as to himself – under the advice of a Detroit banker, managed to bring inflation under control by pushing the Japanese economy to the brink of renewed depression.[29] In the absence of Europe's continent-wide, coordinated management of US aid and access to the deep, global markets of its various empires, America's substantial aid of about $2 billion to Japan – compared to the $4 billion Germany received through the Marshall Plan – did little to ameliorate the situation. Then in 1950, the Japanese were put back to work to feed the American war machine in Korea. In four months, Japan's industry was producing more than it had since the 1930s as the country tried to keep up with US military procurement demands. Like a torrent of water released on the dry bed of a dammed-up river, hard currency coursed through Japan's economy, reequipping its industry and modernizing its factories; Japanese businessmen, using a slightly different metaphor, called the war procurements "blessed rain from heaven."[30]

Ultimately the Japanese had much to thank Mao Zedong for: His victory in China had finally prodded the long-gestating Korean standoff into action, even as it repositioned Japan as the essential bulwark against Communism in Asia, in turn putting pressure on the US government to end the occupation and give Japan sovereignty over domestic affairs. The occupation ended in April 1952; in the summer, the United States was demanding that Japan join both the CoCom and the General Agreement on Tariffs and Trade (GATT).[31] Japan was leaving the blunt subordination of the defeated and formally entering the complex web of international regimes and institutions of American hegemony within which the failed empire learned to thrive.[32]

[29] Andrew Gordon, *A Modern History of Japan. From Tokugawa Times to the Present* (Oxford: Oxford University Press, 2003), 239–41.

[30] Walter LaFeber, *The Clash. U.S.–Japanese Relations throughout History* (New York: W. W. Norton, 1997), 293–95. The businessmen's moniker, along with Prime Minister Yoshida's celebration of the procurements as a "gift of the gods" is in Gordon, *A Modern History of Japan*, 241.

[31] And probably more importantly ChinCom, the restriction lists for trade with China. LaFeber, *The Clash*, 305. For American alacrity in pushing Japan into the GATT we have this for an explanation: "If the Japanese are blocked in their efforts to expand their trade with the free world, they may think it necessary to re-orient their trade toward Communist China and the Soviet bloc," in Memorandum by the Chairman of the Interdepartmental Committee on Trade Agreements (Corse) to the President, 20 August 1952, *FRUS*, 1952–54, Vol. 1, 116.

[32] The best sustained definition of hegemony is Bruce Cumings, *Parallax Visions. Making Sense of American–East Asian Relations* (Durham: Duke University Press, 1999), 205–26. This book takes its cue from Cumings' multifaceted understanding of the term, which owes as much to the work of IPE scholars as it does to Antonio Gramsci.

However, in 1952, few saw the rebirth of the Japanese economy to come, least of all Stalin's Kremlin, which was wont to see the still widespread social distress rather than the resurrection of its business elite.[33] Yet in the measure of sovereignty the Japanese had just gained, the Soviets saw an opportunity. Perhaps Japan could now be induced to stop their trade discrimination and engage its Asian neighbor in mutually beneficial trade, which the Soviets understood as the restoration of the traditional trade between the two countries: Japanese textiles, ships, and industrial equipment in exchange for Soviet timber, coal, asbestos, and medical goods.[34] Stalin would not live to see that restoration, but he might have, had he lived a few more years. Soviet commercial ambitions matched those of many in Japan, where there had long been a transcendent interest in harnessing the resources of Siberia for the Japanese economy.[35]

It was the fishing lobby, however, that was most active in making sure the requisite restoration of diplomatic relations between Japan and the Soviet Union was successful.[36] That restoration came with the visit to Moscow of Prime Minister Hatoyama Ichiro in October 1956, and was soon followed by the first waves of Japanese business delegations. Already in 1956, small- and middle-sized companies in Japan formed a group to study prospects of trade with the Soviet Union, and by the next year business contacts had been well established.[37] All this culminated in a trade agreement between the two countries in December 1957. From this point on, trade turnover doubled every year until 1960, after which it continued to expand at an astonishing rate.[38] Ten years later it had

[33] The Soviet view, once again, was the rule, not the ideologically mandated exception. See for example a British diplomat's observation that "many people were homeless, sleeping rough, under railway viaducts or in the shells of buildings awaiting repair or demolition." Quoted in LaFeber, *The Clash*, 296.

[34] RGAE, f. 413, op. 13, d. 6818, l. 45–46.

[35] A good account of the longstanding geostrategic goal is James Williams Morley, *The Japanese Thrust into Siberia, 1918* (New York: Columbia University Press, 1957).

[36] Kimie Hara, *Japan–Soviet/Russian Relations since 1945. A Difficult Peace* (London: Routledge, 1998), 55–57. The normalization of relations was predicated on resolving the territorial disputes left over from World War II. These were not resolved, and so a peace treaty has never been signed between the two countries. But at the behest of the fishing lobby, which intervened at a delicate time when negotiations were poised to fail, diplomatic relations were restored. Fishing rights in the North Pacific were among the first order of business after normalization.

[37] See for example RGAE, f. 4372, op. 57, d. 380, ll. 45–50 on Japanese offers in late 1957 to exploit Siberian timber. The Japanese made sure to point out that the timber was to be used for paper; Soviet timber could not compete with North American timber for furniture and construction. In exchange the Soviets were carrying out negotiations for fishing boats, as in RGAE, f. 413, op. 13, d. 8057, ll. 9–10.

[38] M. I. Krupianko, *Sovetsko-iaponskie ekonomicheskie otnosheniia* (Moscow: Nauka, 1982).

quintupled, making Japan the Soviet Union's biggest trade partner outside the CMEA – if only for a year.[39]

The Japanese made clear from the outset their goals for their new relationship with the Soviet Union. As Japanese businessmen explained to Viktor Spandar'ian, their Soviet interlocutor, Japan still needed to decrease its deficit with the United States, caused mainly by imports of grain, barley, cotton, coking coal, and oil.[40] Many of these could be replaced with Soviet commodities, since the trade would be carried out on a clearing basis. The main hope for the medium and long term was that Japan "move away from its dependence on American oil, and that in the future Japanese industry should function on Soviet oil," the governor of Niigata Prefecture, Kazuo Kitamura, told Mikoyan on a trip to Moscow in 1959.[41]

As in previous encounters and negotiations, Japanese and Soviet commercial dealers took some time to get mutually acquainted. And as usual, the Soviets had clear ideas about the new relationship while their partners, this time the Japanese, puzzled over the details of what might be gained from the relationship. Could the Soviets not use more dollars and fewer pounds in transactions?[42] Could they not buy more consumer goods?[43] The Soviets had been here before, and their answer was consistent and in the negative. But the Japanese businessmen did pose one novelty. The first two years of trade had been characterized by a rush of different Japanese business groups hurrying to snap up deals with the Soviets. The Ministry of Foreign Trade had quickly learned to play one group against another, sometimes provoking desperate correspondence from Japanese business dealers complaining of Soviet disloyalty and offering ever better terms.[44]

39 Japan was eclipsed by a resurgent West Germany.

40 RGAE, f. 413, op. 13, d. 8324, ll. 26–29. Spandar'ian was responsible for the newly established trade with Japan despite his title as head of the division of trade with Southeast Asia and the Middle East of the Ministry of Foreign Trade.

41 GARF, f. 5446, op. 120, d. 1385, ll. 72–73.

42 RGAE, f. 413, op. 13, d. 8057, ll. 9–10. The Japanese insisted that the pound fluctuated too much.

43 RGAE, f. 4372, op. 58, d. 344, ll. 188–89, or RGAE, f. 413, op. 13, d. 8324, ll. 32–33. This perennial problem for Soviet economic relations went well beyond the initial stage of relations. The British, for example, had been told ten years before, as noted in the last chapter, and they were still trying ten years later, as in RGAE, f. 4372, op. 62, d. 94. ll. 208–11. Or see Mikoyan's talks with a Finnish delegation, in which he holds the planned purchase of more Finnish ships to the Finns' purchase of more Soviet industrial goods, RGANI, f. 5, op. 30, d. 69, ll. 64–67.

44 Such as one from "Progress," an importer of coal, timber, copper, and manganese who complains that they made deals in the early going when the situation was difficult but are now being pushed aside by bigger concerns. They promise that they still have the contacts to get the Soviets the Japanese ships they wanted on a five-year credit basis with "only" 33 percent money down. In RGAE, f. 413, op. 13, d. 8324, ll. 57–58.

When in the summer of 1959 the Japanese tried to rationalize their imports of timber from the Soviet Union by creating an association that would speak for all the different groups involved in the timber trade, the Soviets responded that they would only trade with individual firms – a practice that contrasted with their dealings in the decolonized countries, where they often encouraged such rationalizing associations.[45] The Soviets here appear as champions of capitalistic competition, even as they promoted centralized organization in the global South.

Ultimately, the long-term growth of Japanese relations with the Soviets hinged on oil. Oil was the prize for the Japanese groups and associations of businessmen that had come to Moscow on the heels of the diplomats. Much capital investment would be needed on the shores of the Okhotsk Sea to bring Soviet oil to Japan, the president of the Japanese Association for Trade with the Soviet Union and the Socialist Countries of Europe (SOTOBO) told Spandar'ian in September 1959.[46] Before the Japanese made this investment, they wanted to make sure that the Soviets would deliver the oil reliably and without interruptions. But here again, the obstacle was not the Soviet government. As Spandar'ian pointed out, the Soviets were always ready to sign long-term agreements on oil and all other goods. More problematic was the Ministry of International Trade and Industry (MITI) in Japan, which was often slow and sometimes refused to grant the necessary permits to Japanese businesses to import Soviet oil.[47] Once again, behind the policy were the familiar financial constraints of an incomplete Bretton Woods system coupled with American hostility.

For the Japanese this was not all bad. When Daikyo Oil (now Cosmo Oil) approached the Soviets to buy crude, its director wanted the Soviets to pay a risk premium, i.e. to provide a discount, to hedge for the possibility that the Americans might not buy Daikyo's products because they contained Soviet crude.[48] The larger Japanese oil companies were already tied to long-term agreements with American companies, and only smaller companies, particularly those like Daikyo that had no foreign capital to

[45] RGAE, f. 413, op. 13, d. 8561, ll. 17–18. It is clear that where industrialized countries were concerned, it was more profitable to play one firm against another. What is not clear is whether in the Third World this was an ideological stance. Individual Japanese firms were reliable, obviating the need for an association that would take responsibility for non-fulfillment. This was not often the case in the Third World.

[46] RGAE, f. 413, op. 13, d. 8562, l. 58.

[47] Ibid., l. 59. See for example a July 13, 1959 letter of complaint from the Soviet trade representative in Tokyo, V. D. Alekseenko to the Japanese Ministry of Foreign Affairs about MITI's refusal to increase Tokyo Oil's quota to import more oil, in RGAE, f. 413, op. 13, d. 8561, ll. 19.

[48] RGAE, f. 413, op. 13, d. 8562, ll. 116–17.

appease, had the flexibility to enter into new business with the Soviet Union. These constraints, and its opportunities, were not limited to oil. In these first few years, the Soviets were also having trouble selling their cast iron in Japan. The problem was that Japan had received $101 million in loans from the World Bank from 1953 to 1958, including $73 million in 1958. The main importing firm for cast iron, Kawasaki, received $20 million in 1957, $8 million in 1958, and was hoping for another $20 million in 1959. As a Japanese dealer explained to his Soviet counterpart, Japanese steel mills felt a moral responsibility to their American creditors, bound as they were to a Western financial network that would not look kindly upon business with the Soviet Union. It would seem, however, that such moral qualms could be assuaged if the Soviets could sell their iron at more competitive prices, or so this Japanese dealer avowed.[49]

In March 1959, the Soviet oil export agency, Soiuznefteksport, began to explore the deal the Japanese had been waiting for: an oil pipeline taking Western Siberian oil to the East. In exchange, the Soviets wanted oil pipes and cisterns. At this exploratory phase, the idea was to run a pipe from the Urals to Irkutsk, whereupon the oil would travel by train. The project was to be finished by 1961, but they would first wait for terms from Tokyo.[50] Over the next ten years, the foreign financing of oil pipes in the Soviet Union would become one of the communist power's most important – and consequential – trades. Japan, alas, would have to wait a long time. But that disappointment came later. In 1959, the two partners were still learning about each other. Just recently, in December 1958, Western European currencies – but not the yen – had become fully convertible, ushering in the full promise of Bretton Woods and speeding up international trade.[51] Rumors in Japan were rampant that the ruble would become convertible as well. When asked about it by an excited Japanese diplomat, Spandar'ian was as lucid and direct as usual: "In the Soviet Union there are no such rumors."[52]

The Mikoyan initiative

A 1955 planning report to the Central Committee envisioned in five years a growth in trade turnover of 43 percent, with much of that growth coming

[49] RGAE, f. 413, op. 13, d. 8562, ll. 21–22.

[50] RGAE, f. 413, op. 13, d. 8562, ll. 150–52. Both parties agreed to proceed with caution, lest "foreign circles" intervene and derail the deal.

[51] Japan did not bring about full convertibility until 1964.

[52] RGAE, f. 413, op. 13, d. 8562, ll. 168–69.

in the last two years.[53] More apropos, while it aimed for a 25 percent increase in trade turnover with the Communist Bloc, it hoped for a twofold increase in trade with the rich capitalist countries and an almost threefold increase in trade with the poor ones.[54] Already by 1954–55 the Soviets were working with Canada and Japan to clear up fishing rights in the Pacific,[55] inviting Italian and British businessmen to negotiate new trade deals,[56] and working with the Scandinavian countries to increase trade volume.[57] As they often said publicly and wrote in their own bureaucratic reports, trade with the capitalist countries did not have the scope that it should, mostly because of what they considered trade discrimination against the Soviet Union organized by the United States. "The Soviet Union is ready to expand economic relations with all countries," said a 1958 report from Gosplan's department for foreign economic relations. "In the future we will not relax our efforts to normalize and expand trade and economic relations with capitalist countries."[58]

More importantly, this was a message they tried to convey at every turn during negotiations with representatives of rich capitalist countries, as when Mikoyan met with a group of British businessmen in January 1954.[59] To the Canadians, Mikoyan declared that presently "nothing impedes the expansion of cultural, political and economic relations between the Soviet Union and Canada; to the contrary, there are great opportunities for their growth."[60] And he would often reassure the Japanese that he was still not satisfied with the level of trade between the Soviet Union and Japan.[61]

This was an unshackled charm offensive, led by the Armenian Mikoyan, second in the Kremlin only to Khrushchev and a long-time minister

[53] RGANI, f. 5, op. 30, d. 113, l. 75.

[54] Ibid. The term "capitalist" was one the Soviets used to describe the world outside the Eastern European countries, Mongolia, North Korea, North Vietnam, and China. In fact almost half a decade after its revolution in 1959, even Cuba continued to appear under the rubric "capitalist." Where economic reports and analyses were concerned, the capitalist world was further subdivided into the developed and the "economically underdeveloped," but still capitalist, countries (*slaborazvitye v ekonomicheskom otnoshenii kapitalisticheskie strany*).

[55] See for example RGANI, f. 5, op. 30, d. 116, ll. 101–05 for talks with the Canadians and RGANI, f. 5, op. 30, d. 163, ll. 128–30 with the Japanese.

[56] RGANI, f. 5, op. 30, d. 71, ll. 6–15 for talks with British delegations, which the Soviets were trying to smooth with a fair amount of vodka. See also RGANI, f. 5, op. 30, d. 224, ll. 60–69 for the first Italian stab at Soviet oil, which they would finally regularize in the 1960s with the building of oil pipes directly to Italy.

[57] RGANI, f. 5, op. 30, d. 71, ll. 77–78.

[58] RGAE, f. 4372, op. 57, d. 387, ll. 131–33.

[59] Mikoyan thought them farsighted inasmuch as they understood the use of business relations between both countries better than many British politicians, a sentiment he would repeat to the Japanese. See his many compliments in RGANI, f. 5, op. 30, d. 71, ll. 10–15.

[60] RGANI, f. 5, op. 30, d. 116, l. 102.

[61] See for example RGANI, f. 5, op. 30, d. 274, l. 87.

of trade. In fact, so anxious were the Soviets to show themselves to be reliable partners, that throughout the late 1950s, when harvests were abundant in the Soviet Union, they insisted on fulfilling their commitments to Canada, from whom they had pledged to buy wheat. "The non-fulfillment of our responsibilities in buying Canadian wheat can lead to serious complications in Soviet–Canadian relations, and possibly to the annulment on the part of the Canadians of the trade agreement with the USSR," both the Ministries of Foreign Trade and Foreign Affairs argued in a report to the Central Committee. But perhaps more importantly, it might "undermine the Soviet Union's prestige as a trade partner."[62]

Philip Hanson dates the beginning of large net Soviet imports of machinery from the West to 1958, the same year that Khrushchev started the chemicalization of the Soviet economy, for which even more Western imports were needed. These would only begin to show up in Soviet statistics in 1960 because of the usual time lag between initial negotiation, contract, and equipment delivery.[63] The archival record shows that negotiations started much earlier, and that businessmen from the West played a big role in initiating the economic relationships; it could only be so, given the Soviet leadership's unbroken desire for such relations since the 1920s.[64]

It took time and experience for Soviet policymakers to develop into moderately savvy commercial operators. The Soviet Union had been without important economic relations for more than two decades, discounting the Lend-Lease operations during World War II, which were in essence grants and not particularly conducive to the development of a sagacious sensibility for profit-making. Neither were the 1930s such a time; rather it had been a time of deflating opportunities when Soviet leaders basically pushed such exports as grain ever more unprofitably, and were willing to pay almost any price, including extreme hardship and starvation in their territory, in order to import the necessary technology for their industrialization drive.[65]

Nevertheless it was the late 1920s and early 1930s that briefly became the reference for the first tentative steps in the late 1950s to develop markets

[62] RGANI, f. 5, op. 30, d. 224, ll. 71–72.

[63] Hanson, *Rise and Fall of the Soviet Economy*, 61–63.

[64] See the persistent Bell Punch Company Ltd., which sent and resent letters directly to Khrushchev to get him interested in its industrial equipment. They would not be stayed until they received an audience in Moscow, as it would "stir commercial contacts," which would be "in accord with the spirit of your [Khrushchev's] latest speech." RGANI, f. 5, op. 30, d. 275, ll. 3–6.

[65] See Franklyn D. Holzman, *Foreign Trade under Central Planning* (Cambridge: Harvard University Press, 1974), 39–60.

abroad for the sole purpose of making hard currency earnings. And it was the powerful and able Mikoyan who, drawing on his experience as people's commissar for external and internal trade during the 1920s and 1930s, took the initiative in this endeavor. Now he would do it in his capacity as deputy head of the Council of Ministers, and the general reference in the Soviet government for all things relating to Soviet foreign economic policy.

Among the first such efforts in the late 1950s, Mikoyan commissioned the Ministry of Foreign Trade to look into such possibilities as selling iron pyrite, a sulfide mineral from which copper, sulfur, silver, gold, and even zinc could be chemically extracted before being finally put to use for the smelting of iron.[66] Lacking the technology to gainfully process this mineral, the Soviets had little use for it. This technology existed abroad, however, and from 1929 through the early 1930s it had been exported to Holland and Germany.[67] In 1939 the Soviets tried to sell it in Belgium and Germany, but were unsuccessful, and in 1957, Mikoyan asked the ministry to market it in the West once again, which they did only with late and mixed success.[68]

By the early 1960s, Foreign Trade Ministry officials were more actively taking the initiative in trying to extract profit from the world economy, thanks in part to the world economy's greater willingness to accept Soviet economic penetration. In 1961, the deputy minister of foreign trade alerted Mikoyan to the great demand of railway tracks in developing countries.[69] But here historical legacies intruded on Soviet ambitions. The railway systems of developing countries had begun their construction in the colonial era, with a wide array of track measures, and none of these countries was willing to change its standard to fit the Soviet standard. This made it prohibitively expensive for Soviet factories to allot some of their production for the fulfillment of demand abroad.[70] "Based on the importance of developing trade with underdeveloped countries, as well as the high rewards in hard currency for the sale of railway tracks compared

[66] RGAE, f. 413, op. 13, d. 7931, l. 1000. [67] Ibid.

[68] Ibid., l. 1001. The Soviets approached companies in West Germany, Belgium, the United States, Holland, Japan, and other countries, but without positive results. The ministry ended the report by suggesting that they might be able to sneak it into a long-term trade agreement with West Germany. In fact, six years later they had achieved a measure of success, but were still being routinely turned down by Western firms because of the pyrite's low quality. They were thus still working out ways to market it, with one August 1963 report proposing to categorize the pyrites properly in order to sell the different grades that did meet with Western firms' minimal requirements in quality. See RGAE, f. 4372, op. 65, d. 67, ll. 151–52.

[69] RGAE, f. 4372, op. 63, d. 397, l. 37.

[70] Ibid. The report further noted that only one factory exported its railways, mainly to Finland.

to other varieties of rolled iron," wrote the deputy minister, "the Ministry of Foreign Trade considers it expedient to supply nonstandard railway tracks to those countries. For that purpose it is necessary to lay on one of the iron and steel works the production of nonstandard tracks for export," he concluded.[71]

Later that same year the ministry informed Mikoyan of the great demand in the developing countries in Africa, Southeast Asia, the Middle East, and Latin America for Soviet road-building machines and equipment. However, the ministry's report noted, Gosplan had not allocated enough funds to meet this demand, so that Guinea and Cuba were waiting for spare parts, and an agreement with Indonesia and Greece could not be reached as a result.[72] In a sense, these were easy paths of trade expansion. They did not require the ministry to actively search for the type of profitable market junctures which it was so often admonished into searching. It was rather a very typical passive attitude on the part of Soviet bureaucrats and indicative of the general lack of enterprise that characterized Soviet economic penetration of the developing world. As will be argued in the next chapter, it was mostly the developing countries themselves that took the initiative in expanding commercial intercourse with the Soviet Union.

Be that as it may, Mikoyan's sights in the early 1960s were more firmly set on expanding the more useful trade with the rich and technologically advanced countries. The imperatives for growth in the Soviet Union were much the same as they had been in Western Europe, and these lay in what economists call convergence, that is, growth achieved by closing the efficiency gap between the Soviet Union and the richer, industrialized countries.[73] But to achieve the necessary technology transfer, the Soviet Union would first need convertible currency with which to buy products in the West. Greater openness of Western markets offered opportunities that Mikoyan sought to quickly exploit. Among the Western markets opening to the Soviets at this time was, tentatively, that of the United States itself; typical of the early 1960s was Mikoyan's 1961 directive to the planning and trading agencies, asking that they look into increasing the production of canned crab, as prohibitions against its import into

71 Ibid., l. 38. The ministry wanted, in effect, to commandeer a factory, which would be an unhappy outcome for its manager.

72 RGAE, f. 4372, op. 63, d. 397, ll. 58–59.

73 With respect to Europe's convergence in the 1960s with the more technologically and organizationally advanced United States see Barry Eichengreen, *The European Economy Since 1945. Coordinated Capitalism and Beyond* (Princeton: Princeton University Press, 2007).

the United States from the Soviet Union had just been lifted, and it could become, in Mikoyan's words, a "serious source of hard currency."[74] They succeeded in establishing this export only in 1963, and by 1965 they were exporting 100,000 cans of crab to the United States.[75]

Dreaming of hard currency

Mikoyan's gusto for finding sources of hard currency quickly became the leadership's in general. In the late 1950s, despite a creeping dollar glut in the "free world," the Soviet Union's precarious hard currency reserves were often quickly exhausted, limiting Moscow's ability to satiate Soviet industry's thirst for superior Western products and technology. In 1958, Gosplan's foreign economic relations department started to call attention to the problems with the balance of payments, asking the Foreign Trade Ministry to be more mindful of hard currency reserves when drawing up their plans for foreign trade.[76] At that time, small barter trade disruptions, as started happening in the Soviet Union's trade with China, could deny input materials that put in danger the production of a whole range of articles for the Soviet domestic economy. It happened that year with imports of phenol from China, which the Chinese could not – or would not – provide. The 2,000-ton shortage endangered the production of manufactures in the aviation, automobile, and radio branches of industry, the Ministry of Chemical Industry warned. Lack of hard currency made it impossible to resolve this small emergency by tapping international markets.[77] Even requests by Russia's economic council for imports of oils for the cosmetic industry in Moscow had to be turned down for lack of foreign reserves.[78]

In the first few years of the 1960s, Soviet industrial managers, and the ministerial bureaucrats that catered to them, intensified their requests for imports, overwhelming Gosplan and straining the Soviet Union's reserves of hard currency. Exacerbating the trend, the import of goods from

[74] RGAE, f. 4372, op. 63, d. 397, l. 74.

[75] These were worth 45 million rubles. Ministry of Foreign Trade, *Vneshniaia torgovlia SSSR za 1966 god. Statisticheskii obzor* (Moscow: Izdatel'stvo "Mezhdunarodnye otnosheniia," 1967), 320.

[76] RGAE, f. 4372, op. 57, d. 387, l. 54. This was as part of a general decree that year to improve the planning of the Soviet economy.

[77] RGAE, f. 4372, op. 56, d. 149, l. 10. Gosplan eventually ordered the Ministry of Foreign Trade to go back to the Chinese and ask again, which Ministry officials were reluctant to do, see ibid., ll. 11–12. It seems to have worked, as those 2,000 tons of phenol show up in the published statistics for foreign trade in *Vneshniaia torgovlia SSSR za 1956 god*, 128.

[78] RGAE, f. 4372, op. 57, d. 385, l. 48.

capitalist markets had become an easy way to plug the shortages endemic to the Soviet economic system. The Ministry of Health needed to import vitamins, the district of Odessa needed aluminum for wine vats, China failed to deliver much-needed natrium – used for making alloys and soap, among other products – Moscow needed apples, and Gosplan could not find the hard currency to meet any of these demands.[79]

The lack of currency for these more or less low priority tasks may have been a function of the precedence the Soviet leadership gave to Western goods that were technologically superior and in great demand domestically. The Soviet Union's inability to mass produce the large air conditioning devices necessary to cool airports, for example, led Mikoyan to order Gosplan to look into buying these from an English firm after reports on the distressingly hot conditions of airports in the south of Russia.[80] Likewise, the Cherkassk *sovnarkhoz* required special cables for its mining concern that could only be bought in England or West Germany.[81] This time the *sovnarkhoz* chairman was prepared to address the possible lack of hard currency necessary for the cables, and offered to market for export an extra 400 tons of sugar from the *sovnarkhoz*'s sugar refinery to cover the cost.[82] The request was denied because of the difficulties the Soviets were having at that time in even selling the planned amount of sugar in the international markets;[83] instead, Gosplan proposed the purchase of such cables could be included in the 1962 import plans, which was a standard Gosplan approach for mitigating the strain on Soviet convertible cash flow.[84] The virgin lands initiative in Kazakhstan created demand for

[79] RGAE, f. 4372, op. 62, d. 464, l. 161; RGAE, f. 4372, op. 63, d. 397, ll. 76–77; RGAE, f. 4372, op. 63, d. 399, l. 33; and RGAE, f. 4372, op. 63, d. 399, l. 85 respectively. In all these examples, Gosplan's first reaction was to try to get these products from Eastern Europe, where they could be gotten on barter terms. When denied they simply wrote back to the petitioners that they include the requested material in next year's plan. And so did the growing addiction for imports supply yet another incentive for hoarding, a practice already pervasive and ever-growing throughout the Soviet economy.

[80] RGAE, f. 4372, op. 63, d. 397, l. 158.

[81] RGAE, f. 4372, op. 63, d. 399, l. 44. [82] Ibid., l. 50.

[83] Ibid., l. 52. These difficulties probably resulted from disturbances in the international sugar market caused by the Cuban revolution two years earlier. The Soviet Union promised to buy all the sugar the United States was unwilling to buy from Cuba. However the Soviet Bloc was already self-sufficient in sugar, even if consumption levels relative to the West were low. This resulted in a tremendous expansion of sugar exports every year from 1960 to 1962, expanding at rates ranging from 70 to 90 percent, as the Soviets exported their production of beet sugar and consumed Cuba's cane sugar. See *Vneshniaia torgovlia SSSR za 1960 god*, 24 and *Vneshniaia torgovlia SSSR za 1962 god*, 31. See also chapter 6.

[84] Western cables for the mining industry seemed to have become especially popular around the Soviet Union at this time. The cause of this may have been Soviet scientists' failure to copy the West's high-quality cables; in 1957 the Ministry of Electrical Engineering had specifically requested the import of a variety of cables from West Germany and Sweden for the explicit purpose of reverse

Western diesel generators for the republic's power stations, a request that received a more positive response.[85] Also meriting the effort of financing its import with supplementary exports was polythene, ethylene, and other such chemicals heavily used in the domestic production of consumer goods.[86]

At times, the Foreign Trade Ministry's trade associations could be imaginative, as in August 1961 when they offered a British firm credit in the Soviet economy as a way to purchase that company's products. The firm, The Platt Brothers and Company, refused such advances for its power looms, preferring cold cash instead.[87] Again Gosplan could not come up with the necessary hard money. But more often, the Soviet bureaucracy was slow in conducting transactions and responding to the faster-paced expectations of businesses in the West, as befits large organizations staffed with non-incentivized civil servants. There was ever a sense of urgency when dealing with Western businessmen. When French industrialists in 1961 sent word back to Gosplan saying they were willing to switch to Soviet timber from their traditional suppliers in other countries, they demanded quick and concrete answers. They worked, they explained, "on a strict commercial basis" (*na strogo kommercheskoi osnove*).[88]

Mikoyan, working through the Soviet of Ministers (Sovmin), would sometimes have to intervene to quicken the pace. For example, in the summer of 1961, A. Saalheimer Ltd. wrote a letter to authorities in Moscow complaining that their letters to V/O Raznoeksport on orders the company placed on toys, ceramics, pencils, and tool sets had not been answered in two months. The British company seemed to know how to make the Soviet bureaucracy nervous, noting the possible repercussions such neglect could have on Soviet reputation: "It is no longer a question of money or profit, but becomes a question of principle, and we, who have a first class reputation in most countries of the world, do feel hurt at the attitude of this silence," the director wrote. Sure enough, at Mikoyan's request, the Ministry of Foreign Trade was quick to react, blaming the director of V/O Raznoeksport and establishing control measures for the timely reply to future correspondence from the British firm. Moreover, the ministry promptly dispatched the derelict director to negotiate new agreements with it for the next year.[89]

engineering them and starting production on them as soon as possible. Yet two years later, a combine in Kiev was still asking to have them imported, a request repeated by combines around the Soviet Union. See RGAE, f. 413, op. 13, d. 7931, l. 247 and RGAE, f. 4372, op. 63, d. 399, l. 56.

85 RGAE, f. 7733, op. 49, d. 805, l. 108.

86 GARF, f. 5446, op. 96, d. 1161, l. 60.

87 RGAE, f. 4372, op. 63, d. 399, l. 32.

88 RGAE, f. 4372, op. 63, d. 85, l. 89.

89 GARF, f. 5446, op. 95. d. 1021, ll. 39–42. The Vsesoiuznye Obshchestva (V/O) were the departments of the Ministry of Foreign Trade that actually carried out negotiations and were

The market is a stern teacher: The battle over quality

Given the Kremlin's obsession with hard currency, as well as the expediency of financing growing volumes of imports, the quality of Soviet exports took on a newfound importance. As long as economic exchanges were domestic, the low quality of Soviet manufactured products remained hidden among production statistics of aggregated tonnage and the other quantitative indicators used to incentivize Soviet managers.[90] However, these shortcomings were quickly revealed when they came under the spotlight of international markets, where value was assessed by the laws of supply and demand and prices incorporated a product's quality and relative scarcity.[91]

As early as 1958, a mere few years after the massive unleashing of trade with countries outside the CMEA, Moscow had started to become preoccupied with the message foreign consumers were sending regarding Soviet products. A decree on March of that year was passed by the Council of Ministers ratifying measures to improve the quality of exported goods.[92] The language of the decree is interesting, although it should no longer surprise the reader. It started with an encomium of the growth in international commerce of a country many Western analysts thought – and still think – congenitally and ideologically prone to autarky. It went on to address the problem at hand: the many complaints the Soviet Union was receiving about the quality of its exports. The problems this posed would become very familiar to the Soviets in the 1960s: "a large number of complaints are being received from international companies and organizations, there are considerable losses of hard currency, and damage is being inflicted to the prestige of the Soviet Union in international markets."[93]

There was plenty of blame to go around. An inspection of factories producing for export revealed many problems in the organization of their production, although these problems are familiar to anyone who has studied factory practices in command economies. The finishing and

responsible for the fulfillment of import–export contracts. They each had their competence in different branches of the economy, usually elucidated by the telltale name of each particular department.

[90] See Paul Gregory's discussion on the creation of such a system and the preeminence of quantitative indicators over any considerations of quality in *The Political Economy of Stalinism. Evidence from the Soviet Secret Archives* (Cambridge: Cambridge University Press, 2004), chapter 7.

[91] This argument is fleshed out in Oscar Sanchez-Sibony, "Soviet Industry in the World Spotlight: The Domestic Dilemmas of Soviet Foreign Economic Relations, 1955–1965," *Europe-Asia Studies* 62:9 (2010): 1555–78.

[92] GARF, f. 5446, op. 1, d. 674, ll. 84–90.

[93] Ibid, l. 84.

packaging of equipment was done badly, and technical documentation was sloppily prepared. Managerial irresponsibility and slack party control over production for export were the main culprits. The work of the planning agencies had also been disappointing. Their export plans were generally drawn up too late, and too many factories throughout the Soviet Union were tasked with the production of exported goods regardless of the technological level of their equipment.[94] Meanwhile, the perennial struggle among the transportation agencies created unacceptable bottlenecks.

The measures to be taken were as predictable as they were vague. The regional governments were to improve the quality of the products produced for export in their factories; the party organizations were to establish greater control over these products; the Ministry of Foreign Trade and GKES were to present their trade plans to the Council of Ministers earlier than they had been; all involved were to improve their communication so that the right factories were assigned the right products for export; the transportation ministries were to improve their job. Most importantly to the bureaucratic culture of this highly centralized organization, the paperwork produced by each and every agency involved in the export of Soviet goods was to expand dramatically in an attempt to exercise some control and gain a measure of accountability over implementation and production delivery schedules.[95] Two months after the report, in May 1958, the Soviet government introduced a system of supplementary payments for producers of export goods to induce them to improve the quality of production for export and meet world standards.[96]

A year later, many of the same problems persisted. A follow-up state inspection barred thousands of machinery and equipment parts, as well as other products, from being exported until defects were corrected; a majority of them were deemed unfit for export altogether.[97] In 1958, replacement claims from foreign companies cost the Soviet Union one million rubles of hard currency – these claims, of course, were the only ones the Soviet Union saw cause to redress.

94 Ibid., ll. 84–85.

95 Ibid., ll. 85–88. The paperwork included a progress report from everybody in six months, upon which the follow-up decree a year later was likely based. See Ibid., l. 90.

96 The system is discussed in Vladimir G. Treml, "The Inferior Quality of Soviet Machinery as Reflected in Export Prices," *Journal of Comparative Economics* 5:2 (1981): 200–21.

97 GARF, f. 5446, op. 1, d. 687, l. 4. The document names the particular factories that had failed to provide competitive products. The authors especially single out car parts from the automotive industry, particularly engines and tires produced at the automotive combine in Iaroslavl', as well as tractors from the Khar'kov tractor factory.

Although much of this problematic production involved industrial manufactures, even the low quality of basic Soviet raw materials was exposed. In 1959, Western importers of timber, coal, and chromium rejected Soviet deliveries after finding the timber unseasoned and the coal and chromium riddled with too many impurities.[98] This situation continued into the 1960s, and became a particular concern for officials, especially in times of tight market conditions. Such conditions were in effect in the spring of 1962, when the Ministry of Foreign Trade found itself with tons of unsalable chromium from Kazakhstan at a time when more supply of chromium existed than there was demand for it.[99] The Kazakh chromium, neither assorted nor enriched, was being rejected by French and British companies in favor of the competition's; internationally competitive chromium would require the construction of a completely new factory, the Kazakh Council of Ministers reported.[100] Two years later, however, the problem persisted, and Gosplan was still pushing to improve its quality in order to export it to proven potential clients.[101]

Perhaps inevitably, complaints from Eastern European countries about the low quality of the products the Soviets were bartering with them did not seem to elicit the same degree of alarm. The reports on such complaints were invariably limited to noting the problem, with no prescriptive policy appended, and certainly no suggestion of any further investments to improve the situation. And so 1962 complaints by Hungary, East Germany, Poland, Czechoslovakia, and Cuba about the quality of the Soviet oil delivered to them, which had high levels of salt – up to 100 mg per liter – were not further qualified.[102] In cases such as these, solutions could be simple. When the Czech deputy minister of heavy industry went to Gosplan's headquarters in Moscow to complain about the quality of Soviet iron ore, particularly the ore from Tul'skii – which had an iron content of 43.13 percent rather than the 46.5 percent minimum stipulated in the trade agreement – he asked that the Soviets give them higher-grade ore from a different region. The deputy head of Gosplan turned the request down without further discussion, alleging simply that it was "quite impossible at the moment."[103]

To be fair, Eastern European products were often also of low quality. The Czechs, more than the rest, would habitually try to sell their

[98] Ibid., ll. 5–6. [99] GARF, f. 5446, op. 96, d. 1165, l. 94
[100] Ibid, l. 98. Naturally the Kazakh Sovmin seized the opportunity and asked for more investment funding from Moscow.
[101] RGAE, f. 4372, op. 65, d. 874, ll. 64–65. [102] GARF, f. 5446, op. 96, d. 1165, l. 62.
[103] RGAE, f. 4372, op. 58, d. 28, ll. 3–4.

manufactured goods in the Soviet Union when they found them impossible to sell competitively to capitalist countries.[104] Selling these subpar goods to the Soviets would net the Czechs raw materials such as aluminum, zinc, and grain, obviating the need to buy these with convertible currency and, to some extent, alleviating Czechoslovakia's balance of payments with the West. As often as not, however, the Soviets stalled on these requests or turned them down, particularly when they were made on a supplementary basis after the trade plans had already been worked out and mutually accepted.[105]

Ultimately it was in the fight for convertible currency, rather than for the captive markets of Eastern Europe, that a lack of competitiveness in Soviet manufactures caused the greatest alarm. Time and again the efforts by the Ministry of Foreign Trade to line up a steadfast clientele for Soviet products would be undermined by recalcitrant Soviet factories and their shoddy, uncompetitive goods. In 1962, for example, the ministry's efforts to market foreign currency-earning printing machines in Italy, France, Belgium, and Argentina were undercut by the factory in Leningrad that produced them. In a letter of complaint to the Council of Ministers, the ministry noted that a year earlier the Leningrad factory had failed to deliver 102 printing machines and that those that were delivered were of such low quality that customers, particularly in Italy, were refusing to buy them.[106] Word of Italian companies' refusal spread to companies in other countries, as competitors seized on the information to disparage the quality of the Soviet machines, thus creating even more difficulties for the Soviet position in that market. In an appeal for action, the deputy minister of foreign trade ended by noting that "the position of the factory and the Leningrad *sovnarkhoz* on cutting exports contradicts that of the Central Committee on expanding exports of Soviet machinery and inarguably leads to the loss of markets in capitalist countries."[107] This it did in Italy, where after a peak in 1963 of 258,000 rubles' worth of printing equipment – probably as a result of the delivery of the backlogged orders mentioned in the report – exports plummeted to about 50,000 to 60,000 rubles in later years. Exports of printing equipment more generally also slowed and fell at this time.[108]

104 RGAE, f. 4372, op. 57, d. 385, l. 83.
105 Ibid., l. 84.
106 GARF, f. 5446, op. 96, d. 1165, l. 60.
107 Ibid., l. 61.
108 *Vneshniaia torgovlia SSSR za 1965 god*, 167. I use rubles because there aren't figures in the ministry's statistical publication of how much equipment was sold, which would have been a better record. Although prices for printing equipment may have varied among countries, particularly when sold at market prices in relation to barter agreements, I assume that they did not vary by much when sold to one country over a few years. So printing equipment sold in Italy in 1961 may not have had the same price as printing equipment sold in India that same year as part of a barter exchange, but it should have a relatively similar value to equipment sold again in Italy a few years later.

Another report from the ministry concerned the bad quality and lack of uniformity of Soviet window glass. The ministry reported that the glass was sold in Canada, Italy, Burma, Iraq, Indonesia, Pakistan, Sudan, Ceylon, and other countries, and that it experienced strong competition from England, France, Belgium, West Germany, and Japan, and even from developing countries such as Turkey, Pakistan, and India, as well as some South American countries. In 1962, the Soviet Union exported 3,586 cubic meters of window glass. In 1963 they were trying to sell 4,932, and in 1964 they were planning to sell 6,650, which would bring in 1.5 million rubles in convertible currency. But there were problems. No factories produced "A"-type high-quality windows, and only two produced "B"-type. Mostly, Soviet factories supplied this second type, which was equivalent to "C"-type in the international market. The factories didn't produce especially for export, so that if ten factories exported glass in 1960, fifteen were exporting in 1963.[109] This forced the ministry to sell different types of glass in the same market; for example, an order to Burma of 186,000 cubic meters had to be met by six different factories. "For the gainful use of foreign market conjunctures and the expansion of exports of our glass," the report suggested, "the production of decorated glass, as well as jalousie glass for export should be organized this year." This, however, would require the import of the necessary equipment from the West, which both Gosplan and Russia's economic council approved.[110]

A year later, new opportunities arose in the United States, where there was the possibility of selling 2.5 million cubic meters of glass for 1.3 million rubles in convertible currency. However, there was not enough quality glass to meet American demand. American companies would only accept glass from the Lisichanskii factory of the Donets *sovnarkhoz* in Ukraine; however that factory could only allocate for export 800,000 cubic meters, compared to the two million the ministry needed to cover demand.[111]

[109] GARF, f. 5446, op. 98, d. 1444, ll. 38–39.

[110] Ibid., l. 40. Here the Ministry of Foreign Trade may have been more successful in achieving their goals, as glass exports fell in 1963, in keeping with the ministry's assessments of problems that year, but rose in later years, perhaps as a result of the imported equipment. The amounts still fell well short of expectations, selling less than half the intended amount in 1963 (2,303 cubic meters) and 3,849 cubic meters in 1964, less than they had sold three years earlier, and a little more than half what they planned to sell in 1964. See *Vneshniaia torgovlia SSSR za 1965 god*, 32. Also interesting is the higher number given in the statistical compendium compared to the report for glass sold in 1962. The number is 10 percent higher (3959 compared to 3586). See *Vneshniaia torgovlia SSSR za 1962 god*, 28.

[111] GARF, f. 5446, op. 98, d. 1446, l. 87. Affairs seemed to have remained as they were, with Americans purchasing most of the 800,000 cubic meters the Ukrainian *sovnarkhoz* offered. The next year, however, they doubled their purchases in the Soviet Union and seemingly did so at a higher price,

The lessons of engagement: Polishing commercial practice

A series of reports from the agency for perspective planning (Gosekonomsovet) in the early 1960s detailed the continued enthusiasm for involvement in the world economy, calling for greater Soviet participation in the world division of labor while at the same time trying to devise ways to make Soviet trade more responsive to international markets and hence more profitable.[112] One suggestion was to make foreign trade more continuous. The center's monopoly of foreign trade, along with its insistence in planning it from the beginning of each year, made it less responsive to the real-time needs of the Soviet economy. It also caused the Ministry of Foreign Trade to be less agile in taking advantage of particular profitable junctures in the world economy, a perennial problem that both Mikoyan and Gosplan officials often criticized.[113] One such complaint, for example, had a Gosplan official bemoaning the ministry's unsatisfactory and wasteful efforts in importing oranges, which were more advantageously bought in the first quarter of a given year. In 1962, however, the ministry had been too slow in its work, causing wasteful additional expenses as well as orange shortages "even" in Moscow and Leningrad.[114]

But perhaps most importantly, foreign trade was often not efficiently coordinated, causing sudden interruptions in imports for lack of convertible currency. In drawing plans for imports, the Foreign Trade Ministry, Gosplan, and GKES (the Soviet foreign aid agency) would be made to propose ways of funding those imports with exported goods. When buying advanced machinery on credit, a detailed schedule on how the machinery

indicating some measure of success on the part of the Ministry of Foreign Trade in organizing higher quality exports. See *Vneshniaia torgovlia SSSR za 1965 god*, 320.

112 RGAE, f. 7, op. 3, d. 507, ll. 7–9. The agency in question was Gosekonomsovet SSSR, which took over the function of preparing long-term perspective plans that had formerly been Gosplan's purview as the agency for short-term and long-term plannning. The split of these two functions lasted only a few years, during which time Gosplan maintained its more influential function of short-term, "current" (*tekushchii*) planning.

113 By way of example, a 1963 Gosplan report concisely repeated these criticisms. It complained that the work at the ministry was not yet at a high enough standard of commercial efficiency. The ministry and its subsidiaries "rarely carry out initiatives and do not make enough proposals on the favorable use of market junctures in the selling and purchasing of individual goods, and make mistakes and blunders in their commercial work. The Ministry of Foreign Trade inadequately regulates the balance of payments, and as a result the Soviet Union is indebted to some countries (Argentina, Austria, etc.) and is owed significant debts by others (UAR, Afghanistan, Guinea, etc.)." See RGAE, f. 4372, op. 65, d. 407, ll. 24–27.

114 GARF, f. 5446, op. 96, d. 1161, l. 43. The oranges were imported from capitalist countries, usually in the Mediterranean. Shortages were also being felt in factories that made use of oranges in their products.

was to be brought into use would be strictly required.[115] Furthermore, the Ministry of Foreign Trade was asked to be more discerning in determining the most profitable market conditions when selling foreign currency-earning commodities.[116]

These proposals, along with many others of the same ilk, would be repeated in one form or another, ever more vigorously, throughout much of the decade. They were tied in to the larger economic reforms Khrushchev initiated to make Soviet production more rational and more responsive to domestic demand. They proved to be on the whole rather quixotic, but nevertheless they required the different bureaucratic agencies to establish their purpose and stake their competence. In the case of Gosekonomsovet's perspective planning of foreign trade, the main tasks were to promote the following three points:

1. The development of productive forces and improvement in the well-being of the population; the profitable use of the international division of labor in the interests of guaranteeing the needs of the economy of the USSR in the kind of machines and equipment, raw materials and consumer goods that can be delivered from other countries in exchange for nationally-produced goods, thus economizing expenses in capital, time and labor.
2. The strengthening of the economic base of the world socialist system on the foundation of an expedient and economically effective system of an international socialist division of labor.
3. The broadening of the base of peaceful coexistence with the capitalist countries and above all the strengthening of the political and economic independence of the developing countries, their gradual disengagement from the economic capitalist system and rapprochement with the countries of the communist camp.[117]

The third task harkened back to the optimistic self-righteousness that still persisted in the leadership, especially with regard to the possibilities in the decolonizing world, where the leadership was still convinced the Soviet Union could serve as a model of socio-economic development.

[115] RGAE, f. 7, op. 3, d. 808, l. 27.

[116] Ibid. In the late 1950s and early 1960s, the Foreign Trade Ministry was not very dynamic in showing initiative. The dynamism more often came from the Department of Foreign Trade and Foreign Economic Relationships of the Communist Party, oftentimes from Mikoyan himself, and sometimes from the corresponding Gosplan and state departments, as we shall see.

[117] RGAE, f. 7, op. 3, d. 808, ll. 34–39.

The tremendous explosion of Soviet foreign trade up to then had, after all, occurred under the auspices of central planning, a fact that denoted the seeming superiority of central planning even in the development of foreign trade. Rather than an economic liberalization of current trade practices, the suggestions were to be thought of as a refinement. This was not some form of liberal revisionism, or the convergence toward a more market-oriented system that many in the Left in the West were anxious for. In fact, the changes would require more planning, not less, with the qualification of a more careful consideration for the balance of payments, cash flow, and a generally more informed attitude on the part of the Ministry of Foreign Trade.

In 1961, Soviet officials were still confident in not just the economic, but also the moral superiority of Soviet trade practices vis-à-vis the West. At that early time, an internal Gosekonomsovet report could still posit to the agency's leadership that Soviet foreign trade's obvious lack of weight as a percentage of world trade was not an indicator of its lack of attractiveness. After all, it noted, the monopolistic practices of American companies in the underdeveloped countries were not reflected in the statistics of world trade; as a case in point, the trade of American monopolies with their subsidiaries in South America was one and a half times the amount of trade between these countries and the United States, the implication being that that particular statistical marker – participation in world trade – was oftentimes unhelpful.[118] Despite lesser overall production, the report went on, "the volume of trade between the Soviet Union and East Germany already exceeds the foreign trade turnover between the United States and West Germany," which "directly reflects the advantage of the new type of international economic relations."[119] These were the rightful considerations in determining Soviet success in the economic confrontation between socialism and capitalism, particularly in their coming competition for influence in the former colonized and dependent countries, the report concluded.[120]

The Soviets' first, sustained commercial encounter with the West had begun to challenge some fundamental assumptions in the Kremlin about the efficiency of the Soviet Union's just, egalitarian economy and the bankruptcy of the West's unjust system. But optimism still reigned; transcendent success required only a few tweaks in the system and a little more oversight.

[118] RGAE, f. 7, op. 3, d. 808, l. 6.

[119] Ibid. By "new" one must presume the author of the report meant "Soviet."

[120] Ibid., l. 5.

Conclusion

A 1955 planning report for the Sixth Five-Year Plan laid out the foundations upon which the globalization of the Soviet economy would thrive. Foreign trade would develop "upon the import demands and export resources of the national economy of the Soviet Union during the sixth Five-Year Plan; upon the further development of the national economies of the people's democratic countries and the broadening of economic cooperation with these countries on the basis of a more rational division of labor; upon the development of political and economic relations with the capitalist countries under conditions of the changed international environment; and upon the further widening of commercial relations with neighboring countries and economically underdeveloped countries."[121] It was a simple plan, a general guideline for the political economy of Soviet foreign relations.

It is no coincidence that Soviet trade and world trade in the 1950s followed parallel paths. The Soviet Union was the second or third fastest growing big economy in the 1950s, behind, or alongside, Japan and West Germany, and much like those two celebrated economies, its trade expanded a great deal faster than world trade. As noted earlier, trade turnover growth during the first half of the decade was 87 percent, compared to 38 percent for world trade. Both West Germany and Japan doubled their foreign trade turnover during this time.[122]

I argue that this is more than a mere coincidence. Soviet institutions were well suited for, indeed were founded around, the mobilization of surplus peasant labor and its provision with capital, which was accomplished via soaring investment rates achieved through the extreme depression of consumption.[123] As is usual in large countries, trade did not play much of a role in the Soviet Union's economic growth at this time; in this almost purely domestic achievement, coercion and surveillance were everything, and these only started to be undermined by Khrushchev's reforms late in the 1950s.[124]

121 RGANI, f. 5, op. 30, d. 113, l. 76.

122 RGANI, f. 5, op. 30, d. 113, l. 71. Then again, their benefactor and biggest trade partner, namely the United States, encompassed an aberrant proportion of the world economy at the time.

123 For a good discussion that relates this standard explanation to the end of Soviet growth after 1970 see Robert C. Allen, *Farm to Factory. A Reinterpretation of the Soviet Industrial Revolution* (Princeton: Princeton University Press, 2003), chapter 10. Allen stresses the importance of the end of surplus labor as the main factor in the Soviet Union's declining growth. But there was still plenty in the 1950s.

124 The argument of the collapse of the monitoring regime as the main factor for the decline of the Soviet economy has been most explicitly made by Mark Harrison in "Coercion, Compliance and the Collapse of the Soviet Command Economy," *Economic History Review* 55:3 (2002): 397–433. But it also figures prominently in Khanin's "The 1950s – The Triumph of the Soviet Economy,"

In other words, the Soviet Union did not benefit directly from America's hegemonic supervision of the world economy in the way that some American allies did. But contrary to the precepts of a narrative that stresses the superpower military and ideological confrontation, the Soviets were beneficiaries of a stable and open world economy constructed by America's hegemonic power. The Soviet leadership did not want to stand aside as the rest of the world became more interconnected economically; in other words the Soviets did not consider "an autarkic trade policy as the most suitable adjunct to their development planning," as the current consensus goes.[125] Their position not only on the economic, but also on the political benefits of trade was in effect very similar to that of Western leaders. In fact, in the context of a Bretton Woods system under the constraints of a dollar shortage, Western leaders often proved less liberal in their approach to trade than the Soviets. Nevertheless, the liberal order established in the postwar period, from which Stalin at first was made to absent the Soviet Union for geopolitical security reasons, had started to bear fruit by the mid-1950s. And the Soviets, now led by Nikita Khrushchev, had made it publicly known that they wanted to peacefully coexist. They wanted in, at least to the extent that the Soviet system could participate.

The terms they proposed to the industrialized nations were reasonable. They wanted to resume the Soviet Union's traditional trade with them, which usually entailed an exchange of primary commodities for industrial goods. The main force working against this reconnection was a financial and commercial system that was still gestating. In the second half of the 1950s, dollar shortages, though quickly moving toward excess, were still compelling governments to keep a tight control over their balance of payments. This both constrained economic intercourse – especially relations between private firms and the Soviet government – and paradoxically encouraged Europe and Japan to explore the opportunity to conserve hard currency by establishing trade with the Soviet Union on a clearing basis.

These constraints attenuated with the 1958 move to currency convertibility in Europe. But as trade grew, the Soviets began to experience the challenges of success. Domestic industry clamored for technologically superior foreign products, leading the Kremlin into efforts to rationalize

and even in cruder form as far back as Gregory Grossman, "Soviet Growth: Routine, Inertia and Pressure," *The American Economic Review* 50:2 (1960): 62–72.

[125] A quote from my default standard textbook on the world economy, Kenwood and Lougheed, *The Growth of the International Economy*. I do not mean to insist on my criticism of this particular text because of its inadequacy; to the contrary, I use it precisely because it is a reasonably reliable text and representative of a widely held view.

import priorities. The desire for commercial exchange was fast exceeding the ability of the country to quench it. It is at this point that the Kremlin would begin to more purposefully elaborate a political economy and a relationship with the non-communist world – as a peddler of energy and other primary commodities – that would prevail over the more ephemeral and contrived ideological antagonism of the Cold War.

CHAPTER 4

Maelstrom:
The decolonization vortex

Soviet relations with the former European colonies did not begin in a vacuum. Countries in the emerging Third World were already enmeshed in an intricate web of economic relations with their former colonial masters, and the calculus the leaders of these young countries had to make in seeking new relations was as frequently economic as it was political. The world's political discourse they confronted may have been bipolar, but their economic choices were almost always overwhelmed by the preponderance of the Western economies, which accounted for more than two-thirds of world economic production. The Soviet Union, an economically humble newcomer to the world arena, would quickly see that its options in the Third World were already circumscribed by the overwhelming network of economic relations that extended from long-established centers in the industrialized world. Consider the following three situations.

In February 1958, Indian Ambassador to the Soviet Union K. P. S. Menon, along with a relative of India's Prime Minister Jawaharlal Nehru, visited Iosif Kuz'min, head of Gosplan at the time. The discussion revolved around India's need for Soviet industrial imports and the expansion of Indian–Soviet trade; it had been eleven years since India's independence and a mere seven since Nehru started the country's economy on developmental five-year plans. The Indians explained that the idea was to develop import-substituting industries that would become the catalysts of Indian economic independence from the West.[1] This was music to Kuz'min's ears because it dovetailed quite nicely with Soviet foreign economic objectives in their relations with the South.[2] Kuz'min told the Indian delegation that he supported that policy and the room grew cozy in the warmth of a simple understanding: expanding trade between India and the Soviet Union was to everyone's clear advantage.

[1] RGAE, f. 4372, op. 57, d. 384, ll. 189–92.

[2] As will be discussed later in the chapter.

Was this India's momentous turn toward an economic and geopolitical alliance with the Soviet Union? The snag was this: India's import-substitution strategy had caused the government to incur an increasing amount of debt with Western banks, up to a billion dollars a year during the Second Five-Year Plan, which it would have to start paying off during the next Five-Year Plan.[3] Two years into the Second Five-Year Plan and already dangerously low in foreign reserves, the Indians realized that they were unable to continue purchasing industrial equipment from the West, which was necessary to meet the goals of the plan. The Indians suggested trade with the Soviets could be done on barter terms, and couldn't the Soviets offer credit and consider buying Indian goods right away so that India may buy Soviet industrial equipment later?[4] The air in the room grew frosty and businesslike once more, as Kuz'min offered a diplomatically evasive response.

Or consider this episode in Cairo in September 1962, in an office at the Egyptian Ministry of the Economy. That is where Soviet Trade Representative to Egypt F. K. Kokanbaev found himself seeking an explanation as to why Egypt was not fulfilling its responsibilities to the Soviet Union in deliveries of cotton as stipulated in the long-term trade agreement signed between the two countries, which specified the export of 75,000 tons of cotton. Kokanbaev learned that the Egyptians had been selling cotton in Western markets, even as they continued to vacillate on the exact amount they would export to the Soviet Union, agreement be damned.[5] Well, Egyptian Deputy Minister of the Economy Zakaria Taufik could not tell his Soviet guest anything about that, but he could say this much: either the Soviets lower the prices of their exports, or Egypt will find it hard to keep its prices for cotton and might end up selling less to the Soviet Union than had been agreed.[6] Kokanbaev retorted that prices for Egyptian cotton were already 7 to 10 percent higher than Sudanese prices, to which the Egyptian deputy minister dismissively answered that they had always successfully competed with Sudan. Oh, and before you leave, may I remind the Soviet Union not to reexport Egyptian cotton into the world market?

Finally, consider Cuba in July 1963. The young revolutionary island was asking the Soviet Ministry of Foreign Trade for spare parts for their buses. A mere two years after the United States imposed a total embargo on

[3] RGAE, f. 4372, op. 57, d. 384, ll. 189–92 [4] Ibid. [5] RGAE, f. 413, op. 13, d. 8790, ll. 115–16.

[6] The total sold that year ended up indeed lower. The cotton imported amounted to about 68,000 tons. See Ministry of Foreign Trade, *Vneshniaia torgovlia SSSR za 1963 god. Statisticheskii obzor* (Moscow: Vneshtorgizdat, 1964), 246.

Cuba, Cuba's American-produced GMC buses were breaking down, and they could not be repaired for lack of spare parts. As it turned out, the diesel engines manufactured at the Yaroslavl' Motor Plant were very similar, and the Cubans requested their import.[7]

In every one of these situations, the established economic relationships between the powerful, industrialized countries of the West and the newly independent countries of the South, shaped the affairs and demarcated the limits of the Soviet Union's economic relationships with the South. The Indians had sought complete economic autonomy but only succeeded in incurring debts with the West that encouraged their hesitant turn to the Soviet Union; the Egyptians sold cotton to the Soviet Union only as long as they could get significantly better terms from the Soviets than from the otherwise preferable international markets; and Cuba's close relation with the Soviet Union was forged in its absolute, American-engineered rejection from the world economy, a rejection as essential to Cuba's situation in 1963 as its economic and technological dependence on the United States had been only a few years earlier. And always for the Soviets and their newfound friends in the South, the struggle to circumvent or at least appease the inescapable need for currency printed by the United States Department of the Treasury.

Charybdis

The archival evidence does not reveal any kind of master strategy or even a general aggressive inclination on the part of the Soviet Union to decisively influence the development of Third World countries to their advantage in the 1950s.[8] There was no great Communist crusade. Indeed, the Soviet Union's choice of countries on which to lavish goodwill, countries such as India, Egypt, and Indonesia, were often much too large and politically pluralistic to be easily influenced, as the West had known

[7] GARF, f. 5446, op. 97, d. 1366, ll. 12–13. A previous request had been turned down because the factory did not have the funds necessary to produce spare parts for Cuba. The Yaroslavl plant's engine line had been reverse-engineered during World War II from the GMC trucks that started landing in the Soviet Union in 1943 through Lend-Lease. A second generation of engines was not developed at the plant until 1961, so it was no wonder the Cubans found the engines similar. See Lev Shugurov, "Tri pokoleniia Iaroslavskiikh dizelei," *Za rulem* 11 (1991), 6–7.

[8] A point that has been made by the few scholars who have looked into Soviet archival material on aid. See Ragna Boden, "Cold War Economics: Soviet Aid to Indonesia," *Journal of Cold War Studies* 10:3 (2008): 110–28 and more grudgingly Sergey Mazov, *A Distant Front in the Cold War. The USSR in West Africa and the Congo, 1956–1964* (Stanford: Stanford University Press, 2010). Its latest iteration is in Jonathan Haslam, *Russia's Cold War. From the October Revolution to the Fall of the Wall* (New Haven: Yale University Press, 2011).

for some time – and conveniently forgot when disapproving of developments there. The closest thing to an ideologically determined strategy is the view that Soviet economic relations should generally foster the growth of the public sector, and that economic decision-making should be centralized. This was nothing particularly subversive. The belief in the transformational power of the state to encourage economic development was widespread – even in the rich, liberal countries that practiced economic aid to poorer countries in ways that benefited urban elites and state power.[9] Indeed, for one celebrated economist it was not even a matter of belief, but timing and economic structure; Alexander Gerschenkron described the simple truth that late developers will experience greater centralization in economic decision-making in order to organize fast, industrial development: the later the industrialization drive and the more backward the country, the greater the intervention of the state will be.[10] It would not have surprised him to find in the Soviet archives letter after letter of impatient solicitations of Soviet involvement and industrial technology. Processing this industrial aid through centralized organization was a matter of logistical common sense, though Gerschenkron also calculated that growth ideologies would grow hand in hand with this institutional reorganization. The Soviets need not have responded to these entreaties, but they did. Such was the discursive power of the Cold War mirage. The prestige from which the Soviets derived their legitimacy was on the line. Of course, we have already noted a similar logic in the Soviet Union's accommodation to the technological and developmental hierarchies of the liberal world economy, where Soviets fulfilled contracted agreements without regard to their present benefit. Prestige always seems a fickle mistress to newcomers with no standing, and the Soviet leadership of the 1950s and 1960s was as keen to oblige it in the South as in the West.

It is often intimated in the historical treatments of this period that the Third World was a kind of tabula rasa. Ostensibly lacking the analytical tools and general dynamism to assess the problems besieging their countries, Third World leaders are often depicted as merely trying to copy

[9] A classic example is Walt Whitman Rostow, *The Stages of Economic Growth: A Non-Communist Manifesto* (Cambridge: Cambridge University Press, 1960). A useful retelling of the origins of modernization theory in the state interventions of the New Deal is in David Ekbladh, *The Great American Mission. Modernization and the Construction of an American World Order* (Princeton: Princeton University Press, 2010).

[10] Alexander Gerschenkron, *Economic Backwardness in Historical Perspective* (Cambridge: Harvard University Press, 1962).

one model or the other.[11] Their repeated declarations to the contrary were either ignored or not believed; the only lens that mattered was the one that saw the world in two camps fighting one struggle. In fact, all over the developing world we see generally the outcome Gerschenkron predicted: the growth of strong states that interfered robustly in the social and economic spheres. In other words, implementing one model or the other was not simply a matter of choice for a country's political elite; it had deeper historical and structural roots.

Scholars of colonialism and postcolonialism have pointed out many of the causes for the subsequent political development of the former colonies. One oft-mentioned development is the rise of military regimes in the former colonies. Military organizations had ready-made institutions to ease into, courtesy of the former empires; or they developed locally into formidable institutions during the struggle against colonialism. At any rate, the colonial experience was not conducive to the rise of civil society, economic pluralism, or the development of participatory institutions through which to exercise power.[12] Another general development throughout the Third World, and one that does not necessarily find its origins in the postcolonial condition, is the general rise of expansive civil bureaucracies, which arose to stifle the free market in such disparate places as Pakistan, Brazil, Iran, Taiwan, and Turkey – all of them part of the "free world."

In examining the cultural history of relations between India and the United States, Andrew J. Rotter noted many of the differences among the worldviews of the people of the two nations, and how these marked their relations. He argued that American policy outlook was expansive, based on the American cultural drive for expanding the frontier. India, on the other hand, never looked beyond its borders. For Indians, space was contracted within their borders; they had often been dominated from abroad and had come to see the world outside as dangerous. Their concepts of governance also differed, with the Indians measuring the legitimacy of the state by how well it took care of its people, thus encouraging paternalism, nepotism, and pervasive state intervention in the economy.[13] Needless to

[11] "The 'third world' was in a position to choose during the Cold War," writes Gaddis in *We Now Know. Rethinking Cold War History* (New York: Oxford University Press, 1997), 154, an opinion that was echoed through much of the historiography, one Gaddis himself is echoing.

[12] For a critique on the limits of "postcolonial" studies, but one that doesn't put this standard explanation in doubt, see Aijaz Ahmad, "Postcolonialism: What's in a Name?" in Roman de la Campa, Ann E. Kaplan and Michael Sprinker, eds., *Late Imperial Culture* (London: Verso, 1995).

[13] Andrew J. Rotter, *Comrades at Odds. The United States and India, 1947–1964* (Ithaca: Cornell University Press, 2000).

say, the origins of these developments do not lie in the Cold War. The Indian people did not need the lessons of the Soviet model to convince them of the desirability of a big, protective state.

Yet the lazy Cold War impression that the Third World countries wanted to emulate Soviet success, and built institutions and carried out policy accordingly, lives on. This impression persists even though few countries actually fit this picture, and those that do – Cuba, North Korea, North Vietnam, and China – had one experience in common: intense and sustained American military and economic aggression. No other country in the Third World, and certainly no other country of geopolitical importance, instituted anything recognizably Soviet: an attempt at the allocation of most resources, price-setting for all domestic goods, forced mobilization of labor on an important scale, etc. Most countries of the global South nationalized industry and resources, but in the American imagination this was an ominous sign of Soviet ideological indoctrination only if those countries also accepted weapons or engaged in a vehement, anti-Western discourse (think Saudi Arabia verus Egypt or Senegal versus Guinea). Unfortunately for scholars of the Cold War, who would like to claim all post-World War II history to 1989, the origins and nature of the socio-economic and political changes in these countries do not lie with Soviet subversion and the bipolar competition.[14] The origins of these developments were overwhelmingly domestic as well as systemic of the world economy. Decolonization, not a bipolar struggle of ideas, set the waters roiling. And the effect was that of a whirlpool drawing countries into the vortex formed by rapid political change and social revolution – as revolutions in Europe had done ever since the French invented the concept.

A quick look at the Soviet archives from the mid 1950s reveals the beginning of what would become a constant flow of petitions from the poor nations arriving to Gosplan and the Council of Ministers for aid and advice, not all of which could be fulfilled. When the Afghans were not asking for the Soviets to make haste in helping to organize the production of elevators and mills,[15] it was the head of Burma (now Myanmar) asking

[14] An argument made in Odd Arne Westad, *The Global Cold War. Third World Interventions and the Making of Our Times* (Cambridge: Cambridge University Press, 2005), even if Westad still sees the Cold War as a major perpetuator of conflict during the period.

[15] RGANI, f. 5, op. 30, d. 71, l. 56. See also RGANI, f. 5, op. 30, d. 172, ll. 180–82 on Afghans asking for aid in prospecting for oil and gas. GKES argues that the Soviet Union should feel compelled to help both because it is in the Soviet interest to prospect for oil and gas in countries adjacent to the Soviet Union, and because the request was initiated by the Afghans. Yet again, Soviet prestige was on the line.

for architects,[16] or Guinea asking for whatever the Soviets might offer.[17] As time passed, the flow would grow ever wider, geographically and in volume.

Furthermore, starting in the mid 1950s, poor countries, particularly former colonies, which did not have very diversified trade at the time, were knocking on the Soviets' door to initiate new trade channels. When Khrushchev went on his boisterous first trip to Southeast Asia in 1955 to talk about the successes of the Soviet Union and its commitment to the principle of peaceful coexistence, Prime Minister U Nu of Burma wanted to know only one thing: what concretely could the Soviet Union offer in terms of trade, and how quickly could trade be developed between the two countries.[18] The same went for Indonesia, which in 1954 gave its ambassador the main task of developing direct trade with the Soviet Union so as to weaken the country's dependence on the Dutch for their international commercial needs.[19] This was again the reason the Moroccans approached the Soviet trade representative in Paris in 1957 with a plan to obviate the French and establish direct trade between the two countries.[20] Of course it is true that during the heady years of the 1950s decolonization drive, the Soviet Union certainly had lessons to impart on how best to develop a powerful and reasonably effective centralized state, which we know to have been a popular project throughout most of the Third World. But more immediate and lasting, however, was the role of the Soviet Union in the Third World as a mediator weakening the rigors of a taxing world economy that offered, from the point of view of poor countries, undesirable terms of economic exchange.

Understanding Soviet aid

Semyon Skachkov was the longtime head of the State Committee for Foreign Economic Relations (*Gosudarstvennyi komitet po vneshnim ekonomicheskim sviaziam* [GKES]), the Soviet aid agency. This is what he wrote in a 1959 report to the Central Committee by way of justifying his agency's work: "Foreign economic relations, if built on the foundation of equality and mutual benefit, promote economic progress and lead to a mutual understanding among states and peoples, advance the weakening

16 RGANI, f. 5, op. 30, d. 116, ll. 4–10
17 RGANI, f. 5, op. 30, d. 309, ll. 86–90.
18 RGANI, f. 5, op. 30, d. 116, ll. 228–34.
19 RGANI, f. 5, op. 30, d. 71, ll. 61–62.
20 RGANI, f. 5, op. 30, d. 224, ll. 54–58. The Moroccan case is expanded upon in chapter 6.

of international pressure and improve relations among governments."[21] The historical experience of many governments, the report continued, "convincingly proves that this task of progress cannot be achieved without the construction of domestic industry and the development of a diverse economy."[22] To this end, the Soviet Union was also willing to shoulder its share of the white man's burden and refashion the poor countries of the world in its industrial image.

The parallels in the philosophy of aid between the liberal West and the communist East were striking.[23] They were also not acknowledged; as in almost everything else, the Soviets represented themselves as the converse of capitalism. Their worldview was one dependency theorists would recognize. In their own self-representation, the "goal and terms of Soviet help to underdeveloped countries differs favorably from the help of capitalist countries. Our goal is clear: we strive to help underdeveloped countries ensure their economic independence, more quickly stand on their own two feet, create a modern national industry, more fully utilize their natural resources, lift agricultural production and so contribute to improving the lives of the people of these countries."[24] This, they argued, stood in sharp contrast to the position of capitalist countries, which were interested only in stimulating raw material production for export and reinforcing their monopolistic position so as to draw these economies to theirs in an exploitative embrace.[25]

And yet when put into practice, these policies were the same as those of the West. They both focused on the hardware, as it were, of the developing economies through large-scale infrastructure and industrial projects – a far cry from the microlending and educational "software" approach that is in fashion today. Although both countries tended to emphasize large, engineering projects, the Soviet Union supported import-substitution much more self-consciously than the United States. As Skachkov's report envisaged, Soviet credits, to be repaid in twelve years from the moment of the project's completion at 2.5 percent interest, were directed to the construction of enterprises that would not only pay off the debt in that time, but would also create capital for the further development of the economy.[26]

[21] RGANI, f. 5, op. 30, d. 305, l. 117. [22] Ibid.

[23] A quick rundown of this position can be read in Westad, *The Global Cold War*, 31–35.

[24] Ibid., l. 120.

[25] Ibid. We will see in chapter 5 that this view would change by the mid-1960s, as the Soviets started to focus their aid on the stimulation of the aid recipient's raw material production as well as on the growth of industries that would encourage the importation of Soviet products.

[26] Ibid., l. 121.

Most damningly, as with their rich, liberal counterparts, the Soviets insisted on having their aid credits spent on Soviet industrial products, thus stimulating Soviet domestic production rather than production and employment in recipient countries.

But despite the similarities in worldview, in what they understood to be the role of economic relations in world politics, and in practice, there were several differences. One immediate difference was in the role of recipient governments in economic relations. In extending aid to poor countries, the Soviets sought to strengthen the public sector of the target country, whereas Western countries insisted on strengthening the private sector, even as they often followed a more confused policy.[27] India is the most famous case in point. Aid from the West was usually channeled through the Aid-India Consortium, which included eleven countries and the World Bank, and which disbursed aid to a mix of public and private sector projects.[28] The Soviets, however, supported only large – and conspicuous – industrial projects, sometimes muscling out private Indian consultants and subcontractors that the Indian government wanted to involve in development projects.[29]

Most often, however, Soviet aid-giving idiosyncrasies arose from a lack of power projection capability and a lack of clear interests. A lack of clear purpose was behind one real and important difference between East and West, and it was one the Soviets liked to advertise: Communist investments did not entail ownership of the enterprises they built in poor countries; this meant no repatriated profits and no continued foreign presence.[30] The utility of such a no-strings-attached approach to aid would

[27] RGANI, f. 5, op. 30, d. 272, l. 177. The report also makes clear that in particular circumstances they would also provide aid to private enterprises, as long as they belonged to representatives of "progressive circles" within the country. See also RGANI, f. 5, op. 30, d. 305, l. 123. This is all to be distinguished from the "state sector." By public sector I mean state ownership of industry, rather than provision of services, such as education, that are accepted by all to be within the state's purview, and was often also supported by Western aid.

[28] Jagdish Bhagwati and Padma Desai, *India Planning for Industrialization. Industrialization and Trade Policies since 1951* (London: Oxford University Press, 1970), 185.

[29] A later example, the Bokaro steel plant built in the 1960s, best illustrates this dynamic. The Soviets stepped in to build it after the United States pulled out because of congressional concerns that it was encouraging the wrong sort of development in India. Upon taking the reins of the project, the Soviets controversially forced out of the project the prestigious Indian engineering consulting firm, M. N. Dastur & Co., which had been offering its services to the project for a decade before the Soviets even stepped in. The Soviets preferred to provide turnkey projects, or complete plants, and disliked to work with local partners, particularly if they were of the private, capitalist persuasion. For a good discussion of this aid project see Padma Desai, *The Bokaro Steel Plant. A Study of Soviet Economic Assistance* (Amsterdam: North-Holland Publishing Company, 1972).

[30] RGANI, f. 5, op. 30, d. 305, l. 122.

be reconsidered early in the 1960s, as we shall see. Furthermore, as Khrushchev often pointed out in his memoirs when speaking about aid projects approved during his rule, the Soviets were also weary of having natives work under Soviet management. Direct Soviet management of aid projects might lead to unwelcome conflicts with the recipient country's workers, which would reflect badly on the first proletariat state on earth.[31] And so rather than build on a contract basis, acting as employers as other aid donors did, the Soviet leadership often sent technicians, engineers, and administrators to give technical direction and manage equipment deliveries; the plans were, of course, also Soviet. The only profit they derived, besides the export of goods and services, was the 2.5 percent interest on the money they lent to build the different factories and enterprises. Many scholars have argued, however, that Soviet aid was often geared at introducing Soviet products to new markets and attempting to create technical and technological dependencies. Intended or not, a state of affairs of that sort was achieved in military aid, where even to this day Russia benefits from Soviet-era technological dependencies. Development aid, however, neither produced nor was intended to produce a relationship of dependence; in this matter, as in most others, the conspiratorial argument is not borne out by the archives.

On one issue, at least, Soviet avowed motives had a salutary tinge of self-interest. It had to do with public relations, and GKES laid it out in a set of recommendations for the expansion of economic relations with developing countries given to the Central Committee in December 1958. Not only was profit-making in poor countries against the principles of the Soviet Union, GKES argued, it could disorient progressive circles within these countries and could furnish arguments against the growth of economic cooperation with the Soviet Bloc.[32] That rationale illustrated a modicum of strategic thinking, but also a telling anxiety: Soviet policymakers had a deeply ingrained sense of inferiority when it came to power politics. And why shouldn't they? They were, after all, fundamentally less consequential than the United States, with an economy perhaps equivalent to, or at most slightly bigger than, that of Great Britain or France in GDP terms. The 1958 GKES recommendations bespoke an implicit sense of

[31] Khrushchev mentions this concern throughout his memoirs, but particularly in relation to the Bhilai metallurgical plant and the Aswan high dam in Egypt, both large projects which the Indians and Egyptians respectively asked be done on a contractual basis. See Sergei Khrushchev, ed., *Memoirs of Nikita Khrushchev. Statesman*, vol. 3 (University Park: Pennsylvania State University Press, 2007), 772 and 827.

[32] RGANI, f. 5, op. 30, d. 272, l. 178.

weakness and lack of standing: "In relation to [developing] countries," it noted, "the most important task at the moment is the punctual fulfillment of the Soviet Union's responsibilities according to our concluded agreements."[33] Fear of breaking promises and agreements made with poor countries would become an important theme in prioritizing production for aid. If Western powers were constantly balancing the scales between sticks and carrots, the Soviets seemed to not know what sticks were good for.

The GKES warning on the punctual fulfillment of responsibilities was no idle fear. As was the case domestically, so was it for aid exports; inefficiencies were many, and the power relations at play in domestic inter-industry exchange that often kept a lid on these inefficiencies nationally had little purchase when Soviet international credibility was on the line. Rather than making use of the typically Soviet supply expediter (the famous *tolkach*), GKES or whichever other ministry tasked with export responsibilities, could appeal directly to the top to get the issue resolved, usually to Gosplan, the Council of Ministers, or Mikoyan more directly. While the United States and the European powers could afford to dally and politicize their aid as a tool of coercion and discipline, the Soviet Union fretted over delays, disorganization, and general ineptitude, which, as every Soviet official trying to get something done was so quick to point out, might harm the Soviet Union's image in the eyes of the aid recipients.

The inadequacies in the organization of Soviet aid were many, and they often resulted in complaints from the recipient countries. In 1962, for example, Skachkov wrote to the Council of Ministers to complain about the poor oversight work of the Russian Economic Council.[34] The weight of the Russian Republic's production in Soviet aid deliveries had been steadily growing over the years. In 1961, Russian factories were made responsible for delivering the equipment for metallurgical plants to Finland and Cuba. These deliveries should have been finished by the first half of 1963; however, with no oversight from the Russian economic agencies responsible for these factories, Finland received only 29 percent of the promised deliveries by November 1962, delaying construction. Equipment and documentation for the reconstruction of three factories in Cuba was likewise being held up, so that in the first ten months of 1962 only 1,500 rubles of the 4,800 rubles' worth of equipment promised had actually been sent. This story was repeated in Egypt, India, Indonesia, and other countries, Skachkov grumbled.[35]

[33] Ibid. [34] GARF, f. 5446, op. 97, d. 1377, ll. 9–11. [35] Ibid., ll. 12–13.

Other times, it was the tardiness of the preliminary studies needed to start a project that held back Soviet aid. Three different ministries were involved in such preliminary studies for the construction of a quartz sand quarry and an enrichment factory in Iraq for glass and ceramic production.[36] Their already belated conclusions, however, were disputed by the Vladimir *sovnarkhoz*, which was supposed to deliver the necessary equipment for the projects. Furthermore, a full year after the Council of Ministers had greenlit the quarry project the necessary experiments on the enrichment of the quartz sands had yet to be started. The state construction agency was now asking for two years to finish the basic preliminary work.[37]

The Soviet transportation agencies could also delay aid and cause officials to become anxious over broken promises. Before August 1961, Skachkov had given the Ministry of the Sea Fleet note of the aid deliveries to be carried out of the port city of Odessa that month, which amounted to 28,300 tons of cargo to be delivered to far-flung countries like Guinea, Indonesia, Egypt, India, and Iraq.[38] The Ministry of the Sea Fleet had graciously agreed to grant GKES even more cargo space than that – up to 33,600 tons – which in turn would make up for the leftovers of past undelivered aid. However, poor work at the Odessa transshipment point caused about 2,000 train wagons of export goods to accumulate there. Under pressure to get all those delayed exports on their way, the Ministry of the Sea Fleet refused to carry heavy industrial equipment and agricultural machinery. Furthermore the Ministry of Ways of Communication, responsible for the Soviet railway system, announced a general ban on all transports to the congested Odessa port, stopping in its tracks the transportation of necessary equipment for such aid projects as the stadium in Jakarta, the airport in Guinea, and the Neyveli power station in India.[39] Little had changed three months later, when Skachkov appealed directly to Mikoyan to get the Ministry of Ways of Communication to lift its ban on the transport of exports to Odessa, arguing that the amount of aid production exported by GKES was economically insignificant yet politically important.[40]

To be sure, not all Soviet aid was incompetently delivered. In his memoirs Khrushchev recalls the construction of the Bhilai steel mill in

[36] GARF, f. 5446, op. 95. d. 1031, l. 100. Involved in the project along with GKES were the ministries of geology and construction.

[37] Ibid., l. 101.

[38] GARF, f. 5446, op. 95. d. 1031, l. 103.

[39] Ibid., l. 104.

[40] Ibid., ll. 114–15.

India, of all Soviet aid projects second in fame and prestige only to the Aswan Dam. The Indians had asked the (West) Germans and the British, along with the Soviets for help in building three steel mills respectively, and even had them check each other's plans and blueprints before starting on them.[41] The Germans started right away and quickly took the lead.[42] However, Khrushchev was determined that the Soviet steel mill should begin producing steel and iron before that of the Germans, and, as he reports it, so it did in October 1959. Furthermore, production went smoothly and the Indians soon asked to have its capacity increased, a service the Soviets again provided competently.[43]

Nevertheless, the Bhilai steel mill was an exceptional case. Khrushchev further informs us that he followed this particular project personally and assigned as its manager a renowned and able Soviet engineer, V. E. Dymshitz, who had played a prominent role in the construction of such important projects as the Kuznetsk and Magnitogorsk metallurgical plants in the 1930s. Dymshitz went on to retire as a deputy chairman of the Council of Ministers in 1985 after passing through high level posts at Gosplan and other state committees. Dymshitz reported directly to Nehru on the progress of the plant, and the competitive context of the project, an atypical circumstance, virtually guaranteed the Indians a high-level involvement on the part of the Soviets.[44]

More characteristically, the Soviets ran into schedule problems because of the recalcitrance of their own industry. On such occasions, GKES had to call on the highest echelons to get deliveries moving and avoid "undesirable complaints" from the target country.[45] In a typical reaction in

[41] *Memoirs of Nikita Khrushchev*, 769–70. Khrushchev reports that the British had nothing but high praise for the Soviet plans, while Soviet engineers found many faults that needed to be corrected in the British plan. The British plant was in Durgapur in West Bengal and the German plant was built in Rourkela in east central India. All three plants were finished quickly and started production of steel toward the end of 1959, although Khrushchev points out that the German plant in particular encountered many problems and missed production.

[42] Khrushchev's memory on this particular point, however, may have been faulty. A report dating June 14, 1956 from M. Petrenko of Minmetallurgkhimstroia stated that the Germans were in fact the farthest behind schedule, while the British had not yet taken control of the building site. According to the report, almost everyone assumed from the beginning that the Soviet mill would be the first to get built. Construction had not even been started at the time of the report's writing, so I cannot judge for sure whether Khrushchev was accurate or not. See RGANI, f. 5, op. 30, d. 224, ll. 209–11.

[43] It was done a couple of years later, when the Soviets more than doubled the plant's capacity. It was one of the best-performing steel mills in India for decades.

[44] *Memoirs of Nikita Khrushchev*, 771.

[45] The threat of *nezhelatel'nyi pretenzii* was usually how aid officials tried to get the Council of Minister's attention. See for example GARF, f. 5446, op. 94, d. 953, l. 55 for a case involving delayed equipment deliveries for a steel mill in Ceylon (now Sri Lanka).

1962, Mikoyan had to personally write missives to *sovnarkhozy* in Krasnodar, Leningrad, Volgograd, Penza, Barnaul, Cheliabinsk, Sverdlovsk, and the whole of the Ukrainian Republic to make sure they approached GKES to work out ways to make sure the factories they were responsible for provided all the material and equipment needed for the aid agency to carry out its work.[46]

Yet this record of incompetence was auxiliary to a more important detail: Soviet aid, although certainly generous for a financially humble nation, was simply never very extensive. It is estimated that from the end of World War II until its fall, the Soviet Union offered a total of $68 billion in economic aid, of which about $41 billion had been delivered before the fall; this is about the same as the United States provided Israel alone during a similar period.[47] Again India serves as a good example. It is often asserted as a matter of common wisdom that India leaned toward the Soviet camp during the Cold War, and Soviet aid was alternatively seen as a reason and an outcome of that close relationship.[48] Diplomatic statements by Khrushchev and Indian Prime Minister Jawaharlal Nehru, as well as a high-profile aid project or two, are often held up as proof. This speaks only to the remarkable propagandistic success of Soviet aid, which convinced even the academic establishment – as well as the impressionable CIA. Actual figures, as the graphs in figures 4.1 and 4.2 illustrate, tell a different story.

On the question of aid and the political loyalty of India, the grand framework of superpower confrontation once again leads us astray. As I will argue, with respect to both India and Third World countries more broadly, it is the former colonies' inherently weak position in the world economy that was a much more important determinant in its undertakings in the world economic and political arena. The Soviet Union did not, and could not, hope to replace the West as an aid provider and general economic partner in exchange for a geopolitical alliance; they thought this a presumptuous and ludicrous notion. And neither did Third World leaders really hope for such a change in economic orientation, aware as

[46] GARF, f. 5446, op. 96, d. 1178, ll. 1–16.

[47] Both are estimates for economic aid, as distinct from military aid. Quintin V. S. Bach, *Soviet Aid to the Third World. The Facts and Figures* (Sussex: The Book Guild Ltd., 2003), 79 and Clyde R. Mark, "Israel: US Foreign Assistance." Issue Brief for Congress, October 2002: http://www.adc.org/IB85066.pdf. Aid to Israel has constituted about one-sixth of all US aid.

[48] See for example Frieden's casual description of India as a Soviet ally in *Global Capitalism. Its Fall and Rise in the Twentieth Century* (New York: W. W. Norton & Company, 2006), 322, or Vladislav Zubok and Constantine Pleshakov, *Inside the Kremlin's Cold War. From Stalin to Khrushchev* (Cambridge: Harvard University Press, 1996), 231, where Nehru is the "leader of the Non-Aligned movement and a new geopolitical ally of the USSR."

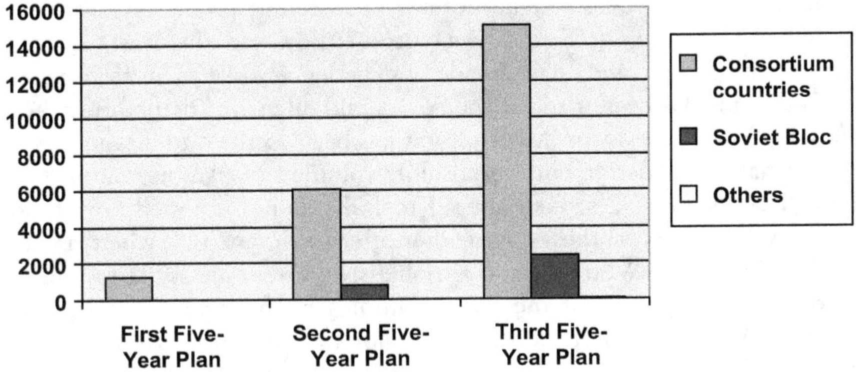

Figure 4.1 Utilized Soviet loans to India, 1951–1966 (in millions of rupees)*
*Calculated from the Economic Survey series, Ministry of Finance, Government of India, available at http://indiabudget.nic.in/previouses.htm

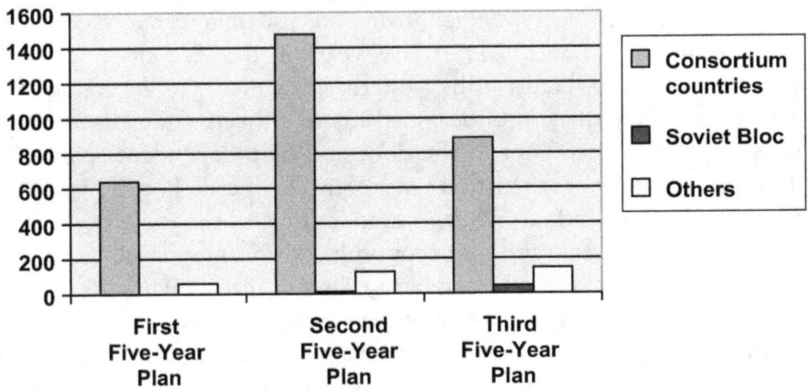

Figure 4.2 Utilized Soviet grants to India, 1951–1966 (in millions of rupees)*
*Ibid.

they quickly became of the limits of Soviet power. Moreover, this would have been anathema to their ambition for full independence. Only the feverish imaginings of American policymakers kept this idea alive – armed as American policymakers were with the lurid estimates of Soviet economic might dreamed up by the CIA. In fact, widening the net of one's trade partners, particularly ones that are not congenitally hostile, has its own rewards; and providing the means that will expedite the realization of normal, profitable trade relations is a reasonable proposition. This is the only immediate context within which the Soviets understood their aid policies. There were also vague notions of fostering a working class that would naturally ally itself to Soviet purpose; however, this was a distant dream, and at any rate a half decade of experience woke them from it.

Too much has been made of the Soviet "aid offensive" that Khrushchev initiated in the mid-1950s. More weight has been ascribed to it than seems appropriate, considering both its absolute volume as well as its volume vis-à-vis Western aid. West German aid to India alone surpassed Soviet aid all the way to 1965, and every year thereafter to the 1980s;[49] where are all the studies on the West German aid offensive? Soviet aid is better understood as a component of the Soviet Union's main strategic priority: its entrance in the world economy as a major trade partner, particularly in the Third World. In fact, Soviet aid barely even passed the threshold of what is considered aid, as opposed to credit-facilitated trade.[50] The United Nations and the Organisation for Economic Co-operation and Development (OECD) define aid as the provision of goods and services with a grant element (GE) of at least 25 percent (an outright grant would have a GE of 100 percent). On average, Soviet aid, usually given as credit with a 2.5 percent interest rate over twelve years, had a GE of 34 percent. This compared rather badly with Western aid, which had an average GE of 90 percent. But then, the idea was not to subvert countries through lavish gifts, but to get a foot in the door and help dependent economies achieve greater autonomy. In this sense, Soviet officials hoped Soviet aid would complement trade to work in tandem toward the same goal.

"The granting of technical and economic aid to underdeveloped countries," argued Skachkov in a December 1958 set of recommendations to the Central Committee, "must necessarily be supplemented and strengthened with the development of extensive trade relations, as only a regulated exchange of goods can serve a stable and fundamental development of economic cooperation between the Soviet Union and the countries of the East. Trade based on the principles of equality and mutual benefit serves as a form of aid from the Soviet Union to the countries of the East, easing for the latter the fight in strengthening their positions in the economic relations with the developed, imperialist governments."[51] Like

[49] Santosh Mehrotra, *India and the Soviet Union. Trade and Technology Transfer* (Cambridge: Cambridge University Press, 1990), 65, as shown in table 4.2. West German aid to the end of the Third Five-Year Plan (that is, to 1966) amounted to 3.42 billion rupees, while Soviet aid was 2.87 billion rupees.

[50] See Bach, *Soviet Aid to the Third World*, 21–26.

[51] Skachkov was writing slightly outside his own competence as head of GKES, the Soviet Union's foreign aid agency. As much as GKES was responsible for exporting aid materials, the institution,

aid, Skachkov continued, trade should support the growth of the public sector, although it should also be used to fortify nationalist elements in the private sector, inasmuch as their strength will lead to the weakening of foreign capital. All these developments would improve the economic position of the Soviet Union because it would give them the chance to buy products they had up to this time been buying in international markets directly from the producing countries, particularly such raw materials and foodstuffs as rubber, cocoa, and leather goods.[52]

Early encounters: Asian whirlpools

We have already noted that the political objectives of Soviet aid were emphatically vague and certainly not building blocks in a global grand strategy for ideological supremacy – or supremacy of any kind. Economic penetration was certainly one of the objectives, and was very much in keeping with the general policy of expanding the network of trade partners, a policy that included the West as much as it included the South. What is not generally noted is the passive nature of this penetration. Admittedly, it is hard to fathom. Under Stalin, the Soviet Union did not seem to care to make economic inroads far from its borders. A change at the top was quickly followed by a string of unprecedented economic agreements with new partners in speedy succession, and unlike Stalin, the new Soviet leaders hurriedly embarked on a series of boastful trips abroad. It stood to reason that the Soviet Union was undergoing a thorough change in its policy toward developing countries, and that this change was undoubtedly the result of a reenergized, internationally-minded leadership seeking to expand beyond its now consolidated empire in Europe. I have been arguing, however, that Soviet trade policy and the ideas around it did not change much from one decade to the other – even if it is true that the last years of Stalin's rule were characterized by a bureaucracy stupefied and petrified with fear. But it's also worth remembering that there was not much of a Third World to trade with before the mid-1950s; in fact, there was not much international trade at all before the 1950s beyond imperial trade, and it was slow to expand and diversify after that. Stalin never lived to see the buds of the coming globalization. More than a change of heart in the leadership, there was a change in the

which itself grew directly out of the Ministry of Foreign Trade, was considered a type of addendum to the latter ministry. RGANI, f. 5, op. 30, d. 272, l. 187.

52 Ibid., ll. 187–88.

opportunities available to them, which breeds its own kind of excitement. If in the 1930s, Soviet discourse on trade had tried to justify a sudden, unwelcome autarky, so it would now try to match the exuberance in the growth and diversity of this renewed age of commerce.

In fact, despite the many narratives that describe the Soviets as active agents in the massive expansion of Soviet economic relations beginning in the mid-1950s, it was more often the governments of the South that initiated and drew Soviet involvement in the form of aid and trade.[53] And it was rare, particularly in the early stages, for the Soviet Union to refuse the requests of these young governments. Decolonization had quickly and inevitably changed perceptions of the world in both Moscow and Washington, and more radically, perceptions of the very identity of Western Europe.[54] Soviet leaders retooled their ideas to match this brisk transformation of the world. They welcomed a change from which they could only gain, given their utter lack of position and influence in the global South. But it would be wrong to characterize the Soviet Union as a superpower expanding its reach and making it global; more often than not, it was the world that was reaching out to the Soviet Union.

The Indonesians were among the first to knock on the Soviets' door. Diplomatic relations with Indonesia were established early in 1950, about a month after its independence from Dutch colonial rule. It wasn't until four years later that the two countries exchanged embassies. The government sent Subandrio, a close associate of President Sukarno, the nationalist leader who had led the revolution against the Dutch. One of his main tasks, Subandrio promptly informed the Soviets upon his arrival in Moscow, was to establish close economic relations between the Soviet Union and Indonesia.[55]

There had been no direct economic relations to speak of between the two countries before, but Subandrio, who had just come from London where he had been ambassador for the last four years, informed the Soviets that in fact they had been buying Indonesian goods in England and Holland for many years. He hoped that direct economic relations with the Soviet Union would weaken Indonesian economic dependence on

[53] A 1959 list of invitations to Khrushchev and their circumstances can be found in RGANI, f. 5, op. 30, d. 308, ll. 95–98. Vojtech Mastny notes this Soviet tendency as well with respect to India in Vojtech Mastny, "The Soviet Union's Partnership with India," *Journal of Cold War Studies* 12:3 (2010): 50–90.

[54] See Kristin Ross, *Fast Cars, Clean Bodies. Decolonization and the Reordering of French Culture* (Cambridge: MIT Press, 1995).

[55] RGANI, f. 5, op. 30, d. 71, l. 61.

Holland and the West more generally.[56] While waiting for the Indonesian secretary of commerce to finish negotiations with the Bulgarians and come to Moscow, Subandrio had been instructed to clarify the Soviet position on that issue, expecting perhaps that Sukarno's harsh treatment of the Indonesian communists might have made all Indonesian overtures unwelcome in the Soviet Union.[57] Furthermore, Subandrio explained, it had been difficult for Indonesia to establish direct trade relations with other developing countries because they were all absolutely dependent on Dutch and English shipping, a problem the Soviets, with their rapidly growing merchant fleet, did not share to the same extent.[58] The Soviets jumped at the chance to get rubber and other raw materials they had been buying in international markets directly from their source, which the Indonesians were happy to exchange for Soviet industrial equipment.

It is difficult to imagine Stalin turning down such a profitable proposition, but then again, he did not. In February 1951, the Indonesian government approached the Soviet trade representatives in both Holland and Sweden to negotiate a trade agreement.[59] They offered rubber, tin, and jute in exchange for agricultural machinery, sewing machines, and other small equipment. They insisted that the Soviets "initiate the issue of a formal request for trade negotiations."[60] Indonesia in Stalin's time was stepping tentatively on the international stage; Indonesian goods were traded mostly through Dutch firms, and Indonesian trade representatives talked with foreign counterparts only as "observers" during Dutch negotiation sessions with other countries. The Soviets nevertheless obliged, and were even willing to talk about military purchases that the Indonesians had requested (although not through the Ministry of Foreign Trade). But the Indonesian government demurred, and Stalin died before Subandrio went to Moscow with a more resolute agenda.[61]

Despite general goodwill on both sides, economic relations with Indonesia did not develop smoothly, and always the initiative remained firmly in Indonesian hands. After Subandrio laid the groundwork, delegations were exchanged with more frequency through 1955 leading to the trade and aid agreement and Sukarno's visit to Moscow in 1956. But the agreement languished in the Indonesian parliament and would not be

[56] Ibid.

[57] See Audrey R. Kahin and George McTurnan Kahin, *Subversion as Foreign Policy. The Secret Eisenhower and Dulles Debacle in Indonesia* (New York: The New Press, 1995) for an account of Sukarno's rule and his policies against the communists.

[58] RGANI, f. 5, op. 30, d. 71, l. 62. [59] RGASPI, f. 84, op. 1, d. 69, l. 61. [60] Ibid.

[61] RGASPI, f. 84, op. 1, d. 73, ll. 53–54.

ratified by factions in government fearful of alienating the United States. Furthermore, by 1957, all imports from the Soviet Union carried out in convertible currency, still the prevalent mode of exchange in Indonesia's largely market economy, were reduced to a minimum. This led to the cancellation of contracts with private Indonesian firms – themselves following government directives to save on hard currency – amounting to about 75 percent of expected Soviet exports to Indonesia for 1957.[62] With the CIA now actively sending covert military and economic help to rebellious army officers on the islands of Sumatra and Sulawesi, the political situation rapidly deteriorated toward the end of that year and into 1958.[63] In the first of many future such instances, cynical American intervention had the effect of sweeping aside the reservations of the army and other members of the Sukarno coalition and creating a consensus in favor of fostering economic relations with the Soviet Union.[64] First the Indonesian government announced it would monopolize the country's foreign trade. Predictably the move proved to be a boon to Soviet exports, which quintupled that year on military purchases and foodstuffs, the latter offsetting the dramatic drop in Indonesia's food production that followed the US-backed military uprising.[65] By April 1958, the domestic political impasse over Soviet aid had been breached and the Sukarno government was finally able to ratify the aid agreement negotiated two years earlier, allowing for the prospective construction of a Soviet-financed steel mill, a phosphate fertilizer manufacturing plant, and the completion of other industrial, cultural, educational, and infrastructural projects.[66] On questions of aid and other industrial exports to Indonesia, the Soviets ceded the initiative to the Indonesian government, which proposed all aid projects in the same manner they bought Soviet goods.[67] In other words, the Indonesians were not shopping around for an ideological guide in a bipolar Cold War market, but rather for a source of capital, industrial technology, and technical know-how. They found it in the Soviet Union after the Eisenhower Administration rejected project proposals and otherwise tightened conditions on aid – another recurrent stroke of serendipity

62 RGANI, f. 5, op. 30, d. 275, ll. 26–27, or 17 million rubles.

63 A concise account of the CIA's involvement can be found in Tim Weiner, *Legacy of Ashes. The History of the CIA* (New York: Doubleday, 2007), 142–54.

64 Boden, "Cold War Economics," 115–16.

65 RGANI, f. 5, op. 30, d. 306, ll. 116–21.

66 RGANI, f. 5, op. 30, d. 305, ll. 137–38.

67 On trade see for example talks from January 30, 1956 in RGAE, f. 413, op. 13, d. 7801, ll. 10–11. Ragna Boden has made this point most forcefully with respect to aid, in Boden, "Cold War Economics," 118, 126.

in Soviet foreign relations around the world.[68] It mattered, however, that the United States and its allies remained the largest providers of aid to Indonesia despite what's often viewed as Sukarno's jump to the other camp.[69]

But despite the hesitant turn to the Soviets occasioned by US hostility to Sukarno, the Indonesian leadership still could not commit to an intimate relationship with the Soviet Union. By November 1959, only two groups of Soviet specialists had been granted visas to conduct their work in Indonesia, one consisting of two specialists to do preliminary work on the famous stadium in Jakarta to be built for the 1962 Asian games, and another group of five specialists to do feasibility studies on a highway; this group was made to wait four months for their entry visas.[70] According to a report to the Central Committee, future delays in the provision of aid would not only depend on the ability of Soviet industry and aid agencies to organize it, but also on the resolution of the financial arrangements in Indonesia's domestic currency necessary for the Soviet purchases in Indonesian markets that would pay for that aid.[71] Ragna Boden has shown with the use of new archival evidence that the completion rate of Soviet projects in Indonesia was much lower than in the rest of Asia, and speculated that this reflected Sukarno's priorities, which lay in military aid rather than economic aid.[72] More likely, it reflected an economy in tatters and utterly unable to pay back those loans, as the report forewarned. The nascent relationship between the two countries was suffering an irreversible blow, as political unrest and war eventually took their toll on the Indonesian economy.

Beginning in 1958, Indonesia suffered a sharp rise in inflation that created difficulties in exporting suddenly uncompetitive primary goods to the Soviet Union. In January, the desperate Indonesian government asked for credit in local currency, a farcical proposal to make at a time of spiraling inflation in that currency.[73] Meanwhile, a licensing system for imports and exports created to deal with the balance of payments crisis was rejecting Soviet exports to private Indonesian firms, which annoyed the Soviets and further depressed bilateral trade.[74] Unable to develop

[68] Ibid., 115.

[69] At least according to a Soviet document dated July 7, 1962, which postulated that Indonesia received about $1.34 billion from the capitalist countries (63 percent of which from the US). By contrast the socialist countries had provided $590,700,000 in aid. See GARF, f. 5446, op. 120, d. 1749, ll. 54–57.

[70] RGANI, f. 5, op. 30, d. 305, l. 139.

[71] Ibid., l. 141.

[72] Boden, "Cold War Economics," 118–21.

[73] RGAE, f. 413, op. 13, d. 8313, ll. 3–4

[74] Ibid., l. 5, or ibid., ll. 28–29.

exports and forced to import foodstuffs and military materiel rather than productive industrial goods, Indonesia was wilting as an economic partner. The resulting debt would have a chilling effect on the future growth of Soviet–Indonesian trade.

This can easily be gauged by looking at the volume and structure of Soviet–Indonesian trade. Indonesian exports remained constant during the next decade, as the Soviets proved unwilling to increase purchases of rubber that was getting more expensive by the month.[75] Meanwhile, Soviet exports to Indonesia decreased precipitously during the next few years.[76] Soviet trade analysts were pessimistic about the prospects for Soviet–Indonesian trade and those of the Indonesian economy.[77] The growth in bilateral trade was unsustainable, they noted, based as it was on debt-fueled purchases of unproductive military purchases. In 1962 they were already asking the Soviet Union to defer debt payments. They asked again in 1964, and expanded the request to other countries in the Communist Bloc. The government had even resorted to borrowing money from the private sector in Indonesia, a severe partner that imposed ever more onerous conditions for its loans.[78] The Soviets reacted by cutting back on exports despite Indonesian requests.[79] In the summer of 1964, the Sukarno government suspended all imports but rice, and the Soviets expected Sukarno to reduce even this by August.[80] Suharto's coup in September 1965 dealt the coup de grace; Soviet exports would henceforth consist only of equipment for the country's energy industry.

Burma (now Myanmar) was also one of the first to show interest, despite the decidedly religious and, in Khrushchev's opinion, "capitalist" inclinations of its leadership, particularly Prime Minister U Nu.[81] The needs of Burma, however, were much the same as those of other Asian

[75] RGAE, f. 413, op. 13, d. 9810, l. 6.

[76] From the *Vneshniaia torgovlia SSSR za ... Statisticheskii obzor* series.

[77] From a report dated July 20, 1963 from the Soviet trade representative in Indonesia: "The economic situation in Indonesia in the first half of 1963 continued to remain extremely taut. Production is still declining, exports during the first four months of the year did not show obvious signs of growth. The balance of trade (excluding oil) for 1962 was again in deficit. Debt on foreign loans and credits increased. The budget deficit at the beginning of the year reached 43 billion rupees; the amount of money in circulation has increased even more. Inflation continued to erode the country's economy." In RGAE, f. 413, op. 13, d. 9810, l. 5.

[78] Ibid., l. 6.

[79] GARF, f. 5446, op. 120, d. 1858, ll. 14–19. This report to Mikoyan is dated June 18, 1964.

[80] RGAE, f. 413, op. 31, d. 306, ll. 34–35.

[81] Khrushchev's thoughts on U Nu are in Sergei Khrushchev, ed., *Memoirs of Nikita Khrushchev. Statesman*, vol. 3 (University Park: Pennsylvania State University Press, 2007), 751–761, where he talks disapprovingly of the many enterprises he owned.

countries, as the Burmese ambassador to Moscow, U On, pointed out to then Chairman of the Council of Ministers Nikolai Bulganin in 1955. The stronger the Soviet Union was industrially the better for Burma, U On told Bulganin, because that meant the Burmese government would have better prospects of receiving economic aid from the Soviets.[82] Earlier that year they had been asking for Soviet architects; this request was met with a warm response from Bulganin, who wanted the Burmese government to know that the Soviet Union would always welcome such requests.[83] Soon after, the Soviets were building a hospital, a technical institute, and a sports center, as well as extending economic development credit to be paid back in rice.

The Burmese case is interesting for various reasons. After that initial burst of interest in the mid 1950s, Soviet–Burmese trade peaked in 1957, falling steadily thereafter to about a fifth of the 1957 volume by the time of the military coup of 1962, where it stayed despite the new government's non-aligned, socialist inclination.[84] Khrushchev's approach to relations with the Burmese government is also interesting. Khrushchev and his colleagues had "no illusions that [U Nu] was going to encourage economic development in Burma along the road of socialist reforms." He hinted at these reservations in a meeting with him in Rangoon (now Yangon) in December 1955, while in the same breath gifting him an Ilyushin IL-14 airplane for official use and offering to expand economic relations and provide economic aid.[85] Indeed, Khrushchev may have felt that the Soviet Union was slow off the mark on trade with Burma: One hot afternoon, while taking a boat ride in Rangoon, his thirst was satiated by a gratifyingly cold beer, a rare sight in an abstinent, Buddhist country. When he took a look at the label, he was surprised to find that "with their trading skills the Czechs had already succeeded in promoting their beer as far away as Burma."[86] So why such generosity when it came to aid? Perhaps the best answer is also the simplest: "Sooner or later new people would come to power in that country and the good seeds that we had sown would sprout and grow and eventually produce good fruit," Khrushchev argued in his memoir.[87]

The seeds did not sprout. And again what is striking here (but why should it be?) is Soviet resignation. It was the Burmese who sought out relations with

[82] RGANI, f. 5, op. 30, d. 116, l. 9. [83] Ibid., l. 8.

[84] Calculated from the *Vneshniaia torgovlia SSSR za... Statisticheskii obzor* series. Burmese strict nonalignment, coupled with a generally withdrawn foreign policy was rewarded in 1961 with the appointment of its representative to the UN, U Thant, to the position of UN secretary-general.

[85] RGANI, f. 5, op. 30, d. 116, ll. 228–34. He also had reservations about U Nu's personal Buddhist inclinations, although he did not express these at the meeting.

[86] *Memoirs of Nikita Khrushchev*, vol. 3, 755. [87] Ibid., 758.

the Soviets and the Communist Bloc more generally in 1954 – prompting Khrushchev's celebrated first trip abroad a year later. During the Korean War, commodity prices – and particularly for Burma the price for rice – had increased substantially. The government had expected the rise to continue, and committed itself to big budgets for economic development during the following years. As the price for rice inevitably plummeted soon after, Burmese leaders sought to expand the marketing of their rice, particularly because they had been hoarding rice in anticipation of a continued worldwide shortage.[88] Faced with huge volumes of rapidly deteriorating rice and world markets unwilling to take it at the prices the Burmese expected, they turned to China and the Soviet Bloc. The Soviets reacted much as they would continue to do in the future, by keeping the doors wide open and providing aid and trade on barter terms, which had the effect of increasing world demand and thus prices. This exchange reached its apogee in 1956, when China and the Soviet Bloc accounted for about a third of Burma's rice exports.[89]

But this passive, non-invasive policy did not work to the Soviet Union's advantage in Burma, as it did briefly in other places in Asia. Already the negotiations proved to be full of friction. The Burmese government hoped the Soviets would buy at least 20 percent of their rice with British sterling, a commodity more valuable for the Soviets than its value in rice.[90] The Soviets, for their part, complained about the poor quality of the rice, which had been stored too long in warehouses and had "become unfit for consumption." Trade negotiations would necessitate several sessions in both Moscow and Rangoon to finally achieve agreement, but that would be only the start of further complications in this economic relationship.[91]

Accustomed to British imports, the Burmese experienced widespread disaffection with Soviet goods. Soviet consumer goods were unmarketable: electrical items did not fit Burmese sockets, delays in deliveries were extensive, and they felt that Soviet goods were generally overpriced.[92]

[88] J. N. Behrman, "State Trading by Undeveloped Markets," *Law and Contemporary Problems* (part 2) 24:3 (1959): 454–81. The price of rice exported by Burma fell by almost 50 percent from 1953 to 1957. See table 1, 455.

[89] Ibid., 456.

[90] RGANI, f. 5, op. 30, d. 113, l. 38. The Soviets complained that throughout the month-long negotiations Burmese demands were a moving target.

[91] Ibid., ll. 39–40. Several compromises were reached, including Burmese acceptance of Soviet assistance in spraying the rice with pesticide before its export to the Soviet Union, and Soviet payment of 20 percent of the rice with British sterling under the condition that the money be spent on the Burmese embassy in Moscow as well as in acquiring further Soviet technical assistance.

[92] Behrman, "State Trading by Undeveloped Markets," 458. Soviet goods were generally priced according to world market prices, often not taking into account that their shoddy quality should have rendered them much cheaper.

In at least one incident that caused some mirth among American observers concerned with "Soviet penetration," Soviet cement hardened into a solid, worthless lump in Rangoon harbor because of improper packaging.[93] More importantly, the price of rice started rising again, obviating the need to barter it away to the Soviet Union. The very feature that had made trade with the Soviet Union so attractive, the possibility of purchasing industrial equipment without the use of hard currency, and one that Khrushchev had advertised aggressively on his trip, had quickly become a money-losing burden.[94] When the Burmese government started demanding hard currency for its rice, Soviet–Burmese trade quickly dwindled despite the long-term agreements that should have locked it in. A 1957 report on Soviet–Burmese trade noted ruefully that given improving terms of trade for Burmese rice in world markets, the government was already starting to slash exports of rice to the Soviet Union. Naturally, they also stopped approaching Soviet agents to purchase Soviet goods.[95] Hoping perhaps for better quality products, the Burmese even resorted to collecting the debt owed them for their rice by buying products in Eastern European countries, with Soviet debt acting as clearing funds.[96] That year trade between the two countries stagnated, falling steadily every year thereafter.

To be sure, not all of these early relations owed as much to world market fluctuations, even when economic cooperation and trade were still the only real, immediate outcome. Witness Afghanistan, a country largely unperturbed by world market junctures. Afghanistan's government was probably even more assiduous than any other in procuring Soviet aid at this early time. Along with other countries bordering the Soviet Union – such as Turkey and Mongolia – Afghanistan had been a recipient of Soviet aid already in Stalin's time. In 1954 it sought to become the second country – after North Korea – to sign an economic cooperation agreement in the post-Stalin era. Afghanistan had already been receiving aid from the United States to build roads, and in that year they called on the Soviets for help in building flour mills, bakery plants, and grain elevators, as well as prospecting for a road-building project.[97] The next year they were building

[93] Abram Bergson, "Russia Turns to Economic Competition," *Challenge* 6:5 (1958): 52.

[94] See RGANI, f. 5, op. 30, d. 116, l. 232 for Khrushchev's sales pitch. The Burmese were also unhappy about Soviet and Czech reselling of their rice in world markets, which meant losses of precious hard currency for the Burmese government.

[95] RGANI, f. 5, op. 30, d. 275, l. 27.

[96] Ibid., to the tune of 46 million rubles.

[97] And demanding that it be done quickly! See RGANI, f. 5, op. 30, d. 71, l. 56.

the trans-Hindu Kush highway, and the year after, again at the request of the Afghan government, the Soviets were prospecting for oil.[98]

Here the Soviet interest was more nakedly geopolitical, and the Afghan government was adept at executing the classic Cold War maneuver of playing on the security concerns of the Soviet Union. Khrushchev feared that American largesse might result in American military bases just south of the soft underbelly of the Soviet Union, so he set his budding aid machinery in motion, as he explained later, that Afghanistan may "establish friendly relations with us and take a trusting attitude toward our policies."[99] He was not far off; although the United States had never really considered establishing a base there, the Americans were busy trying to coax a rapprochement between Afghanistan and Pakistan that would encourage a wider cooperation with the aims of the Southeast Asia Treaty Organization (SEATO), the Baghdad Pact, and other such anti-communist defense arrangements in that region.[100]

It is interesting that in his memoirs Khrushchev ascribes this type of geopolitical consideration only to economic relations with Afghanistan and not with any other country. Equally interesting is the type of economically-minded defensive posture he takes; an American military base in Afghanistan would have meant more spending on the Soviet defense budget, precisely the type of outcome Khrushchev would campaign against throughout his tenure at the top, a campaign that led, partly, to his overthrow in 1964.[101]

Neither to the East nor to the West, the South looks to the South

The Afghan case is one in which there was a real geopolitical objective at stake, which the Afghan government, weary of both the Soviet Union and the United States, clearly and perhaps cynically used to its own economic advantage. The same is often said of other countries whose political and economic evolution became seemingly entangled in the Soviet–American

[98] Bach, *Soviet Aid to the Third World*, 112; on oil prospecting and more road building see RGANI, f. 5, op. 30, d. 172, ll. 180–82. See also RGANI, f. 5, op. 30, d. 272, ll. 127–28 on 1958 Afghan aid requests to build an airport, carry out more oil prospecting, and keep to earlier aid plans to deliver promised industrial equipment.

[99] *Memoirs of Nikita Khrushchev*, vol. 3, 763–64.

[100] There are many statements of policy detailing American aims in Afghanistan. See, for example, NSC 5701, January 10, 1957, in US Department of State, *Foreign Relations of the United States* (FRUS hereafter), 1955–57, Vol. 8 (Washington, DC: US Government Printing Office, 1987), 29–43.

[101] *Memoirs of Nikita Khrushchev*, vol. 3, 765. On Khrushchev's drive to cut spending on the military see chapter 2.

rivalry. At that point, it is often asserted that the Cold War came to country "X" on a particular date or period; in other words, there is a metanarrative like a voracious whale and all other processes and developments that constitute history are irremediably engulfed in its maw. Any goals and objectives existing outside the framework of this metanarrative are of secondary importance – when they are assigned any importance at all – and countries become inert arenas where our two protagonists can fight for influence.

This is why it is difficult to imagine that countries like Indonesia and Afghanistan may, in fact, have been the ones to invite the Soviet Union to play a role in their development. Where the Soviet Union is concerned, this story should be turned on its head. As we will see, these countries were not the only ones to seek out the Soviet Union. Indeed, the potential uses of the Soviet Union were often much greater for the developing world than any geopolitical benefit the Soviets might accrue, and this was anyway none too clearly the reason for Soviet consent to these new economic relations, Afghanistan excepted.

Although Khrushchev's memoirs are often more self-serving than accurate, his description of Soviet aid objectives during his tenure match those stated by the bureaucratic reports written for him and for the rest of the Soviet leadership. Skachkov had written to his superiors in 1959 that the primary objective was to promote mutual understanding between the Soviet Union and the developing countries and, perhaps more immediately, to advance their economic independence. Developing an industrial base might make it less attractive for these countries to import Soviet products, but the Soviets were not thinking of competition, only to weaken international pressure on both those countries and the Soviet Union.[102] In other words, in trying to expand its network of trade partners, the Soviet Union followed a defensive aid policy that befitted its lack of international position all across the global South. Promoting the economic independence of the recipient country would encourage a more neutral political orientation through which mutually beneficial economic considerations would prevail. Economic independence and trust were the two themes Khrushchev stressed: "Although India was not a direct neighbor of the Soviet Union, it was pursuing its own policy of nonalignment with the military blocs formed by the United States, which was attractive to us, and therefore in relations with India we needed to exert every effort to win its confidence even more. The same held true for

[102] RGANI, f. 5, op. 30, d. 305, ll. 117–121.

Burma."[103] Very quickly the idea had permeated the whole of the bureaucracy, their reports, and their practice.

Apparent Soviet success in establishing aid and trade networks is not the only proof historians routinely provide to establish the Soviet Union as a conspiratorial superpower on the march in the Third World. The proof also lies, they assert, in the Soviet Union's power to inspire imitation. The progress of the state sector in many former colonies, the inward redirection of their industrial production, as well as the outright appropriation of typically Soviet institutions such as collectivization in Tanzania or Five-Year Plans in India constitutes incontrovertible evidence of Soviet influence and its power to inspire revolution against the West. Melvyn Leffler's book on the bipolar confrontation, for example, proposes a narrative of such equivalence between the two sides, one so strictly bipolar, that the Soviet Union cannot but be the great inspiration for Third World leaders. "From Cuba to Algeria to Ghana to Egypt to India and to Indonesia, new nationalist leaders voiced their support for planning," Leffler writes. "Most of them were not communists, indeed they sometimes repressed and imprisoned communists. But *planning* was their common vocabulary."[104] The list of countries is always the same when historians want to connote Soviet "advances" in the Third World. In fact where planning was concerned, Leffler might have added Spain and South Korea to the list; after all, India's indicative, largely market-based Five-Year Plans had much more to do with the Five-Year Plans that guided the economy of those two staunch enemies of the Soviet Union than with the strictly mobilizational Five-Year Plans drawn up at Gosplan headquarters. But then the point is to posit the Soviet Union as a pole of attraction and inspiration. The equation is: planning + economic engagement with the Soviet Union = advancement of the Soviet world order. But planning was too universal to belong to that equation, and economic engagement with the Soviet Union was radical only because the American hostility to it made it so. The fact is that many postcolonial governments simply assumed the tasks of planning from their colonial predecessors, and for many of them, American (or Western) aggression determined their economic engagement with the Communist Bloc much more decisively than anything the communists did or stood for.

[103] *Memoirs of Nikita Khrushchev*, vol. 3, 767.

[104] Melvyn Leffler, *For the Soul of Mankind. The United States, the Soviet Union, and the Cold War* (New York: Hill & Wang, 2007), 171. I do not choose the book for its faults, but precisely because it is more judicious than most.

A narrative not so steeped in the determinism of bipolarity affords a more illuminating perspective. Political economist Jeffry Frieden, for one, offers a different point of departure.[105] Rather than looking East, Frieden has the newly independent countries looking toward the Southern Cone of the Western Hemisphere. It was South America that led the postwar world in experimenting with import substitution industrialization (ISI), and the reasons for this, as for much else, can readily be found in the economic crucible of the 1930s.[106]

The 1930s had been a time of economic isolation for Latin America – as in the Soviet Union and everywhere else. Production until then had been centered to a large degree on commodity exports such as coffee and copper, and these commodities had seen their markets dry up during the worldwide turn to autarky of the interwar years and World War II. This in turn reduced imports of manufactured products from Europe and the United States, which fostered local industry to meet demand formerly satisfied by the industrialized nations.[107] "Urban classes and masses expanded to fill the economic, social, and political vacuum left by the disintegration of the traditional open economies," Frieden explains. "Latin America was transformed from a bastion of open-economy traditionalism to a stronghold of economic nationalism, developmentalism, and populism."[108] At this point, the region developed in a similar pattern to that of the United States, where the rise of industry that overtook the cotton and tobacco export farmers in the second half of the nineteenth century was accompanied by protectionist measures. Latin America was merely half a century behind. By the time international trade was revived once again under the auspices of the Bretton Woods system, the social and political context in Latin America had changed decisively against export farmers and miners (the latter in many cases now nationalized), and in favor of domestic industrialists and powerful labor movements that called for protection. As a corollary, much of the communications and energy infrastructure passed into state control, as did many steel mills and other industrial assets. These were often too large for local capitalists to finance,

[105] In Frieden, *Global Capitalism*, especially chapter 13. Frieden is not interested in overturning any paradigms of the Cold War, and so he does not juxtapose this particular explanation with typical Cold War understandings of the issue. In fact whenever his book touches on the Cold War, it shifts to a very traditionalist narrative, a function of the literature he uses.

[106] In fact, one could go farther back in time and build a genealogy for the Third World's anti-free market stance that begins with examples of late-industrializing – relative to Great Britain – countries like the United States and Germany, which successfully deployed ISI-type policies that catapulted their economies to the forefront of economic development.

[107] Frieden, *Global Capitalism*, 302–03. [108] Ibid.

and the Great Depression and World War II had starved them of capital and brought many to bankruptcy. Their production would now work to further national industrial development.[109]

Developments in the colonial world followed a similar path and were compounded by developments in the metropoles.[110] The interwar period and then World War II left a legacy of strengthened urban and local business interests in the colonies. Despite an initial intensification of imperial efforts in the immediate postwar period, the overwhelming success of the Marshall Plan and the general effort on the part of the United States to tear down political and economic barriers among European countries created conditions by the early 1950s that increasingly underscored the economic irrelevance of empire. With Western Europe under American military protection and given the rapid expansion of intra-European and transatlantic trade, the geopolitical justification for empire also waned.

It waned, of course, in the face of the increasing difficulties the Europeans found in their colonies. But it is important to note that these soon-to-be-independent countries were not, upon independence, a tabula rasa on the lookout for ideological direction. With the Europeans and their local allies dominating the agricultural and primary export sectors of the colonial economies, the urban capitalist and working classes that agitated for independence, and which were often close to the military, were far from confused about the national development strategy they would support after empire's end. ISI, Frieden concludes, "was the universal postcolonial solvent."[111]

109 Ibid., 304–05. Frieden also notes the success of these policies in industrializing the South American economies, pointing out that by 1973 the principal countries – Brazil, Mexico, Argentina, Colombia, Venezuela, Chile – were roughly as industrial and urban as their richer counterparts to the north, with industrial output making up 29 and 42 percent of all output, compared to 29 to 48 percent for Europe and the United States. The difference in average income came mainly from the significant inefficiencies of a protected industrial base as well as a larger agricultural sector. ISI had accomplished its goal of industrializing South America, but it turned out that industrialization was not synonymous with affluence.

110 As well as in more informal colonial outposts, like South Africa. See William Martin, "The Making of an Industrial South Africa: Trade and Tariffs in the Interwar Period," *The International Journal of African Historical Affairs* 23:1 (1990): 59–85.

111 Frieden, *Global Capitalism*, 312. See also his discussion on the intellectual underpinnings of ISI worked out primarily by Argentinian economist Raúl Prebisch under the auspices of the United Nations Economic Commission for Latin America. In academia it would be refined under the label of Dependency Theory in the writings of Fernando Henrique Cardoso and Enzo Faletto, *Dependencia y desarrollo en América Latina; Ensayo de interpretación sociológica* (Mexico: Siglo Veintiuno Editores, 1969) and Peter Evans, *Dependent Development. The Alliance of Multinational, State, and Local Capital in Brazil* (Princeton: Princeton University Press, 1979). For a good overview of this intellectual movement and its relevance today see Omar Sanchez, "The Rise and Fall of the Dependency Movement: Does it Inform Underdevelopment Today?" *Estudios Interdisciplinarios de America Latina* 14:2 (2003).

This impressionistic generalization masks a broad plurality of experiences in the former colonial world that also depended on domestic contingencies and the rise of idiosyncratic leaders. Furthermore, the colonial experience of different regions diverged widely one from the other, which in turn helped set different developmental paths. South Korea and Taiwan, for example, opted for a developmental state that replicated their colonial political economy and the export-led success of their late-developing former colonial master, Japan.[112] Unlike those two examples, empire on the cheap in West Africa left woefully underdeveloped state institutions, some of which, such as Nigeria, went on to become rapacious and self-serving.[113] Importantly, however, imperial rule had left them all an authoritarian legacy and a hegemonic belief – shared by many in Western Europe, for that matter – in the transformative powers of the state.

Despite these differences, the analogous consequences of the disintegration of the world economy in the 1930s are nevertheless striking. Indeed, the most meaningful development in the newly independent countries after the liberal world's meltdown was not their position in a Left–Right spectrum that belied their allegiances in a bipolar world. As Frieden points out, the Third World opted out of a liberal system en masse – inasmuch as they reasonably could – and yet did not go for a Soviet-style economy. Broadly, the majority of these countries followed South America's lead in establishing ISI as their preferred economic strategy.

They also looked to start commercial relations with the Soviet Union. Essentially, Third World ISI policies dovetailed quite nicely with the Soviet Union's foreign trade strategy to end the isolation it had lived through. That complementarity of interests led to a convergence of ideas – a rather different starting point of analysis than the ideological capture that is implicitly invoked in the bipolar framework. Both parties agreed that import substitution freed former colonies from dependence on

[112] See Bruce Cumings, "The Origins of the Development of the Northeast Asian Political Economy: Industrial Sectors, Product Cycles, and Political Consequences," *International Organization* 38:1 (1984): 1–40, which places the origins of that development squarely in the colonial period. The term "developmental state" is often used to mean those states that worked closely with domestic businesses to achieve economic development. A wide-ranging discussion can be found in Meredith Woo-Cumings, ed., *The Developmental State* (Ithaca: Cornell University Press, 1999).

[113] Atul Kohli, *State-Directed Development. Political Power and Industrialization in the Global Periphery* (Cambridge: Cambridge University Press, 2004) analyzes state intervention in the domestic economies of Brazil, Korea, India, and Nigeria, and generally finds the origins of future state economic behavior in the latter half of the twentieth century in those countries' colonial experience, particularly during the 1930s – except for Brazil, whose formative experience during the 1930s was not strictly colonial.

Western markets and products, thus weakening international pressure. It also strengthened the role of the state in its economic functions, another desirable outcome that would facilitate further trade expansion with the Soviet Union, as Skachkov had explained in his report to the Central Committee. This was a position that had been well staked out academically in the Soviet Union already by the late 1950s, albeit in a more extreme form than that put forth by the nascent dependency theory being developed in South America.[114]

This point of departure may have been lost on Western analysts, but Soviet analysts were not so ideologically blinkered; moreover, when it came to matters of planning and state-led development in practice, rather than instinctively lumping everything into one sinister category of analysis, the Soviets understood differences in degree and kind, and felt the sting of competition. This was brought to Gosplan's attention – in case it had missed it – in an appeal by the director of its research institute (the Nauchno-Issledovatel'skii Ekonomicheskii Insitut [NIEI]) A. Efimov. The director explained that from the mid 1950s the majority of the developing countries in Africa, Asia, and Latin America had been trying to organize a planned economy, or at least a plan to develop their economy. Many had come to the Soviet Union asking for specialists that would speak their language, but the Soviets were not able to supply enough specialists for such high demand.[115] There might have been a shortage of specialists with language skills in the Soviet Union, but not at the United Nations. In that bastion of centralized development planning, these countries found eager bourgeois economists ready to help them, Efimov warned his superiors. There was also a lack of Soviet academic textbooks on how to plan an economy, so the leaders of these countries were turning to the works of those bourgeois economists.[116] His suggestion to form a special center to render help to officials from developing countries seeking counsel did not seem to come to much, but his general idea to counter the influence of "bourgeois economists" by

[114] See Valkenier, *The Soviet Union and the Third World*, especially chapter 3 on development theory. Mostly using Soviet academic writings as primary evidence, Valkenier documented the Soviet stance in relation to the development of economic independence in the Third World. She assumed these academic studies either guided Kremlin policy or were at least its reflection, and indeed the reports drawn up in the offices of the GKES and the Ministry of Foreign Trade were strikingly similar to those she analyzed.

[115] RGAE, f. 99, op. 1, d. 125, ll. 67–71.

[116] Ibid., Efimov's suggestions were forwarded for further study to the Ministry of Foreign Affairs, but I have not been able to uncover what came of them.

creating Soviet cadres specialized in these issues did receive Gosplan's support. In the end nothing much seemed to have come of that either.[117]

The case of India

The economic trauma of the 1930s, then, decisively shaped the political economy of places as disparate as the Soviet Union and South America, and encouraged the United States to establish a worldwide presence in order to promote international cooperation in the defense of a global liberal order. If the postwar international political economy was not the outcome of an immaculate conception in 1945, neither was India's postcolonial political economy a willful course chosen upon its virgin birth at independence in 1947. Its roots lie also in the period of the Great Depression and World War II. As this chapter has been arguing, the assumption that the leftist rhetoric and the state-centered policies undertaken all over the Third World are a result of Soviet influence and leadership is simplistic and wrong; such an assessment infantilizes Third World societies and their leaders.[118] Scholars of the Cold War require this narrative arc to maintain the overall superpower framework, but the framework proves of little use when looking at the Soviet Union's economic relations with India.

In fact, the postcolonial political economy undertaken by India is a good example of world economic forces shaping national polities in recognizable ways.[119] India's economic growth under British imperial rule was sluggish; Great Britain's liberal policies failed to improve the productivity of India's largely agrarian economy, and it undermined uncompetitive traditional Indian industries such as textiles through a relatively free-trade regime that resulted in the import of manufactured goods from more

[117] RGAE, f. 4372, op. 66, d. 879, ll. 53–54. Both the NIEI and Gosplan, independently, saw in this whole affair a chance to get more funding. The NIEI posited itself as the best positioned institution to conduct that kind of work while Gosplan offered to set aside some of its people, under the condition that courses on development issues and language studies be provided for them, much as was done with cadres preparing for work at the UN.

[118] Any study that hopes to find Soviet ideological hegemony or just a pervasive influence in India needs to start by contending with the findings of Canadian political scientist Stephen Clarkson, which found no real influence of Marxist-Leninist thought in India's state management, and that should that influence grow in India (he wrote in the 1970s) "it would be less because of external stimulation, whether from Moscow or any other communist capital, than from the indigenous flowering of a local communist praxis of the type seen in Kerala or West Bengal." Stephen Clarkson, "Non-Impact of Soviet Writing on Indian Thinking and Policy," *Economic and Political Weekly* 8:15 (1973): 723.

[119] This brief discussion is mostly taken from Kohli, *State-Directed Development*, chapters 6 and 7.

productive European factories. The British colonial state did little in terms of investment in Indian infrastructure and education, and in keeping with its laissez-faire ideology, did little to promote industrialization and economic growth.[120]

This changed briefly during World War I, which transformed India into a strategic provider of some raw materials such as jute for the war effort. The war simultaneously decreased imports to India as shipping became less secure and European production refocused on the war effort. Indian industrialists stepped in to fill the demand for products formerly supplied by the Europeans. The moment was short-lived, and when it was finished they lobbied for protectionist measures to little avail. By the early 1920s these Indian capitalists and their uncompetitive factories had been cast aside once again upon the resumption of trade. But as the world economy unraveled in the 1930s, they saw their fortunes turn again. India's strategic profile had been raised during the war years, and the British government cast about for new sources of revenue to increase defense spending. Furthermore, seeking to maintain the gold standard by stemming the flow of gold from Great Britain, the British sought ways to cut expenditures abroad, on imperial administration for example. Both these goals – and others such as keeping German and Japanese products out of India – could be met through tariffs on imports to India. Protectionism spurred Indian national industry through the 1930s, and World War II provided even juicier state contracts to the resurging class of Indian industrialists.

At the end of World War II, the new class of powerful national economic actors did not find itself as alone as it had been after World War I, when they had fruitlessly lobbied the British government for protection. They had become influential within the Indian National Congress and even came to draft an economic plan in 1943 for an independent India that called for planning, a mixed economy, protectionism, and public investment in heavy industry, all of them prominent elements in Nehru's statist postcolonial economic policies.[121] This grand coalition

[120] The British kept the rupee overvalued, for example, in order to minimize sterling expenditures in India. There were other reasons for India's lack of industry that were not so directly related to British colonial rule, such as the absence of a strong banking system that could channel rural savings to industry.

[121] This was the so-called Bombay Plan, drawn up by the Federation of Indian Chambers of Commerce and Industry (FICCI) with the support of such prominent Indian businessmen as G.D. Birla and J.R.D. Tata, in ibid., 254–55. See also Aditya Mukherjee, *Imperialism, Nationalism and the Making of the Indian Capitalist Class, 1920–1947* (New Delhi: Sage Publications, 2002), 391–432.

of the business, labor, and nationalist elements, forged in the convergence of interests of the 1930s and 1940s, assured that Nehru's India remained unwaveringly in a market-based, capitalist world system, even as Indian leaders sought a measure of economic independence through ISI policies and the development of indigenous industry.

The First Five-Year Plan initiated by Nehru's government in 1951 to industrialize the Indian economy through import substitution was moderately successful, as India saw its economy grow a respectable 3–4 percent annually. It compared favorably with the growth of other underdeveloped nations at the time and, more significantly, it was a historical first for India to see such sustained growth.[122] But then, India was ready for the good functioning of a mixed economy. Even as the economies of many African countries would be decimated with the departure of the Europeans after independence, which often formed the largest portion of the business classes in those countries, India was already well endowed with an entrepreneurial class strengthened during the last two decades of near-autarky and ready to do business under government protection. Soviet–Indian relations during this confident dawn of India's Five-Year Plans were negligible, but it is telling that when the Indians did approach Stalin's Soviet Union in January 1951, it was not for their industrial wares and experience, but for their grain.[123] This was to forestall an impending grain crisis that year that the Truman Administration had decided to use for diplomatic advantage.[124] The Soviets ended up sending 100,000 tons to a grateful India, although not before overcoming the suspicion that the Indians were using them to convince the Americans to sell more grain with fewer conditions.[125] As a report from August 1951 contended, and as the reader should by now expect, it was not the Soviets that were inhibiting Indo-Soviet economic relations.[126] The report indicated that the Soviet Union was open and eager to expand trade with India, but that clear discrimination on the Indian side was holding things back. The report noted that the Indian government had only just taken over the British system of import–export licensing, and that at any rate the financing of India's trade was still monopolized by foreign capital, and both were institutions

[122] Bhagwati and Desai, *India Planning for Industrialization*, see chapter 4 for a breakdown of India's economic performance during the first three Five-Year Plans.

[123] RGASPI, f. 84, op. 1, d. 68, ll. 9–10.

[124] The story is well told in Robert J. McMahon, "Food as a Diplomatic Weapon: The India Wheat Loan of 1951," *Pacific Historical Review* 56:3 (1987): 349–77.

[125] RGASPI, f. 84, op. 1, d. 70, l. 72.

[126] RGAE, f. 413, op. 13, d. 6801, ll. 76–81.

that valued continuity. Some other force would have to intervene before Nehru's government reassessed its exclusionary trade policy.

Some advantages notwithstanding, problems also plagued Nehru's industrialization effort. Population growth speeded up, lowering growth in per capita terms to 1–2 percent, for one. But more pertinently to relations with the Soviet Union, shortages of educated technical personnel quickly became a hindrance to growth, particularly in the fast-growing public sector, which could not fluidly change incentives in order to attract educated workers.[127] More decisively, however, a foreign exchange crisis developed at the start of the Second Five-Year Plan in 1956, limiting planned imports and investment and impressing upon the Indian government the necessity for industries needful of foreign imports to earn their own foreign exchange. It is this squeeze in the balance of payments that jumpstarted relations with the Soviet Union. Imports from the Soviet Union in 1956 more than quintupled from the previous year, and they doubled again in 1957.[128]

The groundwork for this spurt in economic exchange between the two countries had been laid by a couple of Soviet delegations from the Academy of Sciences that traveled to India in January 1954 to initiate cultural and scientific exchange. What they found in India instead was a great interest in getting Soviet specialists in planning and statistics to consult with the Indian government on how to improve Indian planning practices. The Indians asked, however, that these Soviet consultants come from the Institute of Statistics, rather than the Soviet government, so as "not to excite the enemies of India and the USSR" – the English and American press in particular.[129]

Prasanta Chandra Mahalanobis, the famous statistician who played a leading role in drawing up India's First and Second Five-Year Plans,

[127] Ibid., 82–83. For a Soviet version of Indo-Soviet relations in the postwar period to 1958 see RGANI, f. 5, op. 30, d. 302, ll. 61–66.

[128] *Vneshniaia torgovlia SSSR za 1956 god*, 117 and *Vneshniaia torgovlia SSSR za 1957 god*, 116. Soviet exports to India jumped from 29.3 million rubles in 1955 to 161.6 million rubles in 1956 and 338.6 million rubles in 1957. Imports from India lagged behind, but increased by a similar magnitude from 17.6 million rubles to 73.2 million rubles to 167.8 million rubles in those three years, respectively.

[129] RGANI, f. 5, op. 30, d. 70, ll. 1–10. Besides other assorted recommendations involving academic exchange between India and the Soviet Union, the delegation was also asked to consult with the Central Committee on student exchanges. With demand for higher education in India far surpassing the country's educational infrastructure, both Indian government officials and students looked for educational opportunities wherever they could be found. In this case, it was the Soviet Union's financial commitment to the UN and its potential use for education in the Soviet Union that sparked Indian interest.

pressed all the right buttons in his meetings with successive Soviet delegations. In describing India's industrializing intentions, he gave fodder for much of the rhetoric the Soviets would later use in justifying their generous aid policy. India's industrial pretensions were not to be seen as a source of competition to Soviet industry, he argued, but as a means to economic independence that would insulate India from Western pressure.[130] Even as he repeatedly affirmed India's intentions to remain on good terms with the United States as well as the Soviet Union, Mahalanobis explained that the United States' insistence on conditions for their economic cooperation rendered economic relations with them unreliable, which in turn made planning difficult.[131] In contrast, the Soviets had commended themselves in their quick response to India's request for planning consultants. But then Mahalanobis represented only one faction in the great compromise that characterized Nehru's style of governance. As a fellow planner, Mahalanobis saw trade with the Soviet Union as a stable proposition; mirroring the view of the Soviet Union's Gosplan officials, he valued stability and predictability as the foundation upon which to carry out state-driven industrialization.

Indian businessmen, however, another influential political faction in Nehru's grand nationalist coalition, pointed out the problems in an economic relation with the Soviets. A delegation led by prominent industrialist Kasturbhai Lalbhai visited the Soviet Union in September 1954, and their secret report to the Indian government, which was quickly passed to the Soviet government, was a litany of Soviet industrial deficiencies and incompetence (with a sprinkling of praise).[132] The stores suffered severe shortages of consumer products; public buildings were monumental and well-constructed, but the rest were shoddy and

[130] RGANI, f. 5, op. 30, d. 71, ll. 96–97.

[131] Ibid. As an example of the fickle nature of American aid, Mahalanobis offered the United States' 1951 refusal to build a promised steel mill. This was not a simple matter of Indian perceptions; the scholarship on Indian disillusionment and resentment against American conditionality during times of crisis, such as during the small famine of the early 1950s, is substantial. See Andrew J. Rotter, "Feeding Beggars: Class, Caste and Status in Indo-US Relations, 1947–1964," in Christian G. Appy, ed., *Cold War Constructions. The Political Culture of United States Imperialism, 1945–1966* (Amherst: The University of Massachusetts Press, 2000), and, more charitably toward the Johnson Administration, Kristin L. Ahlberg, "'Machiavelli with a Heart': The Johnson Administration's Food for Peace Program in India, 1965–1966," *Diplomatic History* 31:4 (2007): 665–701. For the way cultural perceptions affected trade and aid between India and the United States see again Andrew J. Rotter, *Comrades at Odds*, chapter 2.

[132] The following is from RGANI, f. 5, op. 30, d. 118, ll. 126–39. There was at least one dissident to this assessment, the head of Bengal Chemical and Pharmaceutical S. P. Sen. He felt obliged to send a letter to the Soviets stating his opposition to Lalbhai's report, which had been drawn without consulting the rest of the delegation. It can be found in RGAE, f. 413, op. 13, d. 7624, ll. 47–50.

ill-conceived. The street roads were large and wide, but there were few cars on them and they were outnumbered by trucks. The transportation system left much to be desired, with trams too full, and airplanes chronically late; only the Moscow metro was praiseworthy. Hotels outside of Moscow and Leningrad were badly made and unsanitary. And yet people seemed content, and children in particular looked healthy and well taken care of.

More apropos were their observations on the Soviet Union's industrial capacity. Here the Indian industrialists noted with approval that the factories – as well as many state administrative positions dealing with them – were not led by bureaucrats, but rather by engineers and other experienced, competent former workers in their particular industry. Nevertheless they did not see a single factory that could be described as being on the cutting edge of productive technologies, or that could even be described as modern. Despite being assured by the Soviets that they were being taken to the most modern factories, the Indian businessmen did not see any new technologies or production techniques they had not seen many years before in Western Europe or the United States.[133] They were shown some of the flagship factories, such as Moscow's car factory "Stalin," Leningrad's truck factory, and the machine-building factory "Red Proletariat," and the Indians thought them rather dilapidated and housed in neglected buildings with machinery suffering from widespread disrepair.[134] They were generally unimpressed with the low quality of the production they witnessed and the low productivity of the workers, this despite much state propaganda on the radio and other media to raise productivity and cut down on waste.[135] Moscow State University and the canal project linking the Volga and the Don were evaluated more positively.[136] They were not as impressed with the organization of industry in general, which they noted tended toward autarky, with its many branches aspiring always to be as independent from each other as possible. As economists both in the Soviet Union and the West would later note ad nauseam, the Indians noticed that factory managers cared only for production volume and nothing for quality. In the final outcome, they concluded that there was little in the way of technology and industrial

[133] RGANI, f. 5, op. 30, d. 118, l. 137. [134] Ibid., l. 131.

[135] The delegation was shown one of the most modern textile factories in the Soviet Union, as the textile factory in Tashkent was introduced to them, but they noted that the cloth manufactured there was of lower quality than that produced in India, even if the quantity produced was impressive. See ibid., ll. 135–36.

[136] Ibid., ll. 133.

equipment in the Soviet Union that could not be bought somewhere else, and moreover have it be of better quality.[137]

Even as the Indians were educating themselves about circumstances in the Soviet Union, Dmitrii Shepilov, the then upwardly mobile editor of *Pravda*, was being alerted along with the rest of the Central Committee to the dearth of information on India and the absence of an intelligence gathering infrastructure that could remedy the situation.[138] Despite the thousands of daily publications all over India, the Soviet Union as of the start of 1956 had too few Hindi and Urdu speakers that were familiar with any of them. There was not even a press-attaché among the staff in the embassy in Delhi to do public relations work with the local press in its language, and neither were there daily press summaries carried out at the embassy. Instead, the diplomatic corps relied on the English-language press, which was quickly losing circulation in independent India.[139] This ignorance and lack of preparedness reached to the very top of the Kremlin. Years later, Khrushchev remembered that "our knowledge of India, to tell the truth, was not only superficial, but downright primitive. Don't laugh, but I personally drew some of my knowledge of India from an aria sung by an Indian merchant in the opera by Rimsky-Korsakov entitled *Sadko*."[140]

A corollary to this information deficit and the lack of cooperation with the Indian press was that no effective propaganda work could be carried out in India by the Soviets. Meanwhile, the Indian press was procuring world news from European wires such as Reuters and the Agence France-Presse (AFP). Even the American-based Associated Press (AP) monopolized world news at the *Times of India*, a state of affairs hardly conducive to "objective" reporting on socialist camp news developments in the Indian Press, the report noted.[141] On the commercial front,

137 Ibid., l. 138. Polish industry, which the delegation visited after their trip to the Soviet Union, likewise did not impress them much.

138 RGANI, f. 5, op. 30, d. 161, ll. 53–63.

139 Ibid., ll. 54–55.

140 *Memoirs of Nikita Khrushchev*, vol. 3, 723. "He sang: 'Countless the diamonds deep in our caverns of stone,'" Khrushchev continues. "I knew that the weather there was warm, that the sea did not freeze, that the country possessed countless riches, and that the animal world there was something fantastic. There were jungles. The very word made a very big impression on me, much bigger than now, when we ourselves have seen what the jungles of India are really like. They're not at all as exotic as they sound!"

141 RGANI, f. 5, op. 30, d. 161, ll. 55–56. The same situation also obtained in Burma and other Asian countries, the report observed. Moreover, the report noted, the Soviet Union was consistently described as a threat by the Western providers of information to India, which hindered the Soviet Union from capitalizing on much anti-Western feeling in India over such issues as the status of Goa, a territory still under Portuguese control and a flash point of contention that would only be resolved in 1961 after the Indian government initiated a military conflict with the Portuguese garrison there.

there was an embarrassing dearth of publications on Soviet wares and foreign trade even at the office of the Soviet trade representative, who had not even a brochure to distribute to potential Indian customers.[142]

Deficiencies in the infrastructure for information gathering and propaganda, however, did not do much to deter the budding economic relationship between the two countries. India's complex economy was now feeling the push and pull of world economic fluctuations, which intermittently brought news of Soviet advantages to the attention of interested Indian businessmen of the different economic sectors caught in that ebb and flow. The post-Korean War drop in commodity prices, for example, focused tobacco growers on the potential of untapped Soviet markets.[143] At the same time, the post-Korean War recession in the United States of 1953–54 was making it difficult for India to sell its jute and tea there, denying India the hard currency necessary to maintain imports. A bad harvest in 1953 made that loss of US dollars, and the US grain they could buy, particularly pointed.[144] The year 1954 would have been a good year for the Soviets to aggressively move to get market share in India through barter arrangements. But then, aggressive entrepreneurialism was not a hallmark of Soviet bureaucracy. In fact, the Soviet trade mission was being castigated in September of that year precisely for the poor job it was doing in promoting Soviet commerce in the country.[145] The trade representatives provided no information to Soviet trade agencies on the Indian market, and did not pursue, or even know of, possible Indian customers for Soviet products. The Soviet trade office in India also routinely botched the logistics of finance and shipping when commercial exchange did take place, making for much waste and misunderstanding when Soviet goods arrived at Indian ports without any paperwork to make sense of them. But although the Soviets bungled the commercial opportunities opening up in India in 1954, the following year Indian interest in the Soviet Union would effectively jumpstart the relationship.[146]

142 RGAE, f. 413, op. 13, d. 7624, ll. 55–56. Meanwhile the Communist Bloc countries had their literature in abundance and even translated into English for the benefit of their clients, who by and large did not speak other foreign languages.

143 RGAE, f. 413, op. 13, d. 7429, l. 43, as reported in the *Hindustan Times* on April 11, 1954, and monitored by Soviet trade representatives in India.

144 Ibid., ll. 8–14.

145 Ibid., 92–93, the complaints were specifically from the Foreign Trade Ministry's agency for timber exports.

146 Though the following discussion is based on archival evidence, the statistics clearly indicate 1956 as the year of takeoff in the economic relationship (1955, then, was the year in which most of those deals were negotiated). See Ministry of Foreign Trade, *Vneshniaia torgovlia SSSR za 1956 god.*

In 1955, India was casting about for sources of aid and economic cooperation. The three steel mills built by Germans, British, and Soviets were only the beginning. India's Second Five-Year Plan, starting in 1956, was ushered in by a foreign exchange crisis that accelerated the Indian government's search for export markets and relief from hard currency expenditures. A paper by a newly established Indian think tank concluded that "broadly it can be suggested that the current crisis is the direct outcome of the co-existence of the export structure of an as yet semi-subsistence economy and the changing structure of imports of a rapidly developing economy."[147] From 1954–55, the gap between exports and imports had become a chasm, and the new plan with its emphasis on industrial capital formation – much of which would have to be imported – would only widen it.

This development was not without a touch of irony: The very economic forces that were stifling economic relations with Burma and raising food prices were enabling the foreign exchange crisis in India; the same crisis that had brought India's ambassador to Kuz'min's Gosplan office with the urgent request to increase Soviet purchases in the country.[148] Rising food prices in international markets had thrown off Indian calculations on planned food imports.[149] And that was but one factor. Geopolitical factors also played a role; the Suez crisis had pushed freight rates up by almost 15 percent, and the deteriorating relationship with Pakistan had increased the government's defense appropriations. Poor planning on the part of Indian planners also played a role, as many ancillary investments necessary for the proper functioning of big industrial projects had not been taken into account.[150] Moreover, worried that projects involving hard currency expenditures might be affected by the coming crisis, government ministries and private entrepreneurs in India made arrangements early on to import the requisite capital goods for their particular projects, thus setting in motion a self-fulfilling prophecy and depleting hard currency reserves.

Aid was an obvious salve to the crisis, and the Indian government sought it with vigor. In 1955, foreign aid made up a mere half of a percentage of overall GDP; by 1958, it had reached almost 3 percent of GDP.[151] Even though the majority of the aid came from the World Bank,

Statisticheskii obzor (Moscow: Vneshtorgizdat, 1957), 117. In 1956 exports jumped from 29.3 million rubles the year before to 161.6 million.

147 National Council of Applied Economic Research (NCAER), *Foreign Exchange Crisis and the Plan*, Occasional Papers, No. 1 (New Delhi: Asia Publishing House, 1957), 4.

148 See the introduction to this chapter.

149 NCAER, *Foreign Exchange Crisis and the Plan*, 7–8.

150 Ibid., ll. 8–9.

151 Bhagwati and Desai, *India Planning for Industrialization*, 171–80.

the United States, and Western European countries, the Soviets were also invited to participate. Although Soviet aid constituted a paltry 8 percent of all foreign aid during the First Five-Year plan, the Soviet presence ensured a degree of competition that afforded the Indian government a better negotiating position as well as the realization of projects the West would not fund, particularly in the oil and steel sectors.[152] This was well understood by all involved. When in July 1960 Indian Minister of Finance Morarji Desai went to Moscow to visit Mikoyan and ask him for aid money for the Third Five-Year Plan, he detailed for the aging Old Bolshevik where India stood in their fundraising: The cost of the plan was $21–22 billion, and they would need around $4.75 billion in hard currency – not counting the $1.3 billion they would need to buy grain and the $1 billion they would need to pay back loans from the last plan.[153] They had already agreed with the United States on grain deliveries, Desai continued. Of the $4.75 billion, they had already received $180 million from the United States, and they would soon get another $200 million; this would supplement the $375 million in hard currency already received from the Soviet Union. Ah, Mikoyan interjected, but the Soviet Union was helping in another way: The Americans hope to save India from Communism, he argued, and give help believing that if they do not, the Soviets will. "Help from the Soviet Union obliges the US to increase its own grants, and also those of West Germany, which has lately become very rich," Mikoyan observed wryly.[154]

Aid projects also had the virtue of helping to acquaint Indians with Soviet industrial technology and range of production. But with the intensification of relations in 1955, another bond was formed: Indian intermediaries started offering their services as sales agents of Soviet goods.[155] The process of introducing Soviet manufactures was slow, but the collaboration of Indian agents with knowledge of regional markets, together with frequent trips by Indian businessmen and engineers to the Soviet Union, fostered a steady progress and a more entwined relationship than that forged with fickle governments alone.[156] This development was

[152] Ibid., 182–83. The Soviets had earned a significant amount of goodwill in India with their willingness to do oil prospecting in the country, a costly endeavor that Western oil companies had thought without profit. By 1965, the Soviets had found nine profitable oil fields worth about 100 million tons of oil and 30 billion cubic meters of gas. See RGAE, f. 4372, op. 66, d. 439, ll. 23–30.

[153] GARF, f. 5446, op. 120, d. 1521, ll. 62–63.

[154] Ibid.

[155] RGAE, f. 413, op. 13, d. 7624, l. 107. The year 1955 seems to have been an inflection point in this regard as well.

[156] Ibid., l. 73, for an example of an Indian agent arranging a trip for three Indian engineers to the Soviet Union in the summer of 1955.

wisely encouraged by Mikoyan personally, who preferred to see Indian agents in either the private or public sphere organized to provide sales and services for Soviet products there (and for a good cut, he stressed).[157] Perhaps decades of experience had already convinced Mikoyan that retail and service were not Soviet strengths.

Herein lies the irony in much of the literature that posits ideological affinity as the root of the success of the Indo-Soviet economic and political relationship. If the Soviet relationship with India succeeded where that of Indonesia, Burma, and so many others failed, it was in no small measure because of the Indian economy's liberal elements rather than its economic statism. The Soviet Union persevered as an economic partner to India not only because of its relationship with the leadership – which was strong – but also because of the many Soviet tendrils reaching regional markets that were the fruit of Soviet collaboration with private intermediaries operating within India's private sector. This was necessary in a country where the public sector had grown from 5 percent of GDP in 1950 to a mere 11 percent a decade later – and to 13 percent by 1970.[158] Hard currency reserves fluctuated but remained tight until India's devaluation of the rupee in 1966, yet never so tight that the resulting licensing system strangled the Soviet Union's relationship with private importers, as it did in Indonesia. Moreover the Soviets were able to maneuver in a complex economy that did not suffer from the monocultural characteristics of economies like that of Burma or Ghana, allowing for a broadening of commercial relations that relied less on the whims of a few government decision-makers or the capricious change in the price of a commodity.

The Soviets proved very valuable in mediating the Indian relationship with the West, and helpful in their own right as aid providers. And chronic – but not utterly crippling – pressure on the balance of payments guaranteed the continuity of a relationship of credits and barter that was so very useful to India. But there were also the limits of the economic underdevelopment of both partners. Mikoyan liked to brag that the famous Bhilai steel mill the Soviets built would do away with steel imports from the Soviet Union.[159] But by the early 1960s, competition was just

[157] GARF, f. 5446, op. 120, d. 1315, l. 13

[158] Satish Verma and Rahul Arora, "Does the Indian Economy Support Wagner's Law? An Econometric Analysis," *Eurasian Journal of Business and Economics* 3:5 (2010): 80, table 1. This rate of government participation in the economy is in fact quite natural in underdeveloped economies.

[159] For example in GARF, f. 5446, op. 120, d. 1315, ll. 11–15, during yet another visit, this one in November 1958, by a senior Indian official come to ask for aid money.

as prominent as complementarity, making it difficult to negotiate big increases in trade when both countries produced competing products.[160] And Soviet generosity could be abused, as revealed in a somewhat inelegant exchange in December 1964 between Russian Minister of Foreign Trade Nikolai Patolichev and the Indian ambassador, Triloki Nath Kaul, who was trying once again to raise some funds from the Soviets – anywhere between 1.3 and 4 billion rubles in credit, as the Soviets pleased. Kaul had heard that the Soviet military budget for the new Soviet Five-Year Plan was to be cut by half a billion rubles. He was happy to hear this, he said, as this might free up some capital to lend to India. If Patolichev's jaw dropped to the ground, the document did not record it, but he diplomatically responded by pointing out that whatever savings the Soviet Union realized were to be spent in the Soviet Union, where there also were serious difficulties to overcome.[161]

As the book argues, 1961 proved to be something of an inflection point, when the Soviets began to reconsider their commercial approach in the global South. In India, that added another wrinkle to a complex relationship nicely encapsulated in the following episode, which serves by way of a conclusion: In May 1961, the prominent Indian businessman G. D. Birla went to the Soviet Union to negotiate terms for the import of equipment for a power station and an aluminum factory he was planning on building. His talks with Soviet officials revolved around India's hard currency constraints.[162] During his talks, Birla insisted on reciprocal exchange as the only means through which his planned imports could be acquired. In exchange he offered textile and agricultural equipment, equipment for the paper industry, trucks, and furniture for the many apartments being built in the Soviet Union at the time. It had been six years since economic exchange between India and the Soviet Union had intensified, and the Soviets had started to learn of the limitations of such an exchange with countries that could not offer solid, productivity-enhancing equipment. Perhaps Birla might offer hard currency for his purchases in the Soviet Union, as Brazilian businessmen had started to do? Skachkov asked; it was worth a try.[163] Birla, however, was under strict instructions to offer nothing but barter. After all, one could buy that equipment in the United States

[160] See Spandar'ian's difficulties in seeking common ground in negotiations with the Indians in 1963 in RGAE, f. 413, op. 13, d. 9808, ll. 88–91, 110–12.

[161] RGAE, f. 413, op. 31, d. 305, ll. 19–21.

[162] GARF, f. 5446, op. 95. d. 1034, ll. 69–74. He also tried to negotiate textile manufacturing equipment for some of his colleagues.

[163] Ibid., l. 73.

and England, both of which had offered him very attractive credit arrangements. The limits of the economic relationship were being pushed. The Soviet Union had become an important commercial partner to India, not least because of their cultivation of private sector agents like Birla. But it could never be as important as the West. The World Bank and the consortium countries of the West would continue as the main providers of economic development aid even as India persisted in framing this development within an import substitution strategy that relegated the Soviet Union to an important but secondary role, and moreover, one useful for mediating the liberal world order.[164] The Soviets had learned through hard experience that the effects of their economic magnanimity were invariably limited. As we will see, the Soviets would learn in the coming years to temper their enthusiasm over the possibilities in the Third World with a dose of economic reality.

[164] The weight of Soviet aid in India would remain within the 10–12 percent mark for the whole of the 1960s, with again that number coming from the rest of the Soviet Bloc countries. See Bhagwati and Desai, *India Planning for Industrialization*, 172–73 for a breakdown of aid to India from 1951 to 1968. Exports from the Soviet Union barely passed the double digit mark in India's trade structure, and imports were even lower. See Jadgish N. Bhagwati and T. N. Srinivasan, *Foreign Trade Regimes and Economic Development. India* (New York: Columbia University Press, 1975), 62.

PART III

Integration

CHAPTER 5

Conformity and profit:
The Soviet economy under American hegemony

If the last two chapters have detailed the formation of the wide array of new economic relations the Soviets developed in the second half of the 1950s, the next two chapters will tell of their fates during the 1960s. It is difficult to make sense of this story within the constraints of a metanarrative that emphasizes bipolarity and confrontation. Such a framework necessitates a complete misunderstanding, or ignorance, of world economic dynamics and their import. It requires elements verging on equivalence. It demands unremitting confrontation. It must invent for its two virile poles a cultural and ideological exceptionalism. Yet all these themes are absent when we turn to economy. What we see there is the commonplace, the familiar. In Soviet behavior, we discern the sensuous outline of conformity, the beguiling contour of submission. Soviet economic liaison agents, who lived within these confines, sought refuge in the language of convention, not revolution. What are we to make of this?

The Pax Americana that nurtured the growth of the world economy, despite all Cold War rhetoric, lent an international stability such as the Soviets had not known. The effective subordination of great power struggle under America's security arrangements, a feat as clear to the new Soviet leaders as it was not to Stalin in the immediate postwar years, was much less threatening to Soviet security than the dissolution of international cooperation of the 1930s. As cooperation dissolved throughout the 1930s, European countries, including the Soviet Union, were compelled to fashion themselves into garrison states. In contrast to the 1930s, a time when Soviet leaders enthusiastically followed the Stalinist emphasis on heavy industry and the maintenance of a large conventional army, the 1950s and 1960s saw Khrushchev making cuts to military spending and radically increasing domestic consumption levels. Relatively high levels of military spending were still a requisite because of the nature and general inertia of the Soviet system, and also because of its domination of Eastern Europe. But, as far as Khrushchev was concerned, a nuclear arsenal would suffice for the task of Soviet security; the competition, he clamored, and would clamor until his death, should henceforth be economic and moral.

All the willingness in the world could not actually integrate the Soviet system into the world economy; the impossibility of the ruble's convertibility alone made financial integration all but impossible, not to say anything of other institutional obstacles such as Moscow's monopoly on foreign trade or the country's non-participation in the International Monetary Fund (IMF). So then, why look for the Soviet Union in the world economy, or for the world economy in the Soviet Union? Wouldn't it be more reasonable to see it as a self-contained, mirror-opposite of the West? Did it not signify an economic and ideological alternative to the international liberal system of the West? Was it not an alternate universe, a stance, a hope, an example for the industrializing nations? And if this is all true and we want to understand world politics during the Cold War, wouldn't it be more fruitful to examine the Soviet Union's military capabilities, its ideological precepts, its eccentric leaders?[1] But we have already seen that the Soviet Union closely followed, and indeed was at times profoundly influenced by, the events and developments of the world economy. This process intensified in the global commercial expansion of the 1960s. All political actions and reactions during the period of the Cold War have to be viewed within a general politics of Soviet accommodation of, and adaptation to, the world economy. An obsession with obtaining dollars and the constant mimicking of capitalist practices in their relations with their own "empire" is hard to square with their oft-assumed enterprise of world revolution and general political drive to undermine the West wherever possible.

Let us conduct a thought experiment: What if the tables were turned? What would analysts have made of an American policy of containment that relied for its continuous sustenance on a trickle of rubles, the most widely accepted currency in the world? What would historians have written had they seen infighting and posturing among NATO allies just to get their hands on a few more rubles so they could balance their payments that they may receive more communist credit? What would Americans have thought of their market-based social model had they, along with Third World countries, relied to an important extent on communist technology for productivity gains? In historian Bruce

[1] As the latest rendering from John Lewis Gaddis does, decidedly and irrevocably ignoring a whole scholarly edifice constructed by the revisionists, in *The Cold War. A New History* (New York: The Penguin Press, 2005).

Cumings' formulation on the quiet power of hegemonic arrangements, the experience of this financial hegemony was a "mundane, benign, and mostly unremarked daily life of subtle constraint."[2] In fact, as should have been predictable, the officials that informed and implemented Soviet foreign economic and political policies were well aware of the steep Soviet shortcomings as well as of Western strength and attraction. They felt capitalism's gravity in their bones. More often than not they would try to resolve problems by copying Western practices and/or engaging the world economy in its liberal, market-based form – a political preference that is almost the exact opposite of expansion and aggression. In the first half of the 1960s, as the country's international economic relations deepened and as Soviet officials became increasingly experienced in economic exchanges with the outside world, they readily conformed to the world's economic and technological realities in order to continue a policy of international engagement that they deemed lucrative and desirable.

Learning from the West, competing with the West

Broadly speaking, competition is the key difference between the relative unsuccess of the centralized development of countries like the Soviet Union and the resounding success of the (differently) centralized development of countries like Japan, South Korea, and Taiwan.[3] Despite having developed under Five-Year Plans and a more than cozy relationship with the center, much as its counterparts to the north, South Korean chaebols, which were often as economically disperse as Soviet regional *sovnarkhozy*, were made to feel the full effect of world competition and were allowed to fail when they did not measure up. A convertible and chronically undervalued currency, as well as billions in guaranteed investment from the world's hegemonic power, allowed South Korea the market and financial access necessary for its export-led, "miracle" economic development starting in the 1970s. In the Soviet Union, competition started to have the expected effect on Soviet production for export a decade earlier. The parallel lies in the preoccupations that gripped the Soviet leadership when confronted with this challenge. The difference, of course, was in

[2] Bruce Cumings, *The Korean War. A History* (New York: The Modern Library, 2010), 219.

[3] For the interdependent role of government and heavy industry in Japanese economic development see Chalmers Johnson, *Miti and the Japanese Miracle: The Growth of Industrial Policy, 1925–1975* (Stanford: Stanford University Press, 1982); for Taiwan and East Asia more generally see Robert Wade, *Governing the Market: Economic Theory and the Role of Government in East Asian Industrialization* (Princeton: Princeton University Press, 1990).

the way these preoccupations attenuated in the Soviet Union after exports of natural resources were established in some scale, a luxury South Korea never enjoyed.

As noted earlier, the Soviets were finding the market to be a stern teacher, one quick to spotlight Soviet production's shortcomings, as it did with Soviet chromium, glass, and printing equipment.[4] The Soviets often tried to improve the quality of their products by decree, but just as often they looked to Western practices and Western example. For example, in late 1959 the deputy minister of foreign trade brought to Alexei Kosygin's attention the low quality of an array of oil products exported to Western countries. Its bad quality was rendering oil exports ineffective. "Under conditions of the acute competition being waged with the strongest oil monopolies, the question of ameliorating the quality of oil products and searching for new products takes on important significance," the deputy minister's report asserted.[5] He went on to expound on the example of Shell and Exxon, both of which had well-equipped laboratories and special research bodies that systematically improved the quality of their product to meet market demands. "We practically don't have any organization that especially occupies itself with improving the quality of oil products," the deputy minister noted.

He further informed Kosygin that the Ministry of Foreign Trade, on demand from ministries, *sovnarkhozy*, and research institutes, had been buying models of the latest Western technology in oil refining. However, progress on the reverse engineering of this technology had been slow, costing the Soviet Union millions of rubles in hard currency imports of oil products that could easily have been produced domestically. An example was the antioxidant ionol, employed for the stabilization of oil used in lubrication, transformers, and turbines. That year, the ministry would have to buy 100 tons at a cost of almost one million rubles in hard currency, despite the fact that the technology to produce it was well known and had been bought three years earlier.[6] The solution, the deputy minister concluded, was to imitate Western companies and work out some arrangement whereby Soviet institutes would research ways to improve the quality of oil products to market standards as well as explore new products demanded by the market.[7]

Mikoyan also pushed Soviet ministries to look to the West for lessons on exporting. Noting that the Baltic countries were exporters of potatoes before being annexed by the Soviet Union, as well as the prevailing success

[4] Discussed in chapter 3. [5] GARF, f. 5446, op. 93, d. 133, l. 59. [6] Ibid., l. 60. [7] Ibid.

of Holland, Denmark, and England in this trade, Mikoyan thought it time to develop Soviet exports in potatoes, particularly its profitable early export in spring.[8] This enterprise would require research on capitalist practices in the methods of trade, packaging, and transportation, possibly involving a tour of European exporting countries as well as a trip to possible buyers in Africa and Asia to gauge their interest and the terms on which they would be interested in purchasing Soviet potatoes.

The research was slow in coming. Despite the one- to two-month window Mikoyan had stipulated in June 1962, results did not start coming in until September, and these involved an investigation in the Baltics to learn that indeed the bourgeois government before the war had sold potatoes to European countries and Argentina. The investigation further determined the amount of potatoes to be bought for export – 20,000 to 25,000 tons – and the suppliers' need for wooden containers.[9] Finally, in January 1963 it was the Ministry of Foreign Trade's turn to report that although Western European countries were net exporters of potatoes, they import potatoes in the spring at a price up to five times the price of potatoes in the fall.[10] Refrigerated shipping, a technology the Soviets had not yet mastered, and one they sought to acquire from abroad, would be required for the venture. Mikoyan could have told them that too seven months earlier.

Capitalist business not only provided productivity-enhancing technology, it also provided incentives to cut back on wasteful practices. At the end of March 1964, the Ministry of Foreign Trade reported on the immense waste of timber after it had been sawed and prepared for domestic consumption. The report noted, matter-of-factly and without the dismay that would have been more appropriate, that the remains were often discarded or sometimes even burned. The report's author suggested that they be put up for export.[11] The ministry had already had discussions with Japanese and Finnish firms, and a Finnish firm was willing to buy 50,000 cubic meters of wood a year for 110,000 convertible rubles, which could be increased in the future. The Japanese had expressed interest in buying much more – 400,000 cubic meters a year for one million convertible rubles. However, the report continued, the Soviet Union needed to buy special equipment to prepare the splinter wood so that it matched international standards; this both the Finns and Japanese were willing to provide in exchange for the finished product. The ministry

[8] GARF, f. 5446, op. 97, d. 1363, l. 105. [9] Ibid., ll. 106–09. [10] Ibid., ll. 113–15.
[11] GARF, f. 5446, op. 98, d. 1445, ll. 60.

wanted to go through with this exchange, suggesting that the *sovnarkhozy* that provided the wood could use the money to buy the equipment, since splinter wood that matched international standards had never been exported before.[12] The hapless Ministry of the Maritime Fleet, as always, would have to provide more ships. Khrushchev promptly signed his consent on April 1, and by June, instructions had been passed that stipulated 25,000 cubic meters to be sent to the Finns in 1964, and no less than 50,000 the next year.[13]

It is also true that not all rich countries were created equal. In keeping with the imperatives of their neutrality arrangement, as well as their geographical lot, Finnish firms were politically compelled to maintain high levels of commercial intercourse with the Soviet Union. Although not as constrained in their negotiations as the Communist Bloc countries of East–Central Europe, the Finns would often resort to small demands – similar to tactics used by the East–Central Europeans – that would guarantee them value. Finnish firms could not always follow strict market guidelines in their commercial affairs with Soviet enterprises, but they made do as best they could. If they had agreed to buy 120,000 tons of sugar from the Soviet Union, for example, they might afterward ask that 40,000 tons be of the Cuban cane variety, as they did in 1961 negotiations for the sugar import of the following year.[14] The Finns accepted that the remaining 80,000 tons could still be fulfilled with the lower-grade beet sugar the Soviets had traditionally exported, but the affair showed how keen they were to look for ways to improve, even in small ways, the commercial relationship they had been politically saddled with.[15]

But Finland was the exception. Mostly, the Soviets were more likely to learn than to abuse. When the Japanese decreased their orders of machine tools in 1964, the Soviets took note. Soviet machine tools gained market share in Japan during the recession of 1962, when many small producers of machine tools in Japan went bankrupt. Japanese firms bought Soviet merchandise on the cheap, a decision they regretted when the machines started breaking down. The Japanese dealer of these Soviet machines was

[12] Ibid., ll. 61–62. [13] Ibid., ll., 63, 68. [14] GARF, f. 5446, op. 95. d. 1021, ll. 118–19.

[15] Ibid. The Soviets were happy enough with this arrangement, as they got Cuban consent for the cane sugar's reexport to Finland, for which they could command a higher price. The whole request, however, shows how the Finns had to maneuver within relatively tighter constraints than other "capitalist" countries, working at levels of commercial interaction with the Soviet Union that were probably higher than might have emerged had commercial relations been left completely up to the market.

forced to open up repair shops in Tokyo, Nagoya, and Osaka just to service their clients since the Soviet export agencies sold their manufactures with no service plan.[16] Their losses, the Japanese dealer complained now to the Ministry of Trade, would have sunk a smaller firm. After much effort they got the machine export agency of the ministry to send spare parts, but they turned out to be as useless as the Japanese parts they had first tried to patch things up with. The Japanese dealer's appeal for control experts and better service did not fall on deaf ears, but the experience nevertheless soured the Japanese on Soviet industrial products. Soviet machine-tool exports declined from their peak in 1964 and later failed to keep up with the general growth in trade with Japan.[17]

Furthermore, the lessons were not always successfully applied. In their exports of vehicles in 1963, the Soviets once again followed Western practices and felt they had to emulate them to remain competitive. The models to follow this time were the big three of the American automotive industry: General Motors (GM), Ford, and Chrysler. Compared to the products of those pioneering companies, Soviet cars were obviously technologically deficient, but the problem in question at the moment was warranty. Whereas in 1960 the Soviets guaranteed their cars for six months or 10,000 kilometers, whichever came first, that same year Ford increased their warranty to twenty-four months or 24,000 miles.[18] Skoda, the Czech competition, announced in September 1963 that they would do twelve months or 20,000 kilometers, putting it only a bit short of the rest of the car companies, which had been switching to Ford's arrangement since late 1960. The Soviet Union, however, was still offering six months or 10,000 kilometers at the end of 1963. In order to raise the competitiveness of Soviet automobiles, the Foreign Trade Ministry went around asking the car factory managers to raise their warranties to international standards. Predictably, Soviet managers were disinclined to follow the suggestion, offering instead a modest increase and prompting the Foreign Trade Ministry to seek support from the Council of Ministers against the recalcitrant managers.[19] To return to the comparison that began this section, this episode concerning car insurance points to yet another difference with Korea: In the Soviet Union there was no incentivizing structure for enlisting the cooperation of industrial managers in the export of products.

[16] RGAE, f. 413, op. 31, d. 123, l. 18.
[17] As per the *Vneshniaia torgovlia SSSR za... Statisticheskii obzor* series.
[18] GARF, f. 5446, op. 97, d. 1364, ll. 72–74. [19] Ibid.

A parenthetical note on transportation, or the pangs of commercial growth

Already in the late 1950s the ministries responsible for transportation – primarily the Ministry of Ways of Communication, responsible mainly for the railways, and the Ministry of the Maritime Fleet – were having problems coping with the exponential increase in foreign trade. Complaints to Mikoyan from the Ministry of Foreign Trade and other assorted ministries responsible for the delivery of particular goods for export had risen in tandem with the growth in international commerce. In 1957, for example, the minister of the oil industry complained that the Ministry of Ways of Communication was not providing the train wagons necessary to carry out planned exports of oil.[20] This chronic non-fulfillment stood at 20–35 percent of wagon capacity for planned oil deliveries, hurting oil exports to most East European countries.[21] Meanwhile, the Ministry of the Maritime Fleet was clamoring for more capital from Moscow to fund the purchase in Czechoslovakia of Caterpillar cranes for their ports, as it expected to double sea transit deliveries during the next Five-Year Plan.[22]

As trade expansion moved to encompass a greater geographical area, these sorts of logistical problems intensified.[23] The problems of oil deliveries mentioned earlier notwithstanding, trade expansion occurring in the 1940s and 1950s entailed an expansion of trade with Eastern Europe, and thus mostly land-borne trade.[24] However, by the late 1950s, and particularly during the 1960s, both the absolute level and the share of sea-borne trade as a percentage of trade in general increased, rising from 26 million metric tons in 1958 to about 109 million in 1967, and from 38.1 percent of total trade to 52.7 percent during that same period.[25] The type of strain already apparent after the relatively slow expansion of maritime-borne trade with Eastern European countries in the 1950s threatened to

[20] RGAE, f. 413, op. 13, d. 7931, ll. 9–11. The Ministry of Ways of Communication, then, and in later years, seemed particularly recalcitrant in helping to fulfill export plans, often necessitating the intervention of the Council of Ministers.

[21] Ibid. [22] RGAE, f. 4372, op. 57, d. 384, l. 236.

[23] Along with Gosplan's workload on foreign economic relations. In 1961, Gosplan's department for foreign economic relations was asking for more staff, given the increasing volume of work "and the necessity to establish and expand economic relations with [countries in Africa, Asia and Latin America]." See RGAE, f. 4372, op. 63, d. 400, ll. 7–9.

[24] Citing Soviet sources, Philip Hanson estimated the sea-borne percentage of trade volume with Eastern Europe at 10.5 percent. See Philip Hanson, "The Soviet Union and World Shipping," *Soviet Studies* 22:1 (1970): 46.

[25] Ibid., 46–47. As Hanson notes, this was still well below the world average of a 75 percent share for maritime trade, a result of the continued high share of trade with Eastern Europe.

undermine the exploitation of the Soviets' newfound opportunities in world trade during the 1960s.

This development was anticipated by Gosekonomsovet, the agency for perspective planning. In 1961, Gosekonomsovet officials brought it to the attention of then deputy chairman of the Council of Ministers Alexei Kosygin, writing that "in the last years the volume of Soviet foreign trade turnover and the transportation of import–export cargo grow continuously. Meanwhile the planning and organization of import–export transportation has serious deficiencies, causing great difficulties in the fulfillment of trade plans and the inadequate use of the technical resources of the railways and sea transport."[26]

Tellingly, the Soviet merchant fleet was only the twelfth biggest fleet in the world in 1961, a state of affairs that Gosekonomsovet wanted to see improved if the Soviet Union was going to meet the fast-growing demands of foreign trade.[27] The main issue, according to Gosekonomsovet officials, was to "liquidate the lag of the maritime cargo transportation fleet from demands in the domestic and international sea deliveries in order to provide for the development of trade with foreign countries." To do this, Gosekonomsovet suggested that production of cargo ships in the decade to 1970 would have to be multiplied by three, and by six by 1980, so that in two decades the Soviet Union should have 2,400 cargo ships with a total tonnage of 17,700,000 gross tons of cargo.[28] This would allow the Soviet merchant fleet to become the fourth or fifth biggest fleet in terms of tonnage, which would not only meet Soviet demands for maritime deliveries, but would also allow the Soviet Union to become a net exporter of cargo ships by the 1970s.[29] This immense enterprise would entail the creation of new kinds of productions, such as diesel engines and steam turbines of the latest technology and a whole array of other auxiliary machinery, necessitating the construction of five shipyards and fourteen new machine-building factories.[30]

Gosekonomsovet's estimates were not far off. From 1961, gross tonnage of Soviet cargo ships had tripled as early as 1968, turning the Soviet merchant fleet into the sixth biggest in the world by 1970, a testament to the importance given that industry and to foreign trade in general by Soviet leaders.[31]

26 RGAE, f. 7, op. 3, d. 807, ll. 38–39. 27 RGAE, f. 7, op. 3, d. 814, ll. 9. 28 Ibid., l. 8.

29 Ibid. 30 Ibid., l. 11

31 Hanson, "The Soviet Union and World Shipping," 45, table 1. Hanson's numbers are from the Chamber of Shipping of the United Kingdom. In fact, if one discounts Liberia, whose merchant marine was mostly foreign-owned with the state merely providing the flag, the Soviet merchant fleet would have been the fifth biggest, surpassed only by that of the United Kingdom, Norway, Japan, and the United States.

Cold War-era Western analysts feared that this rapid growth in Soviet tonnage may have been caused by a reaction to the US embargo on ships trading with bloc countries after the 1962 Cuban Missile Crisis, and that the larger merchant fleet would have as an objective the disruption of the world shipping market. But it was economist Philip Hanson who was closer to the mark; he reasoned that the likelier motives had to do with a Soviet need to save on convertible currency and a desire for independence in shipping.[32] After all, Hanson argued, the Soviet Union too was becoming invested in the smooth functioning of world trade. The Soviet archives prove Hanson's less alarmist reasoning to be the wiser, as a simple case of fruit imports illustrates.

From 1952 to 1960 the volume of imported fruits had grown from 69,000 tons to 550,000 tons, a number Gosekonomsovet hoped to increase ten times over the next two decades.[33] To keep up with this growth, particularly when it came to imports of bananas, pineapples, and other such tropical fruits from countries like Vietnam and Guinea that lacked a merchant fleet, the Ministry of the Maritime Fleet needed to buy cargo ships in Western countries. At the end of 1962, the ministry asked Mikoyan for hard currency to purchase seven more ships from West Germany, on top of the three they had already purchased two years earlier.[34] Under the best circumstances these three ships could only carry about 27,000 tons, and for the rest the Soviets had to rely on foreign freight services. This would cost 650,000 rubles in convertible currency for 1963; 800,000 for 1964; and 1,150,000 rubles for 1965, for a total of 2,600,000 for all three years. One ship cost about 2,400,000 rubles, or three million rubles if bought on credit.[35] This high cost of transport convinced Gosplan, which suggested to the Council of Ministers the purchase of at least five ships on credit from capitalist countries from 1964 to 1966; however, that would require a payment of at least 900,000 rubles in 1964 and 2,400,000 rubles in 1965. This made it impossible, as there was no hard currency for it, which in turn prompted the old strategy of having the Ministry of Foreign Trade look into the possibility of buying the ships from socialist countries on barter arrangements.[36] Upon the impossibility of this latest suggestion, however, the Soviets had to find the necessary resources and ended up importing the ships in 1964 on credit.[37]

In other words, there were two considerations in the discussion on increasing Soviet tonnage through imports. The first one, echoed in

[32] Ibid., passim. [33] RGAE, f. 7, op. 3, d. 506, ll. 54–70.
[34] RGAE, f. 4372, op. 65, d. 408, l. 1. 176. [35] RGAE, f. 4372, op. 65, d. 56, ll. 259–60.
[36] RGAE, f. 4372, op. 65, d. 408, ll. 170–74. [37] Ibid., l. 175.

Gosekonomsovet's study on implementing a program for the expansion of the Soviet merchant fleet, was the urgent, unassailable need to implement the trade plan. At no point did any of the agencies involved suggest the possibility of forgoing or at least decreasing the planned imports of fruits. The issue, as Hanson had argued, was always to find a solution to staunch the outflow of convertible currency and how this might best be arranged. Neither was the question of the independence of Soviet shipping ever raised; no officials expressed any fear that the United States would put pressure on other countries to stop all shipping services to the Soviet Union. Although surely shipping independence was desirable, fears of the kind described by Western analysts did not directly prompt the buildup of the Soviet shipping industry. Rather it seemed implicit, and in keeping with the way the Soviets generally dealt with such logistical problems, that if trade was to be increased, building the infrastructure necessary for this outcome was the next, and only, logical step – especially in the absence of information, as was ever the case, on the opportunity cost of investing in that infrastructure.[38]

A 1965 report drawn up for the Council of Ministers by all agencies involved in the planning and execution of the transportation of imports and exports – as well as Gosplan's Institute of Complex Transportation Problems – confirms that these were, in effect, Moscow's main concerns.[39] Transportation, in the study, was viewed entirely as an economic problem needing redress that it may make more efficient use of hard currency. Political consequences, to judge from the report, merely impinged on the economic problems considered, as was the case with the Western shipping cartel that did everything in its power to exclude Soviet shipping and particularly to undermine its cross-trade capacity.[40]

To get the attention of the Council of Ministers, the report started off with statistics that were likely supposed to be understood as denoting a frightening progression. As foreign trade cargo almost doubled from 1960 to 1965, the transportation of foreign trade goods cost 833 million rubles in 1965, compared to 313 million five years earlier, with maritime transportation having taken over the railways as the most important.[41] In two years,

[38] Which Hanson worked out and found to not be very high. In other words, the profitability of Soviet shipping, in terms of convertible currency, compared rather well with the deployment of resources in other hard-currency earning sectors of the Soviet economy. See his discussion in Hanson, "The Soviet Union and World Shipping," 52–57.

[39] RGAE, f. 4372, op. 66, d. 1340, ll. 35–68.

[40] Ibid., ll. 52–53. Cross-trade refers to the use of Soviet ships to transport cargo between two foreign countries, that is, the use of Soviet shipping as a hard currency-earning service.

[41] Ibid., ll. 38–39.

the report predicted, transportation costs would exceed the one billion ruble mark. A significant portion of this expenditure was covered with hard currency, and a lot of it could be saved if the Council would address the many shortcomings in the organization of the transportation of foreign trade. The report went on to list these shortcomings along with suggested solutions in a bid to make Soviet transportation more rational and less wasteful.

These suggestions included the export of oil to Japan through the Siberian port of Nakhodka after the construction of the necessary infrastructure. Oil to Japan was being delivered through the Black Sea and poured into tankers in the Persian Gulf, at a cost of 19.10 rubles per ton of oil. If taken to Irkutsk through oil pipes and then to Nakhodka by train, the authors calculated the transport costs of one ton of oil to be 4.40 rubles. The yearly cost incurred by the then current system would reach 13 million rubles, of which 1.5 million rubles were in hard currency.[42]

The report went on with other examples of the same ilk, every instance suggesting ways to save on cost while paying particular attention to expenditures in convertible currency. These considerations took, in effect, the bulk of the day-to-day operations of agencies such as the Ministry of Ways of Communication, the Ministry of the Maritime Fleet and, of course, Gosplan. As commerce grew, straining the Soviet Union's physical capacity to carry on this growth, Soviet officials in these agencies were concerned with issues of efficiency and economy. By and large trade growth no longer depended on the limitations of other countries' willingness or ability to deal with the Soviets in commerce. With the world economy more open to the Soviets than ever before, the only limitation seemed to be the Soviet Union's own ability to plan and execute expansion in foreign trade. Growth, to judge from the archival evidence, was also their only mandate.

Europe integrates the USSR: The energy peddling superpower

The fact was that the domestic challenges concerning managerial recalcitrance, low-quality production, and inadequate infrastructure were the wages of success. The Soviet system had been forged in the crucible of autarky in the 1930s, and it was slow to adapt to the global demands of the postwar age, even as the leadership in the Kremlin piled on the strain. By the 1960s, several international currents were pushing in

[42] Ibid., ll. 40–41.

the same direction. The US dollar was no longer the obstacle to global commerce it had been a decade before. It was now in abundance in the rich world, obviating systems of state control aimed at husbanding reserves of US dollars. This accumulation of dollars in Europe and Japan greased the financial gears of world trade and intensified foreign interest in Soviet resources.

The dollar glut was also a sign that Europe had recovered vis-à-vis the United States much of the economic and technological terrain it had lost during the upheavals of the first half of the twentieth century; many of those dollars now being wrested from American consumers were obtained through successful competition with US production. This industrial expansion of the 1960s in Western Europe and Japan came with an important corollary: the wholesale switch from coal to oil as the principal source of energy. In 1955, three-fourths of energy consumed in Western Europe was coal-generated, while oil made up the rest; a decade and a half later the weight of coal versus oil had almost reversed. The change in Japan was, if anything, even more dramatic – from the end of the 1940s to the end of the 1960s oil had grown from providing a mere 7 percent of the energy consumed to providing 70 percent.[43] This switch in the industrialized world came with a renewed determination to break free of Anglo-Saxon control of the international oil industry, embodied in the oil majors from the United States and Great Britain that dominated the world's oil production. Europeans needed new and cheaper suppliers of energy. The Soviets, having clamored for this for decades, were only happy to oblige.

Few men fought harder and more successfully to break the oligopoly of the oil majors than Enrico Mattei, head of the Italian state energy conglomerate *Ente Nazionale Idrocarburi* (ENI). Mattei's first attempt to spoil the oil majors' monopolistic hold over the Middle East was to break with the principle of 50/50 profit sharing with the producer countries and to offer Iran a 75 percent stake in his investment. His brazen move into the Middle East spelled the beginning of the end of the domination of the Western oil majors in the region, but it brought him little profit. ENI's exploratory oil wells in Iran came out empty, at least for commercial purposes.[44] Mattei would have to look somewhere else for cheap oil.

The irrepressible Italian next turned east, where there was an even bigger oil industry taboo ripe for the breaking: doing business with the Communists.

[43] Daniel Yergin, *The Prize: The Epic Quest for Oil, Money and Power* (New York: Simon & Schuster, 1991), 545–46.

[44] Ibid., 503–05.

He quickly signed a contract with the Soviet Union in 1958 for the delivery of oil to Italy. On October 12, 1960, however, he finally got his breakthrough in a deal that netted ENI 12.5 million tons of crude oil over five years in exchange for 240,000 tons of large-diameter pipes along with other pipeline equipment, diesel engines, and synthetic rubber.[45] This was the first large-scale pipes-for-oil deal that would become so critical to the future relations between the Soviet Union and Western Europe – and that would fail to materialize for the Japanese. The oil majors were quick to complain to the State Department: "The ambition of Enrico Mattei to use Russia as a means of harassing and forcing out foreign oil interests in Italy; of developing exports of Italian services and goods to Russia; and of using Russian low-cost supplies as a spring-board for entering Western European markets, coupled with the desire of Italy to increase her foreign commerce, threaten to bring Italy into a dangerous position of subservience to the Iron Curtain block."[46] This view came to prevail in the State Department and the White House for the next two decades.[47] If State Department officials understood the hypocrisy of their position, they showed no scruples on the matter: "The average person in Italy gets his oil cheaper because Italy is importing Soviet oil. Industrialists in Europe can produce at less cost because of Soviet oil. It is hard, under those circumstances, to work up resistance to imports of Soviet oil. Our argument has to be the danger of dependence on Soviet oil."[48] The argument was mercenary and fated to fail. When Monroe Rathbone, chairman of Standard Oil of New Jersey (now Exxon), went to northern Europe for an "on-the-spot appraisal of Soviet exports of oil" in the summer of 1961, he came back disturbed. He found that "there is considerable interest in, and pressure for, increased trade with the Soviets, with much of this pressure coming from business interests."[49] The reason was simple: Europe, its security arranged for, was integrating its natural and industrial resources on a continental scale.

45 The deal is laid out in Memorandum of Conversation, 3 November 1960, US Department of State, *Foreign Relations of the United States* (FRUS), 1958–60, Vol. 7, Part 2 (Washington, DC: US Government Printing Office, 1993), 621. American oil companies were especially alarmed at the price, which at $1 a barrel worked out to about half the price of what the oil majors were charging for Middle Eastern oil.

46 Ibid., 622.

47 As recounted in the excellent Bruce W. Jentleson, *Pipeline Politics. The Complex Political Economy of East-West Trade* (Ithaca: Cornell University Press, 1986).

48 Summary Minutes of Meeting, 13 December 1961, FRUS, 1961–1963, Vol. 9, Foreign Economic Policy, 774.

49 Memorandum of Conversation, 18 July 1961, FRUS, 1961–1963, Vol. 9, Foreign Economic Policy, 762.

October 27, 1962 came to be known as Black Saturday, the most dangerous day of the Cuban Missile Crisis. Two airplanes went down that day: a U-2 spy plane flying over Cuba and a private plane carrying Mattei back to Milan from Sicily. Neither crash was an accident. But Mattei's murder did little to change that process of integration. In talks with American Ambassador to Italy Frederick Reinhardt five months before his death, Mattei had insisted that his "only aim was to provide Italy with a cheap power source and to put Italian labor to work" and Soviet oil was the cheapest he could get.[50] This was not the whole truth, as both men knew, but it was a powerful motivation nonetheless. And it was much closer to the truth than the State Department's presumption of a deliberate Soviet ploy to gain market share and subvert the international oil industry. In fact, the price of Soviet oil was the outcome of hardball negotiations. And the main argument Italians and others used to lower Soviet prices was precisely the political pressure the US government exerted on them to stay away from doing business with Communists. ENI's representatives continued to resist Soviet pressure to raise prices by arguing that the company worked in abnormal political circumstances in which they were constantly attacked in the press for dealing with the Soviet Union; as the Japanese had done before them, the Italians argued that Soviet oil prices should reflect the risks and bad publicity that flowed from this.[51]

American-stoked Cold War animosity did little to derail the rapprochement between European countries and the Soviet Union. Business had been the first advocate of this rapprochement back in the mid 1950s, and by the mid 1960s European governments were more or less sold on the benefits of such a policy. This is because they were no longer in the abject financial position of earlier years that compelled them to abide scrupulously by America's wishes. They could now independently offer the main ingredient necessary for any growth in commercial relations with the Soviet Union: capital. Doing business with the Soviets in the days of acute dollar shortage had entailed a strict adherence to a clearing of accounts. In the 1960s, balanced trade continued to be important, but the Italians could afford plenty of slack because, as Italian Foreign Minister Bernardo Mattarella informed his Soviet counterpart Nikolai Patolichev in October 1964, Italy's balance of payments was doing much better and they could afford to have a deficit with the Soviet Union and

[50] Telegram From the Embassy in Italy to the Department of State, 27 May 1962, FRUS, 1961–1963, Vol. 13, Western Europe and Canada, 841–42.

[51] RGAE, f. 413, op. 13, d. 9757, ll. 4–9. The meeting took place on March 16, 1963.

even offer credit.[52] The Italian government was also willing to support credit from private firms to Soviet organizations. This government support became the basis for the two most important deals of the 1960s between Italy and the Soviet Union, indeed two of the most important deals the Soviets signed with anybody that decade: the Fiat turnkey project in Tolyatti that became the AvtoVaz car factory, and the Trans Austrian Gas (TAG) pipeline that piped Soviet gas directly to Western Europe for the first time.[53] The fact that the preliminary talks for both these deals happened in the same month, June 1965, was in this sense not merely coincidental.[54]

In fact, the dollar glut became a great opportunity for the Soviets to use financial competition as a lever to get better terms and quicker results from the rich nations. When in their 1964 meeting Mattarella complained that Soviet–Italian trade was not balanced, Patolichev responded, quite beside the point, that the French government had recently offered more credit on better terms than the Soviets had even asked for.[55] Two years later, Soviet insistence that there was a viable technical and financial deal with Renault in the works finally decided Fiat and the Italian government to meet Soviet financial demands on the AvtoVaz turnkey project, which was signed in May 1966.[56] In commercial operations in Japan this appeal to competition would become the standard stick with which the Soviets progressively obtained ever more capital on ever better terms. The British, quicker on financial matters and in control of the second most international currency in the world, hoped to use their financial advantage to make up for their firms' escalating lack of competitiveness.[57]

[52] RGAE, f. 413, op. 31, d. 82, ll. 91–93. On October 20, 1964 the Italians offered 35–45 million rubles in credit (or 25–30 billion lira) to finance the export of machinery, equipment, and ships to the Soviet Union, while still complaining that Soviet–Italian trade was not in balance. See ibid., l. 95, 101.

[53] In these preliminary talks, which took place on June 28, Fiat President Vittorio Valletta offered to sell Soviet timber in Italy as "an act of friendship." RGAE, f. 413, op. 31, d. 595, ll. 53–56. The preliminary talks between Patolichev and Eugenio Cefis, vice-president of ENI at the time, are in ibid., ll. 64–67, and took place on June 17.

[54] As Lewis Siegelbaum points out, there were low-level talks on the Fiat deal since 1962, but they did not move very far until Valleta's visit to Moscow in June 1965. The story of AvtoVaz is well told in Lewis Siegelbaum, *Cars for Comrades. The Life of the Soviet Automobile* (Ithaca: Cornell University Press, 2008), 80–124.

[55] RGAE, f. 413, op. 31, d. 82, l. 93.

[56] Siegelbaum, *Cars for Comrades*, 91.

[57] Although they still found themselves losing Soviet business as French, German, and Italian firms improved the financial terms on their business deals. See RGAE, f. 413, op. 31, d. 59, ll. 121–24, in which the English foreign trade minister complains about the chronic deficit with the Soviet Union despite English firms' generous lending practices, and Soviet officials' response that British equipment was of comparatively low quality.

The one country that held out the longest was the one country that consumed most of the Kremlin's attention: West Germany. Financial developments worked in the same direction in West Germany as they did elsewhere in Western Europe, but the country was host to a quarter of a million American troops, and West German foreign policy was deeply embedded within an American security structure that remained a constant reference for all West German diplomatic and economic policymaking.[58] Their approach was therefore very conservative and easily overruled by the United States. In fact, the relationship suffered a blow in 1962 when the Americans vetoed an important deal that would have sent 163,000 tons of German wide-diameter steel pipe to the Soviet Union, and imposed an embargo on that pipe. The Soviets needed to extend the *Druzhba* pipeline to countries within the bloc, and the German steel mills of the Rühr were suffering from underutilized capacity and were anxious to find new sources of demand for their steel.[59] This trade was thus the most promising source of commercial growth between the two countries. The effect of the American veto was to stop this burgeoning relationship in its tracks. Soviet–West German trade reached beyond the 300 million ruble mark in 1962, and would not do so again until five years later (see Figure 5.1).

That period of purgatory was filled with familiar Soviet complaints and recriminations. Ludwig Erhard's government had continued the same cautious attitude of the Adenauer government, with similar results. The trade licensing system had been liberalized for trade with most countries including those of the Soviet Bloc, but remained in place for the Soviet Union, a slight that wounded Soviet amour-propre and hurt West Germany's credibility as a trade partner.[60] Meetings at a government level between the two countries took on an irritable tone; mostly the Soviets did the grousing. The preliminary talks in September 1965 for a new three-year trade agreement between Deputy Minister of Foreign Trade Mikhail Kuz'min and a West German delegation led by State Secretary of the Foreign Office Karl Carstens capture the tenor of the relationship during

58 For a careful study of this connection see Hubert Zimmermann, *Money and Security. Troops, Monetary Policy, and West Germany's Relations with the United Sates and Britain, 1950–1971* (Cambridge: Cambridge University Press, 2002).

59 The story of the embargo is recounted in Angela Stent, *From Embargo to Ostpolitik. The Political Economy of West German–Soviet Relations 1955–1980* (Cambridge: Cambridge University Press, 1981), chapter 5.

60 For example in RGAE, f. 413, op. 31, d. 71, ll. 3–4. The Germans often argued that they were afraid to give German exporters too much freedom to sell to the Soviet Union lest the Soviets not be able to pay back their debts. But the Soviets were very right to feel unconvinced by this, given that they had always paid their debts, as they never tired of pointing out to the Germans.

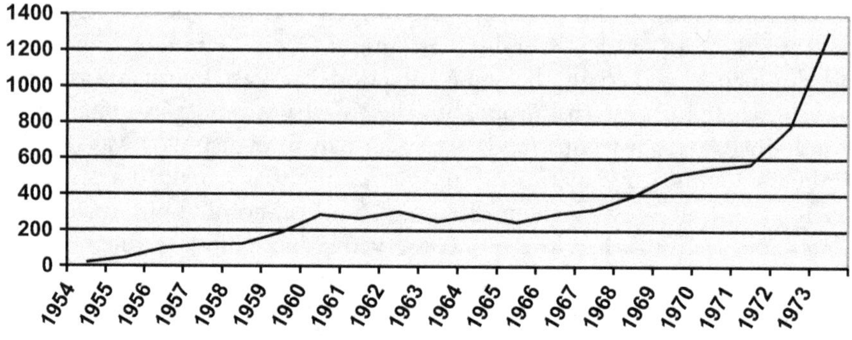

Figure 5.1 USSR trade with West Germany (in millions of current rubles)*
*As derived from the *Vneshniaia torgovlia SSSR za… Statisticheskii obzor* series. The numbers were 304.9 million rubles for 1962 and 319.1 million for 1967. It is important to note that Soviet–West German trade stagnated for half a decade, but did not decline, as the chart shows.

those years.[61] During the meeting Kuz'min complained about the embargo on wide-diameter pipe, remarking that the Soviet Union was already producing it by itself. On a sincere note, he explained that the Soviets preferred to buy it in Germany in order to take advantage of the world division of labor and gain time. He then raised the specter of competition, by now a well-used trope, claiming that if Germany wouldn't sell the pipe, other capitalist countries would. His argument was clear: It is the West German side that was hampering the development of trade between the two countries.[62] The Germans for their part avoided the polemics and informed the Soviets that the West German government was now ready to guarantee export credits. They were three years late, Kuz'min reproached the Germans. West Germany's European neighbors had been offering and guaranteeing credits for a long time. The next piece of good news also failed to placate Kuz'min: West Germany was planning on further liberalizing their trade with socialist countries.[63] And so it went for half a decade, the Soviets sore and bewildered about the tightening of a pointless embargo and the Germans bringing only marginal improvements to the table.[64]

The relationship was much better with the German industrialists. It was almost always the case that Soviet trade and economic officials got along better with businessmen than with civil servants of foreign

[61] RGAE, f. 413, op. 31, d. 71, ll. 18–27. [62] Ibid., 22–23. [63] Ibid., 24–25.
[64] See Manzhulo's recapitulation of 1962 four years later in RGAE, f. 413, op. 31, d. 71, ll. 28–33.

countries.[65] But with German capital flows still subject to extensive government regulation, the main problem continued to be the inability of the German business community to offer attractive lines of credit. In 1963, for example, an understanding had been reached for the export of equipment and expertise for an oil refinery with the capacity to produce twelve million tons of oil products a year.[66] There was no real technical challenge to the project, but the consortium of businessmen that had negotiated it – which was led by steel tycoon Otto Wolff and included Krupp, Siemens, and other flagship companies – could not offer long-term credits to the Soviets. They hoped to use the large export order to put pressure on the government to change the credit policy toward the Soviet Union, and after two years of fighting, the question reached all the way to Erhard, who allowed the consortium to offer a ten-year credit line guaranteed by the government.

The Soviets continued to put pressure on the German government both directly and indirectly through their allies in German business circles.[67] It is clear that German businessmen adopted the Soviet view on the issue of embargoed items and credit arrangements; they continued to hope to change government policy in order to be able to compete for Soviet orders with other European countries.[68] By the mid 1960s, in other words, the Soviets were learning to play the game, substituting diplomatic language about the relationship between trade promotion and world peace for a more aggressive and effective negotiating strategy – assisted with the

[65] With respect to West Germany, Angela Stent notes the difference between the tough public pronouncements routinely made by Soviet officials, and their much more engaging attitude when negotiating deals with German businessmen. Stent, *From Embargo to Ostpolitik*, 144.

[66] The following is recounted in a meeting between representatives from chemical company Imhausen International Company and the Soviet Ministry of Foreign Trade on June 23, 1964 in RGAE, f. 413, op. 31, d. 585, ll. 47–48. Three months later, however, industrialist Otto Wolff was reporting that the government guaranteed only eight-year credit arrangements. In RGAE, f. 413, op. 31, d. 585, ll. 78–81.

[67] See, for example, the foreign trade department's talk with Peter von Siemens: "Such West German government actions as the export embargo of wide-diameter pipe to the USSR, or the refusal from West German firms to fulfill several contracts in the purchase of Soviet goods, have broken the certainty that West German firms can cope with the fulfillment of this or that order." RGAE, f. 413, op. 31, d. 585, ll. 63–65. Or the head of trade with Western countries A. N. Manzhulo's lively meeting in September 1966 with deputies from the Bundestag, in which he complains not just about past grievances, but also a possible new insurance system being negotiated in which West German firms might be insured against losses incurred by sudden government embargoes of Soviet products. This in Soviet eyes would make West German firms even less reliable. In RGAE, f. 413, op. 31, d. 1119, ll. 58–61.

[68] As expressed in so many words by Otto Wolff in September 1965 in RGAE, f. 413, op. 31, d. 585, ll. 78–81.

persistent vocalization of past and current grievances. But it would be neither Soviet griping nor the industrial lobby that finally broke through the impasse. Wide-diameter pipe had been the basis for most of that initial growth during the first half decade of trade, and its embargo had been at the center of its decline during the subsequent five years. Its resumption meant the resumption of the Soviet–West German commercial relationship.

The embargo had always been deeply unpopular in Germany, where it was viewed as a humiliating submission to US priorities – even downright immoral in the way it forced the breach of already existing contracts with Soviet trade agencies.[69] Ultimately, it was the imminent closing to the deal between ENI and the Soviet Union to build the TAG pipeline that made the German government decide to belatedly join the rest of Europe in defying American edict. With talks intensifying between the Soviets and Italians in 1966, the Germans announced an end to the pipe embargo in November.[70] That same month, German Ambassador to the Soviet Union Gebhardt von Walter approached the Ministry of Foreign Trade to investigate whether West Germany could get a hold of some of the gas that would flow through Austria and into Italy.[71] A consortium of German firms had failed to secure deliveries of gas from Algeria, and now they were turning to the Soviet Union to see whether they might divert some of that gas into Bavaria. The understanding was that the Germans would pay for the deliveries in wide-diameter pipe, the largest of which, forty-eight inches in diameter, could only be produced by the Thyssen Group, itself the largest steel company in Europe.[72] It took a few years for the complicated deal to come together, but it was finally signed in February 1970. With a financing of $400 million for twelve years at an interest rate of 6.25 percent, it broke further ground relative to previous arrangements, helping German steel mills with their problems of underutilization and bringing Soviet energy firmly into the core of the Western European economy.[73] It meant the end of the beginning of the continental economic integration that had started with the signing of a three-year long-term trade agreement in 1957. It was also the beginning of the end of a Soviet Union that by the 1980s had become too dependent on energy exports, the price of which proved to be too volatile for the anemic superpower.

[69] Stent, *From Embargo to Ostpolitik*, 109–12. [70] Ibid., 166.
[71] RGAE, f. 413, op. 31, d. 1119, ll. 121–22. [72] Ibid., 123–24.
[73] The deal is detailed in Stent, *From Embargo to Ostpolitik*, 163–68.

Japanese pipe dreams

Japan offers a short-term parallel and long-term contrast to West Germany. Whereas in the long term Europe succeeded in integrating Soviet energy resources into the European economy, Japan's success in integrating Siberia into its rapidly expanding economy was much more qualified. Oil made the difference. But the failure was only comparative, and when it came it was already the 1970s. The short-term commercial development, based as it was on the quick establishment of a Far Eastern timber industry, was rather more successful.

The 1960s were a decade of growth and promise, especially during the mid-decade years of Soviet–West German commercial stagnation. Japanese businessmen, like those in Europe, probed and queried up and down the vast Communist empire. In fact, the competition among Japanese businessmen was such that many were often shunted; Soviet bureaucrats could have the pick of the litter. In the early 1960s, one of the Soviet Union's most loyal Japanese partners, President Noguchi Nosio of the Japan Sea Trading Co., had to wait for a month in Moscow just to get an interview with Mikoyan to talk about the prospects for trade between the Soviet Union and Japan.[74] Yet Japanese businessmen such as Noguchi were nothing if not assiduous. And they were also progressively better informed, often monitoring and seizing on information that might help their cause. For example, upon hearing of a shortage of car tires in the Soviet Union, one Japanese businessman offered to supply that deficit good in exchange for Siberian timber, ever the object of Japanese attentions.[75] As long as he had a willing audience, this time in the department for trade with the countries of Southeast Asia and the Middle East, he further tendered his company's services: "As an all-round trading firm, we handle practically all varieties of commercial products, including

[74] GARF, f. 5446, op. 94, d. 122, l. 102. More concretely on that trip, Noguchi was looking to establish direct air routes between the two countries to facilitate future trade. A year later he still hadn't gotten a deal on the air route, although he had become an important importer of Soviet timber, handling about 10 percent of the exports of Soviet timber to Japan. See GARF, f. 5446, op. 97, d. 1369, l. 10. The direct Moscow–Tokyo route was finally established in 1966, along with the first long-term trade plan between the two countries, after a Japanese economic delegation was finally approved and sponsored by the Japanese government. See Iu. S. Stoliarov and Ia. A. Pevzner, *SSSR–Iaponiia: problemy torgovo-ekonomicheskikh otnoshenii* (Moscow: Mezhdunarodnye otnosheniia, 1984), 19. The relationship with Noguchi only grew warmer. In a warm letter written on the occasion of Mikoyan's eightieth birthday, Noguchi claimed to be the biggest buyer of Siberian timber in Japan, and thanked the now-retired Mikoyan warmly for the faith he had in Noguchi. In RGASPI, f. 84, op. 3, d. 107, ll. 1–2.

[75] GARF, f. 5446, op. 96, d. 1169, ll. 7–8.

textile goods, iron and steel products, machinery and chemical items," he offered, hoping rightly that the Soviets would be attracted to sprawling conglomerates that could accept and supply a wide variety of products, as some large European corporations also did.[76]

The Soviets too became ever bolder in their demands of partnership and capital, sending their own delegation to do business in Japan, including an important one in August 1961 led by Mikoyan himself.[77] A month before that trip, Mikoyan had enthusiastically shown his cards to a visiting group of Japanese businessmen. Prompted by a question from a member of the group on whether they could expect Japan to be part of the plans for the development of Siberia, Mikoyan was clear: "Of course you can. You are the banker. Consequently, everything depends on you. Provide us with credit, and you will get it back with interest."[78] But in 1961, Japanese banks were still not free to provide such loans; government still regulated all international finance in Japan, as another member pointed out. Mikoyan responded with a sales pitch, at least one of typical Soviet vintage (that is, with a shrug at the end):

> You don't trust us? You make a mistake. For your information I'll let you know that in 44 years of Soviet power there has not been a single instance in which a debt has gone unpaid. With us you can work in the broadest scale. We have enormous resources of wood, iron ore, coal, oil. If you allocate capital, we could incorporate into our plans the development of those industries in Siberia and the Far East that ensure the export of the resources you need. If you do not want to give us the credit for this – it's your business. We are still going to develop the economy of these areas, in accordance with our plans.[79]

To belabor the point, Mikoyan repeated himself in answer to a question on the projected construction of an oil refinery in the Vladivostok–Nakhodka region. "Dates have not been determined, but the sooner the Japanese companies provide us with pipes and equipment, the more likely the pipeline will be built. But we do not hurry. You want it to be faster – provide credit to our organizations and they will buy your pipe and equipment."

Delegations by this point were being exchanged with great alacrity on both sides. Two reports from April 1962 show the shared enthusiasm for

[76] Ibid., l. 9. The Ministry of Foreign Trade's department for trade with Southeast Asia and the Middle East was happy to forward the offer to Mikoyan and even advocated strongly for the Japanese businessman's offer.

[77] Covered in RGASPI, f. 84, op. 3, d. 36.

[78] GARF, f. 5446, op. 120, d. 1626, ll. 34–40.

[79] Ibid., ll. 39–40.

the promise of Soviet–Japanese trade relations, and explain how it came to be the most important commercial relation with a capitalist country for the Soviets by the end of the decade. In a report to the Central Committee on their trip in April 1962, one Soviet delegation noted signs of economic friction in the US–Japan relationship. It was the right time for the Soviets to drive "a small wedge" between the two capitalist countries, the delegation argued.[80] That rhetoric was Stalinist archaic, harking back to the now obsolete position of taking advantage of "capitalist contradictions." The report's recommendations, on the other hand, showed little in the way of political calculations, but rather presented a sober appraisal of the economic complementarities of both countries (as well as being an excellent example of Soviet bureaucratese):

> It would be expedient for our country to propose to the Japanese an important increase in purchases in Japan of machinery and equipment, of course under conditions no worse than those presently existing in the world market in terms of price, payment installments, etc. To the list of machine-building production can be added ships, chemical and oil refining equipment, road-building machinery, refrigeration equipment and other types of machines for which there is great demand in the Soviet Union and for which the quality of Japanese versions is sufficiently high. Our industry is also interested in the acquisition of technological equipment, particularly for the manufacture of radio technology, precision bearings and other products… Concomitantly it is necessary to take into account that the expansion of purchases of machinery and equipment will also provide the opportunity to increase the number of our cadres who, upon long stays in Japan, can study there the techniques and technology so as to quickly make use of the favorable experience of Japanese industry.
>
> At the same time we should propose to the Japanese a significant increase in our deliveries of raw materials (in both quantity and nomenclature) as the necessary condition in the expansion of purchases there of machines, equipment, pipes, titanium, high-purity silicon and other materials. It must be said that on the question of the supply of raw materials for their industry, the Japanese fear possible market and political instabilities. Which is why they are interested in: the export capabilities of areas from where they will get their purchased raw materials; the geographical proximity of these sources to Japan; the capacity and continuous operation of the transportation arteries; and other such questions.
>
> This is clearly why Japanese business circles are so keenly interested in our plans for the development of Siberia.[81]

[80] GARF, f. 5446, op. 96, d. 1169, l. 24. [81] Ibid., ll. 25–26.

They were not misreading the mood in Japan's business circles. While the delegation was visiting Japan, the president of the All-Japanese Fishing Association, Takasaki Tatsunosuke, was telling Mikoyan much the same thing, despite the obvious fact that these import–export matters were well beyond the competence of the fishing association.[82] Takasaki, a prominent businessman and politician, cheered the possibility that soon 10 percent of Japanese petroleum demand might be met by Soviet oil. He wanted that tripled. He wanted Soviet oil pipes to reach Nakhodka, and informed a pleased Mikoyan that Japan would be happy to help in the construction of those pipes.

Four months later a delegation of Japanese businessmen was able to put an offer directly to Khrushchev that matched everything the Kremlin had been hearing.[83] The Japanese wanted timber, oil, coking coal, and iron ore, and they were willing to build the necessary factories and power stations on Soviet soil to extract these resources from the Soviet Union – and even went as far as to proposition to fill the sawmills with Japanese workers to ensure the processed timber met their standards.[84] They offered ships, which the Soviets bought enthusiastically. In fact, two years later the head of the Ministry of the Maritime Fleet could still be heard lobbying for them at the Council of Ministers, as they held up much better than Soviet ships over time and cut about 25 to 30 percent of the crew needed to manage them compared to the domestic variety.[85] The Soviet response was businesslike and pragmatic. Soviet economic agencies wanted to get into the details of exactly how much of the raw materials the Japanese wanted that they may factor these exports into their plans.[86] And they continued to push the prospect of building an oil pipe from Irkutsk to the port city of Nakhodka if only the Japanese would commit to sufficient purchases of oil to justify that kind of investment, which would need five to six years to bring into exploitation.[87]

Once in a while, the Japanese were reminded of the systemic and ideational limits of Soviet international commerce. A delegation arriving in July 1963 suggested that Siberian towns be supplied by Japanese consumer goods because it made more sense to transport goods to the Russian Far East from Japan rather than Moscow or European Russia more

[82] GARF, f. 5446, op. 120, d. 1686, ll. 9–17.
[83] GARF, f. 5446, op. 98, d. 1437, l. 35.
[84] RGAE, f. 4372, op. 64, d. 445, ll. 37–38.
[85] GARF, f. 5446, op. 98, d. 1442, ll. 24–25.
[86] RGAE, f. 4372, op. 64, d. 445, ll. 40–41.
[87] Ibid. The Japanese, working under market conditions, could not commit themselves to any particular amount, and limited themselves to stating that Japan was bound to experience a meaningful increase in its demand for oil in the next few years.

generally. Moreover, he advocated, Soviet Siberia should concentrate on exporting its raw materials to Japan unprocessed. With timber, for example, Japanese companies could then process it and sell it back to the Soviets.[88] These brazen suggestions were politely rejected. Non-capital goods (that is, consumer goods) were still not something the leadership sought from international markets – barring cases of absolute necessity. There was no need to start changing the structure of Soviet–Japanese trade, Gosplan officials reasoned. They reminded the Japanese delegation, correctly, that trade relations were being held back by caution on the Japanese side, and anyway they preferred concrete proposals.

The crux, as with Western Europe, was energy. There was always room for growth in the trade of other commodities, and growth would continue apace through the 1960s and beyond. But Soviet oil was the prize, as everyone knew. Without oil, trade growth would be incremental; with oil it would be exponential. The first exchanges of opinion on a Trans-Siberian oil pipe had taken place in 1959. The most spectacular oil discoveries ever made in the Soviet Union, those of Western Siberia in the Tyumen region, had been made in the three years since then. All the while, the Soviets had waited for the Japanese to offer the necessary capital and technology to build the pipeline. The oil was to come on line during the second half of the 1960s, and it needed consumers. It is at this point that the Soviets stepped up the pressure on the Japanese to come through with the necessary financing and planning so that Western Siberian oil may fuel the Japanese economic miracle.

But the Japanese government had not followed Europe in loosening capital constraints and assuming a more liberal approach to business with the Soviet Union. Through the 1960s, the Japanese government was still concerned with trade and current account deficits that might undermine the yen's peg to the dollar, and capital controls remained tighter there than elsewhere in the rich world.[89] These controls grew even tighter during the recession in Japan of 1965, which put pressure on Japanese hard currency reserves. Soviet arguments that Europe's financing of trade was more competitive than Japan's were not as successful there as they were in West Germany.[90] Furthermore, and in the absence of regional catalysts such

88 RGAE, f. 4372, op. 65, d. 412, ll. 85–90.

89 Ronald I. McKinnon and Kenichi Ohno, *Dollar and Yen. Resolving Economic Conflict between the United States and Japan* (Cambridge: MIT Press, 1997), 1–45.

90 In the mid 1960s this became a habitual argument in Soviet–Japanese meetings. The Soviets seemed to tell any Japanese person who would listen, even if it meant berating the head of the Japanese Socialist Party for Japan's offer of a five-year credit arrangement, which compared badly to the

as ENI's open defiance of American desiderata in Europe, Japan's government remained more cautious than its business class.

A second trip by Mikoyan in May 1964 did not shake the Japanese into providing the capital and pipe necessary to bring Siberian oil to the Pacific shore and Japanese markets. His trip had one message: Give the Soviet Union competitive credit terms and we'll go on a shopping spree in Japan. He told leaders of the chemical industry: "We have paid too much attention to chemical science and too little to production. Lately we have decided not to ignore but rather to travel that trail already blazed by the Japanese chemical industry – the purchase of licenses abroad, the use of foreign experience."[91] He told the zaibatsu, the vast conglomerates that ruled Japan's corporate world, first to Mitsui: "Before there was a wall of mistrust, but that it is now destroyed and there is a great deal of mutual trust; when the Soviets sign an agreement, it is impossible that they will not make its payments.";[92] then to Mitsubishi: "The new plan to 1970 will lack hard currency, and although we export industrial equipment to places like India, we do so through the local currency or through barter for local goods; we will need installment plans for large industrial orders from Japan."[93] He told assorted groups of businessmen: "We could place large orders for heavy machinery, complete plants, if only the terms of payments for the orders are suitable, like say, in 10-year installment plans."[94] And he even told Prime Minister Ikeda, who tactfully replied that such details are better left to the experts.[95] The last of the Old Bolsheviks was putting on a dog and pony show.

Mikoyan was not optimistic about the deal that mattered most, as he revealed to Idemitsu Keisuke, vice president of the oil company Idemitsu Kosan Co. Idemitsu Sazo, the company's founder, had been a less flamboyant incarnation of Mattei, defying the oil majors as well as Western governments by dealing with international pariahs – and reaping great benefits. First, Idemitsu picked up oil in Mosaddegh's Iran in 1953 just before the American coup there.[96] Then, in the late 1950s, following in

British offer of twelve-year loans and the French offer of ten-year loans. In RGAE, f. 413, op. 31, d. 123, l. 155. This particular scolding took place on July 13, 1964.

91 GARF, f. 5446, op. 120, d. 1871, ll. 65–69.

92 GARF, f. 5446, op. 120, d. 187, l. 13.

93 Ibid., l. 25. He knew this was a governmental decision, he told Mitsubishi's executives, but he was "sure that such a strong company as Mitsubishi could find a way through banks and other channels to offer long-term credits." They couldn't, as it turned out.

94 Ibid., ll. 44–45.

95 GARF, f. 5446, op. 120, d. 1871, l. 13.

96 But not before the Italians and the Americans had gone in first to scoop up some of the nationalized oil. See Keisuke Idemitsu's comments in "Persian Oil Taken to Italy," *The Times*, April 11, 1953.

Mattei's footsteps, Idemitsu turned to the Soviet Union, becoming the country's main buyer of crude. Unlike Mattei, Idemitsu did not set but rather followed the agenda set by the Japanese government through MITI. So when Sazo's younger brother, Keisuke, told Mikoyan that he would happily buy from the Soviets ten million tons of oil a year if only it came by pipe, he was sincere, eager, and powerless to help.[97] The Japanese government was offering no guarantees that it would allow either the sale of the pipes or the purchase of enough oil to justify the construction project in the first place. Mikoyan's only hope was for businessmen like Idemitsu to lobby for the Soviets, but ultimately both knew that the decision for such a geopolitically sensitive undertaking was America's to make. It might be that the Japanese government would change its mind at the prospect of cheap Soviet oil, Mikoyan told Idemitsu, but the American oil monopolies will not change their minds.[98]

Mikoyan's sales pitch echoed through the halls of the economic bureaucracy of the Soviet Union for years. In September 1965, Gosplan Chairman Petr Lomako could not have been more explicit with Chairman of the Japanese–Soviet Committee for Economic Cooperation Uemura Kogoro: "We are ready to develop oil, meaning to sell it to you, but we would like to have from you a long-term bank credit which we would pay back with oil. Along these lines we can concretely conduct a conversation. There is oil even closer to you. Today there are large oil reserves in the region of Tyumen. We need pipes; we could get them from you on credit. Along these lines can we conduct a conversation."[99] Uemura's suggestion that perhaps that oil could be taken to Japan through Black Sea ports left Lomako unmoved, explaining that even that would require capital investments and Japanese credit.[100]

A year later, Lomako's successor as chairman of Gosplan, Nikolai Baibakov, played the same record to another Japanese delegation that had come to Moscow to find out which areas of the Soviet economy were open for cooperation with Japanese business. "From the Soviet side the doors were open" on the development of oil in Tyumen, gas in Sakhalin, copper mines in Udokanskii as well as Siberian timber and exports of coking coal.[101] "We are ready to cooperate with Japan," Baibakov said, "in the direction and projects that would be mutually beneficial. The difference

[97] GARF, op. 120, d. 1871, ll. 63–64. The meeting took place on May 15, 1964. [98] Ibid.
[99] RGAE, f. 4372, op. 66, d. 87, ll. 88–89. [100] Ibid., l. 89.
[101] RGAE, f. 4372, op. 66, d. 669, ll. 51–54.

in the socio-economic systems is not an obstacle, and the Soviet side would be ready to use whatever possibilities might present themselves."[102]

These possibilities turned out not to include a pipeline to the Pacific Ocean. It was one thing to develop Siberian timber resources. There was a geographical expedience to that endeavor that gave the Japanese both an overriding interest and a competitive advantage vis-à-vis their capital-rich rivals in Western Europe. In the competition for Soviet oil, however, the Japanese remained much too conservative. In 1965, Patolichev tried to prod Miki Takeo, MITI minister at the time – and prime minister ten years later – by explaining Soviet decision-making in the face of a competitive world market environment:

> When foreign trade agencies go to the market, they naturally look to where conditions are most advantageous – price, quality, payment terms – and no one can force the agencies to buy goods where they are not profitable. The Japanese government too cannot force firms to buy there where prices are higher or payment terms and quality are worse. Hitherto we have been able to conclude deals with Japanese companies on better terms than with firms in other countries, and hence the increase in turnover. However, when England, France and Italy offered us long-term credit, Japanese firms were at a disadvantage – less competitive. Please take this into account.[103]

Patolichev then illustrated:

> The Soviet Union is now buying five pulp and paper mills. Some plants could be bought in Japan. The French offer us two plants on credit and we already have a firm agreement on these plants. If they can build two plants then clearly they can build all five. We would like to place some of those orders in Japan, but not on worse terms. We place orders there where conditions are favorable. For example, Italy wanted to receive orders for tankers, but Japanese firms gave us more favorable conditions and a large part of the orders were placed in Japan. In Italy we have ordered six tankers for a gross tonnage of 48,000, and in Japan since 1960, we have ordered ships for a gross tonnage of 1 million and the Soviet Union is now the largest customer of Japanese ships.[104]

But MITI did not move. Mikoyan had been right: Japan would not move without the United States. He had simplified matters a bit, however. It was

[102] Ibid. Baibakov would remain as head of Gosplan for two decades. Other projects he brought up to the Japanese during that meeting were the perennially promised pipeline to the Pacific Ocean from Irkutsk and the development of Pacific ports, both projects finally being brought to fruition in Russia under Putin.

[103] RGAE, f. 413, op. 31, d. 640, ll. 92–93. The meeting dates July 8, 1965.

[104] Ibid., ll. 91–92.

not the oil majors monopolizing the Japanese petroleum market that were the main impediment – although they were not passive spectators either. The main problem was geopolitical, and it affected the United States as much as it did China, with which Japan had lately been cultivating a commercial relationship.[105] An oil pipe would essentially bring Soviet industrial might to the Pacific Rim, significantly increasing Soviet military capabilities in the Far East. It would also require an important readjustment of Soviet trade and credit policies toward the Soviet Union, which the Japanese government was unwilling to undertake. The capital requirements were larger than the Japanese government was comfortable investing in projects abroad, as they continued to make clear to the Soviets well into the 1970s.[106] The government thus waited for one of two developments: either for Japanese businessmen to succeed in negotiating the Soviets down to terms worse than those offered in Western Europe, or to get the Americans involved in the investment, which would bring with it both capital and an implicit political endorsement. Talks dragged on for many years, but the pipe was never built.

Japan nevertheless did finance some important projects, mostly involving timber and coal, as well as an expensive search for gas in Yakutsk and Sakhalin. These were enough to make Japan the most important trading partner of the Soviet Union among the rich capitalist countries in 1970 and 1971. But the relationship, etched in wood and coal as it was, was soon eclipsed once fuel, both viscous and gaseous, began to flow into Europe in the 1970s.[107] By the mid 1970s the relationship had stagnated, even as the Soviet Union was drawn ever deeper into the commercial and financial embrace of Western Europe.

105 For a thorough discussion see Gerald L. Curtis, "The Tyumen Oil Development Project and Japanese Foreign Policy Decision-Making," in Robert A. Scalapino, ed., *The Foreign Policy of Modern Japan* (Berkeley: University of California Press, 1977).

106 Chung Sung-Beh, "Japanese Soviet Economic Relations," *Soviet and Eastern European Foreign Trade* 11:4 (1975): 22–25.

107 Oil and oil products, which had comprised a quarter of all exports in 1963, fell to some 10 percent of all trade by 1970. Coal exports kept up with overall trade and maintained itself at some 10 percent as well. Timber, that linchpin of the economic relationship between the two countries, grew from a third of all trade in 1963 to more than two-thirds by the end of the decade, which in terms of volume in cubic meters entailed a four-fold increase between 1963 and 1970. Calculated from *Vneshniaia torgovlia SSSR za 1963 god*, 234 and *Vneshniaia torgovlia SSSR za 1970 god*, 258. The percentage is in terms of value, given in the tables in rubles. Other raw and semi-finished materials made their appearance in the trading tables during this period and also became important items of exchange, particularly cast iron, aluminum, and some non-ferrous metal ores, as well as cotton and flax. On the other hand, imports from Japan were all manufactured products, particularly machinery and industrial equipment of the advanced technological variety.

Conclusion

Given the complete commitment to standard, profitable commercial exchange that Soviet officials showed in their dealings with capitalist businessmen, it is difficult to sustain any argument that posits Soviet intentions as somehow aiming to undermine the very system of profitable economic exchange that they themselves courted so actively. Their investment in the world economic system was significant and growing. The growth of trade with the rich world during the last three decades of the Soviet Union surpassed that of trade with the "developing" world as well as trade with Eastern Europe. Incidentally, during the 1960s and 1970s the growth of Soviet trade with Japan also surpassed that with Finland. In other words, the rewards the Soviets found in their engagement with the rich countries were more attractive than those of any other relationship. The accommodation to the international liberal system was so complete by the 1970s, that it easily subjugated whatever ideological purpose might have been left.

A small episode of economic diplomacy recapitulates the point nicely. In January 1964, A. Romanov, the head of the advertising department of Vneshtorgizdat, the publisher responsible for publications relating to foreign trade, wrote Mikoyan to ask for his support in a small wrangle with the editor of *Ekonomicheskaia gazeta*, a weekly magazine issued by the Central Committee of the Soviet Communist Party.[108] Twenty-one Japanese businesses had approached Romanov to publish an ad in that magazine extending their New Year's greetings to Soviet citizens, for which they were willing to pay $2,000. Officials at the Ministry of Foreign Trade thought that this could only play a positive role in the development of economic relations between Japan and the Soviet Union. The editor had a different view, however, arguing that publishing such ads from companies from capitalist countries would be "apolitical," given that the magazine was an organ of the Communist Party. He forbade the ad.[109]

Romanov split his argument into two points: the economic and the political. The economic justification was straightforward. The Japanese were willing to pay $2,000. Ads of the same kind from foreign firms had been a good source of hard currency in the last years, bringing in an

[108] GARF, f. 5446, op. 98, d. 1437, l. 10. Romanov was being supported by other officials in the Ministry of Foreign Trade, particularly the heads of the department for trade with the countries of Southeast Asia and the Middle East, V. B. Spandar'ian, and the department for trade with Western countries, A. N. Manzhulo. The editor in question was A. I. Pol'shchikov.

[109] Ibid., l. 11.

estimated 110,000 rubles in hard currency in 1963, an amount that could be increased tenfold in the next few years "under conditions of a rational approach to the question (*pri razumnoi podkhode k etomu voprosu*). Why shut off this source from which our government can derive profit?"[110] Romanov then went on to point to other instances in which Soviet magazines refused to publish advertisements from Western companies. For example, *Ogonek* went back on its agreement to publish an ad for Chanel on its pages, for which Chanel was willing to pay $10,000. This brought him to his second point: Such behavior only sustained the myth that elements existed within the Soviet Union that were bent on obstructing the development of trade with the capitalist world, a myth that the foreign reactionary press loved to trumpet. "The question of the necessity to advertise foreign products in the Soviet Union and to strengthen our commercial propaganda abroad has come to a head, and it must be decided at the highest organs," claimed Romanov. "It is the seriousness of this problem that has made me approach you personally," he pressed Mikoyan.[111] The petition had been made on January 2; two weeks later the issue of *Ekonomicheskaia Gazeta* was published, and Soviet hearts must have warmed that cold winter upon chancing on the cordial greetings from their earnest trading partners to the East.[112]

[110] Ibid. At the exchange rate then current, that was $100,000.
[111] Ibid., l. 12.
[112] Ibid., l. 15. For which Romanov fervently thanked Mikoyan.

CHAPTER 6

Poor relations: The limits of Soviet economic dysfunction

When Fidel Castro finally visited the Soviet Union in the spring of 1963, Khrushchev famously gave him large numbers of weapons as personal gifts.[1] Much more underreported are the ways in which Khrushchev also qualified much of the aid the Cuban leader craved. A request for aid to build an iron and steel works, for example, set Khrushchev off on a tirade on its economic expediency, and this despite its superficial and propagandistic value as a tool toward the economic independence of Cuba, which, as we have seen, was one of the most important rationales for the Soviet Union's foreign aid policy. Khrushchev spoke about the request to his colleagues in the presidium a few weeks after Castro's return to Cuba:

> I SAID: "So you want to build an iron works, well we could build one for you, but how much is a ton of cast iron going to cost you? Do you know how much it will cost you? How competitive would that be? You don't have coking coal. Where are you going to get the coal from? From us? You are going to ship that coal 11 thousand kilometers. So how much is a ton of cast iron going to cost you?"
> He has no understanding.
> "When things are built, you must know what profit you get? So what profit do you get, what goal do you set for yourself? To rely on your own and build a defense industry?"
> "No," he says.
> "So then what?"
> "We need cans to can food."[2]

Khrushchev's lecture to his most valuable new ally is indicative of the type of mindset that slowly came to predominate Soviet foreign policy-making from about 1961–1962. The Kremlin was starting to make a cost-benefit

[1] The story is recounted in William Taubman, *Khrushchev. The Man and His Era* (New York: W. W. Norton & Company, 2003) 597.

[2] Fursenko, A. A., ed., *Prezidium TsK KPSS 1954–1965. Chernovye protokol'nye zapici* zasedanii (Moscow: ROSSPEN, 2003), 722.

analysis of its aid program. The new attitude clearly percolated down the bureaucratic hierarchy – or perhaps it had bubbled up to the Kremlin from below. Either way, a study of the state of Cuban metallurgy and its prospects conducted for Gosplan while Castro was still in Moscow clearly elucidates that state officials were all on the same page. The study analyzed perspective investments in Cuba's existing nickel plant, and compared those to the raising of an altogether new steel and iron works. It concluded that the Soviets would get a full return on their investment in the nickel plant in nine years, half the time it would take for a return on the steel and iron works.[3] Besides the higher rate of return, nickel and cobalt were deficit goods in the Soviet Bloc, "adding to the expediency of quickly investing in the development of the nickel plant in Cuba over the steel mills."[4]

If the nature of the economic relationship between the Soviets and the West took shape in the 1960s – the Soviet Union now committed to peddling its energy resources through an entangling web of wide-diameter pipes – the decade also saw a consolidation of sorts in the Soviet relationship with the global South. This was not so much in the character of the relationship; economic relations with the Third World were as disparate as the members of that sweeping category themselves. It was its volume and value in the structure of Soviet economic relations that congealed. Historians of the Cold War like to make the clever observation that once the bipolar enmity froze in place in Europe, a process that found its culmination in the Berlin wall, the rivalry pivoted out of its European origins and into the international arena. But economically this narrative does not make any sense. The alleged political freeze in Europe was actually the beginning of a continental economic integration, while the economic pivot to the Third World had little to do with a positive development of purposeful Soviet policy. The ambitions that drove that "pivot" are more fruitfully sought in the global South than in the halls of the Kremlin. What the Soviets lacked in strategic vision for the South they made up in their obsession with normalizing relations with the West (see Figures 6.1, 6.2, 6.3, and 6.4).

Trade with the economically developing capitalist countries, as the Soviets called them, did not stagnate in absolute terms (each succeeding pie in the preceding figures is substantially bigger than the one before), but as the figures show, it did stagnate relative to overall trade. This meant that trade continued

[3] RGAE, f. 4372, op. 65, d. 405, l. 53.

[4] Ibid. Furthermore, Cuba already had three small iron works from before the revolution which the Soviets were helping to reconstruct. The study deemed them sufficient for supplying the development of a nascent machine-building industry in Cuba for the next five to six years.

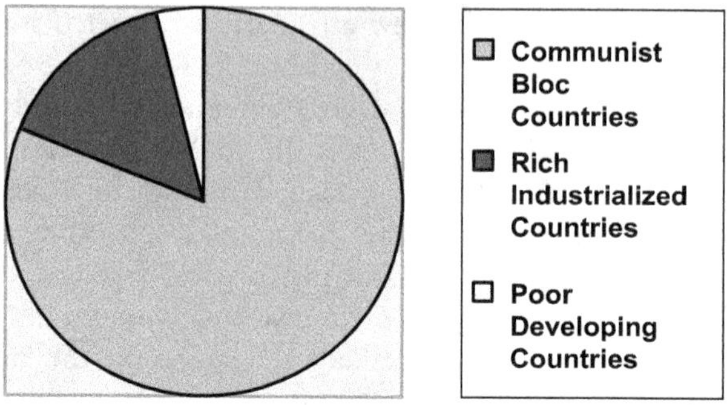

Figure 6.1 Regional weight of Soviet foreign trade, 1950*
*All four tables are calculated from Ministerstvo vneshniaia torgovlia, *Vneshniaia torgovlia SSSR, 1922–81. Iubileinyi statisticheskii obzor* (Moscow: Izdatel'stvo financy i statistika, 1982), 26–27.

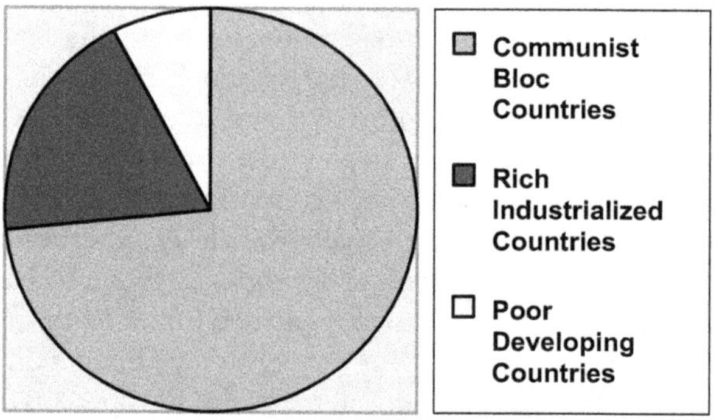

Figure 6.2 Regional weight of Soviet foreign trade, 1960

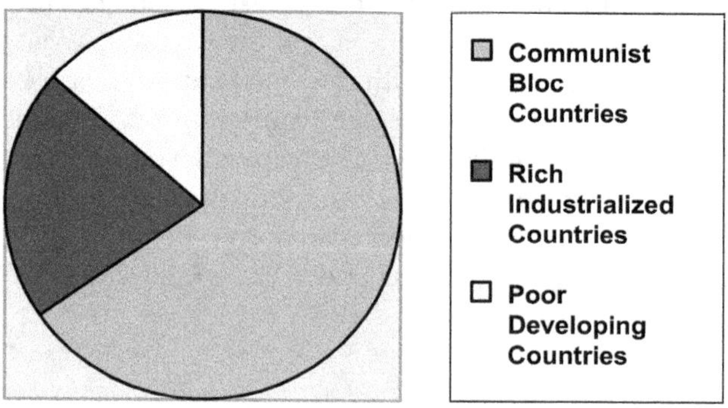

Figure 6.3 Regional weight of Soviet foreign trade, 1970

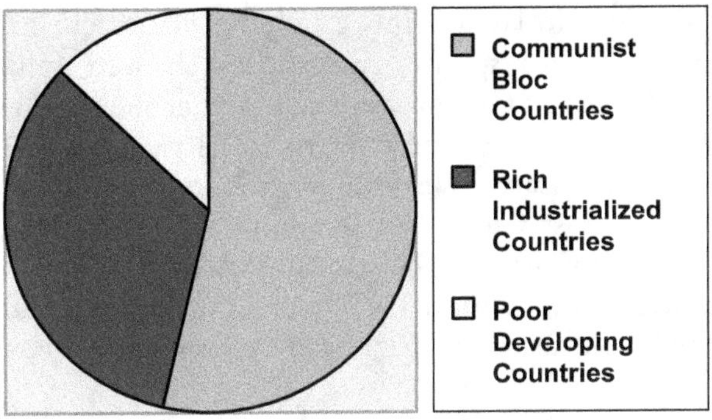

Figure 6.4 Regional weight of Soviet foreign trade, 1980

to grow – after all the Kremlin remained committed to commercial growth – but it did so less rapidly than trade with what the Soviets called the developed capitalist countries. It could not be otherwise; the problem was structural. Underdeveloped economies have by definition a limited foundation upon which to develop a robust economic relationship. The West continued to be the fulcrum that pried open and regulated the Soviet Union's relations with the global South, and the Soviet Union began to learn from experience to curb its enthusiasm there and to develop a more profitable approach.

Cuba and the empire of the banished

What was Cuba? Its newspaper to this day does not proclaim to encompass *El País*, much less *Le Monde*. It is no abstract chronicle of *The Times*, or a messianic missive committed to *Pravda*. It is simply *Granma*, the memory of a boat filled with eighty-two young rebels, taking most to their doom, and only a few to power. *Granma* then gathered all six million people in the island and sailed into the deep and clear of the world economy.

That's where the Soviets found the Cuban Revolution; or perhaps not quite. Before putting out to sea, Fidel Castro sent his brother Raul to Moscow to make sure he would find a harbor to cast anchor. *Granma's* second voyage would not be as reckless as its first. Raul asked Khrushchev to "what extent the USSR was resolute" in following through with his earlier statements on helping Cuba.[5] This was only two weeks after

[5] This refers to Khrushchev's remarks from July 9 claiming that he would defend Castro, in Lars Schoultz, *That Infernal Little Cuban Republic. The United States and the Cuban Revolution* (Chapel Hill: The University of North Carolina Press, 2009), 126.

Eisenhower signed into law on July 6, 1960 a fateful cut to the Cuban sugar import quota. In response, Khrushchev chanced upon the virtue of prudence: "When you Cubans ask what further steps the USSR might take, we want to tell you: Don't hurry to get a precise answer from us. This is not necessary. We will try to do everything to prevent an intervention against Cuba. But we don't want war. And you don't need a war. But we must bear in mind that it is possible, in defending Cuba, to unleash war. And it is possible to defend Cuba without sparking a war."[6] Khrushchev was already planning on bluster, but not yet on missiles.

Here was the perfect Cold War confrontation, one that gave meaning to a discourse on bipolarity that American leaders used to win elections and discipline the free world they led, and that bestowed on the Soviet Union a standing its economy could not underwrite. Here was the battle at its existential clearest. A free peoples were under threat of subjugation, and humanity's beacon of freedom would make a stand – whether for liberty or justice depended on the "camp" you belonged to. But although the discourse emphasized a Manichean equivalence of zero-sum consequences, the situation was of clear American design.[7] The United States had spent most of 1959 waiting for the hot-blooded emotions of the Hispanic revolutionaries to give way to a more rational policy, i.e., one that sought friendly relations with the United States. But Cubans, rather than seeing reason, carried out a land reform that expropriated large American landholders such as Texan cattle baron Robert Kleberg, who quickly discovered that Cuba was "being dominated and run by agents of Soviet Communism."[8] The Eisenhower Administration and the State Department were slower to this discovery, but they got there by October. Representative of the change was Roy Rubottom, heretofore a Castro enabler at the State Department, who on October 23 reviewed the guidelines of US relations with Cuba to counter the "increasingly 'neutralist' orientation in Cuba's

[6] GARF, f. 5446, op. 120, d. 1521, ll. 105–07. The talks took place on July 18, 1960.

[7] A point that is far from original to this book. William Appleman Williams correctly noted many decades agothat "once triumphant behind the leadership of Fidel Castro and the 26th of July Movement, the Cuban Revolution was conditioned by two factors: on the one hand, the internal politics of the Cuban revolutionary coalition; on the other, the dynamic effect of American power and policy upon that Cuban struggle." In William Appleman Williams, *The Tragedy of American Diplomacy* (New York: W. W. Norton & Company, 1972), 4. See also Jacques Lévesque, *L'URSS et la Révolution Cubaine* (Montreal: Presses de la fondation nationale des sciences politiques, 1976).

[8] This was King Ranch's Robert Kleberg, whose lands were seized in June. His reaction is in Schoultz, *That Infernal Little Cuban Republic*, 95–96.

foreign policy and apparent efforts by that country to stimulate neutralism elsewhere in Latin America."[9] They were of course right to worry. Neutralism meant what Americans of another generation might have called the Open Door Policy, which benefited countries with no presence in a particular geography (US, formerly) to the detriment of those that monopolized that presence (European countries). But it also meant more than that; it meant a "distinctly statist and nationalist orientation which, if also adopted by other Latin American countries, would seriously undermine our economic policies and objectives with respect to the Latin American region."[10]

An actual agent of Soviet Communism finally did step on Cuban soil on October 1. When Aleksandr Alekseev made contact with Castro two weeks later, the bearded one asked Alekseev to get Mikoyan, who was in Mexico heading a Soviet cultural and technological exhibition, to bring the exhibit over to Cuba. As for a closer relationship, years later Alekseev recalled Castro's answer that day: "Why be such a burden to you? For Nasser it made sense. First of all, American imperialism was far from him, and you are next door to Egypt. But us? We are so far and hardly can do it. No weapons. We do not ask for any."[11] When Mikoyan finally alighted in Cuba three months later, Castro's "neutralism" turned into an irrevocable transgression. During his stay Mikoyan had negotiated a trade agreement committing the Soviet Union to the purchase of about 20 percent of Cuba's sugar harvest, in other words, the kind of deal he routinely aimed for (see Ghana). For a chastised Rubottom in the midst of changing his mind about Castro this meant that "for all practical purposes Castro could be in the employ of the Soviet government."[12] But where formerly hopeful observers met the news with hysterics, CIA Director Allen Dulles was pleased, hoping in fact "that in the long run the Russian concentration on Cuba would become apparent to the world and that this would be a development favorable to the US."[13] For several months he had been working to dissuade European countries from selling weapons to the Castro regime, with the idea that the Cuban government would eventually

[9] Memorandum, 23 October 1959, US Department of State, FRUS, 1958–1960, Volume VI, Cuba, 636.

[10] Ibid., 636–37.

[11] In an interview with the authors in Aleksandr Fursenko and Timothy Naftali, *One Hell of a Gamble. Khrushchev, Castro and Kennedy, 1958–1964* (New York: W. W. Norton & Company, 1997), 29.

[12] Quoted in Schoultz, *That Infernal Little Cuban Republic*, 114.

[13] Memorandum of Discussion at NSC Meeting, 21 January 1960, US Department of State, FRUS, 1958–1960, Volume VI, Cuba, 749.

turn to the Soviets for weapons and so give his CIA the green light to relive its better days of Iran and Guatemala.[14]

By the spring of 1960, the US government was actively discouraging any attempt at reconciliation with Castro from any American official so inclined, and plotting regime change through covert action.[15] Economic warfare, that bludgeon of first resort, began in earnest when the US government instructed Standard Oil, Texaco, and Shell to refuse to refine Soviet oil in May.[16] This happened in the midst of a visit by a Cuban trade delegation to Moscow led by Antonio Nuñez Jimenez, the future minister of agrarian reform, whose haphazard objectives for the trip crystallized in early June into demands for vastly increased amounts of Soviet oil.[17] This would necessitate an equally enhanced commitment of sugar exports to pay for the oil. The Soviets signed an agreement to send oil with the Cubans in what must have been a record in Soviet bureaucratic alacrity. On their last day in Moscow on June 18, the delegation was told in the morning in a last meeting with Foreign Trade Minister Patolichev that his ministry had agreed to satisfy Cuba's new oil demands, but that it required government approval. This had come before the meeting was even over, and the agreement was ready to be signed by two o'clock that day.[18] With supplies assured, Cuba was free to seize the refineries, which they promptly did on June 29.[19]

The subsequent US suspension of sugar imports a week later had little to do with retaliation for the seizure of the refineries, as a US official later admitted.[20] It was rather part of the plan to overthrow the Castro regime,

14 See Schoultz, *That Infernal Little Cuban Republic*, 116.

15 For attempts at reconciliation see Samuel Farber, *The Origins of Cuban Revolution Reconsidered* (Chapel Hill: The University of North Carolina Press, 2006), 84–85.

16 A thorough discussion of this episode is in Morris H. Morley, *Imperial State and Revolution. The United States and Cuba, 1952–1986* (Cambridge: Cambridge University Press, 1987), 102–07.

17 The reports in RGAE, f. 413, op. 13, d. 8749, ll. 37–42, dating from June 2 and ibid., ll. 78–80, dating from June 18 make clear the mounting focus on oil as Cubans realized during the first half of June that the Western oil companies would hold fast to their refusal.

18 Ibid., ll. 78–80.

19 There was an interesting parallel to this happening at the same time in Ethiopia. When the Ethiopian government approached the Soviets in the spring of 1960 for help with agriculture, by way of aid the Soviets offered to grant oil instead of cash. The idea was for the Ethiopian government to realize the oil in domestic markets for about $15 million. The problem was that the whole of the refining and distribution network supplying Ethiopia was foreign-owned, and these foreign companies refused to accept Communist oil. The Soviet approach to both Cuba and Ethiopia was broadly similar: a general willingness to get a foot in the door and start a new relationship. The Ethiopians, however, proved unwilling to take the same drastic step Castro took. See RGANI f. 5, op. 30, d. 332, ll. 33–36.

20 Farber, *The Origins of Cuban Revolution Reconsidered*, 85–86. The Soviet Union picked up the 700,000 tons of sugar affected by this suspension, at a projected cost – including shipping – of 240

prompting Raul to ask Khrushchev about the extent of a commitment from the Soviet Union the Cubans had refused nine months earlier. The rest of the story is well known. In October, Eisenhower instituted a full economic blockade. In April 1961, John F. Kennedy carried out Eisenhower's project to invade Cuba, with disastrous results. This was followed by a US policy of assassination attempts and economic sabotage that historian Lars Schoultz aptly called "state-sponsored terrorism," and then Castro's sudden declaration that he was a Marxist-Leninist.[21] Castro's new faith, however, did not forestall the deep and lasting resentment Cuba's leaders felt for their Soviet counterparts after the denouement of the Cuban Missile Crisis in late 1962, which had been largely started to further Khrushchev's goals in Berlin and was resolved on Khrushchev's terms and with no consultation with the Cuban government.[22] And if this Soviet-Cuban ideological convergence did not ease personal tensions, neither did it obviate the overwhelming capacity of the liberal world economy to continue structuring the commercial preferences of the Cuban government. These two elements would continue to bedevil the Soviet-Cuban relation.

Yet the American embargo did bring *Granma* quickly to Soviet shores. It would not stray far for as long as the embargo remained in place, but the legacy of a half-century of dependence on its American neighbor shadowed the crew that captained this boat of outcasts. Through the first half of the 1960s their demands were geared to maintaining the industrial and manufactured remnants the United States had left behind in an island that had been moderately prosperous relative to its Latin American neighbors – and probably no poorer than its new Communist benefactor. It was as if an alien civilization had departed and left its technology to decay in the swelter of Cuba. Buses moldered waiting for the 1,250 Soviet engines that might put them back on the road.[23] And when Cuba's American refrigerators began to break down, Cuba found compressors in a Soviet factory suspiciously similar to those at the root of that decay.[24] Furthermore, the contrast between Soviet business practices and those

million rubles, of which about 104 million rubles would have to come from "hard currency goods." Not calculated here is the resale value of that sugar. From RGAE, f. 4372, op. 63, d. 85, l. 183.

[21] Schoultz, *That Infernal Little Cuban Republic*, chapter 7.

[22] This is the interpretation of the most convincing and thorough account of Khrushchev's policy, Aleksandr Fursenko and Timothy Naftali, *Khrushchev's Cold War. The Inside Story of an American Adversary* (New York: W. W. Norton & Company, 2006). For Castro's post-crisis attempt at rapprochement with the United States see Thomas G. Patterson, *Contesting Castro. The United States and the Triumph of the Cuban Revolution* (New York: Oxford University Press, 1994), 261–62.

[23] RGAE, f. 413, op. 13, d. 9006, ll. 46–47.

[24] RGAE, f. 413, op. 13, d. 9007, ll. 8–9.

of the capitalists the Cubans had known so intimately did little to salve tensions. Specialists in different spheres didn't get to Cuba in time and Soviet machines sent to Cuba sat idle for lack of engineers to show the Cubans how to work them. Even Soviet specialists sat idle at times for lack of translators, while all the time Cuban officials impatiently exhorted the Soviets to fulfill their contracts on a timely basis.[25] In Cuba no one ever ceased to be aware of the difference from the efficiency of the American companies that had, once upon a time, managed Cuba's industry.[26]

Even as Cuba was being cast out of from the world economy, the Soviet Union was insinuating its way back into it. In this sense Cuba did not fall into the black hole of an alternative economic universe, rather, its sugar made its way back into it through the ongoing expansion of Soviet participation in global economic exchange. With most of the Communist Bloc indebted to it, the Soviet Union could accept sugar from Cuba for bartering credit, which Cuba could then use to shop around the countries that made up the Communist Bloc; the exports to Cuba from any Soviet Bloc country would then be applied toward debt repayment from that country to the Soviet Union.[27] As the bloc had already been mostly self sufficient in sugar, this exchange and the concomitant surplus of sugar signaled its large-scale entry into the world sugar market. This led a CIA

[25] A. Doluga, chairman of the foreign departures commission, to the CPSU CC, April 7, 1961, RGANI f. 5, op. 14, d. 20, ll. 17–18. Among some of the numbers cited in the document are 300 Cuban instructors waiting for specialists on methods of labor and time-keeping (*metody truda i khronometrazh*). Cubans sent five telegrams to GKES to hurry things up, but only one of the twelve specialists needed had come. Furthermore the nickel industry, second most important in Cuba after the sugar industry, was missing thirty-three specialists and ten translators that had signed up for work in Cuba but never showed. This was likely due to the Bay of Pigs invasion going on at the time, although it also seems that Spanish had become quite an unpopular language to study in the Soviet Union since its heyday in the late 1930s, so that Spanish-speaking translators willing to go to Cuba were hard to come by. See ibid., ll. 19–21.

[26] On the efficiency of North American technical problem-solving when it came to industry, and the dislocation caused by the sudden departure of the more than 6,500 technicians and managers from the island see Louis A. Pérez, *Cuba and the United States. Ties of Singular Intimacy* (Athens: The University of Georgia Press, 1990), 250–52. See also Minister of the Economy Regino Botí's comments on the running of Cuba's industry "by remote control," and the lack of Cuban technical know-how after having relied on American technicians in K. S. Karol, *Guerillas in Power. The Course of the Cuban Revolution*, trans. Arnold Pomerans (New York: Hill & Wang, 1970), 224–25.

[27] More often than not, imports from the more advanced countries in the Bloc like Czechoslovakia and East Germany were more desirable than Soviet imports. The process is explained in a CIA memorandum, "Bloc Economic Support for the Castro Regime," April 27, 1961, NSF Box 51, JFK Library. Cuba's preference for East-Central European aid is clear in the following tally of cooperation projects: The Soviet Bloc was to carry out 116 aid projects as of 1963. Of these, 27 were coming from the USSR, 29 from Czechoslovakia, 27 from East Germany, 14 from Romania, 11 from Poland, 6 from Hungary, and 2 from China. In RGAE, f. 4372, op. 65, d. 405, l. 1.

analyst to conclude in 1963 that "Castro's problems and the Soviet cost of supporting Castro is offset to a considerable degree by the dramatic increase in the price of sugar. The increase in the last year, when applied to 75% of estimated 1963 production of sugar, about equals the estimated economic aid the Soviets are required to give Cuba in 1963. Therefore, it might be said that the Free World is supplying the money with which the Soviets are supporting Castro."[28]

But the Soviet Union made for an unsatisfactory commercial middleman, and Castro's government did not give up in its attempts to go directly to the vastly more desirable world market. They persisted on reneging on their contractual obligations to the Soviet Union, preferring to sell sugar earmarked for the Soviet Union to whichever country would give them hard currency. This meant significant dislocations in the Soviet Union in the planning of sugar production and trade, and they started from the very beginning of the relationship. In 1960, 20 percent of an agreed 1.8 million tons of sugar failed to materialize in Soviet ports, bringing about "a significant decrease in inventories of raw sugar in sugar refineries" and making it difficult to begin the planned mass refining of sugar at the beginning of 1961.[29] The next year Gosplan had to reappraise its input-output tables to accommodate another 15 percent shortfall, and the year had only just begun.[30] According to a 1964 agreement, Cuba was to provide the Soviets with 3 million tons of sugar by 1966, but instead provided a little more than half that number, despite the fact that they had produced almost 5 million tons that year. Another agreement two years later yielded the same results.[31] The Soviet Union, for all its pretentions as a superpower, was often Cuba's dumping grounds for the surplus sugar it could not sell elsewhere.

Inefficiencies on both sides also delayed reciprocal sugar and oil deliveries, and these delays persisted a long time.[32] By the mid 1960s, Cuban leaders undertook more practical economic measures, eschewing the idea

[28] Memorandum on Cuban Policy, April 25, 1963, NSF, Box 51A, JFK Library. The price had shot up because of tight supply, due in part to Cuba's sudden forced withdrawal from the world market. The conclusion is followed by a suggestion that the United States "break the sugar market if possible," since it was a sensitive market "made by middlemen and can be manipulated."

[29] GARF, f. 5446, op. 95. d. 1017, ll. 78–79,

[30] GARF, f. 5446, op. 96, d. 1161, l. 43. The order dates from February 19, 1962.

[31] A. D. Bekarevich et al, eds., *Ekonomika Kuby. Statisticheskii spravochnik* (Moscow: Akademiia Nauk SSSR, 1971), 207. Although they found most of their customers in Europe, they also sold to countries with spare convertible currencies like Egypt and Morocco.

[32] Examples from 1962–64 are in GARF, f. 5446, op. 96, d. 1165, l. 90 on oil; GARF, f. 5446, op. 98, d. 1440, l. 64 on sugar; and GARF, f. 5446, op. 98, d. 1443, l. 117 on Cuban promises to look into organizing their ports better.

of comprehensive central planning and planning instead different sectors of the economy separately.[33] The Soviets, for their part, worked out clearer more delineated objectives for the island and backed off from some of the aid promises deemed, by the Soviets alone, to be inexpedient. However, as Soviet specialists continued the prolonged collaboration with the Cubans and grew closer to them, a new problem arose for the Soviet leadership, namely one of discipline and loyalty among their agents on the island. It is around this time that the Soviet Central Committee started receiving reports of "deficiencies in the work with foreigners."[34] A Soviet advisor from the GKES to the Cuban minister of the economy Regino Botí, for example, instructed the Cuban on how to get around Soviet recalcitrance to provide more cargo trucks to Cuba.[35] He further made irresponsible declarations on collectivization and gave advice on railway construction that was against Soviet interests. He went as far as to tell the minister about secret instructions about the lack of interest on the part of the Soviets to further develop Cuba's nickel industry, a major source of income for Cuba.[36]

The reality of the Soviet seduction, then, had little relation to its depiction in US State Department memos. Admittedly, the Soviet Union had been invited into a thicket of economic and cultural legacies it could not unravel. In his first trip to the Soviet Union in 1961, where he was part of a Cuban delegation to negotiate economic matters, Humberto Lastra was to be unexpectedly regaled with quite a treat. Called to attention by the Spanish-speaking guide's small, shiny bell that quieted the Cuban delegation, Lastra was offered one of the greatest achievements in Soviet consumption; certainly this would show the Cubans the consumer culture that socialism could bring. Lastra was to be treated to Soviet ice cream – although not before a brief introduction to the product, Lastra recalled.[37] Historian Louis Perez has argued that the single most influential factor in the formation of Cuban identity in the twentieth century has been its closeness to the United States.[38] This "singular intimacy" brought Cubans wealth, as rich North Americans invested in Cuban agriculture and turned the island into one of the most important tourist hubs of the 1950s.

[33] Carmelo Mesa-Lago, *Breve historia económica de la Cuba socialista. Políticas, resultados y perspectivas* (Madrid: Alianza Editorial, 1994), 43–52.

[34] "On a few deficiencies in the organization of work with foreigners on scientific-technological exchange," May 11, 1965, RGANI f. 5, op. 30, d. 482, ll. 67–79.

[35] Ibid. [36] Ibid.

[37] Interview with Humberto Lastra, March 12, 2004, Havana, Cuba.

[38] Louis A. Pérez, *Cuba and the United States*, 226–33.

A half-century of interaction, however, also brought economic disparity between Havana and the rest of the country, as well as North American consumption norms that were unattainable by a country that was at the mercy of volatile sugar world market prices. Yet the pale reflection of a cornucopia of consumption shone close, refracted by North American visitors for whom Cuba "was a background for honeymoons, a playground for vacations, a brothel, a casino, a cabaret, a good liberty port – a place for flings, sprees, and binges."[39] Which is to say that Lastra, a highly educated economist from an urban "petit bourgeois" background who had worked in US companies in Havana before the revolution, was unimpressed with Soviet ice cream. Cuba, however, would have to make do with it for the next three decades.

Egypt: The political economy of an alliance failure

"We have long known that Soviet alliances did not do very well during the Cold War," argued Odd Arne Westad a decade and a half ago. "The first Soviet 'empire' – the Sino-Soviet alliance – lasted just about ten years. The second – the Third World alliances with such countries as Afghanistan, Angola, Ethiopia, Guinea, Iraq, Mozambique, Nicaragua, Syria, Vietnam, and Yemen – lasted about as long. Even what Yuri Andropov referred to as 'the special alliance' – with Cuba – was an off-and-on affair for most of its existence."[40] The Soviets simply failed – did not even try – to reproduce the same type of structural ties that bound industrialized economies to each other and to the world economy (mutually beneficial trade, investment patterns, and sustained technological exchange, in Westad's reckoning). Within a framework of Cold War bipolarity, "alliance" becomes necessarily a comparative concept; when the world is divided in two camps, both will seek allies in a zero-sum game of global geopolitical strategy, while some countries may remain neutral.[41] But is this equivalence justified? Mikoyan

[39] Louis A. Pérez, *On Becoming Cuban. Identity, Nationality and Culture* (New York: The Ecco Press, 1999), 490.

[40] Odd Arne Westad, "Secrets of the Second World: The Russian Archives and the Reinterpretation of Cold War History," *Diplomatic History* 21:2 (1997): 268.

[41] Although it is unclear that historians believe in neutrality. For example, writing about Khrushchev's 1959 trip to the United Nations, Naftali and Fursenko note that ultimately, "with one major exception, none of the Soviet Union's third world allies – India, Ghana, Guinea, and the United Arab Republic – supported Khrushchev's call to replace Hammarskjöld with a troika." Fursenko and Naftali, *Khrushchev's Cold War*, 318. Interestingly, the one exception was Cuba. The four countries imagined here as Soviet allies were unrelenting in their proclamations of neutrality. There are few ways in which those four countries could have requited Soviet political support other than in the

did not think so, and he was right. "We are not for the position that friendship with the Soviet Union must damage cooperation with other countries," he told a visiting Moroccan dignitary in 1958.[42] Mikoyan had of course the United States in mind. He may or may not have been personally kinder than American government officials, and he was certainly no liberal, but his approach to international commerce lacked the demands for exclusivity of his American counterparts. And at the heart of that difference lies a simple truth: The United States – with England and sometimes France as junior partners – was hegemonic, and a transgression of the boundaries it set brought with it swift retribution.[43] The Soviet Union, for its part, had none of the same means to bind countries within a hegemonic configuration, and therefore could not fathom doing so (outside the reach its armies in its immediate periphery, or course, i.e. outside of Eastern Europe).

The first wave of colonial independence had come and gone in the 1940s and early 1950s, with many countries driven by political and economic circumstances coming around to look at what the Soviets had to offer. Now a second wave, mostly consisting of African countries, came knocking on the Soviet door, or were similarly driven to it. Morocco was among the first. A Moroccan diplomat from the embassy had at first suggested that direct ties be established immediately. When in February 1957, not yet a year into its independence, the Moroccan chargé d'affaire in France walked over to the Soviet embassy in Paris for a follow-up, he announced that the Moroccan government "very much wanted to develop commercial relations with the Soviet Union," but that at the moment they were constrained by the legacy of economic and institutional dependence on France and the Franc bloc.[44] The French were putting pressure on Morocco so that trade between the two countries for 1957 would be carried out through France on a clearing basis, that is, within the framework of the annual Franco-Soviet trade agreement.[45] They nevertheless invited the Soviets for trade talks in Rabat in April. The Soviets duly obliged, but the pickings there were relatively meager. The Moroccans wanted oil and grain; the latter after a drought had left Morocco with a grain shortage.[46]

forum of the United Nations. But the fact that they didn't in the one of few instances where they could have does not seem to give Fursenko and Naftali much pause.

42 GARF, f. 5446, op. 120, d. 1315, l. 113.

43 This is again Bruce Cumings' formulation, best formulated in Cumings, *Parallax Visions*, 205–26.

44 RGANI, f. 5, op. 30, d. 224, ll. 54–58.

45 RGANI, f. 5, op. 30, d. 275, l. 31.

46 RGAE, f. 413, op. 13, d. 7998, ll. 4–5. In fact, the Moroccan trade minister explained, Morocco was generally a net exporter of grain to France, which the French then reexported to other markets.

They insisted that the Soviets participate in an upcoming international exhibit in Casablanca so that the Moroccan business could compare Soviet tractors to Western ones.[47] And they pushed citrus fruits in payment for the oil.[48] The Soviets would have to be content with having a new partner, but citrus fruits could only get the partnership so far.

More direct ties to Morocco and Moroccan firms were finally established the next year, when in April 1958, upon Moroccan insistence, a direct trade agreement was signed.[49] The commercial relation with Morocco was sizable and constant – as political events never conspired against it – but never really very important.[50] Perhaps because of this, Morocco never made it into historians' lists of countries inspired by the Soviet example. Had they read the stenograph of a meeting between Mikoyan and the Moroccan Secretary of State for Commerce Ahmed Benkirane that April, they might have reconsidered.[51] "We wish to study the planning of our economy and the question of the country's industrialization," Benkirane told the Old Bolshevik. "When we have developed serious economic plans, we will look to friendly foreign countries, particularly the USSR, for their implementation."[52] Then he went further. Benkirane's words were the echo of all newly independent peoples in the global South:

> We are preparing a five-year plan, starting in 1961. But we think it necessary to have a transition plan for 1959–1960, which should allow us to correct the mistakes of earlier plans, to seriously study our wealth, the potential of our capital and people, and possibilities of foreign help. Only after that can we say that we have a national plan. We understand that we must rely on our own strength, although it is also possible that a young country may appeal for help to several countries.[53]

Benkirane then expressed the hope that when Moroccans have a clear understanding of their capabilities and address themselves to the Soviet organizations in charge of economic relations, the Soviets would help Morocco. Was this a paean to the Soviet model? He also admitted that the current transitional plan of 1958 was fully based on the last Four-Year

47 Ibid., ll. 14–16
48 Ibid., 17–21. The Soviets refused an offer of sardines, which the Soviets themselves exported.
49 See RGANI, f. 5, op. 30, d. 274, ll. 100–10 for a post-negotiation meeting between the head of the Moroccan delegation and Mikoyan.
50 The exchange basically continued to consist of Moroccan citrus fruits for oil, timber, and eventually industrial machinery and energy equipment.
51 The stenograph for this meeting, same as above, can also be found in GARF, f. 5446, op. 120, d. 1315, ll. 108–19.
52 Ibid., l. 111. 53 Ibid., 113.

Plan the French had drawn up to administer the economy of their colony. Evils of the colonial legacy, then? Moroccans went on to develop their economy over the next decades under the familiar rubric of Five-Year Plans, a fact that has left Cold War historians unimpressed – as it should.

The relationship with Morocco was every bit as simple as the relationship with Egypt was complex. Here was a tangle of diplomatic, geopolitical, regional, and economic forces that takes much sustained scholarly effort to sort out.[54] Economic ideas and compulsions were intertwined with a more rapidly shifting socio-political panorama here than elsewhere, but the Soviet-Egyptian relationship was not free of the global economy either. As such, Egypt shared in much of the same experience of the Soviet Union as other countries of the global South, inducing familiar opportunities, tensions, and outcomes.

As we've seen, compulsions of hard currency shortages compelled Egyptian leaders to seek trade with Stalin before his death. A more frankly anti-Western government took the reins of power in Egypt in the officers' coup against King Farouk under the leadership of Mohammed Naguib in July 1952. Yet British forces occupying the Suez Canal continued to forestall any semblance of Egyptian independence. Unremitting anti-imperialist discourse notwithstanding, Naguib proved a careful custodian of Egyptian prerogative. It took him a year to approach the Soviets for weapons and industrial goods in exchange for cotton. He explained his caution to the Soviet envoy taking the Egyptian order: "I truly would establish close cultural cooperation between Egypt and the USSR, but I will say frankly that the British and Americans may be suspicious of me, and in response they could crush me and wipe away my regime. Egypt still has neither the strength nor the options to resist them. So I have to make anti-communist statements, although I have no particular predispositions on Communism." And further, "I am forced to play a game with the Americans and the British and between the two blocs."[55] This was to be

[54] One of the keys to understanding that tangle overlaps uncomfortably with the usual Cold War frameworks: The proxy battle between Egypt and Saudi Arabia in Yemen for leadership in the Arab world that consumed all Egyptian ambitions. This is the centerpiece of one of its best treatments, Jesse Ferris, *Nasser's Gamble. How Intervention in Yemen Caused the Six-Day War and the Decline of Egyptian Power* (Princeton: Princeton University Press, 2012). For an illuminating account of American foreign policy in the region that is also more traditionally ensconced within the Cold War paradigm see Salim Yaqub, *Containing Arab Nationalism. The Eisenhower Doctrine and the Middle East* (Chapel Hill: The University of North Carolina Press, 2004).

[55] Vitalii Naumkin et al., eds., *Blizhnevostochnyi konflikt. Iz dokumentov arkhiva vneshnei politiki Rossiiskoi Federatsii*, Vol. 1 (Moscow: Mezhdunarodnyi fond "Demokratiia," 2003), 191.

Egypt's policy in the years to come, even after Gamal Abdel Nasser deposed and arrested Naguib in January 1955.

Nasser's government continued to play the game, though the aim, as for all poor countries, was not so much to play one side against the other as it was to get a better deal from the preponderant West. To this end he approached the Soviets for an arms sale in July 1955 hoping to expedite a decision from the Americans to sell him arms. But when armed riots broke out in Sudan in August and an Israeli raid killed an Egyptian officer in Gaza, he grew anxious at what he considered US vacillation in the face of a British-Israeli plot to undermine Egyptian influence in Sudan and the Middle East.[56] The Egyptians soon utterly changed the tone of the conversation with the Soviet Union. Their ambassador in Moscow, Mohammed al-Kuni, could assure the Soviets in August 1955 that Egypt was committed to "the best relations with the Soviet Union, and to carry out an independent foreign policy, which Egypt could not do under English domination."[57] This time they meant it. They understood the risks involved to Egypt's relations with the Anglo-Saxon powers in coming to the Soviets, but they hoped to gain access to Soviet intelligence to better manage relations with the West. Al-Kuni's Soviet interlocutor had this to say to assuage any lingering Egyptian discomfort with doing business with the Soviets: "Egypt can be sure that the Soviet Union is not a crocodile able to suddenly expand its jaws and swallow Egypt."[58] Soviet diplomats would have to give many such assurances over the years.[59] The next month both parties finalized the famous "Czech arms deal."[60]

From there, the Soviet-Egyptian relationship would wax and wane to the regional ambitions of Nasser and their intersection with European and then American purpose in the region. Indeed Nasser became, in the words of historian Jesse Ferris, "a consultant to the Soviet Union on Arab affairs, an instructor for the newly initiated in the labyrinth of Oriental politics."[61] Nasser's bold redrawing of the geopolitical map of the Middle East with his purchase of Soviet weapons did not incur the expected wrath of the West, to the contrary, in the fall Nasser secured a generous US and

56 The story is told in Fursenko and Naftali, *Khrushchev's Cold War*, 58–74.

57 RGANI, f. 5, op. 30, d. 123, l. 46. 58 Ibid., l. 47.

59 On Nasser's sincere fear of Soviet subversion see Fursenko and Naftali, *Khrushchev's Cold War*, 59.

60 Stalin had refused a similar arms deal to Naguib in February 1953, probably fearing that he was being used as a tool in Egypt's relationship with the United States. But they had left the door open to see whether the Egyptians were serious about the deal. Naguib's government did not follow it up, whereas Nasser did. See Vyshinskii's note in Naumkin et al., eds., *Blizhnevostochnyi konflikt*, 182.

61 Jesse Ferris, "Soviet Support for Egypt's Intervention in Yemen, 1962–1963," *Journal of Cold War Studies* 10:4 (2008), 8.

British commitment to the building of a dam by the southern city of Aswan that was key to the rationalization of Egyptian agriculture and to the industrialization of its economy.[62] That commitment lasted six months. Nasser's persistent pressure on the United States for better terms on the deal led him to one transgression too far: the recognition of the People's Republic of China. American withdrawal from the project, in turn, laid the groundwork for the Suez crisis in the summer and fall of 1956, that final blow to what historian John Darwin has called the British imperial world-system.[63]

Soviet involvement in the building of the Aswan Dam was fraught with Egyptian vacillation. In 1954 the Soviets had agreed to help Egypt build the dam, but the Egyptians had subsequently refused to grant visas for Soviet experts to go to the site and carry out preliminary work.[64] After the American rebuff in 1956, Nasser did not "play the game" but rather resolved to build it with national resources. It was only the post-Suez Crisis economic slump that convinced him to reactivate negotiations with the Soviet Union in their standing offer to finance the building of the dam, in 1958. Not for the last time would the Soviets take up what the United States abandoned in the global South. But the Western refusal to finance the building of the Aswan Dam had been the least important of the consequences that followed the Suez crisis. Much more critical was the economic blockade that had deprived Egypt access to their traditional markets in Europe as well as their traditional sources of finance. A set of guidelines for economic aggression against Nasser's regime had been drawn up even before the crisis. In a March 28 memorandum, Dulles laid out a plan of action to punish Nasser back into America's arms. Dragging out the negotiations on the Aswan Dam was part of the plan, but so was denying Nasser weapons from any Western country and suspending grain exports and any form of aid. A more aggressive follow-up should that fail to change Nasser's mind entailed manipulating the world cotton market so as to block Egyptian cotton exports, jamming anti-Western radio broadcasts in Cairo and pursuing regime change in Syria, Egypt's closest ally.[65]

[62] Nasser's complex exploitation of his intelligence apparatus to play on American fears of Soviet inroads in Egypt to get that American commitment for the dam is wonderfully recovered in Fursenko and Naftali, *Khrushchev's Cold War*, 78–80. A Soviet assessment of the project, its benefits and characteristics, dating from the time of Soviet involvement in the project in April 1958 can be found in RGANI, f. 5, op. 30, d. 272, ll. 232–36.

[63] John Darwin, *The Empire Project. The Rise and Fall of the British World System, 1830–1970* (Cambridge: Cambridge University Press, 2009).

[64] RGANI, f. 5, op. 30, d. 123, l. 196.

[65] Yaqub, *Containing Arab Nationalism*, 42–43.

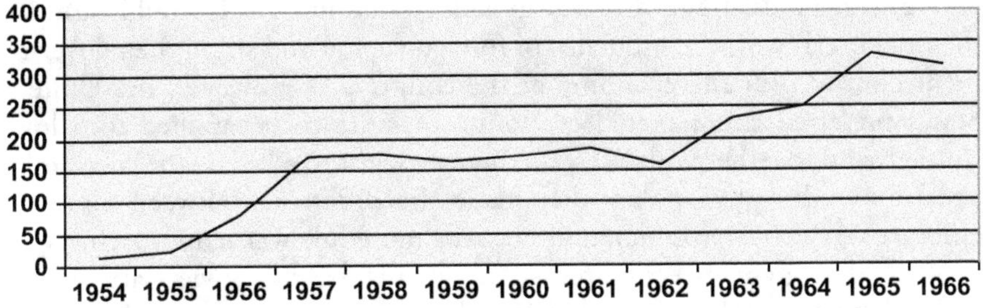

Figure 6.5 Soviet-Egyptian trade turnover (in millions of rubles)*
*Ministry of Foreign Trade, *Vneshniaia torgovlia SSSR. Statisticheskii obzor, 1918–1966* (Moscow: Izdatel'stvo "Mezhdunarodnye otnosheniia," 1967), 219–21.

Not for the last time would American coercion fail to bring a recalcitrant government to heel. But then Nasser was not planning on a complete break and neither did successive American administrations ever countenance extreme escalations of hostility against Nasser, much less a complete break.

Eisenhower's unfriendly but ambivalent approach to Nasser would remain in force even as he worked to build the dissolute King Saud as an alternative to Nasser's leadership in the Arab world.[66] The Soviet Union, exercising no particular centripetal force of its own, would have to wait for the next crisis to move the relationship forward. Trade numbers capture these shifts well. After seeing trade between the two countries almost quadrupled in the pregnant year of 1956 and doubled again the next, it remained in that plateau until 1962, whereupon it doubled once more over the course of the next four years (see Figure 6.5).

That period of substantial but stagnant trade allowed time enough for the two governments to get to know each other. Tension rather than the comradeship feared by Washington was the prevailing mood. European economic pressure on Egypt after the crisis had kept a reluctant Egypt close to the Soviet Bloc. Egyptian cotton had been diverted from European markets to buy Romanian and Soviet oil. An embargo of weapons to Egypt left the door wide open for Soviet armaments sales. British and French capital flight from Egypt left the field open to others as well, although not exclusively to the Communist Bloc. National production had fallen 5–10 percent. Nasser responded to all this by nationalizing French and British banks and

[66] For a detailed study of that diplomatic relationship see Nathan J. Citino, *From Arab Nationalism to OPEC. Eisenhower, King Saud, and the Making of U.S.-Saudi Relations* (Bloomington: Indiana University Press, 2002).

enterprises, a measure the Soviets applauded inasmuch as it would "lead to the final break with the influence of foreign capital and strengthen government control over the economy of the country."[67] However, the United States preferred this targeted economic pressure to be applied to a low simmer, and together with West Germany sought to alleviate the economic situation in Egypt, a policy that made the difference between Castro's embrace of the Soviet Union and Nasser's more lukewarm approach.

With the Egyptian economic situation in flux, the Soviets attempted to implement a policy toward Egypt that "would increase our influence and deprive the United States, West Germany, and others of the opportunity to occupy key positions in the economy of the country."[68] However the Soviets would stop short of subsidizing Egypt. The Egyptians had taken advantage of the Soviet Bloc's willingness to help during the crisis by sharply increasing the price of the cotton they sold to the bloc (by 55–65 percent over world prices and 25–30 percent over those in Egypt's own markets). "In the future this loss cannot be justified and in trade relations with Egypt we must keep to world or mutually-fair prices," the Soviets resolved.[69] This was a fine sentiment, but not shared by an Egyptian side that still preferred to do business with the West and could not find in the Soviet Union an adequate replacement. In the summer of 1960, for example, many of the firms in Egypt that had bought oil drilling equipment from the Soviet Union were finding themselves in acute financial problems, as they found they had backed the wrong horse; the Soviet equipment they were now peddling was no match for that of the United States and West Germany.[70] After the removal from Egypt of the old imperialist West, depriving the new West of the key positions in the Egyptian economy proved to be much more than a simple matter of political will for the Soviet Union, and beyond the country's capabilities.

For the years leading to 1962 it is difficult to find an instance of jovial accord in trade talks between Soviet and Egyptian officials – although the Soviets did get along better with Egyptian businessmen. Consider the men thawing in a Moscow office on February 1, 1960.[71] While Khrushchev, Nasser, and their entourage profess friendship and best wishes, these men, both deputies, are tasked with making trade happen, whether or not it

[67] This economic analysis is taken from RGANI, f. 5, op. 30, d. 224, ll. 73–78. [68] Ibid., 77.

[69] Ibid. [70] RGAE, f. 413, op. 13, d. 8791, l. 62.

[71] The following exchange is taken from RGAE, f. 413, op. 13, d. 8791, ll. 2–5. The document is not exactly a transcript of the meeting, but the report is still probably close to verbatim. At any rate, since the exchange is not verbatim, no quotes have been used. But this reproduction certainly keeps within the spirit of the meeting, and probably much of the verbiage.

brings the peoples closer together, as no doubt was professed repeatedly in welcoming speeches before the meeting:

THE EGYPTIAN: You must increase the assortment of goods; you buy only cotton and last year trade turnover decreased as a result.

THE SOVIET: You haven't given us a list of available products.

ANOTHER SOVIET: And the main problem is that your prices are too high when you barter; take for example your rice.

THE EGYPTIAN: But that's because countries like Yugoslavia are buying cheaply on barter and then reselling for a profit in hard currency.

THE SOVIET (JOKINGLY, THE SOVIET DOCUMENT ASSURES US): But to preempt re-exports by other countries, you are punishing Soviet organizations!

THE EGYPTIAN (PROBABLY SITTING BACK, FIXING HIS GAZE UP TOWARD A DISTANT CORNER OF THE CEILING, EYES GLAZING OVER): The surcharge in our prices is caused by the differences in the domestic and international exchange rates of the Egyptian pound. It should still be profitable for Soviet organizations to buy Egyptian products on a clearing basis, even when overpaying for them. Of course you would get a discount on our cotton if you paid in hard currency and bought it through our cotton committee (and on he goes, reaching the core of the issue after some circumambulatory loquacity). Egypt lacks hard currency but still has to buy spare parts for machinery bought abroad. There are, for example, some 12,000 Fordson tractors, and the railways are all essentially British made.

THE SOVIET: I cannot promise to buy goods with hard currency, but Egypt is delaying the granting of import licenses for Soviet products.

THE EGYPTIAN: Well, for three months you did not buy cotton, and so imports from the Soviet Union had to be decreased.

THE SOVIET: We stopped buying cotton because Egyptian organizations and companies drastically cut their imports, especially oil and oil products, and so we don't have the means to clear the accounts.

THE EGYPTIAN: Well, you practically never use much of the credit we provide, why not increase the credit limit from 1 to 5 million Egyptian pounds and borrow whatever you need?[72]

But this was not the suggestion to break the impasse. In fact, five months later the Soviets were still insisting on the same barter price for cotton as the price the Egyptians quoted in British pounds.[73] Egypt refused to give in, and both sides settled for an understanding whereby Soviet bartered goods could sell for a price that incorporated a premium similar to whatever premium the Soviets paid for Egyptian cotton. However, this left

[72] The reader has actually met our Soviet protagonists: Pavel Kumykin and Viktor Spandar'ian. "The Egyptian" was Deputy Minister of the Economy Shiiati, as transliterated from the Russian. No further information is provided.

[73] RGAE, f. 413, op. 13, d. 8791, l. 47.

a lot of room for misunderstanding and abuse. When the Egyptians complained that the Soviets were selling wire rod at prices 25 percent above world prices – far above the 6 percent premium the Soviets were paying for Egyptian cotton at the time – the Soviets noted that they had no problem selling the rod to private buyers at those prices. There was no "Egyptian price," the Soviets alleged, only a market price.[74] In the Egyptian context of inflation and import suppression of Western products (for lack of hard currency), who was to say the Soviets were unfair? After all, the Soviets pointed out, no one in Egypt complained except for the government.

Relations with the private sphere, the Soviets intimated, were often less complicated. There was less space for a misconstruction of Egypt's political leverage over the Soviet Union, so these calculations did not mar negotiations. However, the usual litany of complaints was soon raised: Soviet goods were offered at too high a price; some deliveries were quite late; other goods did not meet quality standards; and if at times Soviet representatives complained to the Egyptian Ministry of the Economy that the Egyptian firms they dealt with were not obtaining the necessary import licenses, the problem was that agreements with the Soviet organizations were being made without the licenses in the first place.[75] The problems were further complicated by the games Egyptian businessmen played in order to profit from the licensing system. An Egyptian official informed the Soviets that businessmen often gave the Soviets wrong pricing advice to then turn around and argue to the Egyptian government that a similar product can be obtained more cheaply in the West. An import license giving a local businessman the right to obtain hard currency was of much greater value than an equivalent import license for a Soviet product – access to convertible currencies opened opportunities for currency speculation and illegal currency transfers that Soviet Bloc barter licenses did not afford. In order to further rationalize foreign trade, the Egyptian government began to look at the possibility of setting up semi-governmental organizations that could be more carefully monitored.[76]

[74] RGAE, f. 413, op. 13, d. 8791, ll. 65–66. The exchange took place on August 31, 1960.

[75] All of these come from talks held on October 5, 1960 in Moscow between Patolichev and a representative of the Egyptian Ministry of the Economy. In RGAE, f. 413, op. 13, d. 8791, ll. 91–94.

[76] Ibid. The rationing of hard currency along with Nasser's waves of nationalization forced many private companies to fall into line anyway. For example, a tractor dealership approached the Soviets to earn the distribution rights of Soviet tractors precisely because there were few avenues for business growth by 1961 if the company dealt only in Western products. At this time of tight economic constraints, the company told Soviet representative Kokanbaev, business growth was likelier to be found in the barter agreements the Egyptian government was pursuing in the Soviet Bloc. In RGAE, f. 413, op. 13, d. 9042, l.157.

There may have been some basis for this. In 1961, Deputy Minister of Foreign Trade Kuz'min found himself confused by the claim from the Egyptian trade attaché in Moscow that Soviet metals were too expensive, especially compared to Japanese metals. But the Soviets followed world prices in metals assiduously, both as exporters and importers, and Kuz'min was sure that Japanese prices tended to be some 15 percent higher than European prices.[77] How odd then, he thought, for Japanese metals to be the reference against which to judge Soviet metals.

Affairs seemed to improve in the summer of 1961 when the Egyptian government decided to do away with the dual pricing system that incorporated discounts, premiums, and other bartering obfuscations. They would finally offer cotton to the Soviet Union at world market prices.[78] The Soviets promised to reciprocate with pricing reductions of their own for any reduction in the price of Egyptian cotton. But this did little to improve the standing of Soviet products in Egypt, still widely viewed as inferior to American, West German, and even British products. Soviet trade organizations had also quickly established a reputation for providing negligible service for their defective merchandise; pricing changes did not help there either.[79] But most importantly, it failed to forestall the Egyptian state's attempts to cut back on trade with the Soviet Bloc in favor of increased trade with the West. Toward the end of 1961, orders had come from a committee tasked with regulating Egyptian foreign trade to reduce trade with the Soviet Bloc and increase purchases of machinery and equipment in the West.[80] And so, in the first half of 1962, the two countries were back to playing hardball. Egyptian officials passed by Soviet offices to beg for timber, which Egypt could not buy for lack of hard currency. The Soviet Union had not delivered as much as was promised because Egypt had also failed to deliver the cotton under contract, the Soviet trade representative explained.[81] Yet Egyptian officials turned down the Soviet proposal to exchange more timber for more cotton, probably because they had earmarked the cotton for hard currency sales. There were constant rumors of quiet sales of Egyptian cotton in the West that went a long way in undermining Egyptian excuses for refusing to sell more cotton to the Soviet Union.[82] A hostile tone had crept back into their trade talks:[83]

77 RGAE, f. 413, op. 13, d. 9042, ll. 74–75 78 RGAE, f. 413, op. 13, d. 9042, ll. 92–93.
79 As Kokanbaev was told in a meeting on January 17, 1962, in RGAE, f. 413, op. 13, d. 8790, ll. 7–8.
80 Ibid. 81 RGAE, f. 413, op. 13, d. 8790, ll. 40–41.
82 RGAE, f. 413, op. 13, d. 8790, ll. 107–08.
83 The following one took place on November 14, 1962, to be found in RGAE, f. 413, op. 13, d. 8790, ll. 151–52.

THE SOVIET: Why is your cotton yarn so expensive?

THE EGYPTIAN: Because our yarn is made from the highest quality Egyptian cotton and better than those you might find in other markets.

THE SOVIET (WITH NO INDICATION OF JOKING THIS TIME): This is the first time in my life I've heard that in the technical specifications of the quality of the yarn there are also indications of the raw material from which this yarn is produced.

THE EGYPTIAN: It's all true. The Americans and Europeans understand this, which is why they buy from Egypt.

THE SOVIET: Show me those contracts.

THE EGYPTIAN: Egypt has never asked the Soviet Union to show their contracts, but rather has taken the Soviets at their word.

THE SOVIET: Egypt has never had a basis to distrust the information from Soviet foreign trade organizations.

When the Egyptian official tried to change the subject to oranges, he was informed that his prices there were also too high. Well, this is because Egyptian oranges were of higher quality, the Egyptian replied.[84] Yet in the background, Nasser's ambitions were once again seizing the Soviet-Egyptian relationship and thrusting it forward. A coup in Yemen at the end of September had put in place a republican government closely allied to Nasser. He quickly appealed to the Soviets for help, which allowed him to send vast quantities of military equipment to Yemen and project Egyptian influence like never before. But Nasser was overreaching. Egyptian involvement in the Yemeni civil war, often referred to as Nasser's Vietnam, proved disastrous for Egyptian power in the region and wrecked havoc on Egypt's economy.[85] The war amounted to a struggle by proxy for the leadership of the Arab world between Nasser and the Saudis. Its exigencies drove the Egyptians to a dependency on Soviet weapons that finally tipped the scales of Egyptian trade in the Soviet Bloc's favor and created a debt that would become the bane of the relationship.[86] Yet Egypt, like Cuba, continued to fight the dependency by engaging the world economy to the extent that it could. Even as the Egyptian government asked for debt restructuring from the Soviets in order to lessen

[84] Our Soviet hero here is Kokanbaev, while his Egyptian interlocutor was a General Korra, head of the General Organization for Foreign Trade, as per the Soviet document.

[85] A war in which some Soviet airmen fought directly under Egyptian command, illustrating a general dynamic in which "Egypt led the way, the Soviet Union followed, and Yemeni leaders incessantly tried to circumvent the Egyptian gatekeeper to deal with the USSR directly." Jesse Ferris, "Soviet Support for Egypt's Intervention in Yemen," 32. Ferris' attempts at producing parallels between Soviet involvement in Yemen and its involvement in Cuba are, however, less convincing.

[86] This is the main argument in Jesse Ferris, "Guns for Cotton? Aid, Trade, and the Soviet Quest for Base Rights in Egypt, 1964–1966," *Journal of Cold War Studies* 13:2 (2011), 8–9.

the strain on Egypt's balance of payments, it still gave priority to Western buyers of their cotton.[87] Western buyers were allowed to come in September to have first pick of the cotton in whatever quantity and of whatever quality they pleased at prices fixed in July; the Soviets were made to buy later according to strict quotas set by the Egyptian government, rather than to the demands of Soviet consumers of the cotton.[88] All the while, the war in Yemen went on savaging Nasser's relationships first with the British (who had a base in Yemen), and then with the United States, which threatened the deliveries of grain Nasser depended on to feed the population. When in the summer of 1966 the Egyptians went to the Soviets to see whether the latter could take over for the United States in those grain deliveries, the answer was equivocal. The Soviets, after all, were also having problems with grain and had lately been spending much of their hard currency reserves to import it. Soviet resources, Kuz'min noted, were not unlimited.[89] Egypt, unlike Cuba – a large country in the midst of a regional geopolitical struggle of significant proportions – was testing the limits of a superpower that was strong in discourse and will, but far from competitive economically.

East-South relations were usually begun by southern initiative, and terminated likewise. Accordingly, the problem was not that the Soviet Union could not bear the burden of Egypt's deteriorating position. The Nasser regime's accumulation of debt to the Soviet Union and others, and its alienation of the West, created a crude dependency that failed to integrate Egyptian society into alternative economic and cultural structures outside the world capitalist economy. Indeed, the more the Soviet Union insinuated itself in the economic life of Egypt, the greater it was disdained by Egyptian business circles, who continued to prefer a Western orientation – if only it could be stripped of its political and cultural preponderance and arrogance. Furthermore, a cautious Soviet push to use that dependency to obtain discreet calling rights in Egyptian ports immediately undermined the political relationship between the two countries.[90] The Soviet Union gained influence in the global South not because it was an alternative universe to the Western liberal world order, but

87 See for example then Deputy Prime Minister of Egypt Abdel Moneim Kaissouni's talks with Patolichev in Moscow on December 7, 1964 in RGAE, f. 413, op. 31, d. 102, ll. 162–64 and again on December 11 in ibid., ll 173–75.

88 As per complaints aired in a December 9, 1964 meeting in RGAE, f. 413, op. 31, d. 102, ll. 170–71.

89 Even if Soviet goodwill seemed to be, as Kuz'min again made clear. RGAE, f. 413, op. 31, d. 1144, ll. 8–11.

90 As documented in Ferris, "Guns for Cotton?"

because it eased pressures emanating from the West without demanding any political sacrifice. A violation of that general principle – a principle the Soviets loudly and persistently advertised around the world – immediately abrogated the one competitive advantage it had over the West. Yet even without that political misstep, the relationship with Egypt became ever more economically impractical. It underwent a brief respite when Nasser, in a last bout of his singular ambition, sought to lead an Arab coalition against Israel in June 1967. The Soviet Union had worked to prevent the war, and then to bring about peace as quickly as possible so as to salvage what was left from the carcass of a postcolonial moment in a state of quick putrefaction.[91] Perhaps a victory in that war might have salvaged the relationship; instead defeat unbalanced it. Like a sponge, in the span of four years Egypt first absorbed Soviet soldiers to man the defenses at Suez against Israel before they were expressed out by Nasser's successor, Anwar Sadat.[92] Sadat's final rejection of the Soviets in 1972 carried with it no onerous penalty. Repudiating the Soviet Bloc turned out to be quite different from forsaking a complex system of commercial, financial and technological exchange managed by a preponderant and jealous power (in cooperation with equally imperious allies).

The useful superpower in sub-Saharan Africa

In 1956, with the British Gold Coast on its way to independence, the US State Department was brainstorming ideas on how to keep the Soviet Union out of the region. Should they threaten the new country? Should they buy it off with aid? Should they use reliable regional leaders to lobby those with a more independent streak? The answer, of course, was all of the above.[93] Ghana's first prime minister (later president), Kwame Nkrumah, was likewise thinking about how to manipulate world politics to his advantage. His formulation was neither innovative nor complicated, and he quickly set about making an enduring policy of it. He started by sending off a quick invitation to the Soviets to come celebrate Ghana's independence in March 1957. In November, he invited the Soviets to

[91] At least in Michael Oren's telling in *Six Days of War. June 1967 and the Making of the Modern Middle East* (New York: Oxford University Press, 2002).

[92] For an analysis of the Soviet decision to deploy troops to Egypt during the War of Attrition see Dima Adamsky, "'Zero-Hour for the Bears': Inquiring into the Soviet Decision to Intervene in the Egyptian-Israeli War of Attrition, 1969–70," *Cold War History* 6:1 (2006): 113–36.

[93] Sergey Mazov, *A Distant Front in the Cold War. The USSR in West Africa and the Congo, 1956–1964* (Stanford: Stanford University Press, 2010), 43–45.

Ghana for talks on establishing an embassy, a task the Soviets thought would take three days, but which dragged on for more than a week during which Nkrumah very demonstratively paraded around town feting his Communist guests.[94] Then he froze relations with the Soviet Union for two years.

What Nkrumah wanted was his own Aswan Dam on the Volta River that could form the basis for the industrialization of the country's economy. He needed the United States and Great Britain to provide the capital, and so turned to that old chestnut, the threat of Communist "inroads." The fact that the Soviet embassy opened only in August 1959 poses a problem for some Cold War historians. If Cold War dynamism can only be found in the East or West, a major precept of the superpower paradigm, then the wait has to be explained as a Soviet prerogative. The story then becomes one of ideological change in which hesitant Soviet leaders take two years to reevaluate and court Nkrumah as a progressive, noncommunist leader, never mind that they had allegedly made that particular ideological leap many times before, on behalf of Nasser, for one.[95] Indeed, although Ghana had become independent in 1957, the first trade agreement was only signed in June 1959.[96] But there is no basis to suppose that the Soviets had changed their mind about Nkrumah. A report written for the Central Committee in December 1959, after relations were established, described Nkrumah as a petty bourgeois politician rather than a potential ideological or even political ally.[97] It was hard to see it differently, given that Nkrumah had reached out to the United States and Israel for trade and aid. Again the Soviets were not as persuaded as Western analysts would come to be with Ghana's penchant for a prominent role for the state in an incipient industrialization drive. They were unimpressed by Ghana's heavy use of planning. They failed to see in any of this a propitious sign of the African leadership's ideological proclivities. As they pointed out in the report, most of the state and foreign capital used in the construction of industrial projects was channeled through the government's Ghana Holding Company, the successor of an entity formed under British colonial purview in 1951 for the same purpose.[98] Ghanaian officials had also approached the

94 Ibid., 44, 48–50.

95 See for example Geir Lundestad, *East, West, North, South. Major Developments in International Politics Since 1945*, Gail Adams Kvam, trans. (Oxford: Oxford University Press, 1999), 57–58.

96 RGANI, f. 5, op. 30, d. 336, ll. 37–38.

97 RGANI, f. 5, op. 30, d. 305, ll. 263–78.

98 Ibid., l. 265.

Soviet Bloc countries and China, but despite these overtures toward the socialist world "Ghana's foreign policy has a strikingly pronounced pro-West orientation," the report noted.[99]

No, the Soviets did not have a change of heart. Ghana's independence opened the door to the acquisition of cocoa on barter terms rather than hard currency, and that was incentive enough for the Soviet Union to want a relationship, whether or not Ghana presented promising revolutionary conditions. Cold War master narratives notwithstanding, Ghana's national aspirations were not remarkable: plan-based economic modernization and industrialization, a reconstructed and powerful state, and greater economic independence.[100]

So what changed in 1959 that brought Ghana closer to the Soviets? There is a two-part answer. Firstly, three particularly crucial indicators of Ghana's economic well-being changed: the world market price for cocoa, Ghana's production of the crop, and Soviet cocoa reserves – and presumably demand for it. As Figure 6.6 shows, a slump through the first half of the 1960s in the price of cocoa coincided with a sustained rise in Soviet imports of Ghanaian cocoa. As mentioned earlier, Ghana's independence meant that the Soviet Union no longer had to spend precious hard currency on London commodity markets and furthermore could bring its industrial aid to bear on trade, a happy confluence of interests between the two states. Soviet purchases of cocoa quickly climbed from 2 percent of world imports in 1958 to about 8 percent ten years later.[101] But as the reader should expect by now, this was not a smooth development. In fact, in June 1959 the Ghanaians refused to enter into a barter arrangement with the Soviet Union and insisted on hard currency as the only form of payment. A year later, as prices fell ever lower, they were willing to reconsider and accept the Soviet Union's generous terms.[102]

Secondly, the answer has to do with the Volta River dam project. Nkrumah had not been especially subtle in indicating that he would

[99] Ibid., l. 278.

[100] See Westad, *The Global Cold War*, 91–93 for Ghanaian leader Kwame Nkrumah as exemplary in this widespread aspiration in the former colonial world. Although historians tend to mention leaders of the suspicious nonaligned movement when making the point, practically all "western-leaning" leaders that go without much mention, such as a Léopold Sédar Senghor from Senegal, very much shared in the same aspiration.

[101] Philip Hanson, "Soviet Imports of Primary Products: A Case-Study of Cocoa," *Soviet Studies* 23:1 (1971), 67.

[102] RGANI, f. 5, op. 30, d. 336, l. 38. The arrangement was for 10 percent of the cocoa to be paid in Soviet industrial goods the first year (1960), 20 percent in the second year, and so on until reaching 50 percent in 1964.

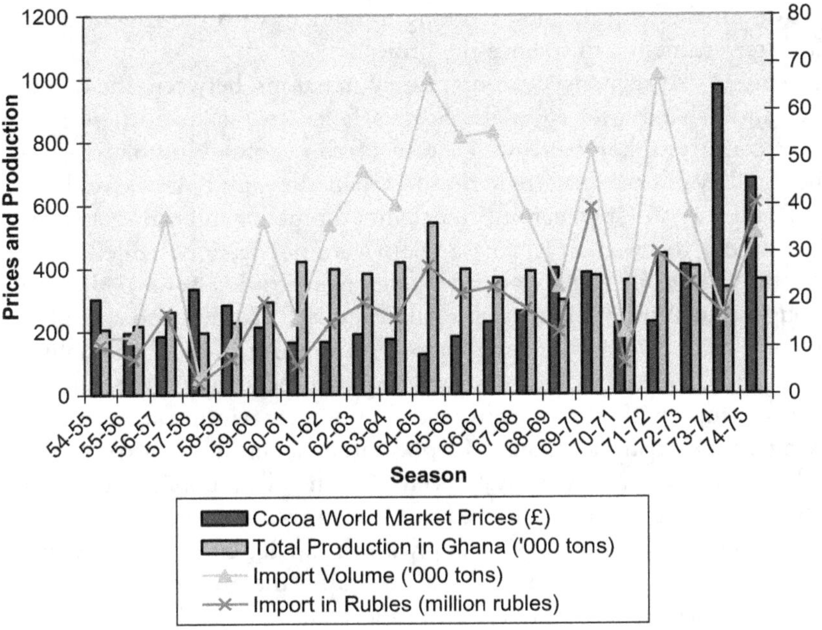

Figure 6.6 Soviet cocoa imports from Ghana*

*Cocoa world market prices are as of the last day of March of each year at the London Cocoa Terminal. Prices and production gathered from Jacques Rolfo, "Optimal Hedging under Price and Quantity Uncertainty: The Case of a Cocoa Producer," *The Journal of Political Economy* 88:1 (1980): 100–16. Soviet volume and ruble imports, in 1961 rubles, are calculated from the *Vneshniaia torgovlia SSSR za... Statisticheskii obzor* series.

keep the Soviet Union out of his country as long as there was progress on the project. However after leading the Ghanaians on, Eisenhower finally decided that capital for the project should come from the private sector.[103] This all but guaranteed a Ghanaian invitation for the Soviet Union to set up shop in the country. Nkrumah wasted little time thereafter asking the Soviets for an offer to finance the dam. In fact, he wanted the Soviets to check the proposal from the American company Kaiser Aluminum and perhaps even to cooperate with the company.[104] Nkrumah's pressure tactics worked. Kaiser Aluminum used a short window of improved US-Ghana relations in the spring of 1961 to lobby for a Western commitment to the project. In the summer, the Kennedy administration gave its

[103] Mazov, *A Distant Front in the Cold War*, 53.
[104] RGANI, f. 5, op. 30, d. 336, l. 35.

approval for the World Bank, working in tandem with the American and British governments, to finance the project.[105]

Despite a subsequent deterioration of relations between the United States and Ghana after 1961, the Soviets failed to make much headway in the country. They were well aware of the games Nkrumah played. When Mikoyan's two-day invitation to Ghana in early 1962 was suddenly transformed upon Ghanaian insistence into a nine-day official visit (which Mikoyan cut to seven days), the Soviets were not terribly baffled. "Such a drastic change in the Ghanaian President's attitude toward the visit, although uncommon in international practice, becomes understandable once one takes into account the absence in Nkrumah of a clear political course and his continuous maneuvering between the imperialist and socialist camps with the objective of obtaining maximum advantage by playing on their contradictions," a report rather superfluously explained.[106] Be that as it may, Mikoyan was received with full honors at the airport in Accra, and the Armenian wasted no time in trying to draw Ghana into a more open and trusting relationship with the Soviet Union. In particular, Mikoyan asked them "not to be shy" in letting the Soviets know if they were dissatisfied with Soviet economic and technical aid.[107]

The next several years of negotiations must have given Mikoyan much satisfaction. Trade negotiations were drenched in candid recriminations and open wrangling. Price was one of the main points of contention. Ghana consistently offered cocoa at a 15–20 percent markup on spot prices at the London commodity markets, which the Soviets accepted as the price to pay for entry into a new relationship that could alleviate an obligatory hard currency expense.[108] The question was over the premium to be paid. Ghanaians, for their part, remained from the start thoroughly comparative, pressuring the Soviets for prices so they may compare with those in the Communist Bloc itself as well as in the West.[109] This is not to say that the world was an open market to Ghana. By 1962 the country had no hard currency reserves to speak of, only the cash flow of what cocoa they could market in the West, where prices were generally depressed and falling through virtually the whole of Nkrumah's tenure as leader. Getting oil under those conditions required a partial reorientation of their trade toward the Soviet Bloc.[110] Yet where industrial equipment was concerned, the Ghanaians insisted on testing purchased Soviet equipment before

[105] Mazov, *A Distant Front in the Cold War*, 200–01. [106] GARF, f. 5446, op. 120, d. 1728, l. 84.
[107] Ibid., 87. [108] RGAE, f. 413, op. 13, d. 9448, ll. 3–5. [109] Ibid., ll. 23–25.
[110] Ibid., ll. 31–32.

ordering more, and mostly used that equipment to complement what was bought in England and West Germany.[111]

Yet unlike elsewhere, the intensification of Ghana's relationship with the Soviet Bloc was not easing the country's financial situation. The Soviet Union and other socialist countries were slow in delivering payments – whether in cash or kind – to Ghana for cocoa deliveries, creating a situation in which the Soviets found themselves chronically indebted to Ghana for a number of years. This prompted recurrent meetings in which the Communist Bloc countries found themselves upbraided by Ghanaian officials.[112] The concern over debt was bundled together with the usual complaints about the absence of service for Soviet products, the lack of any Soviet effort to market their products in Ghana's markets, and the Soviet disregard in retooling the products for Ghana's humid, tropical conditions, which altogether meant that Ghana's government had too difficult a time peddling Soviet goods in Ghana.[113] The usual Soviet response was to say that they were being cheated by both government ministries and private companies that refused to pay for Soviet deliveries.[114] This of course had little to do with the structural problems that Ghana was most concerned about, but it also did little to foster the trust of Soviet officials.[115]

If the Soviet relationship with Egypt was propelled by Nasser's political ambitions while tempered by economic realities, the dynamic was reversed in Ghana: Political choices were propelled by the constraints of world economic developments and Soviet technology and resources.[116] This dynamic came into sharp focus in 1965, at the very bottom of the slump in the international price for cocoa and at the very height of Ghana's cocoa harvest. Not coincidentally, a delegation led by Ghana's finance minister, Kwasi Amoako-Atta, came to Moscow to ask whether they could sell more cocoa than had been earmarked for export to the Soviet Union and whether they could do so at a higher price.[117] The Soviets were likely more amenable to these kinds of requests than the large, profit-oriented

[111] Ibid., ll. 90–92.

[112] See the head of the Bank of Ghana calling all communist bloc representatives on November 6, 1962 in RGAE, f. 413, op. 13, d. 9448, ll. 97–102. And RGAE, f. 413, op. 13, d. 9822, ll. 74–77 for more complaints a year later, this time only to the Soviet trade representative in Accra.

[113] RGAE, f. 413, op. 13, d. 9448, ll. 97–102.

[114] See for example RGAE, f. 413, op. 13, d. 9822, ll. 51–53.

[115] For a snapshot in December 1963, the Ghanaians complained that Soviet debt to Ghana had risen to 1.5 million Ghanaian pounds, while the Soviets complained that they were owed 700,000 Ghanaian pounds by private firms. In ibid., ll. 74–77.

[116] The more usual Cold War narrative wherein Soviet policy "concealed 'superpower' logic" of zero-sum games of control in the global South can be found in Mazov, *A Distant Front in the Cold War.*

[117] RGAE, f. 7733, op. 56, d. 501, ll. 2–4.

companies such as Cadbury that purchased the majority of Ghana's cocoa harvest. Seven years on the Soviets were still struggling to establish a presence and trying to secure their commercial gains in a country that remained stubbornly oriented toward the West (Ghana would like to be more like the United States, but the country's reserves have been wiped out by the sustained low prices of cocoa, Atta told the Soviets, almost apologizing for dealing with them at all). Atta was treated to a lecture on the benefits of trade with the Soviet Union, with its circumvention of hard currency.[118] But that year the Soviet Union did indeed purchase most of Ghana's bumper crop and at higher prices than Western countries were spending on their imports of cocoa.

In a study of Soviet cocoa imports, economist Philip Hanson questioned the competitiveness of Soviet trade, a problem that went beyond the simple issue of price. After all, cocoa beans might be a relatively homogeneous commodity, but the machinery that Ghana was getting in return was markedly not.[119] The exchange was far from optimal, Hanson argued. First, Ghana had to forgo its strict restrictions on imports of luxury goods to accommodate negotiations with the Soviets. Second, Soviet aid deliveries that paid for those imports needed time to be implemented, forming an alleged cumulative surplus with the Soviet Union of $45 million, which adversely affected Ghana's cash-strapped, creditor-hounded government. And finally, Soviet equipment may have been overpriced, the old bane of barter trade. On the whole, however, the Ghanaians must have judged the exchange favorable, as the commercial relationship Nkrumah built with the Soviets survived his overthrow in 1966, when a firmly pro-Western government replaced him.[120] After all, Soviet demand, even if fulfilled on barter terms, had the effect of increasing world demand, and therefore world prices. Hanson concluded that "Soviet primary imports may indeed behave in a rather more 'Western' way than has been supposed," at least in the case of Ghana.[121] Ghana, unlike Indonesia which had mostly rejected

[118] Ibid. [119] Hanson, "Soviet Imports of Primary Products," 69.

[120] For an initiative from the new Ghanaian government to reestablish contact and trade with the Soviets after a half-year hiatus after the coup see RGAE, f. 413, op. 31, d. 1116, ll. 4–6.

[121] That is, he eschews the type of assessment that necessitates a political dimension to Soviet foreign trade. Ibid., 77. He arrives at this conclusion after examining Soviet "grinding" rates, or rates of cocoa bean usage, which was indeed related to its stockpiles and import rates, and ultimately domestic demand. When prices started to rise at the end of the 1960s, skyrocketing after 1973, the Soviet Union went back to pre-1960 purchases patterns, that is, before prices plummeted, lending further credence to Hanson's conclusion, with demand directly related to stockpiles, albeit in the 1970s at a much higher scale of demand.

Soviet aid after Suharto's coup, continued its purchases of Soviet industrial equipment in accordance with its economic goals. The Soviet Union never monopolized Ghana's foreign trade as it would monopolize Cuba's, that other monocultural economy, but then again, Ghana never suffered the same kind of Western political and economic hostility. In time, the Soviet market for cocoa proved convenient to Ghana's balance of payment problems, but its largest customer remained a more or less friendly Western Europe. One wonders what economic system the Cubans would have chosen had they been granted the same political and economic latitude allowed Ghana.

The contrast to Ghana is Guinea. The leaders of both countries had visions of a pan-African movement that dovetailed with Soviet anti-imperialist discourse, but the Kremlin had no particular strategic role for a place like Guinea. The impoverished West African country did not even offer the prospect of saving hard currency on a deficit commodity, as Ghana did with its cocoa. And yet Guinea's relationship with the Soviet Union was more intense. This paradox led both countries to a Cold War cul-de-sac. Guinea's drive to independence in 1958, and its subsequent move toward the Soviet Union, followed an adversarial path similar to that of Indonesia and Egypt, and one that would be epitomized by Cuba a year later. It was an alliance forged not in the magnetism of Soviet power, but in the exclusionary politics of Western hegemony. Unlike Ghana, Guinea did not dally when talking to the Soviets. The two countries became fast friends. But with no economic basis upon which to build an enduring relationship, only a relentlessly hostile political environment could have sustained it. Instead it quickly devolved into mutual acrimony and economic losses on both sides.

The French empire was in full political crisis in 1957–58; French governments rose and fell on the quagmire of Algeria's war for independence. At the start of the summer of 1958, Charles de Gaulle was formally appointed prime minister and he wasted no time in proposing a new constitution that would form the basis for the Fifth Republic. In the fall, an empire-wide referendum was called to approve the new constitution, and de Gaulle made it clear that future friendly relations between France and any given colonial territory would be contingent on a "yes" vote on the part of the colonials. By all accounts Ahmed Sékou Touré, leader of the Guinean Democratic Party, would have liked to comply, but the movement for immediate, unconditional independence inside Guinea was like that of no other colony. It was not until two weeks before the referendum that he finally acquiesced to the trade unions, students, youth organizations, and teachers' union and came out in favor of a "no" vote.[122] Guinea was the only colony to vote against the new constitution, and de Gaulle's wrath came quickly on the heels of that vote.[123] Even as Sékou Touré hoped to negotiate a separate agreement with France and remain in the franc zone, the French government was planning a complete evacuation from Guinea, a cessation of all aid and commercial relations, and the establishment of an economic and diplomatic embargo, all while asking its NATO allies to do the same.[124]

The financial and human capital flight suffered by Guinea at this time crippled its economy, but it was only the beginning. The French suspended all credits and development assistance; the only cooperative endeavor that continued its construction was a port built for the export of aluminum for the benefit of a Franco-American consortium. The rest was best described by historian Elizabeth Schmidt:

> Beyond these economic penalties, technical services were sabotaged and equipment destroyed. Telephone wires were cut, even in the main government building. Cranes at the port of Conakry disappeared. Military camps were stripped of their equipment, and hospitals of their medicines. Soldiers in Dalaba burned their barracks. In Sérédou, formulas for the production of quinine vanished. In Beyla, French doctors absconded with stocks of medicines from hospitals and brand-new vehicles from the health center, all of which were sent to the Ivory Coast. Finally, in a gesture laden with pettiness and symbolism, state dishes were cracked.[125]

This then was the crucible within which the Soviet-Guinean relationship was forged. By the time Cuba knocked on the Soviet door, the Soviets were well-rehearsed in welcoming ostracized states.

The first order of business was to replace French economic assistance and credit now denied to them with that of any country that would provide it. Ghana was an early contributor.[126] The Guinean government

[122] Elizabeth Schmidt, *Cold War and Decolonization in Guinea, 1964–1958* (Athens: Ohio University Press, 2007), 161–62.

[123] The vote was overwhelming. With 85 percent of registered voters voting, 94 percent voted "no" and only 4.7 percent approved the new constitution.

[124] According to Schmidt, "only a small number of contractual workers in the private sector and 150 French civil servants – including 110 teachers – remained in Guinea after independence," Schmidt, *Cold War and Decolonization in Guinea*, 170.

[125] Ibid., 171–72. She further notes that ships carrying food and medicines were rerouted while the French secret services peppered the country with counterfeit currency, creating widespread panic.

[126] Ghana provided 10 million Ghanaian pounds as part of the agreement to form the Union of African States, a brief and failed attempt at Pan-Africanism founded by both countries in November 1958 and later joined by Mali. Sékou Touré would later return the favor by giving Nkrumah refuge and making him honorary president of Guinea after his overthrow in 1966.

cast its net wide, with Sékou Touré eventually traveling to the United States, England, and West Germany, as well as to Czechoslovakia and the Soviet Union in the fall of 1959. He assured his people and international leaders that he meant to carry out a strictly neutral foreign policy.[127] A previous Guinean delegation had arrived to Moscow that summer with the main objective of getting credits and grants from the Soviets – the latter a rare proposition since the Soviet Union did not like granting outright gifts, but preferred to loan funds at 2.5 percent interest to be paid back with domestic products or hard currency.[128] Nevertheless, the Guinean delegation successfully convinced the Soviets to give them grants; although it is not clear to what extent their expectations were met. The Soviets agreed to extend 140 million rubles in credit on the usual aid terms for the construction of unspecified projects. As for the grant, they agreed to give away about 7.5 million rubles for the construction of a radio station, the export of twenty-four cars – four Volgas and twenty GAZ-69 jeeps – and the delivery of some tractors and specialists for a state-owned rice farm.[129]

The enthusiasm for the new relationship was short-lived. After an initial spike in exports to Guinea in 1961, when they reached 24.5 million rubles based on the initial aid agreements, they soon dropped to the 7–10 million range for the rest of the decade. The trade figures tell the tale: Three to five million rubles' worth of coffee, pineapple, and banana imports from Guinea was all the Soviet Union could purchase to keep the relationship going.[130] The Soviet Union could not forestall the shambles that was the Guinean economy in the early 1960s. Guinea's exclusion from the franc zone led to the creation of an inconvertible Guinean franc minted in Czechoslovakia, which isolated Guinea's economy from that of its neighbors. And yet this did not translate into a Guinean commitment to a reorientation to the Communist Bloc. In 1963, for example, the Guineans fulfilled only some 30 percent of their contracted deliveries of goods to the Soviet Union.[131] Mutual trust, never particularly robust, was clearly

[127] RGANI, f. 5, op. 30, d. 305, l. 287.

[128] RGANI, f. 5, op. 30, d. 309, ll. 86–90. At least that is what the translator overheard while taking the Guineans around Baku. Among themselves, they often expressed the necessity of returning to Guinea with "concrete results," particularly in terms of getting outright grants from the USSR. Incidentally, the Guineans also expressed little inclination when invited to go talk to French communists who were visiting Crimea at the time, noting that not a single one of them had ever been to Guinea and that they held mistaken positions in colonial matters.

[129] RGANI, f. 5, op. 30, d. 305, ll. 290–91. For a preliminary list of possible aid ventures see Ibid., ll. 289–93.

[130] See the *Vneshniaia torgovlia SSSR za … Statisticheskii obzor* series.

[131] RGAE, f. 413, op. 31, d. 69, ll. 15–18.

crumbling. Consider the following exchange. Guinea's Minister of Trade Ibrahim Barry complained that the Soviets were counting Guinean exports in Soviet ports, which often meant a 20–30 ton loss in bananas, for example. This meant on average Guinea was losing 5 percent of its bananas and some 3 percent of its pineapples, Barry informed the Soviet trade representative. The contracts were on a Free on Board (FOB) basis, that is, before goods were loaded onto ships at Guinean ports; they were not on a Cost, Insurance and Freight (CIF) basis, in which case shipping costs are the responsibility of the exporter. Guinea could not pay for a representative in Soviet ports to wait for those deliveries and count them together with the Soviets, Barry argued. If that is how the Soviets wanted to do their accounting, then the contracts should be written on a CIF basis. The counterargument was obvious, and the Soviet representative did not lose a beat: If the Guineans find this to be more profitable then please let's do so, but Guinea would have to pay for the shipping costs in hard currency, which it had not had to do under FOB arrangements. Moreover the Guinean export agency was negotiating shipping expenses with Soviet import organizations on a barter basis, whereas with every other country shipping expenses were mostly in hard currency. Barry left this bout with the Soviets in a huff, promising to "study the issue."[132]

The situation with exports did not improve in 1964. That year saw again a 30 percent fulfillment rate of Guinean exports, even as debt to the Soviet Union accumulated. The problem, Guinean officials explained, was that there was a steady leakage of goods in contraband to Mali and Senegal, where Guineans could sell their goods for hard currency, rather than the functionally worthless Guinean francs.[133] Guinea was not Egypt (much less Europe!), where the state was penetrative enough to implement the necessary measures that could help cope with foreign economic aggression. Even sugar imports from the Soviet Union were taken across the border to be sold for hard currency.[134] The years passed, and Sékou Touré's regime kept failing to live up to its progressive credentials. Each year the Soviets found it more difficult to do business in Guinea. Delivery rates did not improve; Guineans would not commit to paying off their debt to the Soviet Union; and they would not even pick up the phone when problems needed urgent resolution.[135]

[132] Ibid., ll. 19–20. The meeting took place on February 15, 1964.

[133] Ibid., ll. 38–40.

[134] Ibid., ll. 86–90.

[135] As when in April 1965 the Soviets redirected an oil tanker after an urgent request from Guinea only to find out that a French tanker from Total was having its oil emptied at port (embargo notwithstanding, apparently). The Soviets spent two days trying to get a hold of somebody in the government to explain what was happening. RGAE, f. 413, op. 31, d. 584, ll. 114–15.

By 1965, Guinea too had adjusted its expectations, both in what the Soviets could deliver and in what Guinea's economy was capable of. That year, the Guinean government scaled down its import demands to keep them in balance with what the country could actually export.[136] In fact, at times they seemed to be backtracking from the relationship altogether, as in their attempt to return three Ilyushin Il-18 airplanes they had bought earlier for Air Guinea. They did not have enough passengers to justify the upkeep of the airplanes and were anyway not competitive with Western airplanes.[137] Despite this readjusted attitude, Guinea again failed to keep its end of the bargain. The great year of diminished but realistic expectations, 1965, still saw Guinea in deficit to the Soviet Union, and subject to another litany of broken export promises.[138] The next year, the Soviets announced that they would withhold all further deliveries until annual debts were paid.[139] Contrived in a paroxysm of revenge by a resentful French state, the Soviet-Guinean romance had peaked quickly before entering a protracted period of spiraling disillusionment that ended in estrangement.

But it would be wrong to lay that disillusionment simply at the door of inadequate mutual commerce. This relationship, as most others the Soviet struck in these years, was driven by the Soviet partner's domestic affairs – which of course intersected more forcefully with the liberal world economy than with any alternative the Soviets could muster. And the Soviet impact on Guinean domestic affairs was far from positive. The newly developed state-owned industries, many of which had been built with Soviet aid and encouragement, suffered from rampant corruption, contributing little to state coffers. Meanwhile, the leading lights remained foreign-owned bauxite and aluminum companies as well as foreign-owned plantations, a fact that guaranteed their continued accommodation by Sékou Touré's government.[140] It is little wonder that rather than continuing to accept

[136] RGAE, f. 413, op. 31, d. 584, ll. 96–104.

[137] Ibid., ll. 60–66. They later reconsidered and asked whether they could return only one airplane. Returning three would have left Air Guinea with only one airplane in its fleet, and they considered it a matter of prestige that the national carrier should have more than one airplane.

[138] RGAE, f. 413, op. 31, d. 1117, ll. 45–46.

[139] This was the message from the head of the African division of the Ministry of Foreign Trade to the Guinean ambassador in a September 7, 1966 meeting. Ibid., ll. 47–49.

[140] In fact, bauxite was the one commodity that could have salvaged the relationship with the Soviets, but the Guinean government kept refusing to commit to its export to cover its debts. It was probably the source of greatest contention between the two, as the Guineans habitually backtracked over promised deliveries of bauxite. Some examples of Soviet pressure for Guinean bauxite exports are in RGAE, f. 413, op. 31, d. 69, ll. 2–11, 19–20, 38–40, 86–90, 135–37, and RGAE, f. 413, op. 31, d. 584, ll. 145, 93–95, 96–104.

turnkey projects from the Soviet Union that increased the country's indebtedness and only led to widespread corruption, Sékou Touré turned to joint ventures with Western companies to exploit Guinea's resources, most notably in a venture with California-based Harvey Aluminium Corporation backed by the US government to create the Boké industrial complex.[141]

Some Soviet conclusions

Soviet institutions and approaches to foreign aid had a marked lack of staying power and lasting influence in those regions of the world where they operated. The problem was analyzed by GKES as early as 1961, but short of a complete overhaul in its approach, there was little to be done that could fix it. The report noted certain trends that became visible even then and which undermined the political effectiveness of Soviet aid, which in turn arrested the profitable development of trade with the Third World. Most markedly, it was found that Western companies were taking advantage of Soviet-financed projects, often a result of the fact that the norm throughout the Third World was the mixed economy. In India, for example, Western companies were lobbying to exploit oil discoveries made by Soviet specialists.[142] Despite the goodwill generated by these discoveries, the Soviets were not able to capitalize on it by exporting competitive equipment for India's oil industry, which in turn gave the Western oil majors the window of opportunity to insinuate themselves into a market they had discounted and rejected only a few years before.[143] But this was only one example of the many wasted opportunities arising from a lack of strategic planning in Soviet foreign trade. A Soviet-built auto-repair shop in Afghanistan that quickly proved unprofitable was allowed to be managed by (West) Germans. More famously, a hotel in Burma built through Soviet grants was handed over to be managed by a consortium of Western companies.[144] Future aid, the report suggested, should be given only after careful consideration of the project's

[141] Lansine Kaba, "Guinean Politics: A Critical Historical Overview," *The Journal of Modern African Studies* 15:1 (1977), 36–41 gives a good critique of Sékou Touré's political economy.

[142] RGANI, f. 5, op. 30, d. 371, l. 228.

[143] See RGAE, f. 4372, op. 66, d. 439, ll. 23–30, for these worries and for Indian assurances of the goodwill the Soviets had garnered for themselves. The Indians were particularly interested in forming more cadres for their oil industry, an endeavor the Western companies were probably not too keen on undertaking.

[144] RGANI, f. 5, op. 30, d. 371, l. 228.

profitability and the end product's quality, or it would continue to be under threat of co-option by Western companies.

At other times, the execution of projects had little to do with the real economic needs of the target country, creating little more than debt rather than economic development. In Laos and Cambodia the Soviets had carried out expensive oil prospecting, likely at the request of states looking for an easy road to riches. The reality, however, was that these countries had little use for oil and none of the auxiliary industry and infrastructure to build an economically viable oil industry.[145] Soviet aid here had left these poor countries with significant costs to pay back for no results, at a generous interest rate of 2.5 percent.

A more important problem, in GKES' reckoning, was the shortage of Third World specialists trained in the technical know-how necessary to take full advantage of Soviet aid, which all too often left these countries vulnerable to the "predations" of Western business.[146] Many of these countries, the agency noted, were weary of cooperating with the Soviet Union in the training of technical cadres, fearing they might become ideologically compromised. GKES suggested doing its utmost to extinguish these fears of subversion, or risk losing projects to Western governments, as was happening in Iraq.[147]

These were all tweaks for a more effective approach to aid. But a more fundamental reconsideration was in the offing by the early 1960s. The days of this type of pell-mell rush to aid Third World countries in sudden need – countries such as Guinea, Indonesia, and Egypt – were numbered. Several scholars have noted a tightening of criteria in the Soviet Union's rendering of aid. Elizabeth Kridl Valkenier dated it to around 1964, but before Khrushchev's fall. Mikoyan had already hinted at a reevaluation of aid practices at the 22nd Party Congress in October 1961, and soon academic institutions were called upon to analyze more carefully the effectiveness of Soviet aid. This development, according to Valkenier, was cemented after Khrushchev's overthrow, when "the pursuit of economic advantage became an important criterion."[148] The economist

[145] Ibid., l. 229.

[146] A situation assessed in the same terms by poor countries such as India, which often appealed to the Soviet Union for help in training cadres that they may raise a competitive, more independent industry along purely national lines. See again RGAE, f. 4372, op. 66, d. 439, ll. 23–30.

[147] Ibid., l. 230–31. As a last suggestion, GKES called for improved propagandistic work to spread information on the generosity of Soviet economic cooperation with former colonies; this was a challenge the Soviet Union was prepared to meet, and did so rather successfully, if we can judge by Western anxieties on the matter.

[148] Valkenier, *The Soviet Union and the Third World*, 12.

Franklyn Holzman was probably closer to the mark in suggesting that there had always been an important economic criterion in Soviet aid and trade, albeit one that became more pronounced during the Brezhnev era.[149]

In fact, in 1961 GKES was already having second thoughts about the Soviet Union's simple aid policies. There was no consideration, for example, for providing aid that would encourage an intensification of trade between the Soviet Union and the target country. In India, they were building oil refineries without stipulating increased crude deliveries to that country, and what's more, their management was being passed over to Royal Dutch Shell. In Turkey, a glass factory built by the Soviets was being supplied by Americans. In Cambodia, Indonesia, and Burma the Soviets built hospitals without insisting that they supply the medicines as well.[150] Furthermore, barter lists were not given due consideration and were often left vague, so that the Soviets ended up accepting products they had little use for, like what happened when the Egyptians insisted that they clear their debts to the Soviets with vegetables. "In the determination of projects in which the Soviet Union is going to cooperate with developing countries, it is necessary not only to take into account their requests, but also our interest in obtaining products from those countries necessary to our economy," the GKES report suggested.[151] With respect to Indonesia, for example, the Soviets were interested in rubber and tin, and yet they had not rendered any aid that would increase the output of those products. Indeed by 1961, there seemed to be little thought on old Marxist reservations on exploitative trade at the offices of the GKES; unadulterated national gain, rather than the economic independence of its partners or the accruement of political goodwill, was an ascendant objective for Soviet foreign trade throughout the 1960s.

In India, for example, the Soviets were starting to withdraw from old relationships that had served them in good stead. A request for aid by an Indian private company to build a factory that would produce four million roller bearings a year received the support of the Soviet trade representative in India, but not of Gosplan officials back in Moscow. Perris Eastern had been Stankoimport's agent in India for almost ten years by 1963, and four roller bearing factories were already being built in India with foreign help, which meant, in the trade representative's opinion, that

149 Franklyn Holzman, *Foreign Trade under Central Planning* (Cambridge: Harvard University Press, 1974), see chapter 16.

150 RGANI, f. 5, op. 30, d. 371, l. 235.

151 Ibid., l. 236.

foreign companies would have no problem picking up Perris' project as well. Despite the trade representative's warnings that such a proposition would hurt Stankoimport's relationship with the Indian firm, Gosplan decided that Soviet resources would be better spent building such a factory in the Soviet Union and exporting the roller bearings as India needed them.[152]

That same year, when BG India Limited approached Prommasheksport asking for technical help in building a factory that would produce 253,000 electrical counters a year, the response was equally pragmatic. BG needed help in organizing the factory's construction, along with the necessary transfer of technology and technological documentation from the Soviets.[153] Gosplan, however, took an economically sober approach. The Soviets already produced enough electrical counters to supply India with as many as were needed, and going through with the technological transfer would only hamper such exports.[154]

There is little question that the political remained important in foreign trade planning, and many examples can always be provided for this thesis; less clear is the proportion of those examples to the whole of trade transactions carried out at this time. Holzman argued rightly that capital invested in the domestic Soviet economy would almost always give a higher rate of return than the 2.5 percent interest rate they were getting on their aid; furthermore perhaps as much as a third of the aid might have been bought by Third World countries as exports anyway, had it not been provided as aid.[155] But then, these considerations were not the ones under debate at the Kremlin. At issue was the economic dependence of the former colonies, and it was thought that as long as that dependence existed, the Soviet Union would not enjoy the fair and mutually beneficial trade they hoped to carry out with developing countries. The outcome would be the perpetuation of a mere commercial subsistence for both Soviets and partners under the unrelenting pressure of a hostile and economically overwhelming West.

This maximum of goals never materialized because most of the economies of the Third World remained stubbornly mixed and always receptive to Western sticks and carrots. Furthermore the Soviets were well aware of the inadequacies of their products in Third World markets, where demand for them tempered a bit a decade after the Soviets broke into

[152] RGAE, f. 4372, op. 65, d. 413, l. 111. [153] Ibid., l. 109. [154] Ibid., l. 110.
[155] Holzman, *Foreign Trade under Central Planning*, 350–53.

those markets for the first time.[156] By the mid-1960s, the share of trade with the Third World as a percentage of total Soviet foreign trade stabilized at around 10–13 percent, even as the share of trade with Europe, Japan, and the United States continued to grow in the Soviet Union's foreign trade structure.[157] It would have been difficult to predict, but it appeared that the mutual economic usefulness of the Soviet-Third World connection had a natural ceiling.

[156] RGANI, f. 5, op. 30, d. 371, ll. 233–34.

[157] This, to repeat, is within the context of overall growth in trade, including trade with the Third World. It's just to note that after the initial enthusiasm and immediate economic connection between the Soviet Union and the former colonies, trade with the West experienced faster growth rates from the mid-1960s.

Conclusion: *Mikoyan's legacy*

Few now knock on the Kremlin's door seeking financial and diplomatic support. There is a profitable legacy of clients of Soviet military equipment that maintain Russia at the top of the list in the arms exporting business. This was a legacy of the Soviet Union's relationships in the global South, so if this book is generally on target, it would be logical to assume that a much more significant inheritance descends from the Soviet Union's dealings with the rich Western countries. And so it does. As this book goes to press, the leadership seating in the Kremlin today is trying to rationalize a gas and oil industry that has stagnated even as it continues to be the government's main source of income and an essential underpinning of its power. This same leadership spent its first eight years at the helm wresting that source of power away from a group of men, the so-called oligarchs, who had taken control of it during the 1990s. These oligarchs, in turn, had been the direct beneficiaries of a peculiar political economy practiced by the Soviet Union at the time of its collapse. When domestic prices were liberalized at the beginning of the 1990s, the Kremlin inexplicably retained price controls in the commodities that Russia exported for its economic well-being. The few, lucky men who bought these commodities at subsidized domestic prices and sold them at world prices became rich beyond all measure or merit. But this was merely a continuation of the same racket that had been run under the management of the Ministry of Foreign Trade (and which benefited the Kremlin directly) for decades. What the 1980s and 1990s had in common was a foreign trade commodity sector that was almost alone in effectively creating immense wealth within the context of a degraded national economy.

If we continue peeling the onion, we find that what the oligarchs had resuscitated from moribundity, and for which they later struggled with the latest tenants in the Kremlin, was the very source of domestic power that had been denied Mikhail Gorbachev at the beginning of his tenure. When energy prices collapsed in 1986, taking with it the earnings with which to manage the patronage networks that Leonid Brezhnev had so deftly handled before him, Gorbachev the conservative reformer became Gorby the radical reformer and destroyer of the Soviet Union. Gorbachev was thus victimized by the world economy to the same extent that Brezhnev was blessed by it. Even before energy prices spiked in 1973 in the wake of the OPEC oil embargo – and again in 1979 following the Iranian Revolution – the Soviet Union had already initiated the construction of an infrastructure that would facilitate the exportation to the world economy of the country's vast resources. The oil shocks of the 1970s had initiated the largest transfer of wealth from the rich world to the lucky poor since the industrial revolution, and the Soviet Union was arguably the greatest beneficiary.[1] This came at a price. The Soviet Union also participated in the global inflation that blighted that decade, and which in the Soviet Union took the form of an intensification of shortages – a paradoxical outcome that partially prompted the mildly reformist policies of Yuri Andropov in the early 1980s and then those of his protégé Gorbachev. And if the Soviet Union had been well placed to participate in that unprecedented transfer of capital, it owed its position primarily to one person whose protagonism in Soviet history has generally been relegated in favor of his more lurid colleagues. More than anyone else's, this was Mikoyan's legacy.

Lenin's famous quip about capitalists selling the very noose with which to hang themselves echoed bitterly in the halls of the Kremlin, even as it reverberated through the spider's web of oil and gas pipes that had immobilized and subverted the very institutions Lenin had helped set up and which had seemed so effective in the 1930s. The pragmatic, sarcastic, good-humored Armenian had taken over Lenin's own legacy in 1925 when he was made to serve as the people's commissar of foreign and domestic trade, a position created to better manage the new amalgamation of internal and external markets produced in the Soviet Union's pursuit of the gold standard. Despite his misgivings, Mikoyan was right for the job.[2] He was unwaveringly one of Stalin's men, but also had a feel for the liberal economic governance that the attachment to the gold standard signified. From that year on, Mikoyan managed the Soviet Union's foreign trade for

[1] As Stephen Kotkin argued, perhaps less dramatically, in his *Armageddon Averted. The Soviet Collapse, 1970–2000* (Oxford: Oxford University Press, 2001), chapter 1. As he points out, it was not just a matter of oil sales alone, but also armament sales to suddenly wealthy petrostates around the world.

[2] Mikoyan's reluctance to take up the post is recounted in the episodic biography by Mikhail Iur'evich Pavlov, *Anastas Mikoyan. Politicheskii portret na fone sovetskoi epokhi* (Moscow: Mezhdunarodnye otnosheniia, 2010).

the next four decades. He did leave his post in the 1930s, when international trade evaporated and ceased to be a factor in Soviet development schemes. He went back to his post promptly after foreign imports became the lifeblood of the Soviet war effort against the Nazis, and he remained there except for a bizarre hiatus during which Stalin inexplicably tried to remove him from the leadership. Stalin died before he could succeed, and Mikoyan became the reference for all things concerning foreign economic exchange until he was finally retired in December 1965, leaving behind him a culture and practice of commerce at all levels of the bureaucracy that survived well into the 1980s.

It is in no small measure because of Mikoyan that this book has argued for a basic continuity in the Kremlin's approach to foreign trade during the Soviet Union's first four decades. It may be that other aspects of Soviet political economy went through many twists and turns, but it is fitting that the longest-serving Soviet politburo member presided over the most constant state policy in Soviet history. Of course there were many twists and turns to the story of Soviet economic exchange as well, but most of them were generated from without, rather than from within. Initial attempts at an accommodation with international finance and commerce foundered in the tempests of the Great Depression, compelling the young state into an autarkic development that unfortunately became one of its defining characteristics in the Western imagination. The real culprit, the collapse of the liberal world order, had been as unexpected as its success would be two decades later.

In a zero-sum, bipolar view of the world, the emergence of the Soviet Union onto the world stage from the mid 1950s might seem like a form of failure of the other camp, a weakening of the "free world." This book has argued, however, that it was in fact US success that brought the Soviets back in. The United States had imposed a vision of the world on its European allies free of empires, while at the same time enforcing a permanent stability on the old continent based on cooperation and the discreet accommodation of tens of thousands of US soldiers on European soil. Freed at last from the burden of securing itself from itself, Western Europe – together with its former colonies – beckoned an obliging Soviet Union out of its unwanted economic confinement.

The world economy quickly slotted the country within its economic and technological hierarchy. The global South found the Soviet Union's experience with state-led development and its penchant for barter very intriguing. In their search for a modus vivendi with the global liberal order, these poor countries saw in the Soviet Union a source of technology and technical know-how, a palliative against the rigors of hard currency constraints (because of the Soviet Union's readiness to barter), and most usefully, a way to scare up better terms from an anxious West. Likewise, the rich, industrialized world was also prompt in taking the measure of the newly reengaged power. The often regrettable experience of Soviet manufactured products soon concentrated minds on Soviet energy resources, which over the course of the 1960s became the Soviet Union's main export category. Japan is instructive here. Japan became the Soviet Union's most important capitalist trading partner by 1970 only to see the relationship stagnate thereafter in comparison with the rest of the industrialized world precisely because it failed to make the transition to energy. With the scrapping of the plans for a pipeline to Japan, timber alone proved no match for the commercial growth that energy was generating in Western Europe.[3]

It is a mistake to move too far away from Western Europe when analyzing Soviet foreign policy, even in the global South. Conventional wisdom too often notes that decolonization seemed to validate Marxist-Leninist doctrine – "the world was going our way" and all that. Certainly Soviet leaders made much of the historical inevitability of socialism, and its apparent advance in the poor regions of the world was propaganda too good to waste. But that development also made a nonsense of Marxism-Leninism. As everyone knew, socialism was something workers built – hence the desperate Soviet fantasy of building an industrial infrastructure in poor countries that would support what the Soviets connoted as "cadres." Privately, Soviet leaders were less sanguine about the nature of the leadership in these regions.[4] Furthermore, socialism's lack of progress in the West went altogether without comment by Soviet leaders, and therefore in most Cold War histories. Yet it was the economic success of the postwar welfare states – a success that had marginalized Communist movements there – that was shaping the Soviet Union's turn toward greater consumerism. And this development itself necessitated an intensified economic relationship with the West. When the Cold War scholarship turns toward what they term "competition" in the Third World, it must temporarily forget that European and American dynamism was informing

[3] Decades later, after the Kremlin could once again countenance the construction of a pipe through Siberia, the project was reactivated. But the Japanese were too late. China too had lifted its head from the misery that was its twentieth century and successfully competed against Japan for the pipe.

[4] Khrushchev tells us as much. See his discussion of Third World affairs in Sergei Khrushchev, ed., *Memoirs of Nikita Khrushchev. Statesman*, vol. 3 (University Park: Pennsylvania State University Press, 2007), 723–887.

a core change in the worldview of Soviet officials away from the triumphalist consensus formed in the 1930s.[5] Furthermore, when writing Europe out of East-South relations while concentrating on the US-Soviet rivalry, historians of the Cold War must begin their stories with the establishment of diplomatic relations, or Khrushchev's trips abroad – a history too often denuded of the sustained legacy of the European presence in these former colonies simply because Cold War histories must fit the bipolar straightjacket. These relations are naturally and without any evidence understood to have been started by the virile Soviet Union; the passive Third World is to be wooed. Of course this is how an irredeemably racist US State Department saw it and unfortunately not all Cold War historians control for this racism when transcribing histories from material produced at the State Department.

What might a more comprehensive analysis that includes Europe and the world economy look like? We might begin with the reaction of a younger Odd Arne Westad after five or six years of digesting the newly opened archives in Moscow: "In terms of economic development, military power, and working alliances, we are discovering that bipolarity may not be the best way of understanding the international history of the Cold War and that the United States formed the core of an expanding system of which we still know far too little."[6] Bipolarity certainly does not account for the deep-seated weakness of the Soviet economic position in the Third World. At every turn this relation was constrained and mediated by the push and pull of a world economy dominated by an economically preponderant West. On the issue of Westad's "expanding system," however, we do in fact know more than he supposed. Indeed the scholarly field of international political economy, which this book has made use of, is dedicated mostly to this question.

More than two decades ago, political economist Stephen Krasner, for one, made a case for Third World initiative to be given pride of place in the developing world's attempts to reconcile its goals with the powerful liberal system constructed by the United States and Europe after World War II.[7] He looked at Third World efforts to secure national control and wealth through the retooling of international regimes that legitimated

[5] As expressed in the changing literature of the Institute of the World Economy and International Relations (IMEMO).

[6] Westad, "Secrets of the Second World," 270–71. In the end, Westad was unfortunately reconverted to the bipolar paradigm that informed his much more influential book, *The Global Cold War*.

[7] Stephen D. Krasner, *Structural Conflict. The Third World Against Global Liberalism* (Berkeley: University of California Press, 1985).

authoritative allocation of resources, rather than market allocation. Krasner analyzed Third World initiatives in such institutions as the World Bank, the IMF, regional development banks, and the United Nations, and examined national regulations for multinational corporations and Third World political leverage in different conventions such as the Law of the Sea, the creation of the Antarctic Treaty system, and the international regime for shipping. He might as well have identified Soviet foreign economic policy as another exploitable tool in the arsenal of Third World international political action. In the Soviet Union these countries often sought shelter from the vagaries of the world economy as well as a catalyst with which to motivate Western countries to meet their anti-liberal objectives.

Soviet comparative economic weakness along with that of the poor countries, however, allowed world market forces to constrain and at times scuttle nascent economic relations even as they at times encouraged their expansion. This book identifies several world economic developments as catalysts for the remarkable growth in Soviet economic relations with the Third World. First, the world economic depression of the 1930s and World War II had the effect of undermining trust in market mechanisms as the basis for economic exchange in much of the Third World, and of promoting a measure of national independence that served as a foundation for the ISI strategies adopted to some degree or another among the bulk of the countries of the South. Legacies of colonialism that promoted state-oriented authoritative rule and left many regions in a state of acute economic dependence on former metropoles and world markets also tended to make the Soviet Union an attractive option when it came to diversifying economic relations and pursuing strategies that favored state-led development. In many regions this attraction was bolstered by the sharp fall in commodity prices following the end of the Korean War in 1953 that had the effect of destabilizing national ruling elites.

Western hostility was often the main engine generating economic relations for the Soviet Union in places like Indonesia, Egypt, Guinea, and Cuba, all of which preferred economic exchange with the West and fell back on the Soviet Union when this was denied them. Ultimately, however, Soviet aid and trade institutions were unable to capitalize on these opportunities and enmesh these countries in economic and political webs that could guarantee a continued Soviet economic presence. But then Soviet aid and trade was not carried out with any such particular strategy in mind, at least not until years of experience operating in the South wised Soviet officials up to the realities of their place in the world economy.

The main motivations revealed by the archival material were political goodwill and the alleviation of western pressure on both the Soviet Union and its economic partners. Of course every country posed its own peculiarity, and many motivations coexisted. But there is little evidence supporting the notion that Soviet economic policies aimed at some specific and immediate triumph of communist principles. Given that in many of these places communists were actively repressed (Egypt) or had no prospect of coming to power (Burma), this lazy assumption, still latent in Cold War literature, is all the more bizarre. Economic inclusiveness in the international community of nations seems to have been the only short and medium-term goal of Soviet foreign economic policy in the Third World.

Here is the problem at the root of the Cold War narrative meme. It created a framework for US officials to understand the world and their actions within a heroic narrative of courage and confrontation, while simultaneously allowing them to claim force majeure should they fail to measure up to the ideals they purportedly defended – a failure that was habitual in the non-white world. These officials operated in an economic world of their making, as befits the preponderant power they served. The discursive universe they built around it and which so many historians have uncritically parroted – i.e., bipolarity – served to discipline the politics and social aspirations of countries around the world as well as the needs of Americans' own self-representation. Bipolarity also happened to be almost accurate in terms of nuclear parity, especially by the late 1960s and early 1970s, lending it a certain plausibility. But it distorted almost all other aspects of the international context. When looking at economy, for example, and as Westad noted two decades ago, bipolarity evanesces.

This is true not only as a matter of economic power, but also the ideational thinking built around it. The dichotomy between US–championed liberal capitalism versus Soviet Communism becomes nonsensical once one looks at global economic developments more deeply. Liberal capitalism was not on the agenda anywhere in the global South, and even the rich countries each opted for their own idiosyncratic forms of less or more liberal economic governance. Soviet-style command economy was somewhat more intriguing in certain countries, but far from an actionable blueprint in most of them. Rather, the institutionalization of a variety of approaches to political economy followed along historical lines of an older vintage than Cold War discourse. The Asian tigers, for example, did not follow North-American–style liberal models, but rather the political economy of the Japanese Empire of the first half of the century, which only became more attractive with its stunning economic success in the postwar period.[8] Elsewhere, the bipolar discourse usefully practiced in the State Department as well as in the Kremlin also leads analysis astray. India, Egypt, Nigeria, and other regional leaders implemented dynamic economic models that had more to do with conjunctural realities, their own economic underdevelopment, and domestic politics than the Cold War superpower ideological frameworks allow. What Cold War narratives, following US officials, have tried to categorize within its simplistic "two-camp" theories has in fact little to do with ideological predilections, and much more to do with whether a country dared to allow the Soviet Union a role in its foreign trade. The fact that India becomes a focus of Cold War narratives while Argentina does not, or Ghana rather than Senegal, has little to do with the economic strategies they employed and the ideological underpinnings these evinced, since they were broadly similar (or at least much more similar to each other than to the two prototypical models of Cold War discourse). Given the paucity of literature on the Third World–Cold War binary, this is a problem that will persist until those countries get their due by Cold War historians.

Western insistence that the Soviet Union was nearly the equal of the West in all things – except, of course, that it was evil – was an unexpected boon to Soviet officials. Stalin had used the two-camp formulation of world politics, new in 1946 when Andrei Zhdanov pronounced it, to initiate the reconsolidation of power that total war had frazzled. But this was part of his modus operandi since at least the Shakhty trials of 1928, or the Kirov murder of 1934. He used it again to bind the lands his army had reached during the war, and many times thereafter in that hapless region. Cold War discourse was a political windfall like no other, even if it also gave the country a stature its economy could not sustain. The price the Soviets paid for maintaining that superpower façade was

[8] See Bruce Cumings, "The Origins of the Development of the Northeast Asian Political Economy: Industrial Sectors, Product Cycles, and Political Consequences," *International Organization* 38:1 (1984): 1–40. Since this work, Cumings has slowly arrived at a more nuanced understanding of Cold War Asia. In a dig at Cold War bipolarity, Cumings describes the Asian wars as an anti-colonialist challenge to American plans to impose a political economy based on the reconstruction of Japanese industrial capacity and its reconnection to its former imperial colonies. The Chinese revolution and the Korean War wrecked those plans, as the United States imposed a division of Asia and maintained it well into the twentieth century. Those anti-colonialist convulsions in the region did not end until the end of the Indochina War, after which China began to be integrated into the world economy and Cold War. Note the redundancy of the Soviet Union to this much more accurate appraisal of modern Asian history. The Cold War, which was brought to Asia in the hull of American bombers, had a military end in Asia before it did so politically in Europe with the financial crises of Eastern Europe. See, for example, Bruce Cumings, *The Korean War. A History* (New York: The Modern Library, 2010), 211–21.

enormous – although not the imperial overstretch of some accounts – but the legitimacy derived from Cold War discourse abroad was also significant. More importantly, sustaining a state of what Mary Kaldor has called "the imaginary war" helped maintain a social discipline within its own empire paralleled only by that of the Atlantic powers, one that, in Kaldor's words, "specified the character of blocs and gave meaning to the sense of belonging to East and West."[9] All the while, its commercial policy bespoke of accommodation and an abiding desire for participation in a Western-dominated liberal world order from which the Kremlin derived tremendous material benefit.

The academic geography of the production of Cold War statistics discussed at the beginning of this book also makes more sense when the Cold War is viewed as a discursive construction rather than the all-encompassing reality of the second half of the twentieth century. The oblique collusion between Soviet and North American economists that conspired to compose an unrealistic statistical picture of the Soviet Union is not accidental. Nor is it chance that challenges to that impossible orthodoxy arose in the margins – in Great Britain and in the dissenting voices within the Soviet Union itself. A semblance of parity in all spheres was the mise-en-scène necessary for the drama of the Cold War to unfold and be sustained. And no one was more interested in spellbinding their respective audiences than the main protagonists.

But a more measured view of the Soviet economy, in all its idiosyncratic importance and limitations, yields a less epic yet more consistent history. It also allows for a truly global history that looks at different regions of the world in the full richness of their complexities and contradictions rather than in the infantilizing simplifications of Cold War Manichaeism. Ultimately the concept that requires the most urgent revision is autarky. The idea that the Soviet Union aspired to be self-reliant, an alternate universe to the liberal world order, has made of the country a Rorschach blot. Unmoored from the world, its history becomes a journey away from and back into the (civilized/rational?) world. But the Soviet Union never left. It shadowed the trajectory of the world economy and participated in all the world's economic trends – and we should not be surprised to find that it participated in its cultural ones as well. We must recover the Soviet Union not just as the important constituent of the global that it was, but also as an inveterate and enthusiastic participant.

[9] Mary Kaldor, *The Imaginary War. Understanding the East-West Conflict* (Oxford: Blackwell, 1990), 4. Kaldor takes her cue from Foucault's idea of "disciplinary technology."

Bibliography

I. Archival Sources

A. State Archive of the Russian Federation (GARF) (*Gosudarstvennyi arkhiv Rossiiskoi Federatsii*)

Fond A-5446: Council of Ministers of the USSR (*Sovet Ministrov SSSR*)

Fond R-403: Council of the Economy of the Russian Republic (*Sovet narodnogo khoziaistva RSFSR*)

B. Russian State Archive of Contemporary History (RGANI) (*Rossiiskii gosudarstvennyi arkhiv noveishei istorii*)

Fond 2: Transcripts and Material of the Plenary Meetings of the Central Committee of the Communist Party of the Soviet Union (*Stenogrammy i materialy plenumov TsK KPSS*)

Fond 5: General Department of the Central Committee of the Communist Party of the Soviet Union (*Obshchii otdel TsK KPSS*)

C. Russian State Archive of the Economy (RGAE) (*Rossiiskii gosudarstvennyi arkhiv ekonomiki*)

Fond 7: State Council of the Economy of the USSR (*Goseconomsoviet SSSR*)

Fond 99: Economic Research Institute of Gosplan (NIEI) (*Nauchno-issledovatel'skii ekonomicheskii institut Gosplana*)

Fond 413: Ministry of Foreign Trade of the USSR (*Ministerstvo vneshnei torgovli SSSR*)

Fond 4372: State Planning Committee of the USSR (*Gosplan SSSR*)

Fond 5240: People's Commissariat of Trade of the USSR (Narkomtorg SSSR)

Fond 7733: Ministry of Finance of the USSR (*Ministerstvo finansov SSSR*)

Fond 8045: Ministry of the Maritime Fleet of the USSR (*Ministerstvo mosrkogo flota SSSR*)

D. Russian State Archive of Socio-Political History (RGASPI) (*Rossiiskii gosudarstvennyi archive sotsial'no-politicheskoi istorii*)

Fond 84: Anastas Ivanovich Mikoyan

E. John F. Kennedy Presidential Library

National Security Files

II. Soviet Newspapers and Journals

Ekonomicheskaya Gazeta

Mirovaia ekonomika i mezhdunarodnye otnosheniia

Pravda

Za rulem

III. Document Collections and Statistical Publications

Anderson, K. M., A. Iu. Vatlin, P. Gregory, A. K. Sorokin, R. Suza, and O. V. Khlevniuk, eds. *Stenogrammy zasedanii Politbiuro TsK RKP(b)-VKP(b) 1923–1938*, 3 vols. Moscow: Rosspen, 2007.

CIA, *Handbook of Economic Statistics*. Washington, DC, 1975.

Handbook of Economic Statistics. Washington, DC, 1991.

Danilov, V. P., O. V. Khlevniuk, and A. Iu. Vatlin, eds. *Kak lomali NEP. Stenogrammy plenumov TsK VKP(b), 1928–1929 gg.* 5 vols. Moscow: Izdatel'stvo Materik, 2000.

Davies, R. W., Oleg V. Khlevniuk, E. A. Rees, Liudmila P. Khosheleva, and Larisa A. Rogovaya, eds. *The Stalin–Kaganovich Correspondence, 1931–36*. New Haven: Yale University Press, 2003.

Dobrokhotov, L. N., V. H. Kolodezhnyi, and V. S. Pushkarev, eds. *Denezhnaia reforma 1921–1924 gg.: sozdanie tverdoi valiuty. Dokumenty i materialy*. Moscow: Rosspen, 2008.

Fursenko, A. A., ed. *Prezidium TsK KPSS 1954–1965. Chernovye protokol'nye zapisi zasedanii*. Moscow: ROSSPEN, 2003.

Jensen, Kenneth M., ed. *Origins of the Cold War. The Novikov, Kennan, and Roberts 'Long Telegrams' of 1946*. Washington, DC: United States Institute of Peace Press, 1993.

Khlevniuk, Oleg V., Arfon Rees, R. W. Davies, P. Kosheleva, and L. A. Rogovaya. *Stalin i Kaganovich. Perepiska, 1931–1936 gg.* Moscow: ROSSPEN, 2001.

Lih, Lars T., Oleg V. Naumov, and Oleg V. Khlevniuk, eds. *Stalin's Letters to Molotov*. New Haven: Yale University Press, 1995.

Ministerstvo vneshniaia torgovlia. *Vneshniaia torgovlia SSSR za 1956 god. Statisticheskii obzor*. Moscow: Vneshtorgizdat, 1958.

Vneshniaia torgovlia SSSR za 1958 god. Statisticheskii obzor. Moscow: Vneshtorgizdat, 1959.

Vneshniaia torgovlia SSSR za 1918–1940 gg. Statisticheskii obzor. Moscow: Vneshtorgizdat, 1960.

Vneshniaia torgovlia SSSR za 1960 god. Statisticheskii obzor. Moscow: Vneshtorgizdat, 1961.

Vneshniaia torgovlia SSSR za 1962 god. Statisticheskii obzor. Moscow: Vneshtorgizdat, 1963.

Vneshniaia torgovlia SSSR za 1963 god. Statisticheskii obzor. Moscow: Vneshtorgizdat, 1964.

Vneshniaia torgovlia SSSR za 1964 god. Statisticheskii obzor. Moscow: Vneshtorgizdat, 1965.

Vneshniaia torgovlia SSSR za 1965 god. Statisticheskii obzor. Moscow: Izdatel'stvo "Mezhdunarodnye otnosheniia," 1966.

Vneshniaia torgovlia SSSR za 1966 god. Statisticheskii obzor. Moscow: Izdatel'stvo "Mezhdunarodnye otnosheniia," 1967.

Vneshniaia torgovlia SSSR. Statisticheskii sbornik, 1918–1966. Moscow: Izdatel'stvo "Mezhdunarodnye otnosheniia," 1967.

Vneshniaia torgovlia SSSR za 1970 god. Statisticheskii obzor. Moscow: Izdatel'stvo "Mezhdunarodnye otnosheniia," 1971.

Vneshniaia torgovlia SSSR, 1922–81. Iubileinyi statisticheskii obzor. Moscow: Izdatel'stvo financy i statistika, 1982.

National Council of Applied Economic Research. *Foreign Exchange Crisis and the Plan*, Occasional Papers, No. 1. New Delhi: Asia Publishing House, 1957.

Naumkin, Vitalii, A. Z Egorin, I. D. Zviagel'saia, G. K. Prozorova, eds. *Blizhnevostochnyi konflikt. Iz dokumentov arkhiva vneshnei politiki Rossiiskoi Federatsii*, 3 Vols. Moscow: Mezhdunarodnyi fond "Demokratiia," 2003.

US Department of State. *Foreign Relations of the United States Diplomatic Papers, 1944*, Vol. 4. Washington, DC: US Government Printing Office, 1966.

Foreign Relations of the United States Diplomatic Papers, 1945, Vol. 5. Washington, DC: US Government Printing Office, 1967.

Foreign Relations of the United States, 1947, Vol. 3. Washington, DC: US Government Printing Office, 1972.

Foreign Relations of the United States, 1952–54, Vol. 1. Washington, DC: US Government Printing Office, 1983.

Foreign Relations of the United States, 1955–57, Vol. 8. Washington, DC: US Government Printing Office, 1987.

Foreign Relations of the United States, 1958–60, Vol. 6. Washington, DC: US Government Printing Office, 1991.

Foreign Relations of the United States, 1958–60, Vol. 7, Part 2. Washington, DC: US Government Printing Office, 1993.

Foreign Relations of the United States, 1961–1963, Vol. 9. Washington, DC: US Government Printing Office, 1995.

Foreign Relations of the United States, 1961–1963, Vol. 13. Washington, DC: US Government Printing Office, 1994.

Whitney, Thomas P., ed. *Khrushchev Speaks. Selected Speeches, Articles, and Press Conferences, 1941–1961*. Ann Arbor: The University of Michigan Press, 1963.

World Trade Organization. *International Trade Statistics 2008*. Geneva: WTO Publications, 2008.

IV. Memoirs

Baibakov, N. K. *Sorok let v pravitel'stve*. Moscow: Izdatel'stvo Respublika, 1993.

Bohlen, Charles E. *Witness to History, 1929–1969*. New York: W. W. Norton & Company, 1973.

Chuev, Felix. *Molotov Remembers. Inside Kremlin Politics*. Chicago: Ivan R. Dee, 1993.

Greenspan, Alan. *The Age of Turbulence. Adventures in a New World*. New York: The Penguin Press, 2007.

Khrushchev, Sergei. ed. *Memoirs of Nikita Khrushchev. Reformer, 1945–1964*. Vol. 2. University Park: Pennsylvania State University Press, 2006.

Memoirs of Nikita Khrushchev. Statesman, 1953–1964. Vol. 3. University Park: Pennsylvania State University Press, 2007.

Mikoian, Anastas Ivanovich. *Tak bylo. Razmyshleniia o minuvshem*. Moscow: Varius, 1999.

V. Secondary Sources

Adamsky, Dima. "'Zero-Hour for the Bears': Inquiring into the Soviet Decision to Intervene in the Egyptian–Israeli War of Attrition, 1969–70." *Cold War History* 6:1 (2006): 113–36.

Ahamed, Liaquat. *Lords of Finance. The Bankers Who Broke the World*. New York: Penguin Books, 2009.

Ahlberg, Kristin L. "'Machiavelli with a Heart': The Johnson Administration's Food for Peace Program in India, 1965–1966." *Diplomatic History* 31:4 (2007): 665–701.

Ahmad, Aijaz. "Postcolonialism: What's in a Name?" in Roman de la Campa, E. Ann Kaplan and Michael Sprinker, eds. *Late Imperial Culture*. London: Verso, 1995.

Allen, Robert C. "Agricultural Marketing and the Possibilities for Industrialisation in the Soviet Union in the 1930s." *Explorations in Economic History* 34:4 (1997): 387–410.

Farm to Factory. A Reinterpretation of the Soviet Industrial Revolution. Princeton: Princeton University Press, 2003.

Åslund, Anders. "How Small is Soviet National Income," in Henry S. Rowen and Charles Wolf, Jr., eds. *The Impoverished Superpower. Perestroika and the Soviet Military Burden*. San Francisco: Institute for Contemporary Studies Press, 1990.

"Russia." *Foreign Policy* 125:4 (2001): 20–25.

Bach, Quintin V. S. *Soviet Aid to the Third World. The Facts and Figures*. Sussex: The Book Guild Ltd., 2003.

Baykov, Alexander. *Soviet Foreign Trade*. Princeton: Princeton University Press, 1946.

Behrman, J. N. "State Trading by Undeveloped Markets." *Law and Contemporary Problems* (part 2) 24:3 (1959): 454–81.

Bekarevich, A. D., ed. *Ekonomika Kuby. Statisticheskii spravochnik*. Moscow: Akademiia Nauk SSSR, 1971.

Berend, Ivan T. *Decades of Crisis. Central and Eastern Europe before World War II*. Berkeley: University of California Press, 1998.

An Economic History of Twentieth-Century Europe. Economic Regimes from Laissez-Faire to Globalization. Cambridge: Cambridge University Press, 2006.

Bergson, Abram. "Russia Turns to Economic Competition." *Challenge* 6:5 (1958): 50–54.

The Real National Income of Soviet Russia since 1928. Cambridge: Harvard University Press, 1961.

Berliner, Joseph S. *Factory and Manager in the USSR*. Cambridge: Harvard University Press, 1957.

Bhagwati, Jagdish, and Padma Desai. *India Planning for Industrialization. Industrialization and Trade Policies since 1951*. London: Oxford University Press, 1970.

Bhagwati, Jagdish, and T. N. Srinivasan. *Foreign Trade Regimes and Economic Development. India*. New York: Columbia University Press, 1975.

Birman, Igor. "The Financial Crisis in the USSR." *Soviet Studies* 32:1 (1980): 84–105.

"The Imbalance of the Soviet Economy." *Soviet Studies* 40:2 (1988): 210–21.

Boden, Ragna. "Cold War Economics: Soviet Aid to Indonesia." *Journal of Cold War Studies* 10:3 (2008): 110–28.

Brandenberger, David. *Propaganda State in Crisis. Soviet Ideology, Indoctrination, and Terror under Stalin, 1927–1941*. New Haven: Yale University Press, 2012.

Breslauer, George W. *Khrushchev and Brezhnev as Leaders. Building Authority in Soviet Politics*. London: George Allen & Unwin, 1982.

Calleo, David P. *The Imperious Economy*. Cambridge: Harvard University Press, 1982.

Cardoso, Fernando Henrique, and Enzo Faletto. *Dependencia y desarrollo en América Latina; Ensayo de interpretación sociológica*. Mexico: Siglo Veintiuno Editores, 1969.

Carr, E. H., and R. W. Davies. *Foundations of a Planned Economy, 1926–1929* vol. 1. New York: The Macmillan Company, 1969.

Cherkasov, Petr. *IMEMO. Portret na fone epokhi*. Moscow: Ves' Mir, 2004.

Chernow, Ron. *The House of Morgan. An American Banking Dynasty and the Rise of Modern Finance*. New York: Grove Press, 1990.

Citino, Nathan J. *From Arab Nationalism to OPEC. Eisenhower, King Saud, and the Making of U.S.–Saudi Relations*. Bloomington: Indiana University Press, 2002.

Clark, Colin. *A Critique of Soviet Statistics*. London: Macmillan & Co., 1939.

The Conditions of Economic Progress. New York: St. Martin's Press, 1957.

Clarkson, Stephen. "Non-Impact of Soviet Writing on Indian Thinking and Policy." *Economic and Political Weekly* 8:15 (1973).

Cox, Michael, and Caroline Kennedy-Pipe. "The Tragedy of American Diplomacy? Rethinking the Marshall Plan." *Journal of Cold War Studies* 7:1 (2005): 97–134

Cumings, Bruce. "The Origins of the Development of the Northeast Asian Political Economy: Industrial Sectors, Product Cycles, and Political Consequences." *International Organization* 38:1 (1984): 1–40.

"Still the American Century." *Review of International Studies* 25 (special issue, 1999): 271–99.

Parallax Visions. Making Sense of American–East Asian Relations. Durham: Duke University Press, 1999.

The Korean War. A History. New York: The Modern Library, 2010.

Curtis, Gerald L. "The Tyumen Oil Development Project and Japanese Foreign Policy Decision-Making," in Robert A. Scalapino, ed. *The Foreign Policy of Modern Japan*. Berkeley: University of California Press, 1977.

Darwin, John. *The Empire Project. The Rise and Fall of the British World System, 1830–1970*. Cambridge: Cambridge University Press, 2009.

Davidson, Basil. *The Black Man's Burden. Africa and the Curse of the Nation-State*. New York: Times Books, 1992.

Davies, R. W. *The Socialist Offensive. The Collectivisation of Soviet Agriculture, 1929–1930*. Cambridge: Harvard University Press, 1980.

The Soviet Economy in Turmoil, 1929–1930. Cambridge: Harvard University Press, 1989.

ed. *From Tsarism to the New Economic Policy. Continuity and Change in the Economy of the USSR*. Ithaca: Cornell University Press, 1991.

Davies, R. W., Mark Harrison, and S. G. Wheatcroft, eds. *The Economic Transformation of the Soviet Union, 1913–1945*. Cambridge: Cambridge University Press, 1994.

Day, Richard B. *Leon Trotsky & the Politics of Economic Isolation*. Cambridge: Cambridge University Press, 1973.

Desai, Padma. *The Bokaro Steel Plant. A Study of Soviet Economic Assistance*. Amsterdam: North-Holland Publishing Company, 1972.

Dohan, Michael R. "Soviet Foreign Trade in the NEP Economy and Soviet Industrialization Strategy." PhD dissertation, MIT, 1969.

"The Economic Origins of Soviet Autarky, 1927/8–1934." *Slavic Review* 35:4 (1976): 603–35.

Dunmore, Timothy. *Soviet Politics, 1945–53*. New York: St. Martin's Press, 1984.

Eichengreen, Barry. *Golden Fetters. The Gold Standard and the Great Depression, 1919–1939*. Oxford: Oxford University Press, 1992.

The European Economy Since 1945. Coordinated Capitalism and Beyond. Princeton: Princeton University Press, 2007.

Globalizing Capital. A History of the International Monetary System. Princeton: Princeton University Press, 2008.

Ekbladh, David. *The Great American Mission. Modernization and the Construction of an American World Order*. Princeton: Princeton University Press, 2010.

Ellman, Michael. "The 1947 Soviet Famine and the Entitlement Approach to Famines." *Cambridge Journal of Economics* 24:5 (2000): 603–30.

Ericson, Richard E. "The Soviet Statistical Debate: Khanin versus the TsSU," in Henry S. Rowen and Charles Wolf, Jr., eds. *The Impoverished Superpower. Perestroika and the Soviet Military Burden*. San Francisco: Institute for Contemporary Studies Press, 1990.

Erlich, Alexander. *The Soviet Industrialization Debate, 1924–1928*. Cambridge: Harvard University Press, 1960.

Evans, Peter. *Dependent Development. The Alliance of Multinational, State, and Local Capital in Brazil*. Princeton: Princeton University Press, 1979.

Farber, Samuel. *The Origins of Cuban Revolution Reconsidered*. Chapel Hill: The University of North Carolina Press, 2006.

Ferris, Jesse. "Soviet Support for Egypt's Intervention in Yemen, 1962–1963." *Journal of Cold War Studies* 10:4 (2008): 5–36.

"Guns for Cotton? Aid, Trade, and the Soviet Quest for Base Rights in Egypt, 1964–1966." *Journal of Cold War Studies* 13:2 (2011): 4–38.

Nasser's Gamble. How Intervention in Yemen Caused the Six-Day War and the Decline of Egyptian Power. Princeton: Princeton University Press, 2012.

Frieden, Jeffry A. *Global Capitalism. Its Fall and Rise in the Twentieth Century*. New York: W. W. Norton & Company, 2006.

Fursenko, Aleksandr, and Timothy Naftali. *One Hell of a Gamble. Khrushchev, Castro and Kennedy, 1958–1964*. New York: W. W. Norton & Company, 1997.

Khrushchev's Cold War. The Inside Story of an American Adversary. New York: W. W. Norton & Company, 2006.

Gaddis, John Lewis. *We Now Know. Rethinking Cold War History*. New York: Oxford University Press, 1997.

The Cold War. A New History. New York: The Penguin Press, 2005.

Gatrell, Peter. *Russia's First World War. A Social and Economic History*. Harlow: Pearson/Longman, 2005.

Gerschenkron, Alexander. *Economic Relations with the USSR*. New York, 1945.

Economic Backwardness in Historical Perspective. Cambridge: Harvard University Press, 1962.

"The Rate of Growth in Russia: The Rate of Industrial Growth in Russia, Since 1885." *The Journal of Economic History* Vol. 7, Supplement: Economic Growth: A Symposium (1974).

Gilpin, Robert. *The Political Economy of International Relations*. Princeton: Princeton University Press, 1987.

Gleason, Abbot. *Totalitarianism. The Inner History of the Cold War*. Oxford: Oxford University Press, 1995.

Goland, Yurii. "Currency Regulation in the NEP Period." *Europe-Asia Studies* 46:8 (1994): 1251–96.

Golubev, A. V. *"Esli mir obrushitsia na nashu Respubliku." Sovetskoe obshchestvo i vneshniaia ugroza v 1920–1940-e gg*. Moscow: Kuchkovo Pole, 2008.

Gordon, Andrew. *A Modern History of Japan. From Tokugawa Times to the Present*. Oxford: Oxford University Press, 2003.

Gorlizki, Yoram. "Party Revivalism and the Death of Stalin." *Slavic Review* 54:1 (1995): 1–22.

Gorlizki, Yoram, and Oleg Khlevniuk. *Cold Peace. Stalin and the Soviet Ruling Circle, 1945–1953*. Oxford: Oxford University Press, 2004.

Gregory, Paul R. *Before Command. An Economic History of Russia from Emancipation to the First Five-Year Plan*. Princeton: Princeton University Press, 1994.

The Political Economy of Stalinism. Evidence from the Soviet Secret Archives. Cambridge: Cambridge University Press, 2004.

Grossman, Gregory. "Soviet Growth: Routine, Inertia and Pressure." *The American Economic Review* 50:2 (1960): 62–72.

Gustafson, Thane. *Crisis amid Plenty. The Politics of Soviet Energy under Brezhnev and Gorbachev*. Princeton: Princeton University Press, 1989.

Hanson, Philip. "The Soviet Union and World Shipping." *Soviet Studies* 22:1 (1970): 44–60.

"Soviet Imports of Primary Products: A Case-Study of Cocoa." *Soviet Studies* 23:1 (1971): 59–77.

"The CIA, the TsSU and the Real Growth of Soviet Investment." *Soviet Studies* 36:4 (1984): 571–81.

The Rise and Fall of the Soviet Economy. An Economic History of the USSR from 1945. New York: Longman, 2003.

Hara, Kimie. *Japan–Soviet/Russian Relations since 1945. A Difficult Peace*. London: Routledge, 1998.

Harris, James R. *The Great Urals. Regionalism and the Evolution of the Soviet System*. Ithaca: Cornell University Press, 1999.

"Encircled By Enemies: Stalin's Perceptions of the Capitalist World, 1918–1941." *The Journal of Strategic Studies* 30:3 (2007): 513–45.

Harris, Steven. "In Search of Ordinary Russia. Everyday Life in the NEP, the Thaw, and the Communal Apartment." *Kritika* 6:3 (2005): 583–614.

Harrison, Mark. "Soviet Economic Growth since 1928: The Alternative Statistics of G. I. Khanin." *Europe-Asia Studies* 45:1 (1993): 141–67.

Accounting for War. Soviet Production, Employment and the Defence Burden, 1940–1945. Cambridge: Cambridge University Press, 1996.

"Coercion, Compliance and the Collapse of the Soviet Command Economy." *Economic History Review* 55:3 (2002): 397–433.

Haslam, Jonathan. *Soviet Foreign Policy, 1930–1933. The Impact of Depression*. New York: St. Martin's Press, 1983.

Russia's Cold War. From the October Revolution to the Fall of the Wall. New Haven: Yale University Press, 2011.

Hewett, Ed A., with Clifford G. Gaddy, *Open for Business. Russia's Return to the Global Economy*. Washington: The Brookings Institution, 1992.

Heywood, Anthony. *Modernising Lenin's Russia. Economic Reconstruction, Foreign Trade and the Railways*. Cambridge: Cambridge University Press, 1999.

Holloway, David. *Stalin and the Bomb. The Soviet Union and Atomic Energy, 1939–1956*. New Haven: Yale University Press, 1994.

Holzman, Franklyn. *Foreign Trade under Central Planning*. Cambridge: Harvard University Press, 1974.

Hough, Jerry. *The Soviet Prefects. The Local Party Organs in Industrial Decision-Making*. Cambridge: Harvard University Press, 1969.

The Struggle for the Third World. Soviet Debates and American Options. Washington, DC: Brookings Institution, 1986.

Jackson, Ian. *The Economic Cold War. America, Britain and East–West Trade, 1948–63*. New York: Palgrave, 2001.

Jacobson, Jon. *When the Soviet Union Entered World Politics*. Berkeley: University of California Press, 1994.

Jasny, Naum. *Soviet Industrialization, 1928–1952*. Chicago: University of Chicago Press, 1961.

Jentleson, Bruce W. *Pipeline Politics. The Complex Political Economy of East–West Trade*. Ithaca: Cornell University Press, 1986.

Johnson, Chalmers. *Miti and the Japanese Miracle: The Growth of Industrial Policy, 1925–1975*. Stanford: Stanford University Press, 1982.

Judt, Tony. *Postwar. A History of Europe since 1945*. New York: The Penguin Press, 2005.

Judt, Tony, with Timothy Snyder. *Thinking the Twentieth Century*. New York: Penguin Press, 2012.

Kaba, Lansine. "Guinean Politics: A Critical Historical Overview." *The Journal of Modern African Studies* 15:1 (1977): 25–45.

Kahin, Audrey R., and George Kahin. *Subversion as Foreign Policy. The Secret Eisenhower and Dulles Debacle in Indonesia*. New York: The New Press, 1995.

Kaldor, Mary. *The Imaginary War. Understanding the East–West Conflict*. Oxford: Blackwell, 1990.

Karol, K. S. *Guerillas in Power. The Course of the Cuban Revolution*, trans. Arnold Pomerans. New York: Hill & Wang, 1970.

Kenwood, A. G., and A. L. Lougheed. *The Growth of the International Economy, 1820–1990. An Introductory Text*. London: Routledge, 1992.

Keohane, Robert. "The Theory of Hegemonic Stability and Changes in International Economic Regimes, 1967–1977," in Ole R. Holsti, Randolph M. Siverson, and Alexander L. George, eds. *Change in the International System*. Boulder: Westview Press, 1980.

Khanin, G. I. *Dinamika ekonomicheskogo rasvitiia SSSR*. Novosibirsk: Nauka, 1991.

Sovetskii ekonomischeskii rost. Analiz zapadnykh otsenok. Novosibirsk: Ekor, 1993.

"The 1950s – The Triumph of the Soviet Economy." *Europe-Asia Studies* 55:8 (2003): 1187–1211.

Kim, Byung-Yeon. "Causes of Repressed Inflation in the Soviet Consumer Market, 1965–1989: Retail Price Subsidies, the Siphoning Effect, and the Budget Deficit." *Economic History Review* 55:1 (2002): 105–27.

Kindleberger, Charles P. *The World in Depression, 1929–1939*. Berkeley: University of California Press, 1973.

Manias, Panics, and Crashes. A History of Financial Crises. Fifth Edition. Hoboken: John Wiley & Sons, 2005.

Kohli, Atul. *State-Directed Development. Political Power and Industrialization in the Global Periphery*. Cambridge: Cambridge University Press, 2004.

Kolko, Joyce, and Gabriel Kolko. *The Limits of Power. The World and the United States Foreign Policy, 1945–1954*. New York: Harper & Row, 1972.

Kornai, Janos. *Economics of Shortage*. 2 vols. Amsterdam: North-Holland Publishing Company, 1980.

The Socialist System. The Political Economy of Communism. Oxford: Oxford University Press, 1992.

Kotkin, Stephen. "Modern Times: The Soviet Union and the Interwar Conjunction." *Kritika: Explorations in Russian and Eurasian History* 2:1 (2001): 111–164

Armageddon Averted. The Soviet Collapse, 1970–2000. Oxford: Oxford University Press, 2001.

Krasner, Stephen D. *Structural Conflict. The Third World against Global Liberalism*. Berkeley: University of California Press, 1985.

Krugman, Paul. "The Myth of Asia's Miracle." *Foreign Affairs* 73:6 (1994): 62–78.

Krupianko, M. I. *Sovetsko-iaponskie ekonomicheskie otnosheniia*. Moscow: Nauka, 1982.

Kumykin, P. N., ed. *50 let sovetskoi vneshnei torgovli*. Moscow: Izdatel'stvo mezhdunarodnoe otnosheniia, 1967.

LaFeber, Walter. *The Clash. U.S.–Japanese Relations throughout History*. New York: W. W. Norton, 1997.

Latham, Robert. *The Liberal Moment. Modernity, Security and the Making of Postwar International Order*. New York: Columbia University Press, 1997.

Leffler, Melvyn P. *A Preponderance of Power. National Security, the Truman Administration, and the Cold War.* Stanford: Stanford University Press, 1992.

For the Soul of Mankind. The United States, the Soviet Union, and the Cold War. New York: Hill & Wang, 2007.

Leffler, Melvyn P., and Odd Arne Westad, eds. *The Cambridge History of the Cold War*, 3 vols. Cambridge: Cambridge University Press, 2010.

Lévesque, Jacques. *L'URSS et la Révolution Cubaine.* Montreal: Presses de la fondation nationale des sciences politiques, 1976.

Lundestad, Geir. *East, West, North, South. Major Developments in International Politics Since 1945.* Gail Adams Kvam, trans. Oxford: Oxford University Press, 1999.

Maddison, Angus. *The World Economy. A Millennial Perspective.* Paris: Development Centre of the Organization for Economic Cooperation and Development, 2001.

Marer, Paul. *Dollar GNPs of the USSR and Eastern Europe.* Baltimore: The Johns Hopkins University Press, 1985.

Martin, William. "The Making of an Industrial South Africa: Trade and Tariffs in the Interwar Period." *The International Journal of African Historical Affairs* 23:1 (1990): 59–85.

Mastny, Vojtech. *The Cold War and Soviet Insecurity. The Stalin Years.* New York: Oxford University Press, 1996.

"The Soviet Union's Partnership with India." *Journal of Cold War Studies* 12:3 (2010): 50–90.

Mazov, Sergey. *A Distant Front in the Cold War. The USSR in West Africa and the Congo, 1956–1964.* Stanford: Stanford University Press, 2010.

McKinnon, Ronald I., and Kenichi Ohno. *Dollar and Yen. Resolving Economic Conflict between the United States and Japan.* Cambridge: MIT Press, 1997.

McMahon, Robert J. "Food as a Diplomatic Weapon: The India Wheat Loan of 1951." *Pacific Historical Review* 56:3 (1987): 349–77.

Mee, Charles L. *The Marshall Plan. The Launching of Pax Americana.* New York: Simon and Schuster, 1984.

Mehrotra, Santosh. *India and the Soviet Union. Trade and Technology Transfer.* Cambridge: Cambridge University Press, 1990.

Mesa-Lago, Carmelo. *Breve historia económica de la Cuba socialista. Políticas, resultados y perspectivas.* Madrid: Alianza Editorial, 1994.

Miller, Margaret. *Rise of the Russian Consumer.* London: Merrit & Hatcher Ltd., 1965.

Milner, Helen V. "The Political Economy of International Trade." *Annual Review of Political Science* 2 (1999): 91–114.

Morley, James Williams. *The Japanese Thrust into Siberia, 1918.* New York: Columbia University Press, 1957.

Morley, Morris H. *Imperial State and Revolution. The United States and Cuba, 1952–1986.* Cambridge: Cambridge University Press, 1987.

Mukherjee, Aditya. *Imperialism, Nationalism and the Making of the Indian Capitalist Class, 1920–1947.* New Delhi: Sage Publications, 2002.

Narinsky, Mikhail M. "New Evidence on the Soviet Rejection of the Marshall Plan, 1947: Two Reports." *Cold War International History Project*, Working paper No. 9, Woodrow Wilson Center, March 1994.
Nove, Alec. *The Soviet Economic System*. London: Allen & Unwin, 1977.
"A Note on Growth, Investment and Price-Indices." *Soviet Studies* 33:1 (1981): 142–45.
An Economic History of the USSR, 1917–1991. London: Penguin Books, 1992.
O'Connor, Timothy Edward. *The Engineer of Revolution. L. B. Krasin and the Bolsheviks, 1870–1926*. Boulder: Westview Press, 1992.
Oppenheim, Samuel A. "Between the Right and the Left: G. Ia. Sokolnikov and the Development of the Soviet State, 1921–1929." *Slavic Review* 48:4 (1989): 592–613.
Oren, Michael. *Six Days of War. June 1967 and the Making of the Modern Middle East*. New York: Oxford University Press, 2002.
Osokina, Elena. *Our Daily Bread. Socialist Distribution and the Art of Survival in Stalin's Russia, 1927–1941*. Armonk: M. E. Sharpe, 2001.
Patterson, Thomas G. *Contesting Castro. The United States and the Triumph of the Cuban Revolution*. New York: Oxford University Press, 1994.
Pavlov, Mikhail Iur'evich. *Anastas Mikoyan. Politicheskii portret na fone sovetskoi epokhi*. Moscow: Mezhdunarodnye otnosheniia, 2010.
Pechatnov, Vladimir O. "The Big Three After World War II: New Documents on Soviet Thinking about Post War Relations with the United States and Great Britain." *Cold War International History Project*, Working paper No. 13, Woodrow Wilson Center, July 1995.
Pérez, Louis A. *Cuba and the United States. Ties of Singular Intimacy*. Athens: The University of Georgia Press, 1990.
On Becoming Cuban. Identity, Nationality and Culture. New York: The Ecco Press, 1999.
Plokhy, Serhii M. *Yalta. The Price of Peace*. New York: Penguin Books, 2010.
Polanyi, Karl. *The Great Transformation. The Political and Economic Origins of Our Time*. Boston: Beacon Press, 1944.
Pollock, Friedrich. "State Capitalism: Its Possibilities and Limitations." *Studies in Philosophy and Social Science* 9:2 (1941): 200–255.
Quigley, John. "Foreign Trade Agencies Abroad: A Note." *Law and Contemporary Problems* 37:3 (1972): 465–73.
Reiman, Michal. *The Birth of Stalinsim. The USSR on the Eve of the "Second Revolution."* Bloomington: Indiana University Press, 1987.
Reinhart, Carmen M., and Kenneth S. Rogoff. *This Time is Different. Eight Centuries of Financial Folly*. Princeton: Princeton University Press, 2009.
Rigby, T. H. *Political Elites in the USSR. Central Leaders and Local Cadres from Lenin to Gorbachev*. Aldershot: Edward Elgar Publishing, 1990.
Roberts, Geoffrey. *Stalin's Wars. From World War to Cold War, 1939–1953*. New Haven: Yale University Press, 2006.
Roh, Kyung Deok. "Stalin's Think Tank. The Varga Institute and the Making of the Stalinist Idea of World Economy and Politics, 1927–1953." PhD dissertation, University of Chicago, 2010.

Rolfo, Jacques. "Optimal Hedging under Price and Quantity Uncertainty: The Case of a Cocoa Producer." *The Journal of Political Economy* 88:1 (1980): 100–16.

Ross, Kristin. *Fast Cars, Clean Bodies. Decolonization and the Reordering of French Culture*. Cambridge: MIT Press, 1995.

Rotter, Andrew J. *Comrades at Odds. The United States and India, 1947–1964*. Ithaca: Cornell University Press, 2000.

"Feeding Beggars: Class, Caste and Status in Indo-US Relations, 1947–1964," in Christian G. Appy, ed. *Cold War Constructions. The Political Culture of United States Imperialism, 1945–1966*. Amherst: The University of Massachusetts Press, 2000.

Sanchez, Omar. "The Rise and Fall of the Dependency Movement: Does it Inform Underdevelopment Today?" *Estudios Interdisciplinarios de America Latina* 14:2 (2003).

Sanchez-Sibony, Oscar. "Soviet Industry in the World Spotlight: The Domestic Dilemmas of Soviet Foreign Economic Relations, 1955–1965." *Europe-Asia Studies* 62:9 (2010): 1555–78.

Schenk, Catherine R. "The Origins of the Eurodollar Market in London: 1955–1963." *Explorations in Economic History* 35:2 (1998): 221–38.

Schimdt, Elizabeth. *Cold War and Decolonization in Guinea, 1964–1958*. Athens: Ohio University Press, 2007.

Schoultz, Lars. *Beneath the United States. A History of U.S. Policy Toward Latin America*. Cambridge: Harvard University Press, 1998.

That Infernal Little Cuban Republic. The United States and the Cuban Revolution Chapel Hill: The University of North Carolina Press, 2009.

Schumpeter, Joseph A. *Capitalism, Socialism, and Democracy*. New York: Harper and Row, 1950.

Siegelbaum, Lewis. *Cars for Comrades. The Life of the Soviet Automobile*. Ithaca: Cornell University Press, 2008.

Smith, Mark B. "Peaceful Coexistence at All Costs: Cold War Exchanges between Britain and the Soviet Union in 1956." *Cold War History* 12:3 (2012): 537–58.

Sontag, John P. "The Soviet War Scare of 1926–27." *Russian Review* 34:1 (1975): 66–77.

Soutou, Georges-Henri. *La guerre de Cinquante Ans. Le conflit Est–Ouest, 1943–1990*. Paris: Fayard, 2001.

Spaulding, Robert Mark. *Osthandel and Ostpolitik. German Foreign Trade Policies in Eastern Europe from Bismarck to Adenauer*. Providence: Berghahn Books, 1997.

Spulber, Nicolas. *Russia's Economic Transitions. From Late Tsarism to the New Millennium*. Cambridge: Cambridge University Press, 2003.

Stent, Angela. *From Embargo to Ostpolitik. The Political Economy of West German–Soviet Relations 1955–1980*. Cambridge: Cambridge University Press, 1981.

Stoliarov, Iu. S., and Ia. A. Pevzner. *SSSR–Iaponiia: problemy torgovo-ekonomicheskikh otnoshenii*. Moscow: Mezhdunarodnye otnosheniia, 1984.

Stone, David R. *Hammer & Rifle. The Militarization of the Soviet Union, 1926–1933*. Lawrence: University Press of Kansas, 2000.

Stone, Randall W. *Satellites and Commissars. Strategy and Conflict in the Politics of Soviet-Bloc Trade*. Princeton: Princeton University Press, 1996.

Sung-Beh, Chung. "Japanese Soviet Economic Relations." *Soviet and Eastern European Foreign Trade* 11:4 (1975): 3–29.

Suri, Jeremi. *Power and Protest. Global Revolution and the Rise of Détente*. Cambridge: Harvard University Press, 2003.

Taubman, William. *Khrushchev. The Man and His Era*. New York: Norton, 2003.

Treml, Vladimir G. "Foreign Trade and the Soviet Economy: Changing Parameters and Interrelations," in Egon Neuberger and Laura D'Andrea Tyson, eds. *The Impact of International Economic Disturbances on the Soviet Union and Eastern Europe. Transmission and Response*. New York: Pergamon Press, 1980.

"The Inferior Quality of Soviet Machinery as Reflected in Export Prices." *Journal of Comparative Economics* 5:2 (1981): 200–21.

"Soviet Dependence on Foreign Trade," in NATO Economics Directorate, *External Economic Relations of CMEA Countries. Their Significance and Impact in Global Perspective*, Colloquium 1983. Brussels: NATO, 1983.

Valkenier, Elizabeth Kridl. *The Soviet Union and the Third World. An Economic Bind*. New York: Praeger, 1983.

Verdery, Katherine. *What Was Socialism, and What Comes Next?* Princeton: Princeton University Press, 1996.

Verma, Satish, and Rahul Arora. "Does the Indian Economy Support Wagner's Law? An Econometric Analysis." *Eurasian Journal of Business and Economics* 3:5 (2010): 77–91.

Wade, Robert. *Governing the Market: Economic Theory and the Role of Government in East Asian Industrialization*. Princeton: Princeton University Press, 1990.

Weiner, Tim. *Legacy of Ashes. The History of the CIA*. New York: Doubleday, 2007.

Westad, Odd Arne. "Secrets of the Second World: The Russian Archives and the Reinterpretation of Cold War History." *Diplomatic History* 21:2 (1997): 259–71.

The Global Cold War. Third World Interventions and the Making of Our Times. Cambridge: Cambridge University Press, 2005.

Wiles, Peter. "Soviet Consumption and Investment Prices, and the Meaningfulness of Real Investment." *Soviet Studies* 34:2 (1982): 289–95.

Wilhelm, John Howard. "The Failure of the American Sovietological Economics Profession." *Europe-Asia Studies* 55:1 (2003): 59–74.

Williams, Willliam Appleman. *The Tragedy of American Diplomacy*. Cleveland: World Publishing Company, 1959.

Woo-Cumings, Meredith, ed. *The Developmental State*. Ithaca: Cornell University Press, 1999.

Wood, Robert E. "From the Marshall Plan to the Third World," in Melvyn P. Leffler and David S. Painter, eds. *Origins of the Cold War. An International History*. London: Routledge, 1994.

Woodruff, David M. "The Politburo on Gold, Industrialization, and the International Economy, 1925–1926," in Paul R. Gregory and Norman

Naimark, eds. *The Lost Politburo Transcripts. From Collective Rule to Stalin's Dictatorship*. New Haven: Yale University Press, 2008.

Yaqub, Salim. *Containing Arab Nationalism. The Eisenhower Doctrine and the Middle East*. Chapel Hill: The University of North Carolina Press, 2004.

Yergin, Daniel. *The Prize: The Epic Quest for Oil, Money and Power*. New York: Simon & Schuster, 1991.

Zaleskii, Eugene. *Stalinist Planning for Economic Growth, 1933–1952*. Chapel Hill: University of North Carolina Press, 1980.

Zhang, Shuguang. *Economic Cold War: America's Embargo against China and the Sino-Soviet Alliance, 1949–1963*. Washington, DC: Woodrow Wilson Center Press, 2001.

Zimmermann, Hubert. *Money and Security. Troops, Monetary Policy, and West Germany's Relations with the United Sates and Britain, 1950–1971*. Cambridge: Cambridge University Press, 2002.

Zubok, Vladislav, and Constantine Pleshakov. *Inside the Kremlin's Cold War. From Stalin to Khrushchev*. Cambridge: Harvard University Press, 1996.

Zubok, Vladislav. *A Failed Empire. The Soviet Union in the Cold War from Stalin to Gorbachev*. Chapel Hill: The University of North Carolina Press, 2007.

Index

For EU product safety concerns, contact us at Calle de José Abascal, 56–1°,
28003 Madrid, Spain or eugpsr@cambridge.org.

www.ingramcontent.com/pod-product-compliance
Lightning Source LLC
LaVergne TN
LVHW011524200926
848484LV00001B/147

* 9 7 8 1 1 0 7 0 4 0 2 5 0 *